Giles MacDonogh is the author of a n\blacksquare works of German history including *A Good German*, *Frederick the Great*, *The Last Kaiser* and *After the Reich*; he also translated the bestselling *The Hitler Book*. He has written for major newspapers in Britain and Europe such as the *Financial Times*, *Guardian* and *The Times*. He contributes to magazines all over the world.

'It would be difficult to attribute Hitler's ascent to any single event, but historian Giles MacDonogh makes a convincing case that 1938 is the crucial year to understanding his reign and brutal hold on power.'

Daily Beast

Praise for *After the Reich*:

'Important and timely. He has a profound understanding of Germany, which he communicates in a humane and engaging style . . . a remarkable book.'

Michael Burleigh

'Brings together many stories that deserve to be much better known in the West.'

Max Hastings, *Sunday Times*

'A gruelling but important book.'

Nigel Jones, *Sunday Telegraph*

'It is not only a fascinating story but a unique and valuable historical document.'

New York Review of Books

1938

HITLER'S GAMBLE

Giles MacDonogh

Constable • London

Constable & Robinson Ltd
3 The Lanchesters
162 Fulham Palace Road
London W6 9ER
www.constablerobinson.com

First published in the UK by Constable, 2009

This paperback edition published by Constable
an imprint of Constable & Robinson, 2010

A copy of the British Library Cataloguing in Publication
Data is available from the British Library

ISBN: 978-1-8490-1338-3

Printed and bound in the EU

3 5 7 9 10 8 6 4 2

Wiedergefunden

Ich ging dann nach draußen, wo die Sterne funkelten und die Abschüsse am Himmel wetterleuchteten. Die ewigen Zeichen und Male – der Große Wagen, der Orion, die Wega, das Siebengestirn, der Gürtel der Milchstraße – was sind wir Menschen und unsere Erdenjahre vor diesem Glanz? Was ist unsere flüchtige Qual? Um Mitternacht, bei Lärm der Zecher, gedachte ich lebhaft meiner Lieben und fühlte, wie auch ihre Grüße durchdrangen.

Ernst Jünger, 31 December 1942

CONTENTS

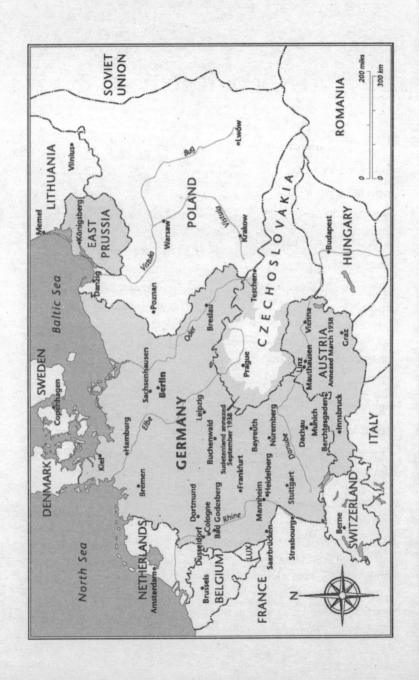

LIST OF ILLUSTRATIONS

ACKNOWLEDGEMENTS

Many people have given me helpful suggestions and references, or have delved deep into their memories of a now distant time: Rupert Allison, John Aycoth, Melanie Barber, Richard Bassett, Angela Bohrer, Ann Bone, the late Gerhard Bronner, Professor Michael Burleigh, Professor Andrew Chandler, the late George Clare, Tim Clarke, Venerable Patrick Curran, Wolf-Erich Eckstein, the late Sir Dudley Forwood Bt, Georg Gaugusch, the late Litzi Gedye, Lydia Hall, Gerhard Heilig, Uwe Kohl, the late Peter Leighton-Langer, Mairin Lodle, Celia Male, Patricia Meehan, Professor Lucien Meysels, Fritz Miesbauer, Gisela Müller, Stefan Popper, Professor Munro Price, Lorli Rudov, the late Arnold Sayers, Professor Hans Schneider, Father Franz Schuster OSB, Henry Wellisch, August Zirner and Ed Zwieback.

Particular thanks are due to people who lent or sent books and papers, such as my friends Christopher Wentworth-Stanley and Sebastian Cody in Vienna. Sebastian also read the typescript and made a number of important points. Michael Smith of the *Daily Telegraph* gave me a copy of an interview with the Viennese MI6 deputy chief, Kenneth Benton, recorded before Benton's death. Peter Ede very kindly sent me his manuscript translation of Gräfin Maltzan's memoirs and other helpful suggestions.

I should also like to thank the staffs of the DÖW archive and the Staatsbibliothek in Vienna; the Bundesarchiv in Koblenz; and the library at Swarthmore College in Pennsylvania for providing me with copies of the Corder Catchpool papers. In London I received wonderful support from a number of institutions: the Public Record Office, Friends House Library, the London Metropolitan Archive for the papers of the British Board of Deputies, the Guildhall Library for the Anglican Church abroad, Lambeth Palace Library, the Newspaper Library in Colindale, the British Library, the Wiener Library and the German Historical Institute.

Thanks too to my agent Georgina Capel and her staff, to Lara Heimert and Leo Hollis, my editors in New York and London respectively, to Douglas Matthews for compiling the index as well as to my wife Candida, who agreed to read the manuscript, and to the rest of my family, for giving me a few moments of peace and quiet.

INTRODUCTION

The year 1938 was one of cataclysmic change for Germany. On 1 January the Reich was administered by a right-wing coalition led by the Chancellor, Adolf Hitler, and dominated by members of the Nazi Party. The army had sworn a personal oath of allegiance to Hitler, but its commanders had managed to retain a degree of independence. The country lay confined within borders decreed by the Treaty of Versailles nearly twenty years before. Hitler had so far contented himself with policing his own house and grabbing back the Demilitarized Zone in the Rhineland. He had yet to pursue any foreign 'adventures'. Although they had been stripped of their roles in German public life, the Jews were still in possession of their property, and many of them continued to lead relatively normal lives. They were evidently in no hurry to leave.

By New Year's Day 1939, all that had changed. The non-Nazis had been purged of all but a few insignificant roles in government; Hitler had assumed total control of the armed forces; Germany had invaded first Austria then the German-speaking areas of Czechoslovakia; the Jews had been robbed, beaten and imprisoned and many had been driven into penurious exile. Hundreds had been killed. Hitler had emerged *deus ex machina* with all the powers of the Nazi regime consolidated in his own person. And worse was to come. That Germans felt an increase in stress and anxiety during those twelve months is perhaps borne out by one telling statistic: their consumption of strong alcohol doubled in the course of the year.[1]

We remember 1938 now above all for Munich, that moment at the end of September when Western leaders apparently gave in to the Führer's demands. Peace was hanging by a thread: Hitler had launched his second foreign 'gamble', and French and British statesmen met their fascist counterparts in a bid to avoid war. We are also painfully aware of the condition of much of Europe in May 1945: a collection of smouldering ruins filled with fresh or festering corpses. In those intervening years some fifty million people had died violent deaths. There is, however, a danger in hindsight, and it would be unfair to seek to draw a direct line between the two situations, for the line is not straight at all. Before the outbreak of war in 1939, no grown man or woman could have accurately predicted the depths to which Nazi Germany would sink by the end.

Nonetheless the events that took place in 1938 make it easy to conclude that Hitler had already mapped out the entire series of conquests by which he would regain the old Imperial German borders in the east, and more besides; but we must not race to such conclusions: Hitler could be more pragmatic than his writings and public utterances suggest and he was probably hoping to get what he could without fighting the great powers. If all went well, and the West made no trouble, other territories might fall into his lap. It was only in the spring of 1939, for example, that he began to make plans to take the Polish Corridor by force, after the Poles refused to agree to Danzig reverting to the Reich. Poland suffered its fourth partition in September 1939.

It is similarly tempting to connect the injustice and violence directed against Austria's and Germany's Jews in 1938 with the industrialized slaughter of the Final Solution. Nazi antisemitism certainly took a new turn in 1938, but it would be difficult to argue that plans had already been drawn up to murder the Jews in specially created camps in east-central Europe. Some would say that Hitler had already made up his mind by 30 January 1939, when he delivered a notorious speech to celebrate the sixth anniversary of the Nazi takeover. Maybe so, but he had to find a means of putting his thoughts into action, and, even then, German leaders were remarkably sensitive to foreign opinion. It is more likely that the speech contained a veiled warning to the Jews in the United States, that there would be trouble for their co-religionists if they continued to stifle German trade and rob the country of the foreign currency it so desperately needed to survive.

Words like *vernichten* and *ausrotten*[i] came easily to Hitler's lips. As a frontline soldier in the Great War he had experienced the effects of poison gas, but even by the end of 1938 it was unlikely that he had made the connection between 'problem' and 'solution'. Wartime conditions vastly accelerated projects that had yet to be formulated; only then was the smoke thick enough to cover the activities of the zealots. Massive troop deployment, inadequate communications and inurement to violent death, brought about by casualties on an unprecedented scale, helped remove the last moral barriers to genocide.

Yet 1938 was the crucial year in the history of Nazi Germany before Europe tumbled into war. Every month resounded with shocks or sensations: the Blomberg–Fritsch Crisis in January, which shook faith in the armed forces; the end of Cabinet government in February; the Anschluss in March that melded Austria to the Reich; the Plebiscite in April that revealed overwhelming support for the Führer; Hitler's trip to Rome in May that laid the keel of a proper alliance with Mussolini; Edda Göring's birth in June, which provided Germans with a welcome social event and demonstrated the popularity of Hitler's chosen successor; the Evian Conference in July, which revealed that the countries opposing Hitler's racial policies were not prepared to put their money where their mouths were; the Kendrick Crisis in August, which destroyed the British intelligence network in Germany; Chamberlain's visits to Berchtesgaden and Bad Godesberg in September followed by the notorious Munich Conference; the occupation of the Sudetenland in October and later that month the expulsion of the Polish Jews from the Reich; Goebbels' recreation of a mediaeval pogrom in November's *Reichskristallnacht*. While the Jews repaired their broken homes and shops in December, the *Kindertransporte* began to ferry their children to safety.

[i] 'Exterminate' and 'wipe out'.

In 1938, the blood was scarcely cold on the battlefields of the Great War and few people were ready for more; yet, in the course of those twelve months, Hitler, Göring and Ribbentrop prodded the West's defences and found out how thin they were. Germany gambled, and with each easy victory they decided they could push even further. Hitler's eyes were already roving, but for the time being he was looking to the southeast. Germany required *Lebensraum* (living space), raw materials and industry. It was Austria and Czechoslovakia that appealed to him at the beginning of 1938, not right-wing Poland, where many people abominated the Jews as much as he did, and which was still considered a useful bulwark against Bolshevik Russia.

In 1938 the deportation of the Reich's Jews began in earnest. Germany gained experience in forcible expulsion with the eviction of the Polish Jews in October, and after *Reichskristallnacht* two weeks later. Following the pogrom of 9–10 November, as many as 30,000 Jews were shoved into the concentration camps that Himmler had been extending and expanding all year. This was the first large-scale, organized strike against the Jews of the Altreich, as Germany north of the former Austro-German border on the River Inn was now called. A few thousand rich Austrian Jews had been languishing in Dachau and Buchenwald since April. The aim was to speed up emigration, but it also oiled the cogs of a machine that would be used again and again once war began. And when that happened it would mostly mean murder.

PROLOGUE

On 5 November 1937 Hitler set out his new vision for Germany. He proposed to smash the shackles of the Versailles Treaty. This programme is revealed in the now infamous Hossbach Memorandum. This was to be his 'political testament'. Hitler's aim was to test his service chiefs and see how ready they were to subscribe to his more radical plans. No notes were to be taken at the session, which was top secret.[1] Field Marshal Werner von Blomberg's adjutant, the staff officer Colonel Friedrich Hossbach, witnessed the meeting between Hitler and the military chiefs: Blomberg, Werner von Fritsch, Erich Raeder and Hermann Göring together with the Foreign Minister, Constantin von Neurath. Hossbach thought the discussion might interest his mentor, the Chief of the General Staff, Colonel General Ludwig Beck, and scribbled down the main points in his diary.[2]

In the course of a two-hour monologue,[i] Hitler told those present that his aim was to maintain the 'racial community' and enlarge it. Germany required *Lebensraum* – not in the country's confiscated African colonies (which did not interest him) but in Europe, where new agricultural land would provide Germany with the self-sufficiency, or autarky, that it craved. He warned the generals that Germany was also painfully short of raw materials. It had to strike before potential enemies such as the Soviet Union could catch up. He predicted that the Russians would be ready to fight some time between 1943 and 1945, which would allow time for Germany to annex Czechoslovakia and Austria. The strike could come as early as 1938. By acquiring these two territories Germany's frontiers would

---

[i] The meeting took place in the Chancellery from 4.15 to 8.30 p.m.

be made that much more secure and the increased manpower would provide him with twelve fresh divisions for the army.

Blomberg and Fritsch were the first to throw up their hands in exasperation, since operations of this sort required minute planning, but Hitler reassured them that there was no hurry. He predicted that the fragile bonds between Britain and France on the one hand and Britain and Italy on the other would collapse by the summer of 1938, leaving Mussolini resolutely in the German camp. He was convinced that Britain would recoil from fighting, and that France would not participate either, as the country would be confined to its bed by yet another political crisis: during the waning years of the Third Republic, French governments came and went with indecent speed.

Neurath was also jittery after the meeting.[3] Much of what Hitler had said may have looked dangerously radical but to nationalists and National Socialists Austria and Czechoslovakia were obvious targets. The Treaties of Versailles and Saint Germain that followed the defeat of Germany and Austria-Hungary had accorded the precious right of self-determination only to the victors in the First World War, or the formerly oppressed peoples of their enemies. Austria had been shorn of all its territories and left in possession of only its German-speaking core. It had been expressedly forbidden to link up with Germany, because the creation of a super-state might have made Germany stronger than the Allies desired.

British politicians had also begun to question the wisdom and morality of the Versailles settlement and were increasingly conscious of these open sores. There was much discussion of the former German colonies, and whether Hitler should be granted an African empire.[4] In general the British were happier with the idea of concessions on the European mainland that did not threaten their empire. Many, particularly in the British Foreign Office, saw revision of the Austrian and Czech borders as inevitable and a German presence in Bohemia and Moravia as preferable to a Soviet one. It was unfortunate, however, that the man who clamoured loudest for such changes should be Adolf Hitler.

Raw materials were vital to Nazi Germany's survival. Austria had the iron ore of the Erzberg, but Czechoslovakia had much more of everything. Both countries could offer foreign currency that was vital for purchasing arms and materials abroad. The German economy was simply not strong enough for the tasks imposed on it by the Nazis. In 1933, Germany had been a modestly wealthy, partly modernized society. The Third Reich had taken steps to change that, but the diversion of so many of the country's resources into the arms programme had left many other areas underfunded: troops slept in bivouacs while money was ploughed into arms construction, and the German railway network, together with its rolling stock, was falling apart.[5] The Finance Minister, Graf Lutz Schwerin von Krosigk, was tearing his hair out over Germany's economic crisis, which he thought would last to 1940 at the very least. He told the Propaganda Minister and Gauleiter (regional party leader) of Berlin, Joseph Goebbels, about it, but Goebbels came out with a typically Nazi line: he did not believe a country could be killed by debt, only by lack of weapons.[6]

On 19 November, two weeks after the meeting with the service chiefs, Hitler received Lord Halifax at the Berghof, his opulent country house above Berchtesgaden in the Bavarian Alps. As Lord President of the Council Halifax was a member of the British Cabinet, and he would shortly replace Anthony Eden as Foreign Secretary. Halifax let it be known that Britain was not opposed to a revision of the Versailles settlement as regards Austria, Czechoslovakia and Danzig, provided it came about peacefully.[7] Halifax clearly had the backing of the British government: in December Prime Minister Neville Chamberlain told the German ambassador to the Court of Saint James's, Joachim von Ribbentrop, that he was prepared to discuss both Austrian and Czech issues.[8]

When Halifax left, Hitler emerged in the best of moods and told his entourage that Halifax was 'a clever politician who fully supported Germany's claims'. He summoned the Austrian Legion, an SS unit composed of Austrian Nazis, and told them, 'The hour approaches when your wishes will be fulfilled.'[9] Hitler did not talk of his need to become absolute master in his own house when he addressed his service chiefs earlier that month, but it was not far from his mind. That meant removing all those who were less than wholly committed to National Socialism. Like a balloonist, he was going to divest himself of the lead weights that impeded his ascent.

Göring took over Germany's finances from Hjalmar Schacht at the beginning of December. Schacht had suggested Göring receive a role in economy in the first place, but Göring was increasingly impatient with Schacht's ways and wanted to use more draconian methods to find money for his projects. Göring now had the job of making Germany self-sufficient while financing German rearmament. Schacht had not thought this autarky feasible. The Foreign Minister, Neurath, was the next victim: he had been appointed by Chancellor Franz von Papen in 1932 and had only joined the Nazi Party in 1937. He was to be replaced by the 'Second Bismarck', Ribbentrop. Four ambassadors were to be jettisoned too: Ulrich von Hassell in Rome, Herbert von Dirksen in Tokyo, Papen in Vienna and, of course, Ribbentrop in London.

It seems unlikely, however, that Hitler had a master plan for these changes or any grand strategy that was specific to 1938. He responded to each crisis as it came along and it was invariably he who came out strongest.

I

JANUARY

'. . . as the silver candelabra had been placed on the table a wonderful light lit up the red and golden wine in all its splendour that was majestically mirrored in the noble wood of ancient furniture and in the wings and clothes of the golden angel together with the balls on the Christmas tree. Every feast day comes and goes in our house as our own new, clear and silent celebration: and the magnificence and the serenity become ever greater with every earthly joy . . . The angels and silver baubles shine from within the dark baroque room: everything is still steeped in Christmas, and therefore from renewed festivity, a new year!'

Jochen Klepper, 1 January 1938.[i]

I n the first weeks of January 1938, much of Germany lay under a thick blanket of snow. Like the snow, the regime's secret police were everywhere. For those who had no reason to love the Third Reich, it was best to keep your head down and talk to no one. Communists, socialists and Jews were among those who had most to fear.

It was not the Germans but the Romanians who had turned up the heat for the Jews at the beginning of the year. A fascist government

---

[i] *Unter dem Schatten deiner Flügel: aus den Tagebüchern der Jahre 1932–1942*, Stuttgart 1955, 542.

led by Octavian Goga had come to power in Bucharest in December. On 12 January he revoked the citizenship of the country's three-quarters of a million Jews, causing large numbers to flee. Some of these surfaced in Austria ('a gift', mocked Goebbels) and there was a fear that they might join the other groups of foreign Jews in Germany.[1]

While the Nazi leaders were delighted to find a new ally in the Balkan state, they were less than pleased to be a haven for its Jews. 'The Jewish question has become a global problem once again,'[2] wrote Goebbels. The Nuremberg-based weekly Der Stürmer celebrated the precipitate departure of the Jews from Romania in a series of cartoons by Philipp Rupprecht or 'Fips'. One showed Jews in France, Britain and the United States weeping impotently over the fate of their Romanian brothers; another, an avalanche of Jews descending on France; and a third, a Jew arriving at an Austrian hotel to find it 'fully occupied'.[3]

Der Stürmer – the unofficial organ for the state persecution of the Jews – also reported that the French Foreign Minister Yvon Delbos had been in Warsaw for talks before Christmas, and had discussed the possibility of despatching Poland's 3.3 million Jews to Madagascar. The editor, Julius Streicher, preened himself: he had been one of the first to suggest the French colony as a new home for the Jews.[4] On 21 January Der Stürmer published a special issue calling for the death penalty for Rassenschänder – Jews who slept with Gentiles. Goebbels – who had slept with at least one Jew – heartily approved. The cover showed the fourteen-year-old starlet Deanna Durbin on the arms of elderly Hollywood Jews. The periodical contained a column in which all Gentiles who continued to have professional or personal dealings with Jews were named and shamed.

Victor Klemperer, a rabbi's son married to a Gentile, had been sacked as professor of romance languages at Dresden University. He was reduced to writing a diary that recorded each new blow levelled at his race. Like many Jews, he was beginning to have second thoughts about having wanted to be more German than the Germans and complained of the 'tragedy of the Jew, misled by his desire to assimilate'. Sometimes it seemed the state's bugbears were Catholic priests, at others Protestant pastors. In January 1938 it was Jews.[5]

THE BLOMBERG–FRITSCH AFFAIR

Hitler might have been looking for a means of securing his position and making himself absolute master of the Third Reich, but it was not always clear how he would bring that about. Time and again, circumstances came to his rescue, and he was able – with (as he would put it) the 'instinct of a sleepwalker' – to turn difficult situations to his advantage. One such began to unravel at the first social occasion of the Nazi New Year, although it was a while before Hitler realized how events could be shaped to his own aims. Indeed, he was so unconscious of the plot going on around him that he was able to accompany Goebbels to see *Die Fledermaus* that evening. The Führer was 'in complete raptures'[6] at the Strauss operetta and wholly unaware that behind his back his underlings were about to provoke a two-week crisis and bring the state to a standstill.

Göring held his suitably gigantic forty-fourth birthday party on the morning of Wednesday, 12 January. His position was emblematic of the peculiar structure of power within the Nazi state: officially Hitler's successor, he was also a minister of state and president of the emasculated Reichstag. He was commander of the air force, therefore answerable to the Minister of War, Blomberg. He was, however, on an equal footing with Colonel General von Fritsch, the head of the army.[7]

The former air ace was one of the oldest in the gang, the same age as his enemy Ribbentrop. Goebbels was forty and Heinrich Himmler was thirty-seven. Hitler himself was only forty-eight. Nazism retained its appeal to an unfulfilled element in German youth – those who had been born in around 1910 and grown up unemployed during the depressed years of the Weimar Republic.

On 12 January Göring was feted in the way he loved best: no one dared to stint on the presents. Hitler had just returned from his Christmas break and gave his old friend a 'splendid' hunting scene by the Austrian painter Hans Makart. The party was interrupted, however, for Göring and Hitler had a solemn office to perform: they were due at the town hall in the Tiergarten district of Berlin at ten to twelve, invited to be witnesses at the wedding of the ageing Blomberg to one Eva Gruhn. As he left the festivities, Göring permitted himself a loud chuckle.[8] For some time he had been looking for a means to extend the Party's influence over the army, and now he saw his chance.[9]

A widower with five children, the noble Blomberg was marrying a much younger woman from the *bas fonds*. Some months before, he had put on mufti and gone to Oberhof in the Thuringian Forest for a cure. Seeing him eating his dinner all by himself, the manager of the hotel had asked him if he would like company. That was when Eva Gruhn sat at his table. Later she informed Blomberg she was pregnant with his child, but he liked her so much that he asked for her hand in marriage.[10] He even went so far as to confess his love to Goebbels, who found the story 'very moving' and promised to help.[11] Eva came from the working-class district of Neukölln in Berlin, where her mother had run a massage parlour. Mother Gruhn had twice been convicted of prostitution and her daughter had followed in her footsteps. She had a police record that documented participation in nude orgies, prostitution and selling pornographic pictures – of herself. She had been on parole earlier that year.[12]

As early as October, Blomberg had cried on Göring's shoulder and told him of his intended's humble origins. He had spared Göring the rest, which he probably did not know himself. He had, however, come under heavy criticism from his own officers. Blomberg had been a stickler for their marrying within their social milieu and was now breaking his own code.[13] Göring reassured him that Hitler's consent would be forthcoming, as he approved any match that struck a blow against the old order. He took great pains to be helpful, going so far as to dispose of a younger rival by packing him off to South America with a well-paid job. Blomberg finally told Hitler after Ludendorff's funeral on 22 December.[14] The marriage went ahead with the Führer's blessing and after their wedding on the 12th the happy couple departed for the island of Capri.[15]

There was a slight glitch a few days later, when they were obliged to cut short their honeymoon, because Blomberg's mother was inconsiderate enough to die. The general was in Berlin on the 17th, the day before her death, when Goebbels saw him and still thought him a 'fine fellow'.[16] The storm broke, however, on 21 January, when an anonymous caller, claiming to be a general, telephoned Army High Command demanding to speak to Colonel-General Fritsch. When he was refused the caller shouted, 'Tell the general that Field Marshal von Blomberg has married a whore!'[17]

The chief of police, Graf Wolf Heinrich von Helldorf, knew the story already. A member of his vice squad, in the course of his duties, had been with a prostitute who had seen the new Frau von Blomberg together with Hitler and Göring in the newspapers and had instantly recognized her as her old friend. The policeman had looked up the file and taken it in to Helldorf.[18] At the Gestapa – Gestapo Headquarters – in the Prinz Albrechts Palais in Berlin, someone showed Franz Josef Huber, later Gestapo chief in Vienna, a picture of a naked woman, telling him the woman was now Freifrau von Blomberg.[19]

Helldorf went to see General Wilhelm Keitel – whose son Karl-Heinz was engaged to be married to Blomberg's daughter Dorle – and asked him to identify the new baroness from a police photograph. Keitel, however, had little to tell the police chief. He said he had not been invited to the wedding, and the only time he had set eyes on her was at the funeral. Keitel had not been able to make out her features as she had worn a heavy veil. After the funeral, the honeymoon couple made preparations to set off for Italy again.[20]

In a style to which Germany was to become accustomed, Keitel passed the buck. He told Helldorf to approach Göring, for the cogent reason that Göring had been at the wedding, and would have had a good look at Frau von Blomberg. Helldorf drove out to Göring's mansion at Carinhall near Berlin. Göring could indeed identify the woman in the picture. He admitted he had known for a long time that Blomberg intended to marry her, and also revealed how he had eliminated a rival. Blomberg, it appeared, had walked into a honey-trap.

While doubt may still hang over his role in Blomberg's fate, there is no question that Göring was behind the removal of the monarchist and anti-Nazi Colonel-General von Fritsch. He was to be pushed out by trumped-up charges of infringing Article 175 of the Prussian Criminal Code by frequenting a Bavarian rent-boy called Sepp Weingärtner ('*der Bayernseppl*'[ii]) in November 1933. Fritsch had allegedly been spotted having sex with Weingärtner in a dark place near Wannsee station by a blackmailer called Otto Schmidt. Posing as a policeman, Schmidt followed him back to town and confronted him on the Potsdamer Platz. According to Schmidt, Fritsch took fright, produced his military pass and asked Schmidt to be discreet. Over the next few weeks Schmidt was able to pump over 2,000 RM[iii] out of the unfortunate officer.[21]

Taking full advantage of the Nazi desire to adhere as strictly as possible to the draconian Article 175, Schmidt earned a living by spying on and blackmailing homosexuals. In 1936 he was arrested and, to save his hide, gave the police some details of his business. Among his 'clients' he was able to name the later Minister of Economics, Walther Funk,[iv] the tennis ace and Wimbledon finalist Gottfried von Cramm and a Graf von Wedel, who was police

[ii] 'Bavarian Joe'.
[iii] Reichsmarks.
[iv] Goebbels recorded rumours of Funk's homosexuality on 31 December 1937. Even Streicher's *Stürmer* alluded to it. See Elke Fröhlich (ed.), *Die Tagebücher von Joseph Goebbels*, Teil 1, Band 5, Dezember 1937–Juli 1938, Munich 2000, 77. Hitler was also aware of it: see R.J. Overy, *Goering*, London 1984, 71.

president in Potsdam.[v] He also named Fritsch. Schmidt was interrogated by Josef Meisinger, the chief of a Gestapo unit called the *Reichszentrale für die Bekämpfung der Homosexualität* (The Reich's Central Office for the Repression of Homosexuality), and told him he met the general in Lichterfelde station whenever he wanted more money.[22] Lichterfelde was home to the cadet school and a natural haunt of top army brass.[23] Meisinger showed Schmidt a picture of Fritsch: '*Det is 'er*', he said in his Prussian idiom – 'That's the man.'

Meisinger had taken the story to Heydrich and Himmler, who had drawn up a report, but Hitler had referred to it as *Mist* (dung), refused to look at it and ordered it to be destroyed. He was still keen to retain Fritsch; it was his entourage who wanted to eliminate him. It is not clear whether it was Göring or Himmler who had been the prime mover in removing Fritsch back in 1936.[24] It was Heydrich who relocated the incriminating dossier and that would point to Himmler, but Göring had been meditating his coup since the end of the previous year, before Eva von Blomberg's shady past had come to light. Himmler wanted Fritsch out because of his opposition to the integration of the SS into the army; Göring because he assumed that Fritsch would be given Blomberg's job, which he coveted. With Himmler's permission, Göring had Schmidt taken out of Papenburg internment camp and brought to his home. Schmidt was shown a picture of Fritsch, whom he once again identified as the man he had seen with *der Bayernseppl*.

After Blomberg's wedding, Hitler had returned to the Berghof and was absent from Berlin until 24 January. The next day Göring represented the Fritsch dossier along with the one Helldorf had penned on the new baroness. When the Blomberg file was produced, the petty-bourgeois Hitler was irate: he had been abused, inveigled into witnessing the ceremony, even kissed the hand of a woman of the streets. He was particularly appalled that the pornographic pictures in

[v] A Graf Edgard Wedel or 'Hofwedel' ('Court' Wedel) had been heavily implicated in the homosexual scandals at the Kaiser's court.

the police file had been taken by Eva's one-time lover, a Czech Jew.

Hitler wanted the marriage annulled. Blomberg immediately refused. Hitler would not allow him to continue as Minister of War. Blomberg seems to have felt well out of it, made little attempt to save himself and went happily into retirement. He still claimed to be madly in love in 1945.[25] Unabashed, he even suggested Fritsch as his successor. Hitler was relieved when Blomberg accepted a generous golden handshake and left soon after for Italy, but he continued to seethe. There is a suggestion that his shattered look was a pose, that he was acting,[26] but Goebbels called it 'the worst crisis for the regime since the Röhm Affair . . . The Führer looks like a corpse.'[27] It is unlikely that Goebbels was misled by Hitler's performance. He saw an 'almost sad and very serious' Hitler on the 25th, but as yet had no details of the Blomberg affair. He noted, however, that Göring was at Hitler's side.[28]

Hitler summoned Keitel and asked him who should succeed Blomberg. Keitel naturally said all the right things: Göring was the man. Hitler, on the other hand, refused to consider Göring, who he thought had enough on his plate already and whom he believed to be 'too idle' to take on the extra work.[29] Keitel then advanced the name of Fritsch. Hitler went to his desk and came back with the Fritsch file. Keitel claims that he responded by saying it could only be 'a case of mistaken identity or slander'.[30] Hitler asked Keitel who should have Fritsch's job. Keitel replied: Gerd von Rundstedt. Hitler thought him too old. Keitel's next suggestion was Walther von Brauchitsch; Hitler parried with Walter von Reichenau. This was a hopeful choice, given Reichenau's loyalty to the cause, but Keitel said he was '*Hans Dampf in allen Gassen*'– a busybody too interested in politics and too little applied to the business of the army. He was unpopular with the other generals. Brauchitsch it was to be.[31]

The bachelor Fritsch had already aroused suspicions among some members of Hitler's elite. He had just been on a long holiday in Egypt where he hoped to cure his bronchitis; he had left soon after the meeting in the Chancellery, together with his second adjutant, a former champion point-to-pointer called Jochen von Both.[32] Göring had had Fritsch tailed, but no proof was forthcoming.[33] Fritsch mistakenly believed the contents of the dossier to be based on malicious rumours about some lunches he had offered an impecunious member of the Hitler Youth a few years before. Other sources mention *two* Youths, and Fritsch teaching them history and rapping them with a ruler on their bare calves when they got their facts wrong. The joke did the rounds of the SS that Fritsch was a calf fetishist.[34]

Hitler gave the file to Hossbach, to find out if there were any truth in it. Hossbach instantly smelled a rat and, against Hitler's orders, confronted Fritsch, who denied everything. He seemed aware that the scandal had been brewed by Göring and Himmler, who wanted to rid Germany of a 'reactionary general'.[35] Hossbach told Hitler that Fritsch denied the charge, and painted Fritsch in such a sympathetic light that Hitler was still keen to make him War Minister. Hitler still had not abandoned Fritsch on 26 January, when the general was asked to come in and see him and Göring in the Chancellery Library. Fritsch entered shouting, 'I really want to look at this pig!'[36] He was not supposed to know that Schmidt would be produced, but Hossbach had told him, thereby incurring the eternal enmity of Göring, who was looking forward to his *coup de théâtre*.

Hitler told Fritsch that he had been accused of infringing Article 175. Schmidt was brought in and promptly identified Fritsch, who in turn vigorously denied the charges. He swore on his word of honour he had never set eyes on Schmidt before and that there was no truth in the allegations. He made the mistake, however, of mentioning the Hitler Youth. Hitler was instantly suspicious: he may have felt there was no smoke without fire, and he was known not to be overly fond of homosexuals. He wrote off Fritsch and Hossbach with him, telling Keitel he never wanted to see the colonel again. The sacking of Hossbach added to Hitler's depression and Goebbels reported the next day that he had been quite tearful.[37] Hitler was not the only lachrymose person around, for Keitel's deputy Jodl reported that his boss was also 'tearful': 'You get the impression of being caught up in one of the German nation's fateful moments.'[38]

Goebbels was finally let in on the Blomberg story by Hitler's former company commander and personal adjutant, Fritz Wiedemann. The two men were joined by Helldorf, who knew the case better than anyone with the exception of Göring and Himmler. When Helldorf brought Goebbels the dossier, he found it 'hair raising'. For a man of honour, there was no alternative but the pistol.[39]

Goebbels finally heard the news about Fritsch's homosexuality too. Positive identification had naturally been sufficient for Göring. The Gestapo-man Huber, however, alighted on a discrepancy: deductions from the bank account of one Captain von Frisch amounted exactly to the sum paid to the blackmailer Schmidt. 'It was like being stung by a bee', Huber admitted later. He went straight to see his superior, Werner Best, who sent him to Heydrich. Heydrich went pale and took him to Himmler. Himmler thanked him: 'You did well.' It was only when Meisinger informed him that the file had been around for a couple of years and had been put away for later use that he realized he had stumbled across a conspiracy.[40] The missing 't' and the lesser rank were not to be allowed to stand in the way of the plotters' desire to block Fritsch's progress.

The apparent strike against the officer corps was causing concern. At midday on Wednesday, 26 January, Helldorf called a meeting at the headquarters of the Abwehr (military intelligence service) on the Tirpitzufer. It was attended by, among others, Admiral Wilhelm Canaris, the head of the Abwehr, his deputies – Colonels Hans Oster and Colonel Hans Pieckenbrock, together with Hans-Bernd Gisevius and Artur Nebe from the Criminal Police.[41] Helldorf defended Fritsch, but in his opinion Blomberg was too compromised, and he was shocked he could have stooped so low.[42] The meeting marked the parting of the ways between the nationalist fellow travellers and the Nazis. The suspicion that the whole affair was no more than an attempt to weaken the Wehrmacht's *esprit de corps* provoked the burgeoning cell of grumblers into downright opposition. The resisters had made an important conquest in the support of Canaris.

Yet the scandal would not go away. On the 27th Fritsch had to endure a four-hour interrogation by Best,[43] again in the presence of Schmidt. Since Schmidt's appearance at the Chancellery, the Gestapo had interviewed a number of young men who had served under Fritsch's command. They included Gottfried von Cramm, who had just returned from America and was later imprisoned for another offence under Article 175.[44] Both Fritsch and Schmidt clung to their stories, but the Gestapo were not interested in recording the fact that Schmidt made various claims that were clearly factually incorrect. Gürtner, the Minister of Justice, who was equally biased against the general, said Fritsch had not proved his innocence and regarded the story of the Hitler Youth as incriminating. Blomberg had thrown fat on the fire before his departure by saying that Fritsch was 'not a lady's man'.[45] Gürtner recommended that the case go before a military court. The interview coincided with the ex-Kaiser's birthday, and the discontent within the officer corps was clear from the number of pro-monarchist celebrations that took place in their messes.[46]

Hitler was distraught: an embarrassing crisis was discrediting the military elite of the Third Reich. His prudish nature found it hard to come to terms with the vices apparently prevalent among upper-class Prussians. He now had three positions vacant – Minister of War, Head of the Armed Forces and Head of the Army – and there was a queue forming: Göring, Joachim von Stülpnagel,[vi] General Graf Friedrich von der Schulenburg (a former Chief of Staff to the Crown Prince, now a Nazi), Himmler and the Nazi General Reichenau.

It was Goebbels, who had risen from the left of the Party and had fewer illusions about the upper classes than Hitler, who came up with the answer: Hitler should take on the first two roles himself. He had

---

[vi] The idea was dismissed – he was too disloyal. He proved Hitler's point on 20 July 1944.

seen the possibilities in divesting the regime of a potentially difficult element in the traditional officer corps.[47] By that stage it suited no one's purposes to exonerate Fritsch, and the process of shaming and removing him went ahead. Goebbels was able to elbow out Göring, who was favoured by the army for the job of War Minister. There was far less planning and a good deal more pragmatism in the decision than has been generally assumed.

The perceived need to protect Fritsch's honour created an Opposition that was to continue looking for a means of deposing Hitler until 20 July 1944. Helldorf was in a position to push the files over the desk to his deputy, Fritz-Dietlof Graf von der Schulenburg (the son of Graf Friedrich), a former Nazi who had lost faith after the Night of the Long Knives of 30 June 1934. Graf Rüdiger von der Goltz went into action as Fritsch's lawyer. On 29 January emissaries from the Opposition set off across the Reich to talk to the leading generals: Oster went to Hanover, Gisevius to Munster and the former mayor of Leipzig, Carl Goerdeler, to Dresden to speak to Generals Ulex, Kluge and List. The message was that the twelve commanding generals needed to make common cause with Fritsch. Some members of the officer corps were out for blood. Oster had to cool the heels of his son Achim and the rest of the garrison in Stettin, who were on the verge of mutiny.[48]

The upheaval caused by the removal of Blomberg and Fritsch left Hitler 'sullen and touchy'.[49] He cancelled his speech to celebrate the fifth anniversary of his coming to power. He had never done so before, and would not do it again until 1943. Rumours ran rife across Germany. The party went ahead for all that, and Hitler appeared on the balcony of the Chancellery to acknowledge the march past of his *Leibstandarte*. A crowd of 100,000 had gathered by candlelight on the Wilhelmsplatz. There were events to distract his followers: national prizes were handed out to the architect Gerdy Troost, the surgeon Ferdinand Sauerbruch and the Nazi ideologue Alfred Rosenberg. There was a Hitler Youth Festival at the Broadcasting House in Berlin. Six million young people were reported to have tuned in. For

Fritsch it was a hard night: he spent it being interrogated by Heydrich, but stuck to his guns.

On the last day of the month, Goebbels spent two hours alone with the Führer, who was still ranting about Blomberg and Fritsch. Blomberg had abused his trust. Hitler was firmly convinced of Fritsch's guilt. The general had been 'all but unmasked'. Goebbels had his own suggestion for Fritsch's successor: Beck, who 'came directly from Schlieffen's school'. Goebbels can't have known the general well. Beck was on the point of throwing in his lot with the Opposition. Had it been Beck and not Brauchitsch who was in charge of the army in September 1938, the year might have turned out very differently, but it appears that Beck didn't want the job.[50]

Rundstedt also saw Hitler that day, and found him in a 'fearful state of excitement such as I had never seen him'. Rundstedt believed that Himmler had 'blackened' Fritsch because the head of the army was a monarchist.[51] That day Hitler revealed to Goebbels that he intended making a huge shake-up in his household in order to create a smokescreen. He planned to appoint Ribbentrop to the foreign office, as suggested by his deputy, Rudolf Hess.[vii] Hitler was not enamoured of his London ambassador, thinking him boring and vain, but he valued his servility. He wanted men like Keitel and Ribbentrop, whom he believed trustworthy.[52] Goebbels was not impressed. 'I consider Ribbentrop is a waste of space. I made no secret of this to the Führer.'[53]

The Blomberg–Fritsch affair was an excellent example of the Nazi speciality of dirty tricks and a temporary alliance between three very ill-assorted men, Göring, Himmler and Heydrich, with walk-on roles by various secret policemen. Hitler – and to a lesser degree Goebbels – was the dupe. The machinations of his underlings left Hitler's faith in national conservative Germany badly shaken, as a result of which he decided he did not need them as much as he had previously

[vii] He came to regret it later. See Reinhard Spitzy, *So Haben wir das Reich verspielt*, new edn 1987, 222.

believed. It is also to be noted that it was not Göring or Himmler but Adolf Hitler who came out on top.

CASE OTTO

As 1937 came to a close, Hitler was more and more obsessed with Austria. At Berchtesgaden, he surrounded himself with the Austrian Legionaries who were trained in sabotage by members of his own Praetorian Guard, the *Leibstandarte* 'Adolf Hitler'. The Legion had paraded before Hitler at the Berghof and he had told them that he would not give up the fight for a Nazi Austria: Austria was his home too.[54] While his hand was often stayed by consideration for Italy, Göring was much more gung-ho, as Austria offered some morsels that were particularly delicious in the form of raw materials, and foreign exchange that he craved for his Four Year Plan. When Austria had been digested the western parts of Czechoslovakia would be surrounded on three sides. Göring stood to inherit property there. Schloss Mauterndorf was being kept warm for him by the widow of his Jewish stepfather. Two of Göring's sisters had married Austrian lawyers, and his anti-Nazi brother Albert lived in Vienna, where he had taken out Austrian citizenship and was employed in the film industry.

Since the beginning of the thirties, Austria had been governed by clerico-fascist Christian Socials who had wound up democracy and replaced the power of the people with seven corporations representing occupational groupings that were allowed to send their advisors to various federal councils. The party had been subsequently abolished and merged into the Fatherland Front. Apart from Italy's Duce, few people – least of all *bien-pensant* intellectuals – expressed any sympathy for Austria's repressive government, and yet the Corporate State was the last bastion to hold out against a merger with German National Socialism.

Chancellor Kurt von Schuschnigg had signed an agreement with Hitler in July 1936 that was meant to guarantee Austrian sovereignty despite Hitler's persistent attempts to destabilize the country. He had had to agree to allow Austrian National Socialists a small role in government, but Hitler had not kept his word and the terrorist activity had continued. Most recently the Nazis had been afraid that Schuschnigg intended to restore the monarchy under Archduke Otto, eldest son of the last Emperor Charles. According to Goebbels, the Austrian monarchists were becoming increasingly impertinent. Hitler was beginning to fear that if he did not move quickly, they would get there first.[55] In June 1937 the German General Staff had been asked to draw up plans for an Operation Otto to seize Austria.

Every day Hitler's men let off bombs around the country in a bid to make Austria ungovernable; the Corporate State was visibly crumbling, partly as a result of Nazi harassment, partly from its own internal contradictions. Schuschnigg had assumed some of the apparel of the Duce and the Führer, but he did not conform to the image of the strongman: he was more like a cross between Neville Chamberlain and a Jesuit. As the Nazis sought every opportunity to destabilize the state, Vienna became the principal stage of history for the very last time.

At the start of 1938, Schuschnigg's police had discovered an extensive Nazi plot against his government, and plans to assassinate him and stage an uprising in the spring. The papers were signed by Hess. On 25 January the police raided the Nazi Committee of Seven and arrested the civil engineer Dr Leopold Tavs, who was deputy to Hitler's Gauleiter for Austria, Josef Leopold. Tavs had been boasting a little too loudly of his invulnerability and was arraigned for high treason. As the Germans did not want Hess's role made public, a great deal of pressure was brought to bear by Berlin to scrap the trial.

The German ambassador to Vienna, Franz von Papen, was also to be assassinated. The Nazis would make it look like the work of the Fatherland Front, killing two birds with one stone, as Hitler had been wanting to get rid of Papen for some time, since, like Neurath, he opposed the Anschluss.[56] The former chancellor had only narrowly escaped death on the Night of the Long Knives in 1934. The Nazis were goading Schuschnigg to use his army against them; then they would have a pretext to march in.

Schuschnigg had already dissolved his own Praetorians, the *Heimwehr*, who had been the equivalent of the SA. The leader was Mussolini's protégé Prince Ernst Rüdiger von Starhemberg, 'a man of winning appearance, very modest political gifts, immense ambition and little love of work'.[57] Mussolini, however, who had protected Austria at the time of Dollfuss's assassination in 1934 by moving his troops up to the Brenner, had now decided that his bread was better buttered with Hitler and jilted Schuschnigg. He needed Hitler now that the British and the French were ganging up against him over the invasion of Abyssinia, and he wished to avoid the embarrassment of Hitler bringing up the 250,000 or so Germans who had been living under the Italian flag in the South Tyrol since 1919, and had been persecuted by his government for wishing to remain German. Besides, Schuschnigg himself had once told Mussolini that the majority of Austrians would be in favour of a German occupation and that, if Italy sent troops, the Austrians would unite with the Germans to fight them.[58] The Austrian Chancellor was clearly on his own.

2

FEBRUARY

Hitler dithered for two more days before coming to a decision about who was to lead the army.[1] Fritsch was asked to submit his resignation on 3 February.[i] The French ambassador, André François-Poncet, who had been invited to dinner that night, received notice that the party was cancelled the day before. He had been surprised to be asked, as Fritsch was not socially gregarious. The only place he encountered the 'ursine' army chief was at the races.[2]

On the 3rd Hitler confirmed to Goebbels that Neurath's days were numbered too. He was looking to pull a rabbit out of a hat to deflect attention from the farce in his armed forces. This reshuffle could be passed off as 'rejuvenation'.[3] Schuschnigg was also in the firing line;[4] as Hitler put it, 'Schuschnigg should not take courage, he ought to be quaking in his boots.'[5]

On Friday, 4 February, the German cabinet met and Hitler announced that he was to abolish the title of Minister of War and take over the leadership of the armed forces himself. The War Ministry's functions were to be assumed by the OKW (*Oberkommando der Wehrmacht*, i.e. armed forces high command). This was to be administered by another pliant figure, Keitel, who was accorded ministerial rank; meanwhile Keitel's nominee Walther von

[i] Fritsch was exonerated by the court on 18 March, but he was not given another role. He volunteered to lead his regiment in the Polish Campaign and died before Warsaw on 22 September 1939. It has been suggested that he had intentionally sought death.

Brauchitsch was moved in to lead the army. Hitler had personally examined him on a number of issues and found him politically sound.[6]

Both Keitel and Brauchitsch were reputed 'God-fearing',[7] but despite his traditional credentials Brauchitsch promised to lead the army towards National Socialism. He was not entirely morally clean either: he was keen to divorce his wife and marry a woman from a humble background. Göring was able to sort things out again, as Brauchitsch's son Bernd was one of his adjutants, and he sweetened the pill by offering the first wife enough money to buy her consent. Another advantage for Hitler was that Brauchitsch's paramour was '200 per cent rabid Nazi'.

The army were not to be spared. Inspired perhaps by the Soviet Union's Great Terror, which took place that year, and the purge of the Red Army, Hitler pushed twelve senior generals into retirement and transferred another forty-four to new roles, where they could no longer make trouble. One of the announcements made it clear that Himmler would now be allowed to create his own armed SS of 600,000 men, the ancestor of the Waffen-SS.

Walther Funk became Minister of Finance. Göring had kept Schacht's seat warm for him but Funk had far less power than his predecessor. Göring had naturally made off with the plums, saving them for his Four Year Plan. Göring was compensated with the title of Field Marshal, while Neurath was to be given a sinecure and Ribbentrop moved across the Wilhelmstrasse to take his place as Foreign Minister; he already had his own National Socialist 'Ribbentrop Bureau' putting its feet in the more delicate ballet of diplomatic process. One of his pet projects was a German–Japanese alliance.[8] As the French ambassador François-Poncet put it, Ribbentrop 'had a prodigious ignorance of diplomatic matters'.[9]

Ribbentrop was beside himself with excitement at his appointment. He had been a singular failure in London: sent to seal an alliance, he had come back empty-handed. He had spent all of December concocting a report in 'miserable German' in which he advocated a tripartite alliance with Italy and Japan.[10] Goaded on by his sparkling-wine heiress wife Annaliese, his former Anglophilia had now turned to hatred.[11] Since his return he had been doorstepping Hitler, who had affected not to notice him.[ii] He was finally summoned to appear before the Führer in the Chancellery conservatory on the 2nd. While Ribbentrop was closeted with his master, his Austrian secretary Reinhard Spitzy was kicking his heels outside as an SS servant congratulated him that he was no longer adjutant to an ambassador but to a minister. After his appointment, Ribbentrop's hubris returned and he repaired to his expensively rented wing of the Kaiserhof Hotel opposite, ordered a whisky[iii] and called his wife.[12]

As *Reichsaussenminister* (generally contracted to RAM[iv]) Ribbentrop added the old Presidential palace to his collection of residences. He promptly tore it down and replaced it with a neo-baroque edifice designed by Hitler's architect Albert Speer that was more to his taste. He told Spitzy, 'My good fellow, now we are going to pursue a proper German policy . . .'[13] As much as possible, policy was to be dictated by ideology, although the Nazi leaders still wanted to avoid alarming foreign governments, which explains the moderate changes at ambassadorial level. The secretary in the Chancellery, Lammers, informed the ambassadors in Rome, Tokyo and Vienna of their dismissal by telephone that day.

There were some positive results from the shake-up in the Wilhelmstrasse. The ambassador to Rome, Ulrich von Hassell, was retired. His dislike for Hitler and his regime had been only too

---

[ii] In his mendacious memoirs, Ribbentrop claimed his appointment had come as a 'complete surprise' (*The Ribbentrop Memoirs*, London 1954, 78).

[iii] Possibly a Johnny Walker. Ribbentrop was a close friend of Alexander Walker, the descendant of the original Johnny. See Giles MacDonogh, 'Walking Tall: From Grocer to Whisky Powerhouse', in *Cigar Aficionado*, Winter 1996.

[iv] Ribbentrop was known as 'Groraz' behind his back – *größte Reichsau-ßenminister aller Zeiten* – 'The Greatest Imperial Foreign Minister of All Time'. Hitler was 'Grofaz' – *größte Führer aller Zeiten* – 'The Greatest Leader of All Time'.

apparent and the Italians had complained. Ciano, the Italian Foreign Minister, in particular loathed his habit of quoting Dante – 'I distrust foreigners who know Dante.'[14] The fairly neutral, old-school Dirksen in Tokyo was not dropped but shifted to London. He owed his retention to his mother having once been useful to Hitler in Berlin society.

Significant changes came at a lower level of the diplomatic corps that was little permeated by the Party. The leading anti-Nazi, Erich Kordt, became the head of Ribbentrop's secretariat in the Foreign Office, and was instrumental in having his brother Theo shifted from Athens to take over his old job of counsellor at the embassy in London. Finally, on 2 April, Ernst von Weizsäcker was promoted to become Permanent Under-Secretary of State. The Opposition was now in position to alert foreign governments to Germany's intentions. Despite many threats, the Nazis were never able to bring the Wilhelmstrasse wholly under their control.

On 4 February the changes that had taken place were explained in a wireless broadcast. The 'strongest concentration of all political, military and economic forces' was to be placed in the 'hands of the supreme leader'. On the 5th the new structure of the Reich was the main theme in Germany's newspapers and the source of a great deal of gossip and conjecture. It was believed that there had been a plot against the government and an attempt on the Führer's life. Hitler told his closest retinue not to let the public know that the real reason for change had been the fallout over the Blomberg–Fritsch Affair.[15]

The writer Jochen Klepper read all about it when his Jewish stepdaughters handed him the morning newspaper: 'This is completely unexpected . . . It is a day so heavy with destiny that it can only be compared to 30 January 1933: it is much more significant than June 1934.[v] It is as if the last barrier is gone . . . '[16] On the afternoon of the 5th Hitler gathered the generals around him and read them parts of Gürtner's report on the Fritsch case. In the

[v] i.e., the Night of the Long Knives.

circumstances they could only agree that Hitler had done the right thing. That evening he told the story to his ministers, in an emotional address that brought cabinet government to an end in the Third Reich.

SCHUSCHNIGG IN BERCHTESGADEN

Hitler turned his attention to Austria. With Austria amalgamated into the Reich, Germany could bring Hungary and Jugoslavia into economic subservience. He had been hesitant about Italy, but now the Duce's opposition seemed to have abated and the meeting with Prime Minister Chamberlain's envoy Lord Halifax had assured Hitler that Britain would not stand in his way. Halifax had intimated that the British government would be prepared to accept the reversion of Danzig, and border alterations in Czechoslovakia too, with time.

Since then the redoubtable anti-appeaser Sir Robert Vansittart had been removed as Permanent Under-Secretary at the Foreign Office, and the Foreign Secretary, Eden was on his way out too. He resigned in a huff on 20 February after a tiff caused by Chamberlain's meddling in foreign affairs. His departure came as a relief to Hitler, especially as he was replaced on the 26th by the selfsame Lord Halifax who had given him so much encouragement at Berchtesgaden.[17]

Göring was egging Hitler on to invade Austria if Schuschnigg would not yield. Göring's Four Year Plan was responsible for providing the funding and resources for German rearmament. Germany was seriously short of steel, which was such an important commodity to the Nazis that Hitler was the sole arbiter of who got what. On 8 February Göring complained to Hitler that the Four Year Plan would never be complete. He was looking around for a means of achieving autarky in the shortest possible time.[18]

As it was, Austria's steel production was small, just 4 per cent of Germany's, but there was a greater potential in working the iron-ore mines of the Erzberg. Perhaps an even greater incentive to conquest was the reserves in Austria's national bank. With 782 million RM in foreign exchange, Austria possessed twice as much cash as Germany for shopping abroad and purchasing raw materials needed for war. On 10 February Göring met his economic advisors. The German balance of payments was 'bleak', and there was talk of cuts to high-priority projects. Göring's gaze turned greedily towards the River Inn that separated Germany from Austria.[19]

The idea behind the Berchtesgaden talks between Hitler and Schuschnigg had been Papen's. The meeting had been on the cards for some time, but had been postponed as a result of the Blomberg–Fritsch Crisis.[20] Papen had visited Hitler on 5 February following his dismissal, since he was anxious to restore his status as Hitler's personal representative in Austria.[21] Hitler had put Papen's recall on hold, depending on his ability to bring him Schuschnigg. On Saturday, 12 February, Papen took Schuschnigg to see Hitler in Berchtesgaden in the company of the Austrian Foreign Secretary, Göring's new protégé, Guido Schmidt. Göring did not attend the meeting as he felt the moment for negotiation was over.

Schuschnigg was anxious, and told the Mayor of Vienna, Richard Schmitz, that if anything were to happen to him he was to assume the Chancellorship. He gave orders that the border be closed if he were not back by 9 p.m.[22] As they made their way up to the Berghof, Schuschnigg, Schmidt and Papen passed a unit of Austrian Legionnaires, stationed to humiliate Schuschnigg. They found the Führer in no mood for small talk. When the Austrian Chancellor tried talking to Hitler about the beauty of the view, it was brushed aside. Although the conversation was conducted behind closed doors, Hitler's rants could be heard on the floor below: 'I, an Austrian by birth, have been sent by Providence to create the Greater German State! And you stand in my way! I will crush you!'[23] He, Hitler, was the better Austrian; he, Hitler, had no Slavic blood – an allusion to the Austrian Chancellor's Slovenian name. In one report, Hitler threatened to invade Salzburg.[24] He told Schuschnigg that no one would come to his defence.[25]

He demanded that the dismayed Austrian Chancellor include in his cabinet the moderate Austrian Nazi lawyer – Schuschnigg's former comrade-in-arms – Arthur Seyss-Inquart.[vi] Schuschnigg was also to amnesty all Nazi terrorists in Austria's jails and concentration camps.

Austrians were to be allowed to be Nazis. Hitler also required the dismissal of the Austrian General Staff Chief, Lieutenant Field Marshal Jansa, who possessed a viable plan for protecting the country against German aggression.[26] For his part Schuschnigg asked that two of his bugbears be removed from Austria, Tavs and Leopold.

Schuschnigg then had to endure lunch, ending with an *Apfelstrudl* – no tribute to the visiting Austrian but prepared to please the vegetarian Führer's irrepressible sweet tooth. During the meal Schuschnigg looked pale, while Hitler talked on general matters, avoiding politics.[27] The Austrian was desperate for a cigarette, but Hitler delivered one of his monologues against smokers and smoking. He had to wait until the meal ended before he could light up, and then only one cigarette, negotiated for him by a compassionate but wholly unbriefed Ribbentrop,[28] whose one contribution to the debate was to propose a currency and customs union between the two countries.[29] That afternoon Hitler continued to dictate a settlement to him in a way that would become increasingly infamous.

This settlement was based on the Keppler Protocol, named after Wilhelm Keppler, the Nazi 'Commissioner for Austria', who was also present that day.[30] The Protocol went much further than the demands made before lunch, calling for a partial removal of Austrian sovereignty. It encapsulated the slow, 'evolutionary' Anschluss favoured by Hitler at the time. Schuschnigg was to hand over some of his independent foreign policy to Hitler, inasmuch as it touched on matters of mutual German-Austrian interest; there was to be a lifting

[vi] Seyss had been born Arthur Zaytich to a Bohemian schoolmaster and his German wife in Moravia. When the family moved to Vienna, the father changed his name to one with a more Germanic allure. Goebbels thought him 'no Nazi in our sense of the word' and a 'great dud': *Tagebücher I*, V 170, 181.

of all bans on National Socialist activity, which was declared 'compatible with Austrian sovereignty'; Seyss-Inquart was to be named Minister of the Interior to ensure that National Socialism was allowed full liberty; Schuschnigg had to sack his press secretaries; Glaise-Hostenau was to be made Minister of War, and there were to be regular exchanges between the two armies; finally, the Austrian economy was to be integrated into that of Germany and Dr Hans Fischböck made Minister of Finance.[31]

Schuschnigg conferred with his Foreign Minister before informing Hitler that such decisions had no value under the Austrian constitution: nothing could be done without the agreement of the President. Hitler showed his displeasure by shouting to his butler, 'Get me Keitel!' According to one account, Hitler's general was buckling on his sword in the conservatory below, one of a trio of military men who had been brought in to intimidate Schuschnigg, along with the air force General Hugo Sperrle and Reichenau. Keitel claimed later that he had no idea why he had been asked that day.[32] The Austrians feared they were about to be arrested when Keitel appeared asking for orders. Hitler grinned and said, 'There are no orders. I just wanted to have you here.'[33] Hitler later told his circle that he had asked Keitel how many divisions Germany had at the Austrian border, and what sort of resistance they were likely to encounter from the Austrians. Keitel had allegedly replied, 'Not worth mentioning, my Führer.'[34]

Papen intervened and managed to make Hitler agree to only a partial implementation of the Protocol by the 18th, as the rest would require the President's consent. Hitler told Schuschnigg he had given him three days to put the agreement into effect and that it was to last five years: 'That is a long time and in five years the world will look different, anyway.'[35] Hitler recovered his composure and hinted at darker plans: 'In tanks, planes and motorized vehicles we are the leading power today. It would be completely irresponsible and unjustifiable merely from an historical point of view not to use a magnificent instrument like the German Wehrmacht.'[36]

Schuschnigg appeared prepared to cooperate. According to Papen, the inclusion of the Nazi wooden horse[37] Seyss-Inquart in the Cabinet was the only concession that he had not planned to make before arriving in Berchtesgaden.[38] Other sources suggest that he had been negotiating with Seyss since Tavs' arrest.[39]

The Austrians left at 11 p.m. after signing the Protocol. On the way back to Salzburg, Papen was the only one to speak: 'Now you have some idea, Herr Bundeskanzler, how difficult it is to deal with such an unstable person.'[40] Schuschnigg returned to Vienna at once. The next day he conferred with the President, Dr Wilhelm Miklas, who reluctantly agreed to give in to German demands, including the appointment of Seyss-Inquart as Minister for Security and an amnesty for the Nazis then languishing in custody. Austrian Nazis in uniform were free to roam the streets again.

Hitler turned up the heat. The Abwehr chief Canaris was summoned to see Keitel, who told him to step up the campaign of sabotage[41] until Tuesday the 15th.[42] Canaris, who was still deeply involved in the dirty tricks in Austria and in whipping up the ethnic Germans in the Sudetenland, was provided with the detailed plans for 'Case Otto'. Hitler also appointed Major Klausner as Gauleiter to replace Leopold, who was perceived to have overstepped the mark. Despite reservations, the Austrian parliament approved the agreement.[43]

The Italian Foreign Minister, Ciano, got wind of the talks. He had been pleased with the news of Ribbentrop's appointment as Foreign Minister because '. . . he has made clear his hostility to the English, who have treated him badly'. The Anschluss, on the other hand, he thought inevitable and 'The only thing to do is delay it as long as possible.' Mussolini thought much the same; he was irritated, but believed the merger a *fait accompli*.[44] Goebbels didn't learn the details of the meeting at Berchtesgaden until the following week. Like Göring, he deemed cannons more articulate than words but noted that Hitler was happy, and that neither London nor Paris would raise a finger to help. Heydrich told him that Schuschnigg was 'crushed'.[45]

Nazi bureaucrats were already carrying out the preliminary spadework for the assimilation of Austria. In 1937, SS department II-112 had drawn up lists of the most important Jews outside the Reich; the aim was to build a huge personnel index of Austria. Jews were not picked at random, as Adolf Eichmann made clear:

> For weeks before the Anschluss, as far as Department VII was concerned, the Austrian campaign was prepared on roll-file cards . . . We looked at Jewish civil servants and freemasons in every ideological corner. We sat like schoolboys on benches and copied the information on to the cards; then they were arranged alphabetically, letter by letter, and anything that was not urgent was put to one side. With this card-index the first wave of the SD [Sicherheitsdienst – the SS's own secret service] stormed into Austria.[46]

Information had been supplied by Keppler, who also had close contact with the Freundeskreis Heinrich Himmler – captains of industry who courted the leader of the SS. Keppler was also in touch with the Dresdner Bank, which was keen to mop up the Austrian Mercur Bank in the event of an Anschluss.[47] The cards for Austrian Jews were completed in June 1937 and in September that year the head of the department, Herbert Hagen, and his expert on Zionism, Adolf Eichmann, undertook a trip to the Middle East. The two men had already hatched the idea of creating a central bureau for Jewish emigration to speed up the process of evicting the Jews.[48]

The aim of the trip was to reach Palestine, where they wanted to send the Jews too, but the British were reluctant to let them in. On 2 October 1937 Eichmann and Hagen docked in Haifa and were given authority to land for only twenty-four hours. They hired a droshky and drove around for the allotted time, even going to the top of Mount Carmel to admire the view. On 3 October they landed in Egypt and made for Cairo, where they spent twelve days. There they met Arab leaders and a couple of Nazi agents who had travelled down from Palestine to talk to them. When they tried to obtain visas for a better look at Palestine, however, the two Germans were thwarted by the British authorities.[49] The District Commissioner for Galilee, L.Y. Andrews, and a policeman had been killed by Arab terrorists, and the ensuing unrest proved a useful pretext to keep them out.[50]

Victor Klemperer in Dresden had a fairly good idea what Hitler was going to tell the Reichstag on the 20th. He noted in his diary 'that he has been his own Minister of War since 4 February, that he has dismissed Blomberg and Fritsch and that he was halfway towards annexing German-Austria'.[51] Hitler spoke for three hours that day, addressing the issues of the return of the colonies, the League of Nations, Germano-Polish friendship, Russo-German hatred and the need to protect the Sudeten Germans. The overture to Poland was significant. He needed them on his side if he was to get away with the plans expressed in the Hossbach memorandum.[52] The shambles in the armed forces was to be covered up by Caesarist foreign policy: '. . . The German Reich is no longer willing to tolerate the suppression of ten million Germans across its borders . . . I am glad to say, however, that the Austrian Chancellor has shown insight and satisfactory agreement has been reached with Austria.'[53]

In general the speech was mild and expressed warm feelings towards Austria. After his performance there was a social gathering at the Chancellery. Papen thought Schuschnigg would resign soon. Goebbels noted, however, that Papen also stood up for religion while he, Goebbels, had been busy closing religious newspapers – one Catholic and one Protestant – for the sake of balance. He was itching to strike harder. On 24 February he noted about a 'cheeky speech' made by the Cardinal Archbishop of Munich, Faulhaber: 'Our revenge will not be long in coming.'[54]

In the Austrian provinces, National Socialist demonstrations greeted Hitler's speech. Reading the newspaper, Jochen Klepper wrote that 'Austria was being spoken of as if it were already ours.'[55] Seeing the same news, Klemperer seized on the threat of war implicit in the promise of a stronger army.[56] From that moment onward the Austrian city of Graz and the rest of the province of Styria effectively fell to the Nazis. In Britain the Foreign Secretary, Eden, resigned that day. 'This is good for us,' noted Goebbels.[57] He wasn't wrong: the British Foreign Office had already written Austria off.[58] Appeasement was now official policy, it seemed, and the British government felt the need to buy Germany off. The ambassador, Sir Nevile Henderson, brought the Wilhelmstrasse an offer to return Germany's African colonies with the exception of South West Africa, which was now owned by South Africa. Goebbels joked that they would offer them Portuguese colonies instead. Eventually Henderson reappeared with a suggestion that they might like the Congo.[59]

Schuschnigg was able to redeem himself before the Austrian people to some degree with his speech to the diet on the 24th – a holy day in Germany as the anniversary of the Party's foundation. He declared 'Rotweissrot bis in den Tot',[vii] and thereafter, in his patriotic announcements in various Austrian cities, he whipped up a last-ditch enthusiasm for the independent Austrian cause. Schuschnigg had moved too late, however, to unite the country. He needed to bring the socialists and the trade unions back within the pale of the constitution and they told him that they could not fight the country's enemies with their hands tied. Even the former Emperor's son Otto urged him to bring in some socialists.

In Berlin, Goebbels noted renewed activity among the legitimists behind Otto.[60] When the crunch came, however, there was no serious attempt by the left or the right to move against the Nazi menace, which might have been brought down by a general strike, after the model of the 1920 Kapp Putsch in Germany. Schuschnigg's assertion of Austrian independence incensed Hitler and his circle. Goebbels thought him 'a little pig'. Schuschnigg's resistance, however puny, forced the Nazis to abandon the evolutionary method: 'In the end we are really going to have to use force.'[61]

Some read the signals correctly. On 17 February the temperamental

---

[vii] 'Red, white, red until we are dead' – the colours of the Austrian republic.

Italian conductor Arturo Toscanini cabled the Austrian government
to inform it that he would not be conducting at Salzburg, or anywhere
else in Austria. He had flirted with Mussolini, but enough was
enough. The musical director of the Vienna Philharmonic, Bruno
Walter, urged him to reconsider.[62] On Sunday, 27 February, Walter
conducted the Vienna Philharmonic for the last time. The music-
loving Chancellor Schuschnigg was in his box. He was at the height
of his popularity and was cheered wherever he went. In Berlin,
Goebbels was playing cat and mouse with the conductor Furtwängler
again. Goebbels had not foreseen that Austria would fall to Germany
so quickly: 'I will let him get up again, otherwise he'll leave for Vienna
or Salzburg.'[63]

As the Reich's cultural supremo, Goebbels was concerned about
painting as well as music. The 'Degenerate Art' exhibition that
pilloried avant-garde German painting was opening in the partly
ruinous Reichstag building in Berlin, and he was in close contact with
the curator, the painter Adolf Ziegler. On Sunday the 27th he went
along to have a look. There were new elements to the show, which
had opened in Munich the year before. 'What rubbish!' noted the
former collector of progressive modern artists such as Emil Nolde and
Ernst Barlach. Still, he did not feel that the message struck hard
enough, and ordered that the paintings be rehung.[64]

In the second week of February, Goebbels was angry that the courts
still failed to grasp the fact that they were meant to act according to
the wishes of the government. Some homosexual members of the
Party had been arraigned in Stuttgart: 'I hope there will be the most
draconian sentences.' Another case was refusing to go as planned.
Pastor Martin Niemöller of the Confessing Church was in the dock
for subversion. He had managed, however, to make use of the
courtroom and freely air his criticisms of the regime. 'Just wait until
I get hold of that pig Niemöller. The lawyers are incompetent twits.'
Goebbels was particularly livid that the pastor had spoken for seven
hours about his 'heroic life'.[65] Goebbels succeeded in having the case
heard in camera, and Niemöller was transferred from Moabit Prison

in Berlin to Sachsenshausen on 2 March after being sentenced to seven months' 'fortress detention'.

With Niemöller out of the way, the Opposition lost one of its most important early leaders, but others arose to take his place. At the very end of the month Fritz-Dietlof von der Schulenburg returned from his skiing holiday in Bergen, and Helldorf put him in the picture about Fritsch. That very day, Monday the 28th, Helldorf informed General von Stülpnagel of the activities of the Opposition to date. Fritsch's agony had not ceased: a few days later he was interrogated in a Wannsee villa. The theme was no longer his purported homosexuality, but also his political reliability. Fritsch protested that these sessions were a disgrace to him *and* the army.[66]

3

MARCH

On 1 March – Shrove Tuesday – Hermann Göring received his new field marshal's baton from his Führer. The portly former air ace had failed in his bid to yet further expand his portfolio of offices. The carnage lay all around him in the form of the shattered careers of Blomberg and Fritsch. He had been fobbed off with a bauble. Klemperer noted bitterly, 'They have no sense of how ridiculous they are.'[1]

The Austrian plum was ripening, but Seyss-Inquart was warning Berlin that Schuschnigg was not intending to play straight. There was still a nagging fear that Mussolini would come to Austria's aid, as he had done four years before, when the Nazis murdered Chancellor Dollfuss. Meanwhile Hitler's underlings were as disunited as ever, with Goebbels increasingly critical of Himmler's methods. Berlin's Gauleiter thought making Germany into a police state bred 'cowardice, fear and hypocrisy'.[2]

Goebbels was also annoyed about the proceedings against Fritsch, which he thought 'no longer decent. There is hardly a shred of evidence. In any case, they should never have drawn the Führer into the business.'[3] Hitler had continued to agonize right up to the moment he dismissed his army chief. At much the same time, Fritsch's defence lawyer Rüdiger Graf von der Goltz at last learned that the evidence the Gestapo was using against Fritsch was actually from the Rittmeister von Frisch dossier. The following day Helldorf took that file to Oster at the Abwehr. On Sunday, 6 March,

Schulenburg appeared at Goltz's house to warn the lawyer that he might be being watched by the Gestapo. Were his servants reliable? He also checked the telephone for listening devices.[4]

The court of honour was to sit in judgement on Fritsch at the Preussenhaus, or old House of Lords, on the 10th. The judges were Göring, Raeder and Brauchitsch. Goltz, who had been able to offer Fritsch some solace at the end of February, now possessed the proof that the case was as leaky as a sieve: 'Colonel-General,' said Goltz, 'you may now celebrate your victory.' The lawyer brought the general a bunch of red roses.

A few days before, Schulenburg paid a call on General von Witzleben to assess the possibility of an armed revolt. Witzleben had been ill in January but was now open to representations of this sort. He told Schulenburg that Colonel Paul von Hase was prepared to march on Berlin with his regiment, and that he himself had already talked to Hase about this very subject. Witzleben was still smarting from the murders of the former Chancellor Schleicher and General von Bredow during the Night of the Long Knives. An old-fashioned Prussian officer who wore his heart on his sleeve, in 1937 he had sounded out several generals on the need to prevent Hitler from taking Germany to war. As he was fond of saying: 'I know nothing about politics but I certainly don't need to in order to know what I have to do.' He almost certainly made contact as well with Oster, who was able to put him in touch with Schulenburg and Ulrich Wilhelm Graf von Schwerin-Schwanenfeld.[5]

On 10 March, the president of the court of honour, Göring, was preoccupied with Austria, and the Fritsch case was adjourned until the 17th. Initially Schmidt continued to stick to his story, but when it proved to have been a case of mistaken identity he finally broke down. On the 18th he admitted, '*Jawohl, ich ha' jelogen*' ('Yes, I was lying').[6] Some of the leading Nazis begrudgingly admitted that the case against Fritsch was null and void. On 1 April, Hitler even went so far as to send Fritsch a goodwill message congratulating him from recovering from an illness. Goebbels rightly called it 'cold comfort' for the loss of his entire world.[7]

THE ANSCHLUSS

On 5 March, two Nazis, Seyss-Inquart and Glaise-Horstenau, were admitted to the Austrian Cabinet. The *Deutsche Grüss*, or raised-arm salute, was permitted in private circles. Yet Chancellor Schuschnigg had evidently decided that he could go no farther down the road designated at Berchtesgaden and felt he needed to summon his parliament. The agreement framed in 1936 was as far as it went. 'Austria can and will live. It will never voluntarily give up its national existence.'[8] Austria was German, Schuschnigg was convinced of that, but he was not prepared to become part of a National Socialist or 'Prussian'-dominated Germany. The mention of Prussia was yet more evidence that Schuschnigg was trying to manipulate his people: there was nothing Prussian about Hitler or his regime, but after the victories of Frederick the Great in the eighteenth century and the Austrian defeat at Königgrätz in 1866, the Prussians were loathed in Austria.

Austria was falling apart. There was a demonstration in Schuschnigg's favour in Vienna, but Nazis ran up a swastika flag at Graz town hall. Ciano heard that Seyss would soon become Chancellor: 'The Duce is now strongly critical.'[9] Otto von Habsburg implored Schuschnigg to appoint him instead. The writer and director Ernst Lothar went to see Schuschnigg on Sunday, 6 March, in the little house he lived in at Upper Belvedere. Lothar voiced the fears of Austria's Jews in the light of Schuschnigg's appointing Nazis to his cabinet. He suggested that Schuschnigg should make Bruno Walter director of the National Opera. The Chancellor agreed and asked Lothar to talk him round. They then lapsed into a pleasant conversation about Walter's interpretation of Bruckner.[10]

Lothar saw Schuschnigg again two days later, on Tuesday the 8th, at the Ball of the Vaterländische Front. He and his ministers were dressed in the black uniforms of the *Ostmärkische Sturmscharen*.[i] Lothar thought they looked like SS-men and said so. The party secretary, the poet Guido Zernatto, merely shrugged his shoulders.[11] Schuschnigg's policy was to remove the attractions of Nazism by offering his people an imitative homegrown version. He had decided on a radical course of action, possibly encouraged by the French, who wanted evidence that there was no majority for unification with Germany: Schuschnigg was going to hold a plebiscite instead. He went to Innsbruck on 9 March for a meeting of the Front and made the announcement from the balcony of the royal palace. The poll was to be held on 13 March 'for a free and independent, German and Christian Austria'.

Schuschnigg was becoming brave, encouraged by the international response to his defiant speech of 24 February.[12] For most people, his decision to call a plebiscite came as a bolt from the blue. He had sounded out Mussolini on Monday the 7th, but the latter had given him no leave to hope: 'C'è *un errore*,' the Duce told the Austrian envoy Colonel Liebitzky. Mussolini had been pleased to hear of Schuschnigg's resistance, but he was aware that Italy was in no position to fight Germany to maintain Austrian independence. Now there was a risk of losing everything.[13] Halifax thought much the same: 'foolish and provocative', he dubbed it.[14] Hitler was not expecting it at all and was initially at a loss to know how to respond. He had sent Ribbentrop to London, so now he would pretend that the RAM was seeking British agreement to the Anschluss.[15] Goebbels was also caught unawares: Schuschnigg, he thought, was a nasty peasant who was trying to catch them out. Once he had recovered, Hitler realized that it was just the provocation he was looking for.[16] The Anschluss would be accelerated.

---

[i] The Stormtroopers of the Ostmark, i.e. Austria. This was also the name awarded to Austria after Hitler reduced it to a province of the Greater German Reich.

When the news broke in the Berlin Chancellery, Spitzy likened the mood among its denizens to an angry swarm of hornets. His master Ribbentrop was away in London, saying his adieus, and Schuschnigg was very probably aware of this. He ran into Hitler's adjutants Julius Schaub and Wilhelm Brückner, who were rude: 'No one is interested in you diplomats,' said Schaub – 'and not in the slightest bit in your boss', added Brückner. They were wrong: Hitler wanted to see Spitzy and vent his fury about the plebiscite: 'Listen to me. This Schoschnik [*sic*], he wants to betray me . . . and by the foulest tricks like public polls, the exclusion of younger voters, an embargo on propaganda from the opposition and so on. That is an outrage, and I shall not tolerate it.'[17]

Jodl noted in his diary that the plebiscite would bring in a 'strong majority for the monarchists' who were backing Otto Habsburg.[18] That would have added to Hitler's fear of a restoration, and not just Hitler's: the Czechs too were petrified by the idea of the return of the monarchy. The Austrian Chancellor sent out feelers to European capitals to see if there was support for military action against Germany. Ciano thought it bad news: 'The Nazis are rising against the Plebiscite . . . Schuschnigg has made a fatal mistake . . . The Plebiscite bomb is fated to explode in his hands.'[19] The subject was brought up in the French Chamber, where there was a desire to take 'positive' steps to preserve Austrian independence.[20] The British Foreign Office were still resigned to what they perceived as Austria's inevitable fate.[21]

Schuschnigg and his men threw all the energy of the Corporate State into the poll. Huge numbers of flysheets were printed and distributed by its various organizations, the *Jungvolk* (the Corporate State's version of the Hitler Youth) in particular. Some were scattered by aircraft in Austria's most remote and snowbound corners, where many voters would have been Nazis. Lorries trundled about, transmitting the message of Austrian independence by loudspeaker. Planes trailing banners carried the word '*Ja*' over the cities. A flysheet showed Schuschnigg and the Austrian *Kruckenkreuz*, the Corporate

State's version of the swastika.[ii] Another displayed a group of three men, partly wearing Austrian folk costume, again with the *Kruckenkreuz*. Everywhere the German theme was pushed home: to be a good Austrian was to be a good German; to be German was to be free. Austrians were better Germans than the Nazis.[22]

The plebiscite almost certainly accelerated the end of Austria,[23] which raises the question: was there an element of provocation? The age qualification was raised to twenty-four to make it impossible for young Nazi thugs to register their views. The electoral roll was not up to date anyway and there was no possibility of revising it in so short a time. Voters simply had to produce identification to register. Moreover, the ballot slip was printed with the word '*Ja*'. Anyone who did not want to keep an independent Christian Austria had to cut out a piece of paper himself and write the word '*Nein*'. 'Devious and shabby' was how one contemporary described it.[24] Göring gleefully pointed out at his trial that there were plenty of opportunities to rig the ballot – it was not in any way fair.[25]

On 10 March, German Heroes' Remembrance Day, Goebbels arrived at the Chancellery in Berlin to find Hitler bent over maps of Austria. The leader of the Austrian Legion, Reschny, was worried that the Austrian army would fight if Schuschnigg told them to.[26] Lothar went to Linz and noted that Schuschnigg's popularity was running high: a boy who shouted '*Heil Hitler!*' was all but lynched.[27] Schuschnigg returned to Vienna that day and a furious Hitler ordered his military chiefs to prepare for an invasion on the 12th. Göring postponed the Fritsch trial *sine die* and rushed off to join Hitler. He was delighted that he could control German foreign policy during Ribbentrop's absence.

The humiliated RAM was stuck in London with instructions from Hitler not to move. He was to represent the German government in the course of the crisis. Like many of his contemporaries,

[ii] A Greek cross with long flat tops to the arms. It was not the only Nazi-style trapping of the Corporate State. Schuschnigg ended his speeches with a rousing '*FrontHeil!*' The equivalent of *KraftdurchFreude* was *Neue Leben*.

Chamberlain had a low opinion of Ribbentrop's intelligence. It was not just with Britain that Ribbentrop was prone to putting his foot in it. In his passion for signing a German-Japanese alliance, he destroyed a profitable Sino-German trading relationship that provided Germany with wolfram, among other things.[28] The RAM learned of the Anschluss from Chamberlain, Halifax and Cadogan in the course of lunch at Downing Street, and followed its progress on the BBC.[29] To add insult to injury, his predecessor Neurath was temporarily brought back to the Wilhelmstrasse to deal with the flak from abroad. Many other important members of the gang were missing too. Brauchitsch was on leave and Reichenau in Cairo. Keitel was asked to produce the Case Otto file and Beck to move two army corps to the frontier. Hitler still wanted a pretext for going in. Göring thought that was eyewash: they should go in anyway.

Schuschnigg issued the news to government and ministers as late as he could. The headquarters of the government party, the Fatherland Front, also had a visit from Dr Desider Friedmann of the Jewish Congregation or IKG (*Israelitische Kultus Gemeinde*), who brought a cheque for 500,000 Schillings. The following day he brought them another for 300,000.[30] It was a reflection of the degree of anxiety that was going through the community. As the writer Gina Kaus put it, they hoped to win, 'but we were worried for all that'.[31] They were conscious that if Austria fell they would suffer a terrible fate. For Hitler, the affirmation of an independent Austria would amount to a humiliation.

On 11 March Hitler performed the first ever invasion by telephone. The Chief of Police, Dr Skubl, rang Schuschnigg at 5.30 a.m. to tell him that the border had been closed at Salzburg. The pious Austrian Chancellor's first reaction was to take himself off to Mass at the cathedral. When he reached the Chancellery he discovered that German forces had been mobilized in Bavaria and that Seyss-Inquart had disappeared. As it transpired, the German mobilization had been chaotic: the General Staff possessed no proper plans. Later many units actually broke down on the road between Linz and Vienna. It was a godsend that the Austrians offered no resistance.

No one had had much sleep in Berlin. Goebbels had been scribbling propaganda for most of the night, preparing to drop thirteen million leaflets on Austria in response to Schuschnigg. Papen arrived from Vienna to find Neurath, Interior Minister Wilhelm Frick, Himmler, Brauchitsch, Keitel and their retinue. He was kept in the dark in an antechamber of the Chancellery while the others took decisions. Around midday Hitler sent word to Mussolini, through Prince Philip of Hesse, that Case Otto would go ahead whatever the Duce said. He took the trouble to sugar the pill: his letter contained 'a precise declaration about the recognition of the Brenner as the frontier of Italy'.[32]

Hitler was a furious bundle of nerves, unable to issue coherent orders, and it was Göring who directed the Anschluss. At 9.30 a.m., Seyss-Inquart and his fellow Nazi minister Glaise-Horstenau arrived at the Austrian Chancellery in the Ballhausplatz. Göring issued an ultimatum at around 10 a.m.: he wanted the plebiscite postponed within the hour and another one announced, to be carried out under the system established by the Germans in the Saar.[iii] When Schuschnigg made inquiries in Graz he learned that the postponement had already taken place and that he had apparently resigned. When the Chancellor asked if he could rely on the police to defend Vienna he was told that, since the amnesty, the Nazis had been reinstated, and that their loyalty to the Austrian Republic was doubtful. Schuschnigg was sure that the army was reliable, but he was convinced that Austria should not go to war with Germany – there was to be no repeat of 1866. He decided at 2.45 p.m. to postpone the plebiscite, and called the loyal members of his cabinet to inform them. The scene in Vienna must have been rendered all

---

[iii] The Versailles Treaty had awarded the Saar region on Germany's western border to the French for a period of fifteen years, after which its destiny would be decided by a plebiscite. In January 1935, over 90 per cent of the Saarländer voted to return to Germany.

the more absurd by the ubiquity of loudspeakers blaring out the national hymn *O Du mein Österreich*. Within a few weeks most of his ministers and senior bureaucrats would be breaking stones in Dachau.

Seyss-Inquart went to report the decision to Göring, who was closeted with Hitler. Communication was not helped by a faulty telephone connection between the two countries. As there was insufficient power to take the calls to his private apartments, Hitler and Göring had to wait for news at the Berlin Chancellery switchboard. Göring's prodigious girth meant there was scarcely room for anyone else in the small room. Hitler was standing with one knee on a sofa nervously twisting the curtain cord with his hand when Seyss finally came on the line. In his excitement he managed to pull down the curtain. 'Yes, he should act!' Hitler shouted.[33]

At 5.30 Seyss returned to Schuschnigg with a notebook containing the Reichsmarschall's prescription: 'The situation can only be saved if the Austrian Chancellor resigns immediately and if Dr Seyss-Inquart is appointed Chancellor within two hours. If these conditions are not fulfilled, German armies will move on Austria.'[34] In Berlin it was still not certain whether the army would go in.[35] Other conditions in the ultimatum had to be carried out by 7.30 and Seyss grumbled that he was being treated like a receptionist. German forces were already mustered at the border. In Austria, public Tannoys told men born in 1915 to report to the colours: a partial mobilization.[36] Troops were positioned here and there and morale was good, but nothing more came of it. A unit moving up to the border from the Neusiedlersee was greeted with mild enthusiasm in some places, and at others – like the small towns of Melk and Amstetten – by a population that had already gone over to Hitler. The general inspector of the Austrian army, Sigismund Schilhawsky, described military resistance as 'pointless' because Austria could not hope for any immediate support from outside. By 6 p.m. the troops were sent back to their barracks.[37]

Lothar experienced this at first hand in Amstetten. There was a

Nazi parade in the town and the firemen's band was playing the
Horst-Wessel-Lied. At that moment the Austrian army arrived, making
for the Austrian-German frontier. Lothar talked to the captain, who
told him, 'We left Vienna to avoid bloodshed. From tomorrow we will
be no more than a unit in the German armed forces.'[38] At that stage
Hitler had not fully decided on his course. The idea was to make him
Federal President and the rest could come gradually.[39] State Secretary
Hornborstl madly telephoned potential saviours. The Italians had
already washed their hands of Austria.[40] No one was prepared to
guarantee the state. Halifax replied that he could offer nothing. In the
circumstances Schuschnigg meekly did what was required of him and
went, but he insisted on the correct form and tendered his resignation.
In his memoirs Schuschnigg allowed himself a reflection: 'That day
meant not only the end of Austrian independence, it also meant the
end of international morals.' It is a wonder it took him so long to
realize the gravity of the situation.

While the Austrian Chancellor slowly divested himself of his
offices, Seyss-Inquart and Glaise-Horstenau sat in a corner of the
Chancellery and received messengers with closecropped or shaven
heads, 'most of them with heavy sabre scars across their faces'.[41] The
Nazis had moved in. One was Gauleiter Joseph Bürckel from the Saar,
who was meant to take over Papen's job.[42] Keppler had landed at
Aspern in his private aeroplane. Hess came by train.[43] The new
brooms snatched telephones from the hands of loyal officials and
slammed them down. After tendering his resignation, Schuschnigg
returned to the Ballhausplatz to clear his desk. He was observed by the
images on the wall: the death mask of Dollfuss, murdered in the office
next door, and the Empress Maria Theresa. He rehearsed the golden
moments of Austrian history, prompted by the same pictures of the
great and good, and the hall that in 1814 and 1815 had witnessed
the glory days of the Congress of Vienna.

A retainer entered to tell him that the Germans were broadcasting reports of a communist uprising in Austria. The government
was said to be helpless, and there were hundreds of casualties.

The announcement of his resignation was broadcast at around 7 p.m. Miklas was still fierce in his reluctance to appoint Seyss-Inquart Chancellor, but he ultimately gave in half an hour later. Schuschnigg's departure was the signal to the Nazi thugs to take over: the violence began as local bosses were ousted from their offices and the barracks of the Fatherland Front were taken over. Avoiding bloodshed did not enter into the Nazi agenda.

At the cabaret Simplicissimus, the German comedian Fritz Grünbaum made his last appearance before he and his partner Karl Farkas were banned. The lights had already been switched off. 'I can't see a thing, nothing at all. I must have stumbled on to the Nazi cultural stage.'[44]

In the Jewish-owned Café Herrenhof, the German exile Walter Mehring was sitting with his agent when Seyss-Inquart and Glaise-Horstenau came in to confer. It was Seyss-Inquart's *Stammlokal*.[iv] The waiter told Mehring, 'Seyss ordered only soup. Now it's getting serious.'[45]

Schuschnigg made his last broadcast at 8.15 that evening. He had postponed the plebiscite as he had been determined to avoid bloodshed at all cost. Gina Kaus lived above the Jockey Club. She listened to the speech and went to the window and looked down on to the Lobkowitzplatz, where she saw a policeman put away his red, white, red armband and put on a swastika: evidence that the police played a crucial role in the death of Austria's First Republic. Her lover Eduard Frischauer, a baptized Jew whose uncle owned a Sunday newspaper, said, 'We leave tomorrow.'[46]

Austrian army units received orders to withdraw towards the east – they were not to open fire. Hitler was also cheered by the news from Austria: now that he knew the army had been muzzled, he gave the order for his troops to march at 8.45 p.m.[47] At 10.30, he received the information he had been waiting for: Mussolini gave him the go-ahead. Hitler was delighted. He told Göring's friend

---

[iv] Like the 'local' pub to an Englishman.

Prince Philip that he would never forget Mussolini's gesture, and he never did.

Hitler's Austrian agent, Keppler, had already moved into his office. The initial arrests were going ahead, and Mayor Schmitz was the first to be taken into custody. He had refused to fly a swastika from the town hall and had armed the municipal militia. The Nazis also captured and consumed 166 brace of sausages they found in the Rathauskeller.[48] Miklas finally summoned Seyss shortly before midnight. The President was now in no position to object, having been confined to his villa by the SS-man Otto Skorzeny, the discovery and protégé of the Austrian SS chief Ernst Kaltenbrunner. It was Skorzeny's first appearance as Nazi Germany's chief daredevil. His career would include liberating Mussolini from Il Grand Sasso in 1943, and leading the storming of the Bendlerstrasse after the plot of 20 July 1944.

Seyss appointed a Cabinet of conservative Nazis. Göring insisted on the inclusion of Dr Franz Ulrich Hüber as Minister of Justice. He was the husband of Göring's sister Paula. Seyss's reign as an independent Austrian Chancellor proved to be shortlived. When the German military attaché, General Muff, rang Berlin at Seyss's request to inform Göring that everything had been carried out according to his wishes, and he could now recall his forces, Göring told Muff that, on the contrary, he was to demand the assistance of German troops to re-establish law and order. Göring had been enjoying his sport. That evening he was the host at a Winter Ball at the Air Ministry in Berlin. He arrived fashionably late after his exertions on the telephone. He found an opportunity to talk to Sir Nevile Henderson, who delivered a predictable protest, and the Czech minister, Mastny, who, despite Göring's anxieties, gave him the assurance he wanted: Czechoslovakia would not mobilize to save Austria.

When, around midnight, Göring heard that Miklas had given in, he collected Goebbels from his table and together they drove to Hitler to listen to the first broadcast of the *Horst-Wessel-Lied* from Vienna. Only one thing marred his enjoyment of the evening: the news that Himmler was already on his way to Vienna. Göring called Seyss to say that he did not want the wire-tapping services to fall into the hands of his rival.[49] He alone held the bugging monopoly for the Reich. Expatriates and German Jews were also tuning into Austrian wireless to learn of the country's fate. Schuschnigg's broadcast had ended with the Austrian national anthem followed by some Austrian classical music. When they heard the *Horst-Wessel-Lied* they realized 'Austrian freedom was dead'.[50] Goebbels naturally thought otherwise: 'The bells of freedom have struck for this land too.' In Nuremberg, Julius Streicher's *Stürmer* exulted in the emergence of 'Greater Germany' and the end of 'Jewish rule'.[51]

In the luxurious 'Zu den drei Husaren' in the Weihburggasse that evening, the atmosphere was jubilant. A Mr and Mrs Friedrich Frankau of Montreal, Canada, signed the restaurant's golden book: 'We are both very happy to have been in Vienna the very day Austria became a part of the greatest country in the world. God be forever with the Austrians.' Over the next few weeks others would make their way to Vienna's best (and still Jewish-owned) restaurant. On the 15th Edmund Veesenmayer, who achieved fame later for his role in deporting Hungary's Jews to Auschwitz, praised the day when 'our Führer's homeland returned to our great, ethnic-German Reich. After a hard struggle the finest day of my life and at the same time the day of commitment towards our Sudeten-German brothers.' A table full of German railway officials decorated the book with a swastika. They had witnessed the parade of the German and Austrian forces in the capital. Göring's friend Udet was there on the 27th, Viktor Lutze of the SA on 3 April and two days later General Kesselring.[52]

AUSTRIA'S JEWS

On 12 March an excited Göring called his friend Prince Philip of Hesse in Rome. He wanted to ascertain if Mussolini was happy or was going to rock the boat. Prince Philip told him that a swastika was already flying from the Austrian Consulate. The King of Italy (Philip's father-in-law) had informed him that Colonel Jozef Beck, the Polish Foreign Minister, had relayed the news that 25,000 Viennese Jews had asked for passports. 'The view is here that it's best to open the frontiers for a while so that the whole scum gets out . . . !'

Göring made no secret of what he wanted in his reply: 'All right, but not with any foreign currency. The Jews can go, but they will kindly leave behind their money, which they have only stolen.'[53]

The Anschluss not only scattered the political elite of the Corporate State, it struck terror in the hearts of the Jews. Up until 1938, Austria's Jews could be broadly divided into Zionists and assimilators. After Hitler's arrival, however, assimilation was to prove a dead letter, while for Zionists the dream of a Palestinian homeland became a possibility. The assimilated Jews realized that their Gentile manners availed them nothing. The Nazis hated them even more than they despised the Zionists. Some Jewish communists headed for the Soviet Union, joining those who had left for fear of imprisonment by the Corporate State in 1934. This was risky, however, as there was every chance that they might end up in the gulag.[54]

A.R. Penn, the Secretary of the Church Mission to the Jews, arrived in Vienna from Romania and Poland on 11 March to find the city in a state of overexcitement about Sunday's plebiscite. When he woke the next morning Schuschnigg had resigned and the SA had occupied the political vacuum. The air rang with cries of 'Heil Hitler!' On 12 March, while he sat talking to Hugh Grimes, the British embassy chaplain, Penn heard Hitler proclaim the Anschluss. Before he left, a Jewish friend took him up to the hills that overlook the city. She told him, 'I feel as if I were looking at my beloved Vienna for the last time.'[55]

As of 11 March 1938, there were 185,028 Jews in Austria of whom 176,034 lived in Vienna: just under 10 per cent of the city's population or 2.8 per cent of Austrians. Vienna had a hefty Jewish infrastructure with ninety-four synagogues and 120 welfare organizations under the umbrella of the IKG, an organization dominated by Zionists since the twenties; both the president, Friedmann, and the vice-president, Dr Löwenherz, were Zionists. Another significant Jewish body was the 8,000-strong *Bund Jüdischer Frontsoldaten* or Jewish Old Soldiers' League, founded in 1932 and led by Captain Siegfried Edler von Friedmann.[56] In addition there were those who no longer admitted to Judaism, and many who were racially Jewish yet who had converted to Christianity or were simply agnostic or atheist.

Hitler's antisemitic policies were bound to find favour in Austria, for they had been developed there in the first place. Young Adolf had come up from Linz and been appalled by the sight of Vienna's Jews: the city was the most Jewish in the German-speaking world. The party behind the Corporate State – the *Christlichsozialen* or Christian Socials – had been founded by the same Mayor Karl Lueger who coined the phrase 'I decide who's a Jew.' He meant that in a few cases Jews could aspire to social acceptability.

When Austria became a republic, Vienna's Jewish population filled the social and political vacuum created by degradation of the imperial nobility. There was a large influx of so-called *Ostjuden* from Poland and Russia – strange apparitions with beards and kaftans whose lives had been wrecked by pogroms and war and who had headed west to seek their fortunes. They were greatly resented in Germany and Austria, not only by the Gentiles but by the more assimilated Jews, who found them primitive, and felt they held up a grubby mirror to their more refined selves.[57]

In 1921 there was a three-day meeting of antisemites in Vienna and in 1923 between 50,000 and 100,000 marched around the Ringstrasse protesting against the Jewish 'dictatorship'.[58] When the Corporate State arrived some Jews were already able to see the writing on the wall. Stefan Zweig's house on the Kapuzinerberg near Salzburg was searched for weapons in 1934. The writer was so scandalized that he turned his back on Austria and went to live in England.

A year later, on 16 September 1935, Austria introduced racial law under the *Blutschutzgesetz*.[v] It was no longer permitted to enter the description *konfessionslos* (non-denominational) on a birth certificate. Any Jews who had lost their religion without gaining another were obliged to list themselves as Jewish. The law was more in keeping with Catholic thinking than with Nuremberg, but undoubtedly prompted by the latter.[59]

Although the Corporate State was not officially antipathetic to Jews, there was a cold persecution as they were squeezed out of public life. There were now very few Jewish members of the National Council, as the legislative body was called. Contracts in Viennese hospitals were not renewed when the doctor was Jewish; publishing houses refused to print books by Jews and newspapers were increasingly reluctant to employ Jewish journalists. The *Neue Freie Presse* had been purged of Jewish staff by 1937. Film production companies did not employ Jewish actors and actresses, as they needed to be able to sell their films across the border in Germany; and Jewish sportsmen could not compete if there were Germans about. It was believed that Schuschnigg intended to reduce the percentage of Jews in the professions to reflect their share of the population.[60]

Many of Vienna's assimilated Jews were virtually indistinguishable from the German elite: they read their Goethe, Schiller and Nestroy, and went to concerts to listen to Beethoven, Schubert, Brahms and Franz Schmidt. Believing themselves to be good 'Germans' (people spoke seldom of being 'Austrian' then), they had no desire to leave. The *Ostjuden*, lately come from the *shtetls*, were more likely to be attracted to the idea of Zionism and the establishment of a Jewish state, preferably in Palestine.[61]

After the Anschluss, it was calculated that 20 per cent of potential refugees were non-Aryan Christians: ethnic Jews who had been baptized.[62] The Quaker Emma Cadbury, who was based in Vienna, estimated their numbers at 60,000 Catholics and 10,000 Protestants, although the official figure was a comparatively modest 24,000.[63] The

---

[v] Law for the protection of blood.

philosopher Karl Popper, for example, had been baptized a Protestant in infancy.[64] Conversion was gaining popularity among Jews. Between 1928 and 1934 there had been 447 baptisms. The arrival of Hitler in power across the border in Germany seems to have provided a further spur: there were forty-two baptisms in 1932 and 102 in 1933, but in the first half of 1934 there were 152.[65]

Baptism was a way round the various kinds of *numerus clausus* that limited Jewish entry into branches of public life. With the *Taufschein* or baptismal certificate, the Jewish *Taufjude* could become a judge, a professor or a highranking civil servant with far greater ease.[66] A measure of how many members of the Jewish elite were Christians is the fact that a third of the Jews in Dachau were baptized, and not only for political reasons: many of them had a Christian grandparent or two.[67] The British chaplain Grimes reported at the beginning of 1937 on the success of the Swedish pastor Tarrel, who carried out thirty to forty conversions every year. 'He [Tarrel] thinks there would be many more if it were not for the pressure exercised by the Jews themselves who will not employ Christian Jews.' Tarrel had converted a hundred Jews in 1934, possibly because of the creation of the rigidly Catholic Corporate State.[68]

THE DICTATORSHIP OF THE GUTTERSNIPES[vi]

The birth pangs and infancy of the First Austrian Republic had been aggravated by chronic unemployment. While Germany had been able to solve most of its problems, at the time of the Anschluss anything up to 300,000 chiefly young Viennese were out of work.[69] They gravitated towards extremist organizations that purported to be able

[vi] A favourite phrase of the sports journalist Maximilian Reich. It was first used by an unnamed Scandinavian diplomat. Maximilan and Emilie Reich, *Zweier Zeugen Mund. Verschollene Manuskripte aus 1938 – Wien – Dachau – Buchenwald*, Vienna 2007, 74 n1.

to solve the problem one way or another. One of the promises delivered by the Nazis was the 100 per cent elimination of unemployment.[vii] As one contemporary put it, 'Hunger drove millions into the arms of the Nazis.'[70] The Jews were, as ever, considered to be the principal enemy: idle and rich, feeding off human misery.

On 11 March the Hitlerites were already out and about in the largely Jewish Second District, shouting slogans and flailing fists hours before the German army had reached Vienna.[71] The sportswriter Maximilian Reich saw the Nazis in the Kärntnerstrasse, Vienna's chief commercial boulevard: HJ[viii] members aged between ten and sixteen, chanting against Schuschnigg, the Jews and priests.[72] Schuschnigg's resignation was the signal for the revolution to begin. Illegal Nazis donned swastika armbands or SA uniforms and took over key offices. Jews were immediately sacked or sent on extended leave. That same day, Emma Cadbury wrote to Alice Nike in London: 'The Jews here are very much worried and there has been an increase of antisemitic propaganda, but I hope this may quiet down. . . .'[73]

The *Morning Chronicle*'s man in Vienna, Eric Gedye, recorded disgusting scenes where the Viennese showed the Jews the pent-up hatred seething within them:

> It is the heartless, grinning, soberly dressed crowds on the Graben and the Kärntnerstrasse . . . fluffy Viennese blondes, fighting to get closer to the elevating spectacle of an ashen-faced Jewish surgeon on his hands and knees before half a dozen young hooligans with Swastika armlets and dogwhips that sticks in my mind. His delicate fingers, which must have made the swift and confident incisions that had saved the lives of many Viennese, held a scrubbing brush. A storm trooper was pouring some acid solution over the brush – and his fingers. Another sluiced the pavement from a bucket, taking care to drench the surgeon's

[vii] It was one of the messages in Göring's speech in the North West Station on 26 March.

[viii] Hitler Jugend, or Hitler Youth.

striped trousers as he did so. And the Viennese – not uniformed Nazis or a raging mob, but the Viennese Little Man and his wife – just grinned approval at the glorious fun.[74]

The Czechs prudently sealed their borders to prevent an influx of Jews;[75] only those with the appropriate entry visas could pass.[76] The Vienna–Prague train arrived in the Czech capital that night with no Austrians on board. It left Vienna at the usual time of 11.15 and was due to reach Czech soil forty minutes later. The numbers on board were progressively whittled down by a succession of brutal searches. The few who made it to the border at Breclav were crushed to learn that the Czechs would not let them in. The Czechs were not unhappy about the Anschluss; they were happier to see the Germans in Vienna than face a Habsburg restoration.[77]

Those Jews who had fled on four wheels abandoned 'a whole car park' and hid in the woods closest to the frontier. The cabaret artist Jura Soyfer tried to cross the Swiss border on skis but was arrested and taken to Innsbruck. Other Jews boarded trains to Romania but were turned back at the border; even those who had Romanian papers were refused permission to return.[78]

Naturally the wisest ones made for the borders as quickly as they could. That was particularly important for anyone on a Nazi black list. Malwine Dollfuss, the widow of the murdered Chancellor, two Habsburgs and Guido Zernatto of the Vaterländische Front were successful, as was the comedian Karl Farkas; but many found no way through. Brno was often the goal. It contained a large German minority even in 1938, and many of Vienna's Jews had family in southern Moravia. Once in Czechoslovakia, they could catch the 'flying Moses' from Prague, the aircraft that flew the children of Israel away from the Nazi peril.[79]

Writers whose works had been burned on the Opernplatz in Berlin were advised to go before the Germans took hold of the city. One of them was the German dramatist Carl Zuckmayer, who had been living near Salzburg for years, but happened to be in Vienna at the time of the Anschluss. He was in the theatre all day and oblivious of political developments until he heard Schuschnigg's resignation broadcast that evening.[80]

Zuckmayer had survived a dozen battles on the Western Front, as well as the terrible upheavals of the postwar years; he had been on the streets at the time of the HitlerPutsch in Munich, and witnessed the Nazi takeover of power in Berlin; but nothing compared to those days in Vienna. 'It was the witches' Sabbath of the plebs that laid all human values to rest.'[81] That night he was travelling in a taxi when the mob decided that he and his companion were Polish Jews and needed to be beaten up. Zuckmayer only escaped by shouting out something that sounded like '*Heil Hitler!*' in his best Reich German accent, like a sergeant-major drilling his squad. When the skies blackened with German bombers making their way to the airport at Aspern, a new, equally sinister noise joined the screams of the tortured. After a while you got used to that too. All those new sounds merged into one: 'The air was filled with the cacophony of Armageddon.'[82]

Zuckmayer's play *Bellmann* was shortly to open at the Theatre in the Josefstadt, directed by Ernst Lothar. In the middle of rehearsal on Sunday two actors came to Lothar and declared they represented the theatre's National Socialist cell: Zuckmayer's play could not be performed because the author was part Jewish. Lothar promptly resigned and went home to his flat on the Beethoven Platz, next to the Imperial Hotel, where Hitler was staying that night. Shortly afterwards, the police arrived to impound his passport. Lothar's wife, the actress Adrienne Gessner, lost her temper: 'Go to Mr Gauleiter, or whatever title the idiot uses, the fellow who sent you . . . and tell him that I threw you out.' Lothar apologized for his wife and gave the policemen his passport. He sensed that he would have considerable problems getting the papers back and promptly negotiated an exit visa from the local police for the vast sum of 25,000 Schillings, then set out for his brother in Switzerland with his daughter in a new, chauffeur-driven car.[83]

Everything went well until they approached the border at St Anton in the Vorarlberg, where they were flagged down by the local gendarme. He had been told to look out for the car. He was perfectly polite, and had even read Lothar's novels, but he had been told to inform the SA. Lothar waited upstairs in the police station while his daughter and the driver stayed by the car. The SA-men rolled up soon after. They were not polite and said the Lothars would have to undergo a strip search. They grabbed the daughter and prepared to tear off her blouse. Lothar was quick on the uptake: they too wanted to be bought off, in this instance with the car. The Nazis were in raptures over their booty. As soon as he had signed an affidavit to say that he had given it them of his own free will, they drove the Lothars to the border in Feldkirch. The SA headed off in the car, leaving the theatre director and his daughter at the station. Fortunately the border official was a fan and had been to several of Lothar's productions: he waved them off to freedom with a friendly '*Auf Wiederschauen in Österreich.*'[84]

Austrian officials weren't all so friendly. As Lothar discovered, the western borders were being more carefully watched than the east. Schuschnigg's friend, the Education Minister Hans Pertner, who had suggested that he bring in the socialists, made his way to Czechoslovakia.[ix] It was not always that easy to settle matters, and the thought of an impoverished exile made people postpone the decision until it was too late. Gina Kaus, a Jewish writer whose books had been burned in Berlin, had an Italian passport by virtue of the fact that her former husband had been born in Trieste. Together with her son Peter and her lover Eduard Frischauer, she managed to board a train on Monday that was full to bursting. They were delayed five hours at the border. An outraged English skier related that she had been 'gynaecologically investigated'.

[ix] His intermediary was the journalist Anton Kuh: '*Jetzt weiss ich dass wir verloren sind. Ein Staat, der mit einem Kuh verhandelt, der ist am Ende!*' The pun is untranslatable: 'Now I know that it has come to an end. A state that negotiates with a *cow* (i.e. Anton *Kuh*) has had it.'

When they reached the Swiss border she felt like hugging the conductors.[85]

As a rule only Jews or Mischlinge (persons of mixed Jewish and Gentile blood) made haste to leave. Exceptions were the Gentile writer Franz Theodor Csokor[86] and the musicians Erich Kleiber and Ralph Benatzky. The Nazis wrongly thought the latter was a Jew. Those who went, or preferred to remain abroad, make an impressive list: musicians like Robert Stolz, Fritz Kreisler, Arnold Schoenberg, Hanns Eisler, Erich Wolfgang Korngold or Egon Wellesz; conductors such as Bruno Walter and Joseph Krips; singers of the calibre of Lotte Lehmann, Maria Jeritza, Alfred Piccaver and Richard Tauber; men and women of theatre and cinema like Max Reinhardt, Otto Preminger, Fritzi Massary, Elisabeth Bergner, Oskar Homolka and Anton Wohlbrück (later Walbrook).

In Berlin, Goebbels was hatching plans to 'de-Jew' Vienna and located a few collaborators in the process, such as the actor Attila Hörbiger, who was able to report on his wife Paula Wessely with her many Jewish friends. Vienna's music was all 'Jews and Jew-lovers'. A desire to set some traditional Aryan composers on the pedestals formerly occupied by Brahms and Bruckner led to Franz Schmidt's commission to write Eine deutsche Auferstehung (A German Resurrection) in 1938. Goebbels wanted the pro-Nazi Karl Böhm for the opera, while Hitler favoured Hans Knappertsbusch. When Goebbels visited Vienna on 30 March he gathered the remaining Austrian artists around him in the Hofburg.[87]

Bruno Walter had had the good fortune to be in Holland for the Nazi triumph. He took out French citizenship, and the new powers in the land made off with the contents of his flat. Arnold Rosé, for fifty-seven years leader of the Philharmonic, fled to London, where a new Rosé Quartet was founded. The portraits of Mahler and Walter and an engraving of Rosé disappeared from the historic wall of the offices of the Philharmonic. Mahler's bust was removed from the foyer at the Opera. The Gustav Mahlerstrasse became the Meistersingerstrasse.[88] The wife and children of Hugo von Hoffmannsthal emigrated in

March. Hermann Broch spent months in prison before he was able to reach England. Robert Musil left in August, clutching the manuscript of *A Man without Qualities*.

Jews were made scapegoats for the last acts of the Corporate State and had to wash the pro-Schuschnigg graffiti off the walls and pavements. At the Café Herrenhaus, the owner and his wife, together with seven customers, were forced to scrub the – presumably unsullied – walls. The chief rabbi, the Zionist Dr Israel Taglich, was philosophical about cleaning the streets, saying, 'I am washing God's earth.' They called themselves *Araber* (Arabs), because they were '*a raber*'(*reiber*) or scrubbers.[89] This was not a Nazi invention; it was the Fatherland Front that instituted this form of punishment, and meted it out to illegal Nazis, when they were caught daubing slogans.[90]

The plebiscite had been largely funded by Jewish money, something that made the Jews appear particularly culpable. The first acts of bestiality were carried out by the homegrown SA, although they were quickly joined by Himmler's men, who carried their own hitlists. Before Eichmann's arrival, the most important body in Vienna was Department II-112, SS-Oberabschnitt Donau. There were two days of 'wild' persecution between 11 March and formal annexation on the 13th.[91] Franz Rothenberg, president of the Creditanstalt bank, was hurled from a car at top speed but survived. Others were not so lucky. Isidor Pollack, managing director of the Pulverfabrik chemical works, died of the wounds he sustained from his beating. Later the Deutsche Bank would take over the Creditanstalt and I.G. Farben would appropriate the Pulverfabrik.[92]

As in Zuckmayer's case,[x] it was still possible to impress some Nazis by flashing a medal for bravery. The writer Leo Perutz, for example, escaped a nasty scene on the 13th by pointing to his EK1.[xi] Later even this would have no effect on the Viennese thugs. The huge amount of booty they accrued was taken to 36 Prinz-Eugenstrasse, the HQ of

[x] See below, pp. 56–61.
[xi] *Eisernes Kreuz Erster Klasse* – Iron Cross 1st Class.

the SA group Donau-Wien, before being transferred to the Hotel
Metropole, which had been seized from its Jewish owners and turned
into Gestapo HQ. The Prinz-Eugenstrasse was the city home of the
Rothschild family and their vast fortunes naturally concentrated the
minds of the Nazi brigands. The young Dudley Forwood, equerry to
the Duke of Windsor, knew the Rothschilds well, and had the run of
their country house. He was on holiday there on 12 March prior to
leaving for Paris the next day. A footman brought him a message: the
gnädige Baronin had called. He was not to show surprise if anything
strange were to happen on the train. He found the station filled with
troops. At Feldkirch the passengers were ordered off. Over the
loudspeaker he heard: '*Alle Leute raus. Juden auf der linke Seite*'
('Everyone out, Jews on the left'). At that moment he saw the
Rothschilds' English nanny coming towards him with the children.
They pretended to be his. He remembered what the servant had told
him and went along with the game. He got them out.[93]

The mask had fallen. In an officers' mess in Neudiedl am See, a
subaltern suddenly refused to play billiards with another officer
because he was a Jew. The latter walked out of the mess. No one
attempted to hold him back.[94] On 14 March the army was purged of
Jews, and officers and men had to swear an oath of loyalty to Hitler.
The Jewish General Sommer appeared on the street in full rig with
medals. This time the SA showed respect and saluted him. It did not
work twice.[95]

It was not just violence: 'confiscations' were the order of the day –
shops were emptied of their wares, garages of their cars. Rich Jews
were incarcerated for months until they were convinced to hand their
property over to the Gestapo. This was important if there were art
works and collections to steal under a dubious cloak of legality.
Money disappeared into the pockets of Nazi thugs. The Zionist Leo
Lauterbach expressed his astonishment at their ferocity: 'Nobody who
knew the average Viennese until that moment would believe that he
could sink to such a level.'[96]

When the Austrian authorities sought to atone for the violence after 1945, the Viennese were found to be suffering from collective amnesia. In Erdberg they tracked down the chief perpetrator, Josef Breitschneider. Despite the almost total lack of witnesses for the prosecution, he was sentenced to eighteen months, and released after six. In the Twentieth District, Josef Graf had taken it upon himself to visit the cafés, beat up Jewish customers and make them drink from the spittoons. On the 14th he was leading a squad of Jews towards the North West Station hall to perform physical jerks. A group of SA-men coming in the opposite direction decided he was going too far and liberated the Jews. Graf had earlier forced a Gentile to carry a panel up and down the street after visiting a Jewish café. It read 'Arisches Schwein geht zum Judencafé rein' ('Aryan pig goes into Jewish cafés').[97] The gymnastics were extended to Jewish children, who were assembled and forced to perform until they collapsed. The purpose was to extort money from the parents, who could not bear to watch their offspring being abused in this way. Once the torturers had been paid off, more Viennese appeared and took over where the others had left off.[98]

Rich Jews were arrested and prepared for the first transport for Dachau. As the police and the SA had drawn up their own lists, there was a certain rivalry over their prey.[99] The Schiffman brothers, department store owners, were seized in the Taborstrasse and their staff dismissed; likewise Gerngross and Herzmansky in the Mariahilferstrasse, the shoe magnate Krupnik, the carpet merchant Schein, the stocking manufacturer Schön with its eighty branches, the industrial baker Anker, the lightbulb producers Kremenzky and Pregan, the jeweller Scherr, the men's fashion merchant Katz and the clothier Gerstel. The emptying of the Schiffman stores lasted three days.[100] Jews with valuable art collections, like various members of the Gerngross family, found their possessions put up for auction.

At least some of these had made large donations to Schuschnigg's plebiscite funds. Gerstel's name was unfortunate: it was the slang word for cash. As the local Nazis put it at the time 'Darr Jud muss weg und sein Gerschtl bleibt da!' ('The yid must get out, but he has to leave his dough behind').[101] The Nazis took over prominent businesses and arrested the owners, like the Kuffners, proprietors of the famous Ottakringer brewery. Of assets totalling 9 million marks, 2.5 million were confiscated at once, and when the Kuffners sold out, they gave a further 35 per cent to the Nazis.[102] Restaurants were obliged to hang up signs banning Jews.[103]

One of those who tried to cross the Czech border on the 13th was Fritz Grünbaum, but the train was sent back and those on board plundered. The unlucky ones were also arrested, including Grünbaum, who was sent to the new prison in the Karajangasse where he shared a mattress with the later Austrian Chancellor Bruno Kreisky. Grünbaum died in Dachau after a bungled suicide attempt. His wife Lilly was murdered at Maly Trostinec.[104] His huge art collection was sold for a song, and the money went into the coffers of the Reich.

In the provinces the atmosphere was calmer. With the exception of Burgenland, there were few Jews. Graz had the reputation of being the most Nazi city in Austria. The Jewish legal clerk Helmut Bader observed on 13 March that all his judges had donned swastika armbands. He was summoned before the head of personnel and summarily dismissed.[105] The physiologist Otto Loewi, who had won a Nobel Prize for medicine in 1936, was arrested. The money he had been awarded was placed in a closed account.[106]

A *razzia* (raid) mopped up Austria's Jewish journalists on the 17th when Maximilian Reich was arrested. The Black Maria went on to pick up the others. One of them evidently refused to come. Reich heard a shot. When the Gestapo men returned to the car they told the driver, 'The chap didn't want to come with us. Now he can stay at home.'[107] They laughed. Reich was taken to the *Liesl*, the police prison on the Elisabeth Promenade, where he found his friend, the amateur boxer Willy Kurtz, the mayor and numerous prominent Viennese.

The carnage continued unabated: on Tuesday, 15 March, the critic and cultural historian Egon Friedell hurled himself from the fourth floor of his block of flats as the Nazis came to claim their game. He apparently told the Gestapo men to wait, went into his study and shouted down to the people in the street to clear a space. It is possible they had only come in the tradition of good *Adabeis*[xii] to enjoy the spectacle of Friedell's arrest.[108] He had refused to flee, feeling that he would cut an absurd figure as an exile. In one account, the Gestapo men had not come for Friedell at all, but to visit a maid with whom one of them was dallying. He had jumped to conclusions and then to his death.[109]

The Gestapo arrived at 19 Berggasse, the home and surgery of Sigmund Freud, and proceeded to search the flat. His daughter Anna was taken away for interrogation a few days later. Freud was powerful enough to be able to take his family and most of his possessions into exile when he left in June. The building Freud lived and worked in for forty years was eventually turned into a *Sammelwohnung* – a Jewish collection point – from which Jews were deported to their deaths. Freud's five sisters were all murdered in the east.[110]

Zuckmayer finally left on the 15th. Wilhelm von Ketteler at the German embassy had told him that he would be safe, and that the Austrian version of National Socialism would be gentle. Ketteler was almost certainly a decent man, and an opponent of National Socialism who was involved in a plot to kill Hitler. He was murdered by the SS-man Horst Böhme on Heydrich's orders and fished out of the Danube two weeks later.[111] He had been deemed politically unreliable, having removed all Papen's political files to Switzerland.[xiii] Stubborn to the last, Zuckmayer was finally talked into flight by his Austrian wife. It was literally the last moment: the Nazis had already occupied the family house near Salzburg and they were to arrive in his Vienna flat the next day, 'confiscating' in the process around a

---

[xii] From *auch dabei*, the traditional Viennese gawper, but there is a malicious implication too.

[xiii] It wasn't the first time that a close association with Papen had proved fatal: both his speechwriter, Edgar Jung, and his press secretary, Herbert von Bose, were killed following the Night of the Long Knives in 1934.

thousand books signed and dedicated by the great and good, and for the most part by 'degenerate' authors of the time.

Zuckmayer reckoned his chances at fifty-fifty. Everything went smoothly until he reached Salzburg. He was even able to see his own bathing hut at Henndorf, and thought he could hear his dogs barking. They stopped while a troop train passed. The Austrians lowered the windows and obsequiously shouted 'Heil Hitler!' at the conquerors. The soldiers reminded the writer of himself in 1914. They looked embarrassed at this effusiveness and carried on eating their soup.

Salzburg station resembled an armed camp. The cigarette woman, who had provided for Zuckmayer's needs for years, was running after the soldiers, squawking 'Daitsche Brieder'xiv ecstatically and sticking cigarettes in their pockets. It was a repellent vision that made it easier for him to accept the need to quit his adoptive land. There was no passport inspection until the train stopped in Innsbruck, some three hours from the Swiss frontier, at which point a fat man in plain clothes and a swastika armband with a police badge in his lapel came in, accompanied by two Brownshirts with revolvers in their belts.

All went well until he saw Zuckmayer's profession: writer. 'Get off the train and take your luggage.' Zuckmayer wanted to know why.

'Our Führer does not like the press.'

'I am not from the press.'

Attempts to argue with the man were of no avail: Zuckmayer and other 'delinquents' left the train and were taken to the police station, where they sat and waited. He was angry when his turn came to face his interrogators and barked at them in military German. He threw down his German passport and continued to perform his version of an offended member of the master race. He showed them a telegram from the film director Alexander Korda, indicating the time he was due to be in London, and noted that they were unable to understand the English. The man who had taken him from the train insisted that

---

xiv 'German brothers', in the local accent.

Zuckmayer was a writer: 'That is suspicious . . . Our Führer does not like the press.'

'But I am a screenwriter . . . The Führer likes films.'

The events that followed had a typically Austrian quality. The man at the desk agreed that Hitler was a film fan, and admitted that he knew Zuckmayer's house and had swum in the lake there. 'A lovely spot,' he said. Zuckmayer agreed. 'What more do you need from me?'

The official rose from his desk. 'In times like this errors occur, but we try to do our job. Go quickly, but through the back door. Those people out there,' he said, gesturing towards the queue outside, 'they won't escape so easily. They're all Yids.'

He had not got far before he heard one of the Brownshirts coming up behind him. A hand was placed on his shoulder. His body went cold. The Nazi drew a small book from his pocket. Zuckmayer recognized it as the novella he had published the previous year, *Ein Sommer in Österreich* (*A Summer in Austria*). 'I have just read this . . . would you sign it for me?' Zuckmayer did so with the fountain pen provided. The Brownshirt was standing close and leant over him. 'There will be no more "Summers in Austria" . . . Goodbye and make sure you don't come back. Take care at the border.' With that he clicked his heels and disappeared.

Zuckmayer got on the next train. It was stuffed with people trying to leave. He was bathed in sweat and, as he opened a carriage door, unbuttoned his coat for the first time. There was a sudden silence. A man of Jewish appearance jumped up and offered him his seat. 'But that is your seat. Please sit down again,' said Zuckmayer. The others moved up to create some room. Then Zuckmayer caught on: they were staring at his buttonhole. He had bought a swastika at a newsagent in Vienna. Only Party members wore swastikas in Germany, but in Austria they were on sale everywhere, and people put them on simply to tell the thugs they were not Jews.[112] On 11 March they had cost 35 Groschen, but the price had risen since.[113] It was a simple device to ensure a modicum of peace, but he had done more: he had also put on his war medals, including his EK1. The combination of Nazi and war hero was not easy for the Jews in the carriage to decipher, but they offered him schnapps and told him of their fears at the approach of the border.

The closer they came to the frontier the more the carriage panicked. There were constant patrols in the corridor. The doors were opened and they were asked over and over again how much money they had on them. They were allowed ten RM or twenty Austrian Schillings, the precise sum Zuckmayer had brought with him. The playwright studied those around him: there was an Aryan football player with his Jewish fiancée, and a supposed general's son, the one who had offered him schnapps, who, just before the train reached the border, threw all his money out of the window. A Polish woman recognized Zuckmayer and wanted to ask him about forthcoming theatrical events.

Then the train arrived in Feldkirch and, when he saw the spotlights, Zuckmayer's hopes all but vanished. He concentrated his mind on survival.

'Everyone out with their suitcases. The train is to be evacuated.'

'Porter!'

'Carry it yourself . . . there are no porters for the likes of you.'

The station was teeming with men in black and brown uniforms. There were tables on to which the contents of suitcases were being poured out and pored over, while cases were tested for false bottoms. Everything was examined with a finetooth comb. Some of the passengers were being stripsearched. Zuckmayer recalled that his case contained a number of autographs by fellow writers, most of them 'degenerate'. He feared the worst.

The official looked at his name for a long time, then tossed his head back as if he had been suddenly struck by lightning. 'Zuckmayer? . . . *the* Zuckmayer.'

'What do you mean by that?'

'I mean the notorious.'

'I don't know if I am notorious, but there is certainly no other writer with my name.'

'Come with me.'

'I must stay with my luggage.'

'You don't have to do that.' And he laughed a mocking laugh as if to say: you won't need any luggage any more where you are going. He was led away to a hut at the end of the platform. Another man was being taken into custody. Behind the desk sat an SS-man with steel-rimmed spectacles. 'Carl Zuckmayer, ah ha!'

He examined his passport. It was valid for five years. Jews received theirs for six months. The SS-man was vaguely aware that Zuckmayer was racially Jewish – his mother's family were converts – but the passport appeared to contradict this. He reached for a printed list, but could not find Zuckmayer's name on it. 'Funny . . . I had heard something about you once, but I can't remember now what it was. So you are not a Jew at all.'

He laughed and Zuckmayer permitted himself a smile. He did not feel it was incumbent upon him to tell the official that his mother was born Goldschmidt. The Nazi read from the passport: 'Catholic . . . na ja. We are going to deal with those priests too.' He became chatty, and looked as if he might be going to give him back his passport. They talked about his screenplays. The Nazi had seen his latest film. He asked Zuckmayer if he were a member of the Party. Zuckmayer said no. Then the tone changed: 'German writer and not in the Party?' Nor was he a member of the Nazi writers' organization. Zuckmayer admitted that his works were actually banned in Germany, and then regretted it.

The SS-man reacted queerly: he reached out his hand and shook Zuckmayer's. He said he was impressed by Zuckmayer's honesty: most of the people who came before him lied. He volunteered to smooth his way into the Party. The writer thanked him, but said that would not be necessary. Zuckmayer took the opportunity to snatch his passport back and asked if he might have his luggage now.

The SS-man offered to come with him, expressing the hope that that there would be no difficulties occasioned by the search. Zuckmayer envisaged problems for all that: the manuscript, the autographs. He decided to open his coat again and pretend he was looking for something in his pocket. It did the trick: the Nazi wanted to know if he had been at the front, if he had held a commission. He stared at the EK1. 'Then you must be a hero,' he said, staring wide-eyed at him. Zuckmayer played down his heroism, but told the SS-man that medals could not be bought for tuppence ha'penny on the streets all the same. He was alluding to the price of a swastika in his buttonhole.

The SS-man was now eating out of his hands. Not only did he understand the reference to the 'opportunists', he relished Zuckmayer's wit. He bellowed out to the SS- and SA-men around him that they were to honour a hero with a rousing cry of 'Heil Hitler!' They did just that, 'as if I were the Führer himself'. Zuckmayer admitted to feeling like Captain von Köpenick from his own play.[xv] The SS-man told his soldiers to take Zuckmayer's cases on to the train. They had not even been examined. He countermanded the strip-search as well. Zuckmayer was the only person on his train to be exempted.

As the SS-man took him to the station buffet to wait for the rest to pass or fail the examination, an acquaintance of Zuckmayer's wife came up to him and identified himself. His Jewish wife was on the other train waiting in the station; she had a broken leg. Zuckmayer now chanced his luck again. Omitting to tell the SS-man she was a Jewess, he said she was not able to come to the interrogation. 'If you testify for these people, then it is all right,' the Nazi said. The couple were placed on the Swiss train.

There were agonizing moments before it left. Zuckmayer sat in the buffet with the SS-man and they drank their way through the former's last twenty Schillings. The Nazi told him he wanted to prove himself in the field. Zuckmayer comforted him, saying there would be a new

[xv] In *Der Hauptmann von Köpenick* an unemployed cobbler and petty crook dresses up as a Prussian officer and manages to commandeer the petty cash in the town hall of Köpenick near Berlin. It was based on a true story, and particularly loathed by the Nazis.

war soon. He did not hate the Nazi; he pitied him. He saw him as he had seen so many, lying ashenfaced in a pool of blood. Every now and then an SA-man interrupted their drinking to report a big haul in marks or valuables. Dawn was breaking when Zuckmayer's train finally began to move and he was able to quit his sinister companion. Only when Swiss guards entered his carriage did he know for certain that he was not going to Dachau.[114]

Not just the Jews, but all the Corporate State's elite was tainted with the crime of *lèse majesté* against the Führer. Zuckmayer records that aristocrats were forced to scrub the streets, because they too had stuck up for an independent Austria.[115] Both the former Vice-Chancellor and head of the Fatherland Front, Emil Fey, and the Minister of War, General Wilhelm Zehner, apparently 'committed suicide'. Fey allegedly killed his wife and son first. Their bodies were removed from his flat in sealed tubes and taken to the anatomical institute. His corpse was reported to contain twenty-three bullet holes.[116]

Göring saved the Foreign Minister Guido Schmidt by sending his own aircraft to collect him. He was later appointed to the board of the Hermann Göring Works. Around 15 per cent of the judges were dismissed; both the Minister of Justice, Robert Georg Winterstein, and the senior judge, Alois Osio, perished in the camps. Other victims of the new broom were monarchists. Otto von Habsburg was still perceived as a threat. They naturally had no time for the upstart Hitler. Many of them were arrested and despatched to Dachau.[117]

BURGENLAND

There were only tiny pockets of Jews outside Vienna: some 2,000 in Styria; in the Vorarlberg just eighteen.[118] There was a significant community in Burgenland, however, where 3,632 Jews inhabited seven acknowledged, protected old communities: Eisenstadt,

Matersburg, Kobersdorf, Lackenbach, Deutschkreuz, Frauenkirchen and Kittsee. They amounted to a little more than 1 per cent of the population in Austria's easternmost state, but had lived there for several centuries, whereas many Austrian Jews had only quit the *shtetls* of the east a generation before.

It was one of the Nazis' pet projects to rid the province of its Jews as quickly as possible. Whole villages were cleared. In one, 300 were driven from their homes. An American Quaker who witnessed the expulsions recorded, 'We have never seen anything as bad as that in Germany.' In the monthly meeting of the British Board of Deputies the sentiment was echoed: 'The situation in Austria is even worse than the situation in the German Reich. What took the Nazis five years to accomplish in the Reich has been done in five weeks in Austria.'[119]

Until 1921 the region had been a part of Hungary and the Nazis wanted to assert its 'Germanity' before all else. The older expellees were often in possession of Hungarian papers. The violence against the Burgenland Jews began as soon as Schuschnigg announced his resignation. It frequently took the form of rounding them up and driving them over the nearest frontier. The Czechs, Hungarians and Jugoslavs responded by closing the crossings. The leader of the Frauenkirchen Jews, Ahron Ernst Weis, managed to escape on a tourist visa to Palestine. His dentist brother committed suicide. Most of those expelled found refuge in Vienna. Lauterbach and the Christian Zionist Brigadier-General Sir Wyndham Deedes visited three families from the dusty border town of Deutschkreuz who had been expelled 'with a few trifles' by the local gendarmerie. In Rechnitz there were brutal murders.[120]

The ancient Jewish community rapidly became a cause célèbre. On 3 May 1938 a Czech rabbi, Michael Dov Weissmandl, visited Lambeth Palace to drum up support for the Burgenländer. He had a letter of introduction from Isaiah Porritt, the senior Orthodox rabbi in Vienna, and Samuel Epp, the senior rabbi in Burgenland. They were seeking a safe haven for 3,000 Jews. Lang's secretary, Alan Don, wrote to Samuel Hoare at the Home Office to ask if a special favour might be granted in this instance.[121]

The plight of the Burgenland Jews is the subject of Franz Werfel's short story *Die wahre Geschichte vom wiederhergestellten Kreuz* (*The True Story of the Remaking of the Cross*) of 1942. Werfel conceived it as part of his unfinished novel *Cella*, which was set in northern Burgenland. The Catholic priest Ottokar Felix relates the martyrdom of the rabbi of Parndorf, Aladar Fürst, on the night of 11 March, and his own role in seeking to protect the Jews in his village and accompany them into exile. Aladar Fürst did not exist, but the other events described in the story took place on 20 April. The local SA, drunk with power – and wine – threw between twenty and thirty Jews out of their homes and took them to the Hungarian border at Mörbisch on the Neusiedlersee. There they spent four nights in no-man's-land, as the Hungarians were not prepared to accept them. They were eventually allowed to go to Vienna.[122]

Another event that was later dramatized was the expulsion of the Jews from Kittsee, which formed the basis of Friedrich Wolf's play *Das Schiff auf der Donau* (*The Boat on the Danube*). In Kittsee the Jews were forced across the border into Czechoslovakia but, as they had no papers, they were made to endure weeks on an island and later a boat before the Czechs would take them in.

In the state capital, Eisenstadt, an exception was made for Alphons Barb,[xvi] the director of the state museum. The commissioner for cultural issues in Austria asked for a stay of two or three months in his case as the archaeologist had made an important contribution to knowledge of German prehistory in Burgenland through his excavation of gravesites, and had proved that the Germans got there first. Barb had been making an unconscious contribution to *Ahnenerbe*, the research into Germanic roots that was replacing religion for Nazi extremists. He was allowed to continue to live in Vienna until 1939, when the British Museum organized his transfer to London.[123]

[xvi] The author's godfather. In Britain he found work in a bicycle factory in Leeds.

HIMMLER, HITLER AND EICHMANN ARRIVE IN VIENNA

Heinrich Himmler was the first Nazi VIP to arrive in Vienna. His two Ju 52 aircraft touched down in Aspern at 5 a.m. on 12 March. On the way down from Berlin he slipped and almost fell out of the aircraft, and his intelligence chief claimed he had saved his master's life. He was accompanied by the lofty figures of Heydrich, Wolff, Daluege and a large team of SD and Gestapo men dressed in grey uniforms; this was to be the unveiling of the new Waffen-SS kit. They were met on the tarmac by the Austrian police chief Skubl with a police guard of honour. The Germans then went about their task with proverbial efficiency. A willing civil servant was able to provide Himmler with all the state's police records, above all the criminal records of the banned left. Very few wriggled through the net.[124]

Skubl's attentiveness did no good: he was replaced by Kaltenbrunner, one of the few Austrian Nazis ever to achieve high rank in Berlin. Himmler set up his base in the Hotel Regina. Bürckel moved into the Regina in his wake, before opting for the defunct Parliament building on the Ring. The Gestapo were the first to take up residence in the Hotel Metropole after leaving their offices in Vienna's 'noble' street, the Herrengasse. With Schmitz gone from the town hall, the huge square in front of the building was renamed the Adolf-Hitler-Platz two days before the arrival of its new dedicatee.

Himmler and Heydrich immediately unleashed a week of the 'wildest manhunt' followed by wave upon wave of arrests. Between 50,000 and 76,000 people were arrested in March. Classified as 'damaging to the nation', they included intellectuals, public figures and businessmen. Most of them were released after the plebiscite was carried out under Nazi scrutiny on 10 April.[125] Communists were also at risk. The Communist Party had been banned by the Corporate State, and its members were locked up in the concentration camp at Wöllersdorf. There were still active cells, however, and the Nazis took over the job of hunting them down with renewed vigour.

Well-paid police narks went about their business. Kurt Koppel and his mistress Grete Kahane were thought to have been responsible for the arrests of around a thousand communists, leading to about a hundred executions. The fourth central committee of the Communist Party was probably founded by police spies.[126] Himmler went to look at some of his catch in person. He was rather surprised at the aspect of Louis von Rothschild, who had been arrested at Aspern airport. He did not look sufficiently like a Jew, with his bright blue eyes and uncowed manner. When Himmler asked if he knew who he was, Rothschild replied, citing name and rank. The Reichsführer SS was so taken aback that he ordered that Rothschild's cell be made more comfortable. He was to get fresh furniture and a new lavatory seat and basin.[127]

Himmler and Wolff joined their master in Linz. Himmler then accompanied the chief of his economic administration, Oswald Pohl, as he travelled to Upper Austria to look at suitable quarries where they might establish concentration camps. Their eyes lighted on Mauthausen and Gusen. Between April and August various plots of land were bought and the site in Mauthausen rented from its owners, the city of Vienna. (Mauthausen stone was used to make Vienna's pavements.) On 8 August the first prisoners were transferred from Dachau. Mauthausen was to gain the reputation of being one of the grimmest of them all.

Hitler's desire to bind his old country to the land he had adopted had incurred fresh problems. Germany had now acquired 200,000 or so more Jews, who needed to be encouraged to get out. Certain Jews were to be made an example. One of those singled out in Linz was a Dr Eduard Bloch, whose sign was smeared with the word 'Jude'. In 1907 Bloch had taken care of the Führer's mother, Clara Hitler, who was suffering from cancer. Hitler had expressed his gratitude in a letter he wrote to the physician at the time. The desecration of the sign came to the attention of Kaltenbrunner, who sent two SS-men to clean it up.[128]

Department II-112 was responsible to Himmler. It dealt with

emigration, and Eichmann was installed as the expert on Zionist organizations. Ironically, the Nazis and the Zionists had shared aims, and Eichmann was keen to make this work in his favour. They both wanted the Jews to go, and they both were keen on choosing Palestine for their promised land. Eichmann promoted Zionism 'with all means'.[129] Members of the Zionist organization B'nai B'rith topped his list of possible collaborators. The assimilated Jews, on the other hand, were the principal enemies of the National Socialists. As Eichmann's colleague Dieter Wisliceny put it, they were there to 'crush the assimilatory organizations'.[130] With the Nazis' favourite tactic of divide and rule, the assimilated Jews and the Zionists could be played off against one another; there was little love lost between them.[131]

Hitler had been making slow progress. Leaving Göring to manage the shop, he flew to Munich with Keitel. It was Keitel who witnessed his telephone conversation with Mussolini: 'Duce, I will never forget what you have done . . . never, never, never . . .'[132] Hitler reached the Austrian border at around noon and stopped to confer with General Fedor von Bock and receive a report from his press chief Otto Dietrich. At 4 p.m. he crossed into Austria at his birthplace, Braunau on the Inn, where he was received by the mayor; then he drove on to his adopted home town of Linz.

For the first time he was revisiting the country he had quit as a 'penniless vagabond'.[133] The reception accorded him by the Linzer was so ecstatic that he was moved to tears. Indeed, the Austrian response to the Anschluss surprised Nazis and non-Nazis alike. Most people had shared Schuschnigg's optimistic view that a clear majority of Austrians were opposed to the merger. In Berlin, Klepper noted that the larger and most active part of the population must been in favour, 'otherwise these scenes of brotherhood would not have been possible'.[134]

Beds were hastily prepared at the Hotel Weinzinger.[xvii] It was not ideal: there was just a small porter's lodge and one telephone.

[xvii] Pulled down in the 1960s.

Ribbentrop, who was angry and frustrated in London, could not get through to Spitzy until 7 a.m. on the 13th. The RAM was told to stay put. Seyss together with Glaise-Horstenau had travelled up from Vienna to await Hitler's arrival. Seyss later made a speech in which he announced the scrapping of Article 88 of the Treaty of Saint Germain, which forbade the unification of Germany and Austria. In Nuremberg, 'Fips' of *Der Stürmer* celebrated the end of the 'shameful' treaties of Versailles and Saint Germain, while in another cartoon a Jew was concerned at reading that 'Italy was not at all opposed'.[135] On 13 March Hitler indulged in a moment of filial piety when he went to nearby Leonding to put flowers on his parents' grave and visit their home.

While Hitler was in Linz, he had a change of heart about maintaining Austria as a separate state. It seems he may have been swayed by the enthusiasm of the crowds.[136] He chose to 'manage' the revolution instead. He had originally planned to create a National Socialist Austria, closely linked to Germany with himself as Federal President. Now he decided that he was going to incorporate Austria as a self-governing province of the Greater German Reich.[137] The federal states were to be replaced by Nazi territorial divisions or *Gaue*, under the control of a Party boss or Gauleiter. Vienna, expanded to take in much of the land to the south, was placed under the command of Odilo Globocnik, and the controversial Burgenland disappeared altogether as it was incorporated into the *Gaue* Niederdonau and Styria. Seyss legitimized the constitutional changes and Austria duly became a province of the Reich on the 13th. Even the prime mover behind the Anschluss, Hermann Göring, was amazed at the speed at which the changes were made. A plebiscite conducted under Nazi rules was now ordained for 10 April.

Seyss was to relinquish his post as Chancellor of Austria under the new constitution, and become Reichsstatthalter (governor). Under him served a small group of ministers.[138] Bürckel was brought in from the Saar-Palatinate as Reichs Commissioner for the Reunification to manage the plebiscite, as he had done successfully before in the Saar.

His appointment from outside was significant: Austrian Nazis were to play a paltry role in the new territory. Bürckel imported his own men, who were surreptitiously mocked as members of the *Pfalzer-Postenjäger* or 'Palatinate-Job-Hunters' Regiment, while Austrians dubbed their drunken Gauleiter *Bierleiter Gaukel*. The man who would have been Gauleiter, Leopold, ended up as a lowly Party inspector in Munich, before dying with his ambitions in the Russian campaign. Walter Riehl, who had founded the NSDAP in Austria after the First World War, was actually imprisoned on 18 March and only released on Hitler's orders. He was given no work by the new administration. Theodor Habicht, who had been the strong man in Austria before the Anschluss, was compensated with the town hall of Wittenberg in Saxony.[139]

Hitler did not trust them, and preferred to have Germans from the Altreich (as it was now called) occupy almost all the important positions.[xviii] He may have doubted, and even had cause to question, their loyalty, but he used a rather more German justification: laziness. As he had said in his first speech in Linz, the Austrians needed to lose their fondness for *Gemütlichkeit* and put their shoulders to the wheel. The only exceptions were Carinthians such as Klausner and Globocnik.

The cold-shouldering of home-grown Nazis led to considerable resentment in Austria, where the Nazis from the Altreich were quickly transmogrified into 'Prussians', the traditional enemies, although most were no such thing. Bürckel very rapidly became a more powerful figure in the land than the 'governor', Seyss, who was shifted off to Poland when the war started, then to Holland in 1940. Reich law, on the other hand, was only gradually brought in to replace elements in the constitution of the Corporate State.

As Hitler had hoped, there were no great international

[xviii] In the directorate of finance in Linz, for example, thirty of the sixty-five staff were from across the border. Gerhard Jagschitz, 'Von der "Bewegung" zum Apparat', in Talos et al., *NS-Herrschaft*, 101.

repercussions. The Duce was satisfied that Hitler would not create problems in the South Tyrol. Britain declined to act to secure Austrian independence. Chamberlain told the Commons on the 14th that Britain had no obligations towards Austria. The British confined themselves to a pious hope that the Germans would not take revenge on their political and racial enemies. Two days later Lord Halifax told the Upper House that Austria's status had been bound to change in the long run. The French could not respond, for the simple reason that their government had resigned. They were in no position to act on their own anyway. The United States' Secretary of State, Cordell Hull, forbore from comment until the 19th, when he more or less recognized the Anschluss by saying that the Germans were now responsible for Austria's debts. On 17 March, the spokesman for the Soviet regime, Maxim Litvinov, called for action against German aggression, but had nothing specific to say about Austria.[140] Only two countries protested: republican Spain, which was shortly to be eclipsed by Franco's forces, and Mexico. The Austrian Second Republic later renamed a Viennese square in Mexico's honour.

On 15 March, the *Daily Mail* published an interview with Hitler that George Ward Price had conducted in the Weinzinger.[xix] Ward Price had been waiting for the Führer in Linz and as a keen Hitlerian had enjoyed the privilege of mounting the tribune and offering the Austrian people his warmest wishes for the future. His view was that Hitler was a man of peace who represented the only bulwark against bolshevism, a view echoed by many high-ranking officials in the Western world.[141] Four days later Ward Price was in Prague and in his cups he told officials that Hitler's next move would be to recover the German-speaking parts of Czechoslovakia.[142]

On 14 March, Hitler finally drove from Linz to Vienna via Amstetten. Vienna was seething with excitement over the prospect of his arrival. He was a day late, hindered by the unpreparedness of his

[xix] '. . . he is close to the Führer'. Göring to Ribbentrop, 13 March 1938.

army and his own desire to create a frenzy of anticipation. Even then, no one could explain the massive enthusiasm of the population. The city was filled with 40,000 Hitler Youth and *Bund Deutscher Mädel* (German Girls' League) waiting to salute their leader. His cavalcade made for the Imperial Hotel on the Ring. Once upon a time he had earned a few *Kreuzer* digging snow in front of the hotel, and he had always cherished a desire to stay there. Also in his entourage was his mistress, Eva Braun. Her presence did not prevent him later that day from visiting the grave of the previous incumbent, his niece Geli Raubel.[143]

Hitler had left word that he was 'too tired' to address the public, but after repeated requests from the crowd he appeared on the balcony of the hotel to enormous acclaim. There was no denying the enthusiasm of the Viennese, although some maintained that they were less delighted to see the German army, and turned away in silence.[144] Others have pointed out that the crowds were swollen by hordes of provincial Nazis who had been bussed in to boost numbers. Quite a lot of those who came out to gawp were mere *Adabeis*, but that does not account for all of them by any means. Certainly appearances supported Göring's view that 'apart from the Jews in Vienna and part of the black ravens, the Catholics, there is nobody against us'.[145]

One black raven, Cardinal Theodor Innitzer, paid Hitler his respects at the Imperial Hotel on the 15th.[xx] He had been meditating a fitting reaction to Anschluss. The Sudetenländer Innitzer had been a minister in the clerical government of Ignaz Seipel and was seen as one of the pillars of the Corporate State. When local Nazis demanded a gesture, the Cardinal ordered the bells rung in Vienna's churches. He prudently expressed his 'delight at the old dream of German unity', and sent a telegram to Hitler on the road to that effect. He was walking on eggs, however. On 12 March the *Primas Germaniae*, Cardinal Sigismond Waitz, Archbishop of Salzburg, had been placed

---

[xx] He was not alone: the new rector of Vienna University, Fritz Knoll, did the same.

under house arrest, and the Prince Bishop of Graz and Sekau, Ferdinand Pawlikowski, was taken to prison by a jeering crowd. Elsewhere the Abbot Ambros Minarz of Altenburg Abbey refused to fly a swastika flag, causing the SA to occupy the abbey on the 17th.[146] The Bishop of Linz, Johannes Maria Gföllner, had famously said it was impossible to be a National Socialist and a Catholic. He took no notice of Hitler's presence.[147]

The Church was second only to the Jews in unpopularity and the mood was explosive. Innitzer must have felt a need to prevent it blowing up in his face. Everyone in the Church feared a new *Kulturkampf*.[xxi] On 13 March he had offered prayers of thanks for the bloodless transformation.[148] Such behaviour appeared to mar a good record. As rector of the university he had been sympathetic to poor Jewish students, when many of his fellow bishops had been openly antisemitic. Innitzer had taken advice from the Catholic former German Chancellor, Papen, who was anxious that the relationship between Hitler and the Cardinal should start on the correct footing. Papen and Seyss convinced Hitler to see Innitzer. The Church had been hand-in-glove with the Corporate State, and the Nazis wanted to see its influence curtailed. Papen believed that Austria would soon become ungovernable if the Church were not treated properly.[149] Innitzer would later regret it when he realized that the Catholics had been duped.

Innitzer made his way to the Imperial at 9.15 a.m., accompanied by two clerics, his secretary Joseph Weinbauer and Johann Jauner-Schrofenegg. There was an ugly crowd of Austrian Nazis outside, whistling and shouting '*Pfui*' and '*In den Kanal mit dem Kardinal*' ('Throw the Cardinal in the canal'). They were received first by Papen, then ushered in to see Hitler at 10 a.m. Spitzy wrongly maintains that Innitzer performed the 'German salute';[150] rather, Hitler made to kiss the Cardinal's ring, but Innitzer raised the chain

---

[xxi] When Bismarck tried to break the Catholics after the creation of the Second Reich.

on his chest and made the sign of the cross. Hitler reassured Innitzer that provided the Church remained loyal there would be no trouble.[151] Innitzer suggested that loyalty was conditional on the maintenance of the Concordat guaranteeing the position of the Church. Hitler was impressed by the behaviour of the Austrian prelates, whom he compared favourably to the Germans. The SS scattered the hostile crowd as Innitzer left.[152]

The Vatican was outraged by Innitzer's fifteen-minute audience. The Pope condemned the Cardinal for 'breach of loyalty and treason' although this was later rescinded.[153] Austria's small Evangelical Church had declared the Anschluss 'blessed' the day before the Catholics. Certain Evangelicals had been hoping that the Nazis would launch a new Reformation and free Austria from the power of the Catholic Church.[154] The Cardinal was not the only person to see a rosy future in the Greater German Reich: there were also the usual sycophants, and a number of 'Aryan' poets who put their joy into verse. One of these was Josef Weinheber, a member of the Party since 1931. He committed suicide when Germany lost the war.

After the Cardinal left, the devoted Ribbentrop was finally given leave to join his master for his moment of glory in Vienna. At around noon on the 15th, Hitler addressed an audience of some 250,000 people on the Heldenplatz. Goebbels thought it 'a popular uprising in the truest sense of the words',[155] but to some extent he had connived at it by making it a public holiday.[156] Hitler returned to the Heldenplatz after lunch to lay a wreath at the Burgtor. This was the moment when Austria's army and police were paraded before him to swear their new allegiance. On returning to the airport at Aspern, Ribbentrop got lost and ended up in a farmyard.[157] Hitler flew to Munich. As the aircraft passed over the Austrian Alps, he turned to Keitel and said, 'Now that is all German again.' After a quick snack with Keitel at the airport, he repaired to his own flat. The next day, he returned to Berlin, where he was met by Göring, proudly waving his baton. Goebbels had ordered that the factories and places of business be closed at 1 p.m. so that the people could be on the streets to welcome the conquering hero. It was to be a reception 'such as the capital has never seen'.[158]

The Austrian 'revolution' had gone too far, even for the Nazis. On 17 March Heydrich threatened Commissar Bürckel with disciplinary action. He would send a Gestapo unit to deal with Party members who had allowed others to act in a 'completely undisciplined manner'.[159] At the time of the plebiscite in April there was a half-hearted attempt to blame the communists, who had been dressing up in Nazi uniforms and robbing people.[160] The next day Berlin reaffirmed its authority in Austria with a second regulation: power was in the hands of the Reichsführer SS.[161] Bürckel took the hint and threatened to expel the plunderers from the Party. On 29 April he thundered in the Austrian edition of the Nazi *Völkische Beobachter*, 'Germany is governed by the rule of law. That means that nothing happens that has no foundation in law . . . There will be no organized pogroms,[xxii] not even by Frau Hintenhuber[xxiii] against Sara Kohn in the third courtyard, one floor up next to the taps.'[162] Himmler too vented his fury on any Reichs German SS-men found working for their own personal profit. They were to be arrested and ejected from the SS.[163] Once again the Nazis were conscious of foreign opinion and the fragility of German exports.[164]

On the 18th Hitler addressed the Reichstag to report on the union with Austria. He promptly dissolved the assembly before fresh elections on 10 April. This time the poll was to give total power to the Führer: 'then we'll throw away the last democratic-parliamentary eggshells'.[165] A rumpus between the Poles and the Lithuanians was closely studied in Berlin. Lithuania backed down on the 19th, but Hitler now saw the time was ripe to wrest Memel from the small Baltic state which enjoyed good relations with Moscow. The territory had been awarded to Lithuania at Versailles, although it had been a German port before then. The Polish Foreign Minister Beck's policy

---

[xxii] Later certain Nazis would ignore this, particularly Goebbels.
[xxiii] A typically Aryan Austrian or South German name.

was dictated by the German–Polish rapprochement of 1934.[166] The Poles coveted Memel too, and Lithuania was barring their access to the port, but Beck wanted to hold both Germany and Russia at arm's length and maintain Danzig despite the signs that Halifax had informed Hitler that Britain was indifferent to its fate. Hitler therefore needed to make concessions. The Teschen pocket in Sudetenland, with its largely Polish population, was a gobbet to dangle in front of the Poles to gain their support for the dismemberment of Czechoslovakia.[167] In the meantime any German claims to the Corridor were played down: the price of cooperation from Warsaw.[168]

Goebbels found Hitler studying the map. 'First comes Czecho. We are going to split it with the Hungarians and the Poles. And we are going to exploit the next opportunity should Warsaw come to blows with Kovno to pop Memel in the bag. Good, but not yet: we are a boa constrictor digesting its prey. Then the rest of the Baltic [and] a piece of Alsace-Lorraine . . .'[169]

In Vienna, the Austrian bishops were being subjected to all the bullying Bürckel could muster. They met on the 18th and were given a draft document urging all Austrians 'as Germans to recognize the German Reich'.[170] Innitzer objected to an article in the text that had them agree to assimilate the Church's youth organizations. The document passed to and fro, until all six bishops gave in. Innitzer even added 'and Heil Hitler' in his own hand at Bürckel's insistence. The message was doubtless put out to try to ease the situation and to create a *modus vivendi*. After four years of 'clerical fascism' the clergy had a great many enemies, and Austrian priests had already suffered physical violence.[171] Bürckel passed as a man sympathetic to Catholics. Waitz wrote of his astonishment that the bishops had submitted, however, and the bishops were not proud of their pusillanimity: only two published the text in their diocesan organs, and Gföllner had boycotted the session.[172]

Eichmann arrived in Vienna on 16 March to take up the job of directing Department II-112. Two days later he took part in the *razzia* at the IKG building in the Seitenstettengasse, seizing documents relating to Jewish support for Schuschnigg. Friedmann, his two assistants, the architect Robert Stricker and Jakob Ehrlich, and the office director Löwenherz were arrested together with the president of the Zionist National Union, Oskar Grünbaum. Eichmann slapped Löwenherz, telling him that he had been to Palestine, and that he had been born in the old Templar colony of Sarona.[173] This was evidently a fantasy: he came from Solingen near Düsseldorf, but had been brought up in Linz. Others taken into custody were the presidents of the Jewish freemasonic lodges and sixteen high-ranking Jewish masons.

The Duke of Windsor was supposed to have intervened in an attempt to save Louis von Rothschild and the ear specialist Professor Heinrich von Neumann. The Duke was told that Rothschild would be released when he had compensated the state for the losses that occurred with the collapse of the Creditanstalt bank, although Rothschild had resigned a year before the crash. There was a rumour too that Freud had been taken into custody, but that proved unfounded.

Other prominent Jews to be locked up were the eighty-two-year-old Professor Salomon Frankfurter, the seventy-five-year-old Professor Ferdinand Blumenthal, Dr Armand Kaminka, Dr Karl Lothberger, Professor Viktor Frankel, the former minister Arnold Eissler, the editor of *Der Morgen*, Maximilian Schreier, the former editor of the *Neue Wiener Tagblatt*, Dr Loebel, the journalist Erwin Honig, the playwright Louis Hirschfeld, the actors Fritz Grünbaum and Ludwig Stoessl and the cabaret artist Hermann Leopoldi.[174] They also mopped up the head of the Jewish old soldiers' league, Friedmann. The IKG was asked to raise a contribution of 500,000 RM, more than half of what they had paid out to the former Chancellor's fundraisers.[175]

The university was purged on 17 March, the same day that the formal machinery of the Corporate State was wound up. Out went the professors of physics (Leo Ehrenhaft), ethnology (Wilhelm Koppers) and Romance languages (Alfred Kurzbach). They also expelled Stefan Meyer and Karl Przibaum together with Ernst Zerner, the professor of organic chemistry and an old front-line soldier, and the chemist Fritz Feigl.

Eichmann was a relatively lowly Nazi then, a significant cog in a larger wheel. The formal machinery of terror was established with the Gestapo office, responsible to Himmler and Heydrich. The chief was the Bavarian Franz Josef Huber, assisted by the jurist Humbert Pifrader. Huber was a favourite of Heydrich's and a personal friend of Heinrich 'Gestapo' Müller, the big man in Berlin. He had run the Austrian branch of the Gestapo since 1934, and had probably been involved in the planning of the *putsch* against Dollfuss. He was also one of the three greatest enthusiasts for the extermination of the Jews, together with the future Gauleiter, Schirach, and Huber's later assistant Karl Ebner.[176] Heydrich and Himmler were probably quite keen to move Huber out of Berlin, as he had inadvertently rumbled them during the Fritsch Scandal.

The Gestapo operated from the piano nobile of the former Metropole. The secret policemen were mostly young, educated people, many of them lawyers with doctorates. Half of Prussia's 4,000 articled lawyers had been out of work in 1932, and the number of Austrian advocates who were désoeuvré in 1938 must have been similar. The Gestapo provided work of sorts.[177] Othmar Trencker was head of the SD, and Dr Viktor Siegl of department II/E was appointed to the task of making sure the Jews left all their valuable possessions behind them. This was a serious position. The Gestapo had an office that dealt with the location of hidden assets, and they stopped at nothing. They didn't wear kid gloves: the writer Erich Fried's father had his stomach kicked in by the Gestapo man Göttler from Düsseldorf because he wouldn't tell him where his money was concealed.[178]

At the Gestapo's department II/D, Rux and Heger had responsibility for the imprisonment of Jews, while department III dealt with illegal emigration. Eichmann took the portfolio of legal emigration, the interpretation of the Nuremberg Law and the issue of passports and passes, helped by Emil Komers of the Emigration Office. The Vienna Gestapo grew to become the largest in the Reich, with 850 of the 2,000 men active in Austria. As many as a third of them were German, as Austrians were often dismissed as 'soft and spineless'.[179] Every day between 450 and 500 people were examined in the Metropole. The Gestapo could avail themselves of a network of between 600 and 800 police spies. The Café Viktoria was often used to lure the unfortunate victims to their fates, as it was close to the Gestapo headquarters. The Gestapo's work was massively assisted by the Viennese propensity to denounce all and sundry. There was a mythical Viennese saint called 'Sancta Denunziata'.[180] After the war it was reckoned that a quarter of all investigations came from information provided by private persons. They even sneaked on the assistant Gestapo chief for allowing his Russian maid to go out without the statutory 'Easterner's Badge'.[181]

GÖRING

The stars of the Nazi scene now came to visit their new province and its capital, Vienna. Göring loved Austria and was popular there. After visiting the former home of his Jewish godfather, Epenstein, he arrived by boat from Linz and spoke in the decommissioned North West Station on the 26th. He claimed 300,000 Jews had caused the impoverishment of Vienna. In a radio broadcast he mentioned the increasing numbers of Jews who were taking their own lives. He said he could not put a policeman behind every Jew to stop them. If they were unhappy they had only to go to Palestine. Everyone knew of a good Jew, but that would not solve the Jewish problem.

The real message behind Göring's speech was that he was expecting to be able to fund German arms production by making off with the coffers of the state and fleecing Vienna's Jews. On the other hand, he was keen to avoid anything that would disrupt trade, particularly the export trade, and left instructions with Bürckel to preserve it at all costs.[182]

He had come wearing his Four Year Plan hat, which was formally introduced on 19 March. On 23 March Austria's economy was brought into line with that of the Altreich. The federal reserves would provide a brief respite for the German economy and allow the country to run its highest trade deficit since 1929.[183] Jewish businesses were to be Aryanized without further ado.[184] The Four Year Plan had been acquiring chunks of Germany's most important industrial concerns. Göring, it seemed, had only to ask, and a part of the empire was made over to him. In the case of Jewish factories, he was not content with a slice of the action: he wanted the whole lot.

There were three huge Jewish concerns that had eluded him to date. These were the empires of the Rothschild, Petschek and Weinmann families. Their acquisition was made all the more difficult by their international ramifications. Shortly before he left, Göring had had a letter from Queen Mary of Great Britain asking him to intercede in favour of Louis Rothschild.[185] Her appeal would fall on deaf ears, for Göring was especially interested in getting his hands on Rothschild's money. The Rothschilds owned businesses in Austria, France and Czechoslovakia and the assets were divided up among branches of the family in Vienna, Prague and Paris. Sensing danger, they had transferred ownership of their Witkowitz steelworks to London in 1937, together with its Swedish subsidiary. The company was now British, and Baron Louis was being held as a hostage in the Hotel Metropole until a means could be found of giving it to Göring.[186] Göring was not even going to get close until German troops occupied rump Czechoslovakia a year later, and only then by paying around a third of the asking price of £10 million. The Rothschilds agreed to the deal chiefly to liberate Louis, and also because the Czech works were now effectively imprisoned too. The deal was still not tied up when war broke out, leaving the Germans with no claim to the Swedish subsidiary and in illegal possession of the Czech works.

Keppler's time was taken up with the appropriation of Jewish big business. He had cut his teeth on the holdings of coal baron Ignaz Petschek. Old Ignaz had died in 1934 and the firm was in the hands of the founder's heirs. Several non-Jewish firms were interested but were prepared to pay only a percentage of the company's worth. In July Göring ordered the Aryanization of 200,000,000 RM of Petschek property in Germany. The Petschek empire owed some 30,000,000 RM in taxes, which proved the lever for the appropriation of the whole business. When Germany walked into the Sudetenland, the Nazis grabbed the firm's headquarters in Aussig. The Foreign Minister of the rump Czech state promised his help in tracking down the money. The business was eventually split between Göring and Flick.[187]

In Austria, Keppler Aryanized the Hirtenberg weapons factory and the mammoth Bunzl & Biach paper concern. Göring's problem was that he had come two weeks too late to catch the smaller fry. Many valuable Jewish possessions had already disappeared into other people's pockets. The Viennese wanted the money for themselves, and were even refusing to pay their debts to Jewish businesses, which led to a further shortfall in Göring's expectations. It was important that the state itself should receive the Jewish businesses at the lowest price and then have the ability to sell them to respectable interested parties at a profit.[188]

In the event, the new *Vermögensverkehrsstelle* (Office for the Traffic of Assets) was helpless in the face of the Viennese desire to plunder their Jews. When they sought to find out what had happened to the fortunes of their victims they discovered that the money had disappeared during the 'wild' time, and there was no hope of relocating it. From now on the Nazi authorities had to make sure that they got there first.[189] This made Göring's plans conflict with those of Eichmann, who wanted the Jews out as quickly as possible and was prepared to use the money from the rich to finance the departure of the poor. Göring desired that money for himself. The result was a push-me, pull-me situation whereby the Jews were being held back from emigration until they could be proved to have turned over their assets. Their passports were therefore impounded until they had paid their dues to the conquerors. Such conflicts were rife in Nazi leadership where Hitler delighted in the principle of divide and rule.

The Jews were feeling the heat from the new masters. This is borne out by the figures: in January that year there had been eighty-eight suicides, of whom five were Jews; in February sixty-two and four Jews; in March 213, of whom seventy-nine were Jews; in April sixty-two, of the 138 were Jews.[190] Suicide among Viennese Gentiles was also a daily occurrence. An anti-Nazi Colonel Deloge had been offered the editorship of a pro-Nazi organ. He was found dead with a revolver in his hand and a note beside him that read, 'I cannot serve the Godless.' A senior judge called Meyer poisoned himself and his wife and four children. Before he died he put up a sign in his window saying, 'I cannot take responsibility for bringing up my family in the spirit of atheism and crime. God forgive me!'[191]

Another package of measures introduced by Göring's ministry was meant to cure the unemployment problem in Austria. Jobs were to be created on the German model: new fast roads, dams and motorways were to be built; the mines were to be developed; there was to be a reform of agriculture with improvements to the soil; new cooperative dairies were to be created; new housing was to made available.[192] This was meant to lure the old socialists over to the Nazi side: giving them work would make them the new brooms and superior to the 'Blacks' (supporters of the Corporate State) whom they had replaced.[193]

*

On the same day that Göring spoke at the North West Station, the 26th, the Gestapo appeared at Schuschnigg's home to interrogate him for the first time. The reasons for the visit were given in Goebbels' diary. It had been decided that Schuschnigg was to be subjected to a show trial on charges of breaking the constitution, abuse of power and murder. He was to be sentenced to death and then suffer the ignominy of the Führer's pardon.[194]

> Four men in SS uniforms sat round around the table. I noticed the new style of things, for instance that these officials kept their hats on during the interview. The speaker was an Austrian who . . . had been in the police department of Salzburg until 1932. After offering my cigarettes around and telling me that I was also allowed to smoke, he began the hearing.

Schuschnigg was asked about his possessions and his bank accounts ('My truthful answers were met with complete incredulity') and his attitude to the monarchy. He was also asked if he were a freemason, an extraordinary question to put to such a pious Catholic. They wanted to know what his relations were with Baron Rothschild and the Cardinal. Then they began to search the house.[195]

Göring's visit was followed by those of a handful of Nazi bigwigs keen to reassure the Austrians of their goodwill: Goebbels, the women's leader Gertrude Scholz-Klink, Hans Frank, Funk, the labour leader Ley, Rosenberg and Hess. Goebbels spoke for three hours at the Station three days later. In his own account, he was received with 'storms of excitement'.[196] Many stressed the fact that the Nazis had nothing against the Church: they had their business, the Church had its.

SUDETENLAND

With Austria in the bag, and no blood spilled on the German side at least, Hitler proceeded to the next territorial objective mentioned to the service chiefs on 5 November: Czechoslovakia. That other creation of Versailles, Czechoslovakia had begun life in the rosy light of the idealistic conception of its founder, Tomás Masaryk. As in Jugoslavia, the Allies had bundled a number of incohesive peoples together. In Jugoslavia there was an overwhelming Slavic majority in all its constituent parts (although they didn't necessarily get on with one another), but in Czechoslovakia the non-Slavic element was more than a third. For a while there was a small degree of accommodation, but matters changed after Masaryk's retirement in 1935 when Edvard Beneš took over as head of state. Beneš was opposed to any accommodation with Germany over its non-Slavic minorities.[197]

The Czechs and the Slovaks were both Slavs, but they had no previous history of cooperation. Prague had been ruled from Vienna; Bratislava (formerly Pressburg) was a Hungarian city, ruled from Budapest. In practice the Czechs looked down on their rustic cousins to the east. The two minorities that rocked the boat the most were the Germans in the Czech lands and the Magyars who had been stranded in the Slovak provinces. There were 3.5 million Germans in western Czechoslovakia, living mostly in northern Bohemia (the so-called Sudetenland) and southern Moravia. There was also a small but prominent minority in Prague and Brno (Brünn) and a number of islands deep in the Czech-speaking core, such as Iglau, south of Prague.

The Hungarians were mostly to be found in southern Slovakia, disgruntled at being estranged from their motherland, and at the fact that Versailles had awarded Pressburg – the coronation capital of Hungary – to Czechoslovakia, henceforth to be known by its Slovak name of Bratislava. Ragbag it might have been, but Czechoslovakia had acquired considerable strength since 1919: the French had guaranteed its borders in 1925, and the Soviet Union ten years later – although the Soviets required the French to act first. The Czech flirtation with the Soviet Union, however, sealed its fate in the eyes of some Western conservatives, who would rather have seen the Germans occupy the country than bolshevism establish an outpost in Central Europe. Even without the promised Soviet aid, however, Czechoslovakia also had a powerful army, an exemplary chain of border defences (all of them in the German-speaking regions in the north, and none facing Austria in the south) and a thriving arms industry.

The pretext for Hitler's intervention was the treatment of the German-speaking minority in the Sudetenland. Goebbels had been let in on his plans, but most of Hitler's entourage did not learn of them until the end of May. Hitler, however, had already taken the trouble to square the Jugoslav minister Stojadinovitsh on 17 January: he did not want the Jugoslavs walking into Hungary if the latter came to his aid in Czechoslovakia.[198] From Halifax he had learned that the British had already looked at the problem, and decided – realistically enough – that military intervention on their part was practically meaningless. The most they could do was starve the Germans out with a naval blockade, which would require two to three years to take effect.[199]

With Hitler's men in Vienna Goebbels thought the time was ripe to evict the large Czech element of the city's population. He thought Göring had been wrong to reassure Mastny on 11 March. Two and a half weeks later, on 28 March, Ribbentrop, Lorenz and Hess, together with an impressive bevy of diplomats, had a meeting with the Sudeten German leader Konrad Henlein, whom Germany had been subsidizing since 1935. The Czech 'Führer' was a school PE master, scoffed at in SS circles for suspected homosexuality.[200] He was not the tough man: by all reports that title went to his second-in-command, Karl Hermann Frank.[201] Hitler had told Henlein to refuse all blandishments from Prague, and the Czechs were now becoming aware that what had previously been an annoying domestic matter had more serious implications. The Anschluss had also raised the Sudetenländers' hopes of becoming part of Greater Germany, and there had been Nazi demonstrations in some of the smaller German-speaking towns. The Nazis hoped for post hoc verbal protests of the sort delivered after 12 March.[202] On 29 March Goebbels flew to Vienna. From the aircraft the Gauleiter of Berlin could make out a large chunk of Czechoslovakia. 'Just wait!'[203]

CANARIS, THE WILHELMSTRASSE AND GOERDELER

Protest over the treatment of General Fritsch had given birth to a new Opposition within the old German elite. Its two most important recruits were Admiral Canaris in military intelligence and Ernst von Weizsäcker in the German Foreign Office. Although Canaris had little questioned Hitler's government at first, with time he became increasingly anti-Nazi. When he recruited the Austrian military intelligence man Erwin von Lahousen-Vivremont after the Anschluss, he warned him, 'You may not, under any pretext, admit to this section . . . or take on your staff any member of the NSDAP, the Storm Troopers or the SS, or even an officer who sympathizes with the Party.'[204]

Canaris communicated with the Chief of Staff, Beck, through Oster, a Christian monarchist who had fallen foul of the army after a bedroom scandal. He was outspoken in his attitude to Hitler, whom he referred to as 'the pig', and made no bones about the fact that he needed to be slaughtered. It was Oster who recruited Beck – again, probably as a direct result of the Fritsch affair. Many rallied to the cause for similar reasons, even some who on the face of it seemed unlikely opponents of the regime, such as the Berlin police chief Helldorf, a one-time antisemitic thug and playboy. Helldorf had access to all sorts of useful material from the police files.

Another of Oster's key contacts was Hans von Dohnányi, the son of the Hungarian composer Ernő, and a departmental chief in the Abwehr. Dohnányi was part of the legal team defending Fritsch at his 'court of honour'. Dohnányi painstakingly assembled material on the crimes of the Nazi state, which he stored in an old filing cabinet in the corner of his office. Neither he nor Oster took much care to conceal their activities. Dohnányi was also instrumental in bringing in a host of like-minded contacts, starting with his own relatives by marriage, the Bonhoeffers.[205]

Ernst von Weizsäcker was the Permanent Under-Secretary of State at the German Foreign Office in the Wilhelmstrasse in Berlin. His concern led him to secure appointments for like-minded persons in German embassies and legations, and to maintain contacts with Canaris. Two of his most trusted diplomatic sources were the Kordt brothers, Erich and Theo.[206] Ulrich von Hassell, the sacked ambassador to Rome, was another foreign policy expert. He was sponsored by Krupp's son-in-law, Thilo von Wilmowsky, and his position as advisor to a European economic think-tank afforded the cover he needed to travel. Both Hassell and Beck were brought together by the venerable *Mittwochs-gesellschaft* or Wednesday Society, together with other opponents to the regime such as the Prussian Economics Minister Johannes Popitz and the economist Jens Jessen.

That spring, the former mayor of Leipzig, Carl Goerdeler, went to London. Goerdeler had been suggested as a successor to Brüning as Chancellor in the Weimar Republic, and was a universally respected politician. He served the Third Reich as a Commissar for Price Control, and managed to tolerate the regime inasmuch as it furthered his own causes.[207] He was not enamoured of the left and lived in profound fear of Soviet Russia. As a former deputy mayor of Königsberg he wanted to see a revision of the Polish border drawn at Versailles, and Danzig regain its place in the Reich. He had resigned from Leipzig town hall in 1937 over the removal of the statue of Mendelssohn and the failure to place a church at the centre of a new housing estate. He was kept in funds by the Stuttgart industrialist Robert Bosch, which allowed him to carry out his work abroad.

Goerdeler's 'grand tour' started in June 1937, taking in various parts of Europe and the Americas. In March and April 1938 he was off again, this time travelling only to France and Britain. In August he went on another trip, to Switzerland and the Balkans.

His problem, however, was discretion – or lack of it. He was distinctly verbose, and insisted on writing extensive reports which

were copied to hosts of people. While he was in London he revealed
the fact that he had had some assurance from Brauchitsch that the
general would confront Hitler after the court of honour dismissed the
case against Fritsch. The loose talk proved too much for the fickle
Brauchitsch, who ran to Hitler to clear his name of involvement with
the *frondeurs*. The gaffe threatened to blow Goerdeler's cover too, as
his mission was under the aegis of Canaris and Weizsäcker.[208]

Goerdeler had made the trip with former Chancellor Brüning.
Brüning had thought Chamberlain a non-starter, but was anxious to
put Goerdeler together with Churchill, and a talk was arranged in
Sussex on 3 April at the house of some English friends. At the last
moment a suspicious telephone call scotched the meeting. It
eventually transpired that there was a Gestapo agent in the
household. The lunch went ahead without Goerdeler. Brüning was
able to fill Churchill in on recent events in Germany.

At the same time as Goerdeler emerged as the civilian leader of
the Opposition, Ludwig Beck moved into the position of military
chief. Beck was opposed to Hitler's military 'adventures', but he was
probably less outraged by some of the border revisions that Hitler was
to make: few if any Germans believed that the Versailles settlement
was just. Beck's chosen weapon was the memorandum. Examples were
despatched to Brauchitsch and mocked by Hitler. In the first half of
1938, Beck must have believed that Hitler could be made to see the
light. In one famous paper written at the time he informed officers of
the limits to their oath of obedience, when their consciences and
responsibility would not allow them to carry out orders.[xxiv] Beck
feared the growth of the paramilitary elements in the Third Reich
and called for a new programme 'for the Führer, against war, free
expression, and end of secret police practices, the return of law to the
Reich, the halving of all levies, the end of palace building, the

[xxiv] It is interesting to note that even the most blinkered Wehrmacht officer
of the Third Reich had come round to his point of view in the end. At his
trial in Nuremberg Wilhelm Keitel regretted 'that he had not seen that there
were limits to a soldier's sense of duty'. Keitel was hanged.

construction of homes for the people and Prussian cleanliness and simplicity'.[209]

Another who joined the ranks of the Opposition was the President of the Reichsbank, Hjalmar Schacht, encouraged by his wounded vanity as his importance declined in the Third Reich. Schacht could see better than anyone that autarky was leading the German boat on to the rocks. The country was pathetically short of foreign currency, which merely encouraged the gangsterlike Göring to steal it from the enemies of the regime, the Jews. Schacht's impatience cannot have been helped by the Anschluss, which had required him to rescue his sister and her non-Aryan husband, then ferry them to Holland together with their money.[210]

Some of the opponents of the regime were monarchists, which did not go down well in Britain, where some felt they should have finished the First World War by hanging the Kaiser. One was Ewald von Kleist-Schmenzin, a Pomeranian squire and a member of the right-wing DNVP. He was connected to the plotters in the Abwehr through his brother-in-law, Ulrich von der Osten.[211] In March he approached the British journalist Ian Colvin in the Casino Club in Berlin's Bendlerstrasse and revealed details of Hitler's aggressive programme. The message from the Opposition was always the same: that Hitler needed a firm approach that was the very reverse of the policy of appeasement pursued by the British government. Colvin took the message to Sir George Ogilvie-Forbes, the Chargé d'Affaires at the British embassy. By the time Kleist set out for London in August, his credentials had been properly screened on both sides of the North Sea.[212]

RED TAPE

Hitler had made it plain from the start: the Jews had to go.[213] Göring had added that they should leave their *Gerstl* (dough) behind. There were a dozen or so methods of transferring money abroad, but in almost every case the sums involved were pitifully small. Any emigrant who had satisfied all the requirements could leave with ten marks, or twenty Schillings, or double that amount if going to a country with no common border with Germany. They could also bring 1,000 RM worth of goods. Personal belongings could also be removed, providing the emigrant had submitted a list for approval.[xxv] Jewels generally had to be smuggled, as the state was particularly interested in impounding them.

One-way tickets could be paid for in RM. Travelling – for example, to South America – would require a huge sum. Until 1938 there had been *Altreu*,[xxvi] which had permitted Jews to transfer anything up to 50,000 RM to Palestine. This had been created to encourage trade between the two countries, like the Ha'avara Agreement, which allowed for a complicated system of exchange whereby the emigrant paid his money into a closed account in RM and received it in sterling once he had landed in Palestine. It amounted to a favoured trading status for Germany in the Mandate: an extraordinary situation in the circumstances, and one that allowed German Jews numerous commodities from the old country.

Jews with foreign nationality could sell interests in a foreign company. Money that was not exported by one of these methods had to be paid into a closed account that could not be touched, which was later raided by the Ministry of Finance. Smuggling was a possibility, but German currency was virtually worthless on foreign exchanges. There were various schemes whereby the money could be given to a poor Jew and recouped from a rich friend or relative at the other end.[214]

On 26 March the IKG in Vienna was dissolved, together with all the other organs of the Jewish congregation,[215] greatly adding to the

[xxv] When the author spoke on the telephone to Emeritus Professor Hans Schneider in his Milwaukee home, he was informed that Schneider was surrounded by furniture from his parents' Viennese flat. He had no idea how they had got it out.

[xxvi] Allgemeine Treuhandstelle für die Jüdische Auswandering.

panic among the Jews 'who were besieging the various foreign consulates in an effort to get out of the country'.[216] One of those trying to obtain a visa from the British was the writer George Clare. He was refused.[217]

The process was Ulyssean. The first paper required was the *Steuerunbedenklichkeitsbescheinigung*, [xxvii] a certificate proving that all taxes were paid. The process of obtaining it was as long and clumsy as the word itself. It involved visits to and payments to the *Bezirkshauptmannschaft* – the directorate of the applicant's district – where the *Kleiner Meldenachweis*, a certificate of domicile, was to be obtained; the next stop was the *Magistratsabteilung*, the District Commissioner's department in the town hall; this was followed by the Accountancy Department or the central tax office; and the tax office of the district where the applicant lived. If the forms had been filled in properly and the right sums paid, the applicant received his *Steuerunbedenklichkeitsbescheinigung* and could proceed to stage two.

That is, if he had enough money to pay for emigration tax or could raise it by selling off his goods. Jewish assets were technically worthless and many people were reduced to borrowing money to finance their departure, when a few weeks before they had figured among the richest inhabitants of the city.

Stage two consisted of a visit to the *Devisenstelle*, where the Jews' assets were released and the department granted certificates of good conduct. The long queues outside both offices provided a means of making a little money for both the Nazis and unscrupulous Jews. The corruption did not abate. In December Gertrude Löwenhek complained that she had spent six nights camping outside the British consulate in the Wallnerstrasse while Nazis with swastika armbands took 100 RM bribes to issue numbered passes.[218]

Doing a little business on the side was not restricted to the consulates. Certain Jews styling themselves 'documentation experts' stood outside offices and offered to obtain papers for you for a fee.

[xxvii] Literally 'certificate of fiscal harmlessness'.

'They knew every back door. It was the poor Jews who queued for hours outside the front doors.'[219] Those waiting in the queues were sitting ducks: they could be picked out and sent off to clean up a barracks by SA-men or Hitler Youth boys. When they reached the top of the queue they were told the form was incorrectly filled in, and that they had to do it all again.[220]

Stage three was the passport itself from the emigration office. You first went to the police station of your district, where you had to answer questions as to the nature of the passport: new, for all lands, a *passepartout*, and extension of an existing document. Then the applicant went off to the emigration office in the Herrengasse, then to the *Passamt* in the Wehrgasse, where the appropriate visas had to be obtained.

The passport office in the Wehrgasse in the Fifth District was one of the most feared stations of abuse and humiliation. One witness recounted, 'How frightful this Wehrgasse was! A much too narrow room in an old Viennese house, a narrow suburban street, in which thousands pushed, shoved, sweated and cursed . . .' On average, people waited for a day and a half before receiving their papers.[221]

The applicant still needed some money. 'The only foreign exchange he can obtain is that put at the disposal of the community by outside refugee organization, which is completely reserved for the purpose. In return for his last Marks he obtains the necessary dollars or pounds: if he has none, he receives an advance from the community.'[222]

For many countries a certificate of moral probity was required as well as proof of residence. For the moral certificate two witnesses were necessary. From 23 July a new ordeal was established: the applicant had to provide a photograph with an exposed left ear, and register his or her fingerprints. Once the *Ausreisebewilligung* (exit visa) was granted, the applicant had to promise never to darken Austria's doors again.

It would be hard to argue that there was no element of sadism in the long-drawn-out business of obtaining the relevant papers to leave, even if Eichmann could justify it by saying that it ensured that the Jews left their money behind. The crucial interrogations of would-be immigrants took place in the Palais Rothschild in the Prinz-Eugenstrasse. Queues gathered several hundred metres away on the Schwarzenberg Platz at nightfall in order to make sure of being seen the following day. There were two queues: one for 'normal' Jews and the other for those who had been bought out of Dachau and were recognisable by their shaven heads. The Dachauer took precedence.

By the end of September Eichmann could boast that he had rid Austria of 50,000 Jews.[223] It was much tougher for Austrians to find a safe haven than it had been for the Germans after 1933. Visas had been abolished for Germans and Austrians in 1927, but the Home Office in London changed the rules in response to the Anschluss, reinstating the restrictions. The new rules came into force on 21 May. The British government did not want to see the country flooded with poor Central European Jews; once they were in, it would prove very difficult to send them back. There was even a suggestion that MI5 had warned the government that the whole thing was a Nazi plot to flood Britain with Jews and create a 'Jewish problem' in the United Kingdom.[224]

At first discretionary powers were left with the Passport Control Officers, who were often more sympathetic to the cases before them than the government would have been. The argument behind this was that they had the ability to find out more about individual cases than an immigration officer at the ports; and by then it would be too late. It also shifted the onus of guilt from the Home Office to the Passport Control Office, which was nominally under the control of the Foreign Office.

Later the Home Office changed its mind, perhaps because too many Jews were being let in. The PCO had to forward all applications to the Home Office for their approval. The Home Office clearly did not trust the PCO. There were accusations of favouritism, and the Consul-General in Vienna, Gainer, admitted that all his officials seemed to have some 'pet Jew' they wanted to see admitted.[225] In December the Home Office finally proposed that all applications be made in Britain, provided that the persons in question give the right assurances that they can maintain themselves. The distrust might have been occasioned by the occasionally pragmatic approach of MI6 and the PCO.[226]

FURTHER ADVENTURES OF EICHMANN

Adolf Eichmann was the model Nazi civil servant, 'a totally obedient receiver of orders'.[227] Hitler intimated the broad lines of policy; the Nazi satrap filled in the detail in such a way as to please his master. Austrian Jews were to be treated with a good deal more savagery than had been experienced in Germany up to then. Despite rough handling, however, Eichmann had yet to advocate the 'final solution'. For the time being his policy was an 'economic solution': fleeced first and driven into exile.

Eichmann was to create the 'Viennese model' for forcing Jews out, preferably to Palestine. His concern was how that could reasonably be funded. Rich Jews could get themselves out, but not the poor. The Ha'avara Accords of August 1933 were defunct by the time of the Anschluss.[228] Of the 170,000 Jews who left German lands between 1933 and 1939, 50,000 of them found their way to Palestine,[229] taking their home comforts with them, furniture, household equipment, paintings and *objets d'art*.[230]

At the beginning Eichmann wanted emigration to Palestine to be carried out according to the rules. A Palestinian journalist called Mosche Krivoschein, codename 'Galili', had a plan to assist Revisionist Jews to Palestine. He had won round Dr Kagan, the president of the Makkabi. Money would be found to get round the quotas imposed by the British. Galili had contacts with Greek ship owners who had formerly been involved in gun-running during the Spanish Civil War. Now that it had become legal, there was no money to be made any more and they were looking for new business. They were prepared to transport Jews for a price, in small and not particularly seaworthy vessels.

Galili's organization Af-Al-Pi ('Despite everything') brought together the services of the Viennese lawyer Willi Perl and the industrialist Hans Perutz, together with an 'extremist' called Paul Haller. They operated transports in 1937 and 1938, of which the last to leave was on 25 April 1938. Perl went to see Eichmann to suggest ways of shipping Jews to Palestine illegally. He drew attention to the risks involved, for the British were liable to compensate for illegal entries by docking their number from the number of legal entry visas. Eichmann was scandalized by the suggestion: he did not wish to create 'centres of crime'.[231] He was apparently so angry that he told Perl, 'I'll put you up against a wall and shoot you!' Perl replied, 'We need your cooperation for a more important matter.' In time Eichmann was convinced.[232]

Perl did not abandon his project. After he was forced to give up his legal practice in the Stubenring, he dedicated himself to emigration. Together with Galili he went to Berlin to promote his ideas. It was a dangerous game, as he was incurring the wrath of numerous London-based Jewish organizations that were there to seek legal ways of increasing the number of people allowed into Palestine.

Another organization that grew up at the time was Mossad, or *Mossad leAliyah Bet* (Institute for Immigration). As the name implies, it was created to facilitate illegal entry into Palestine. In a report dated 17 August 1939, the Zionist Norman Bentwich, representing the Council for German Jewry, related an interview he had had with 'Captain' Eichmann in Vienna. The British had formally ended Jewish emigration to Palestine, but Eichmann persisted: '[The Nazi authorities] systematically foster illegal transports to Palestine, and for this purpose do provide a certain amount of marks from the confiscated Jewish property.'[233]

Eichmann's plan was to drive out 7–8,000 Jews a month. That way he would have eliminated the Austrian Jews by the beginning of

1940. 'They prefer a disorderly to a planned emigration, as a means of making trouble for Jews in other countries,' Bentwich noted when he attended the meeting with Dr Löwenherz from the IKG. Eichmann claimed to be acting on orders from the 'highest quarters'. He was prepared to allow that 20–25,000 Jews could remain. They were to be made up of old people 'who could not be emigrated', 'pensioners of the government or the municipality' and 'very poor persons'.

Bentwich was told that Eichmann was retraining the Jews for their new lives. Most of it was for menial work, an intentional humiliation: 'There is a class, for example, for bar-mixers, and several for butlers, which are attended by lawyers, doctors and industrialists. The possibility of domestic service in England has been a Godsend. Thousands of children and adults are learning English somehow . . .'[234]

The outside world was not necessarily ready for the brutal treatment of the Austrian Jews. In Germany the persecution had cooled down after the boycott and the Nuremberg Laws, and during the Berlin Olympics of 1936 the obvious signs had been cleared away. The Aliens Committee of the British Board of Deputies had been more concerned with other Jew-baiting nations, such as Poland, Romania and Russia. On 23 March the Aliens Committee held an emergency meeting. Austrian Jews seeking refuge in Britain had been turned back at the frontier. The Home Secretary was determined to 'treat each case on its merits'. Even those who managed to cross the border were, in theory at least, to register their presence in Britain with the German Consul.[235]

OFF TO PALESTINE

The popular board game '*Juden raus!*' sold nearly a million copies between 1936 and 1940. The aim was to bring as many Jews as you could to one of six *Sammelplätze* (collection points) and then it was '*auf nach Palästina*' (off to Palestine). You threw a die and if you were in luck landed on the shops of Kohn, Gorstein or Stern. There were homely instructions for the children written on the board such as '*Zeige Geschick im Würfelspiel/damit Du sammelst der Juden viel*' ('Throw the dice with all your skill/and with sundry Jews your baskets fill'). And finally '*Gelingt es Dir 6 Juden rauszujagen,/so bist Du Sieger ohne fragen!*' ('Should you manage to drive six Jews out,/you'll be the winner, there is no doubt'). The board was covered with caricatures of Jews in the style of *Der Stürmer*.

But the British didn't want the Jews to go to Palestine, first choice for 90 per cent of Austrian Jews.[236] The Balfour Declaration had stipulated the creation of *a* Jewish homeland (as opposed to *the* Jewish homeland) but after 1935 the British had had a change of heart, partly based on the levels of street violence in the Mandate. In March 1937 there had been a spate of bombings of Arab cafés and buses. Official attitudes had also changed after the Italian attack on Ethiopia. Between 1936 and 1938 immigrant levels had fallen. For the time being immigration was limited to around 12,000 per annum. There were 'strong Arab demands for the complete stoppage'.[237]

To obtain a permit to go to Palestine, Jews needed to visit the British Passport Control Office. Many years later, Kenneth Benton, Kendrick's second-in-command at the Passport Office, described a typical day of dealing with Jewish hopefuls:

> They used to fill up the courtyard by about nine o'clock in the morning and I used to stand on the steps and give them a lecture on what chance they had of getting away. 'Your only chance of getting to Palestine now is either if you've got relatives or a capitalist visa. But you might be able to get to Grenada. You might be able to get to Jamaica. India will only take you if you are a qualified dentist,' and so on.
>
> Then during the day they were coming in one after the other. I had a whole lot of women who were examiners working for me spread through the office. But the stories were so terrible: that

they had been separated from their children; that they had seen loved ones go off in a Nazi convoy with the Gestapo and so on and it just went on all day and at the end of it it made one desperately unhappy that you could do nothing. The American vice-consul who was a pal of mine said: 'I've got to the point where if any woman leaves my office not in tears, I feel I haven't done my job.' It was a dreadful, dreadful time.[238]

The British clung to their policy despite the crisis brought about by Nazi racial law. A British White Paper published in May 1939 outlined the government's new policy: Palestine was to be a state with an Arab majority and a Jewish minority, to which no more than 75,000 further Jewish settlers could be added before 1944, unless the Arabs consented to more. Meanwhile the Secretary for the Colonies, Malcolm MacDonald, looked at the possibility of establishing a Jewish state in British Guiana. By the end of the year, however, the Foreign Office had illegally decided that British Guiana was 'climatically unsuitable'.[239] The new policy was as leaky as a colander: 51,186 managed to reach Palestine between 1 April 1939 and 31 March 1945.[240]

Lucian Meysels' case was typical of many Jews who realized they had to act fast:

On the evening of 11 March we knew we had to get out – *hic et nunc*. My father had been cultural editor of the *Neue Freie Presse*, a job for life, he thought. This had the advantage that he had not written a word on politics under his by-line for the past three years and at the same time had contact with several legations. We immediately started to get visas – a prerequisite for getting an exit visa. The first visa we got was Czechoslovakian, which we intended to make use of although my father never intended us to stay there: 'Fifty miles between us and Hitler is not enough.'

A couple of weeks later, a friend of my father in the Wallnerstrasse told us to apply for a pilgrim-cum-tourist visa for

Palestine *since that quota had not been used up by the spring of '38.* After all, who wanted to make a pilgrimage to the unruly Holy Land then. 'Gesagt, getan'[xxviii]: my father got us three visas for a deposit of £30 or £40 each, to be refunded 'on our return'. We could have gone direct, but my mother wanted to say goodbye to her brother before leaving Europe. We stayed in Bratislava for three weeks and took a train by a circuitous route via Hungary, Yugoslavia and Italy, after the travel agent where we had bought the rail tickets told us we would not need any transit visas. However, hardly had we been on the train, than we were bounced off by the Hungarian Frontier Police. Fortunately we had left a day earlier than required . . . My father sent my mother . . . to the Hungarian Consulate to get transit visas. No sooner had she met the consul, than the man told her: 'We don't give visas to Jews!' Whereupon she told him: 'I'm not Jewish'; putting her baptismal certificate, which she had wisely taken with her, under his nose. Minutes late she had three visas. We caught the train the next morning and this time got through in time for the boat.[241]

It was nonetheless easier to go to Palestine than it was to enter the United Kingdom in the immediate aftermath of the Anschluss. After consulting MI5 and MI6, among others, Halifax issued new instructions to the Passport Control Officers:

Such persons, particularly those who appear to be of Jewish or partly Jewish origin, or have non-Aryan affiliations, should be discreetly questioned as to their family circumstances, and how their business or employment has been affected by recent events; and if it is suspected that emigration is intended, the applicant should be invited to say so frankly. If he persists that a visit only is intended, he should be warned that if he overstays the period

[xxviii] Sooner said than done.

allowed, steps will be taken to compel him to return to Germany or Austria.[242]

As a result of the Anschluss and the tightening of passport controls, emigration became more difficult from the Altreich too. Long queues formed outside the offices of the Jewish *Hilfsverein* in Berlin, the Palestine Agency and the British consulate in the Tiergartenstrasse. In a great many instances it was the Passport Control Officer in Berlin, Frank Foley, or his counterpart in Frankfurt, Robert Smallbones, who found some means of issuing them with the precious papers. Many Viennese Jews went to Berlin, where the atmosphere was calmer and there was as yet little or no violence directed towards them.

OTHER HAVENS

The British were not the only people helping to save Jews. The Chinese Consul-General Ho Fengshan is credited with issuing 4,000 visas to Jewish residents between 1938 and 1941. In the first three months of his posting he is supposed to have helped 1,200 Jews reach Shanghai.[243] Ho was Christian, and believed this was the natural thing to do. Once in Shanghai there was an infrastructure to help the Jews, but it was quickly stretched. The Sassoons were Shanghai Jews, and might be expected to take an interest. Sir Victor Sassoon was President of the Central Jewish Council. The chairman of the Committee for the Assistance of European Jewish Refugees was Ellis Hayim. Shanghai was open, but the immigrants needed transit visas. Iraq, for example, could not be crossed unless the Jew was in possession of a British or Palestinian passport. By June 1939 there were 9,500 Jews registered and another 1,500 unofficial migrants. It was thought the town would have 25,000 by the time the influx slackened off. Only 350 had found work.[244]

If you bought a one-way steamship ticket, the right of abode was thrown in with it. A visa for Shanghai did not necessarily imply that the possessor was serious about going to China. In many cases it was simply a means of leaving German territory, and the ultimate objective would have been to enter Britain or the United States.[245] It was a precious opportunity to get out of a concentration camp after 10 November.

Wolfgang von Weisl operated the New Zionist Organization from the rue de Bassano in Paris's affluent *seizième*. He reported that there were already 24,000 applications lodged at the French Consulate in Vienna by 26 April.[246] Some Jews got stuck in India, where there were 26,080 towards the end of the war, 10,000 in Bombay alone and 2,000 of them acknowledged refugees from Hitler.[247] Desperate Jews set their sights on different countries that they thought might offer them a refuge. 'Unscrupulous persons' set about selling bogus visas. Paraguay appeared to encourage immigration, but then it turned out that they wanted recruits for a war against Bolivia.[248] Some countries responded by setting quotas. Australia was one of these, fixing the number of possible places at 500 in March. By the end of the month there were already in excess of 6,000 applicants. The first to arrive landed in October: twenty-two Austrians, three Germans and two Czechs.[249] Australia looked like being the only one of the dominions to respond to the plight of the Jews, but hope soon petered out, when the government began to renege on its promises.[250]

THE ANGLICAN CHURCH AND THE JEWS

The Foreign Office in London thought there could be as many as a million baptized Jews on the Continent.[251] No one was clear about what was in store for them. Bishop Bell of Chichester had responded to the threat by creating the Church of England Committee for Non-Aryan Christians in 1937. It was ready to provide travel expenses, grants and tuition fees for non-Aryan Christians deemed to be at risk.[252] The Committee was founded on the idea that there was no specific body looking after non-Aryan Christians other than the Quakers. The Jews had their own organizations, whereas the Christians' 'number was as great, if not greater, than that of Jewish victims'.[253]

This seems doubtful now, but assimilation had indeed led to a great many conversions and as yet it was also not clear how much risk the *Mischlinge* ran. Bell was, as ever, sympathetic, but that was not true of all bishops. The most pro-German of the prelates was Headlam of Gloucester, who thought the Jews 'clever, malicious and untruthful, and they have excessive influence on the press of Europe'.[254] On the other hand he was capable of ticking off the Nazi ideologue Alfred Rosenberg: 'We find by experience that a strain of Jewish blood may strengthen a race.'[255]

The unsung hero of the British bishops was Basil Staunton Batty, Bishop of Fulham, who was responsible for the British parishes in northern Europe. As early as 12 March 1933 he told the Cosmo Gordon Lang, the Archbishop of Canterbury, to put pressure on the Nazis over their treatment of the Jews and to oblige the German Protestant Church to react:

I am asking for further information from those I can trust . . . My object in writing is to suggest that if I can stir up the church in Germany to protest against any persecution on religious grounds . . . we might make some pronouncement in England which would show them we stood behind them in this matter.[256]

At the end of the month, Batty wrote to Lang again about the persecution of the Jews. 'My own opinion is that a protest should be made by the Lutheran Church and that the Christian Church throughout the world should support it but I fear that the Lutheran Church will not take action through fear of Hitler.'[257]

He was right: the Lutheran Church in Germany was largely silent. As its foremost martyr, Dietrich Bonhoeffer, wrote at the time:

She was silent when she should have cried out because the blood of the innocent was crying aloud to heaven. She has failed to speak the right word in the right way and at the right time. She had not resisted to the uttermost the apostasy of faith, and she has brought upon herself the guilt of the godlessness of the masses.[258]

Batty sat on the Foreign Committee of the Church of England and two years later he took Headlam to task over the Confessing Church in Germany, the only Protestant organization that was resisting Hitler: 'The Confessional Church deserves our sympathy. It is putting up a good fight for the essentials of the Christian faith . . .'[259] In Canterbury, Lang was also quick to condemn British policy. On 22 March 1938 he wrote to the Home Secretary, Samuel Hoare, to protest against the entry restrictions placed on Austrian Jews, pointing out the dramatic rise in Austrian suicides. Jews had been turned back at Croydon airport.[260] Both Hoare and Chamberlain were at pains to tell the Commons that indiscriminate immigration would cause difficulties at home and that they did not believe there were grounds 'for an alteration of the laws'.[261]

Lang had been measured in his approach to the Anschluss. On 29 March he told the Lords he was aware that the Austrians had sought just such a merger after the Great War, and thought that it had been inevitable. The statement was interpreted in Germany as approbation.[262] On the other hand he believed the manner in which it had been carried out was 'reprehensible', even if he was thankful that it had taken place without bloodshed. That last line caused him some considerable embarrassment and he regretted it later; several peers were better informed than he was about the murderous nature of the German occupation.[263]

Lang atoned for his error. On 17 July he was one of the church leaders to institute Sunday prayers for the Jews. The Chief Rabbi of Great Britain, J.H. Hertz, asked for Jews to assemble at 5 p.m. that day, so that Jews and Christians could be united in prayer. The Jews

said prayers for imprisoned Christians such as Pastor Niemöller, while
the Christians prayed for the Jews. In the Anglican Church in Berlin
a similar service was held. Bishop Batty was naturally behind the
latter, and reported on the service to Lang.[264] By the end of the year,
not only had Lang lost his reputation for sympathy for the Nazis but
Der Stürmer had made him the subject of the cover story for issue fifty-
two for 'standing up for Jewish assassins'.[265]

NON-ARYAN CHRISTIANS AND GILDEMEESTER

According to the Nuremberg Laws (enacted in Austria on 20 May
1938) baptized Jews were still Jews and the Quakers played a leading
role in helping non-Aryan Christians to safety. Later a third of the
places on the *Kindertransporte* were reserved for their nominees. The
idea of bringing Jewish children to safety had been mooted by Richard
Cary, Secretary of the International Secretariat, as early as the
summer of 1933. The British and American Quakers maintained an
office for the German Emergency Committee in the Singerstrasse in
Vienna, dealing mostly with Catholic converts. After November they
were besieged by applicants: 11,000 applications were made for
15,000 people. The Quakers succeeded in getting as many as 4,500
out by the time war broke out in September 1939, including around
1,200 children.[266] Sixty per cent of these went to Britain, with
somewhere between 200 and 300 going to America and about 150 to
Australia, where the colonial government required £200 before
granting a visa.[267]

The Quakers succeeded by sheer doggedness, trying to bend the
Home Secretary's ear in every instance, or to find someone who
would sponsor the Jew, so that he would not be a burden on the
taxpayer. In May, the Quakers asked Corder Catchpool, Secretary
of the Friends International Centre in Berlin, to go out to Austria
to see what could be done. He wanted to talk to the 'highest

authorities . . . It appears that efforts for relief are being made difficult, if not deliberately obstructed, and that little can be done until the position is cleared . . .' Catchpool had been in touch with Sir Wyndham Deedes and Norman Bentwich. Sir Robert Vansittart put him on to Sir Ernest Holderness, who gave him an introduction to Thomas Kendrick, the Passport Control Officer in Vienna.[268] The Quakers' brief was severely limited. As one official[xxix] wrote on 27 August, 'I can only help non-Aryans, Mischling [sic] and Confessionslos [sic] . . . I never take up an entirely Jewish case unless, for instance, a married pair where one of the couple is Aryan.'[269]

The other bodies that dealt extensively with Jewish Christians were the Swedish Church and the so-called *Gildemeester Aktion*. Frank van Gheel-Gildemeester was a fifty-seven-year-old Dutch pastor's son, an idealistic charity worker who wanted to see the Jews settled in the Harrar Province of Ethiopia, where they would have been reunited with Jewish Fellashas. He had been in and out of Vienna for years, working for charities and latterly as a prison visitor for Nazis imprisoned in Stein or at the Corporate State's concentration camp in Wöllersdorf. They included Rintelen, the Austrian Nazis' chosen successor to Dollfuss.[270] His charitable work had brought him into contact with leading Nazis, making him an ideal front man for a scheme that would benefit Vienna's Jews. By his own testimony, he had no interest in race or nationality. He was interested only in humanity.

His activities were not confined to Austria. Catchpool said Gildemeester had been responsible for the release of the pacifist Fritz Küster from Buchenwald. If this is true, he was playing a similar game to Catchpool himself, operating a humanitarian trade, seeking favours in return for looking after German nationalists imprisoned abroad – although Catchpool annoyed the Nazis so much that they locked him up for a while.[271]

[xxix] 'HNN' – possibly Alice Nike.

Gildemeester's close links with the Nazis in general and Göring and Eichmann in particular led to his being distrusted then and ever since. The organization smacked of a profitable business, hiding 'under the cloak of charity'.[272] There is no evidence that Gildemeester profited from it, but there remains a slight whiff of sulphur about him. Somehow Rintelen's son-in-law, Erich Rajakowitsch, managed to work his way into the machinery of the *Gildemeester Aktion*.[273] Rajakowitsch was an 'ambitious Nazi', and his role was probably to make sure that Gildemeester remained in with those in power.[274] Professor D. Cohen of the Dutch Committee for Special Jewish Affairs warned the British Board of Deputies not to trust him.[275] The American Quaker Florence Barrow noted that Gildemeester worked 'closely with the Gestapo', extorting rich Jews to give their money to the poor. She wondered 'whether Mr Gildemeester was being "used"'.[276]

He was probably just naive. The Zionist Norman Bentwich called him a 'well-meaning but eccentric Quaker'.[277] On his visits to Vienna he stayed in a simple room in the Dom Hotel in the Singerstrasse, close to their offices. He had been involved with the Friends during the First World War, when he had lived in Chicago, and it may well have been the American Friends' Service Committee that sent him to Vienna in 1918 when he worked for Herbert Hoover. One woman who was employed by him after the Anschluss thought he had been in Vienna during the First World War, and had helped bring undernourished children to Holland.[278] Nothing is known about his activities in the twenties and early thirties, but he remained in touch with the Quakers and visited their offices in Berlin in 1938 with a view to cooperation.[279]

Willi Perl was also suspicious of Gildemeester at first, but he came to the conclusion that he 'was most likely genuine, otherwise he wouldn't help baptized Jews' who were anathema to Orthodox ones. He came to the conclusion he was 'a Christian who was truly concerned for all humans'.[280] The first test cases for what was to become the *Gildemeester Aktion* were the Kuffner brothers, Moritz and

Stephan, owners of, among other things, the huge brewery in Ottakring. Moritz Kuffner was also a director of the Reitler private bank that was liquidated on 17 March by the lawyers Heinrich Gallop and Pollak. The Kuffners had been imprisoned after the Anschluss. Under the scheme, the Kuffners offered to pay 10 per cent of their total fortune to finance the emigration of poorer Jews. They had, of course, to discharge the other taxes too. That meant 25 per cent emigration tax, another 20 per cent *Judenvermögensabgabe* (Jewish fortunes forfeit) and any unpaid arrears. If they were lucky they could escape with something under half of their money, but that was rarely the case. Once the Kuffners offered to pay over the required sums they were released and allowed to emigrate. Gildemeester was brought in to be the front man in a scheme that would ultimately bring together between 120 and 180 rich Jews who would hand over similar sums to finance the emigration of poorer Jews. All but one of the rich Jewish families who participated left the Reich in safety.[281]

Few banks were interested in acting as trustees for the scheme. They feared that the Nazis would revoke the project and they would lose their money. On 30 May, however, Krentschker & Co. of Graz agreed to take on the business. They charged 3.5 per cent for fortunes over 300,000 RM and 3 per cent for anything below. The lawyers demanded another 1–1.5 per cent. By the time the scheme was wound up, Krentschker had turned over 25.7 million RM of Jewish assets.[282] Others earned themselves small fortunes out of the misery of the Jews: an SS-officer called Fritz Kraus made between 1.7 and 1.8 million RM. There was a brisk trade in Gildemeester application forms.

The charity was based at Wollzeile 7. Arthur Kuffler, the chairman of Mautner textiles, acted as joint chairman along with Gildemeester, the non-Jewish front man. The real power resided in the then office manager, Hermann Fürnberg. The charity had a staff of eleven or twelve. The basis for the *Aktion* was the so-called Ha'avara Accords, which had allowed German Jews to ship their money out to Palestine after 1933. The drawback with Ha'avara was that it only allowed the big fish through, while the little ones remained caught in the net. The *Gildemeester Aktion* set out to let the big fish help the little ones. The elimination of the smaller fry through emigration was exactly what Eichmann had foreseen, and the *Gildemeester Aktion* can only have been good news as far as he was concerned. The advantage for the richer Jews who availed themselves of the *Aktion* was that it arranged everything for them: passports, visas, preparation for emigration and so on.

Another area where the Gildemeester charity could help was in releasing Jews from 'protective custody' in a concentration camp. A man might be bought out of Dachau for sixty RM. Gildemeester also provided affidavits for emigration to the United States. Altogether they sold 24,500 questionnaires, and 8,378 Jews received grants amounting to 905,936 RM, not including the children who left on the *Kindertransporte*. Of the 2,675 non-Aryan Christians who left Vienna before 21 October, all seemed to have been sponsored by Gildemeester's charity. All in all about 30,000 Jews profited.[283]

Gildemeester's more idealistic vision – financing 13,000 plots of land in Harrar Province in Ethiopia – remained on the drawing board. To this end he intended to create a Gildemeester Bank in the City of London. Mussolini, on the other hand, showed no interest in having Germany's rejected Jews in his new African Empire. When the Germans brought the subject up, he told them he would not part with so much as a square inch of territory, but thought a Jewish homeland might be established in Russia, Brazil or the United States.[284]

BAPTISMS

Not everyone by any means was sympathetic with the Jewish émigrés.[285] 'Some, a few,' wrote *Times* correspondent Douglas Reed,

> have had themselves baptized; but they remain Jews. In three Central European capitals that I know the baptism of Jews, since

the annexation of Austria, has become an industry. The step is taken in all cynicism, as a business proposition, a means of getting into countries that have banned the admission of Jews, a device to tide over the years until the antisemitic wave subsides again. The Jews joke about it among themselves, and the Jews I know, who talk frankly with me because they know that I understand the racket, joke about it with me. One Jew, discussing it with me, told me of an acquaintance who, to his annoyance, found that he had to pass through a period of instruction in the faith he was about to acquire before he received the coveted baptismal certificate, and how he cut short the priest's explanation of the immaculate conception with the words '*Schaun S, ich glaube ihnen sämtliche sachen*' ('Look here, I believe everything'). This was thought very funny and sent a roar of laughter around the table. In one of the capitals I speak of, several hundred Jews were baptized as Church of England Christians in the summer of 1938, and by a trick they succeeded in pre-dating the baptismal certificates, so that the reason for the conversion should not be too apparent. The convert is usually re-converted to the Hebraic faith when the antisemitic period passes.

These baptized Jews, who have no belief whatever in Christianity, join the community of 'non-Aryan Christians' for whom your Church leaders constantly appeal.[286]

Streicher's weekly *Der Stürmer* ran a cartoon of Jews racing towards a baptismal font – 'Only if the Jews might live more Jewish lives.'[287]

Reed and Streicher naturally overstate the case. Some Jews had been edging towards Christianity for some time. One example was the Viennese Jew Karl Josef Balner, who went over to Catholicism in May 1938 and was baptized by a priest in Erdberg called Franz Brenner. Balner chose to live the life of an *U-boot* (submarine) rather than emigrate, and during the summer months he inhabited a tomb in the Jewish part of the Central Cemetery. In the winter he was hidden in a monastery by men working for Father Bichlmair's *Pauluswerk* charity, which was responsible for Jewish Christians. Balner survived the war.[288] Marriages were also a means of getting out. In 1938 there were advertisements in Prague newspapers offering the services of Christian grooms for Jewish brides. Such gallantry did not come free of charge.[289]

At the end of March, Eichmann convened a meeting of the most important representatives of Zionist bodies who were still at liberty. He told them that he was going to solve the Jewish problem, but he needed obedience and cooperation. Alois Rothenberg was appointed his collaborator to head a twelve-member *Dachverband* (umbrella organization) for Palestine.[290]

*

March had been a good month for Hitler: everything was going swimmingly. His plebiscite campaign began with a speech on Königsberg on 25 March. He was going to show the outside world that Germans were the true democrats. Much of his time was spent in Austria. On the 31st, a speech in Frankfurt filled with mystical deism was broadcast over the airwaves. Hitler continued to spice his language with references to the All Highest: 'I believe that it was also God's will that from here a boy was to be sent into the Reich, allowed to grow to manhood, and be raised to become the nation's Führer, that he might lead his homeland into the Reich. There is a divine will, and we are nothing but its tools.'[291] Germans remember hearing this speech assembled in the halls of their schools.[292]

This messianistic and self-congratulatory tone was music for certain Austrians. The Socialist leader and former Chancellor Karl Renner let it be known on 3 April that he would vote yes in the plebiscite. There is a suggestion that his decision was horsetrading, and that he wished to arrange the release of leading socialists.[293] On the other hand, the Austrian socialist had always been in favour of the merger. The Anschluss would end the 'stray wandering of the Austrian people'. He was not alone in breaking ranks and joining the fellow travellers: ex-President Miklas and Ernst Rüdiger Prince Starhemberg both tested positive.

On 3 April, Hitler was in the faithful city of Graz in Styria where on 13 March 60–70,000 people had formed a parade to celebrate the Anschluss. Graz was close to the border with Jugoslavia, which had received large areas of Lower Styria in the Versailles settlement. Styrians and Carinthians resented their Slavic neighbours. That very day the Austrian concentration camp at Wöllersdorf, which had been used for Nazis, mysteriously burst into flames. In Berlin, Goebbels gloated: 'a shameful blot swept from the horizon'.[294]

4

APRIL

THE FIRST DACHAU TRANSPORT

By April Jews' rights had reverted to what they were before 1867, when they were first accorded permission to settle in the Austro-Hungarian capital. In 1868 they had also been granted leave to renounce Judaism. This had been revoked. The Gestapo chief Huber had made it clear that 'unpleasant' Jews and 'above all Jews with criminal records' would be arrested and sent to Dachau. Jews aged over fifty were not to be sent unless their cases were deemed serious, as they were unlikely to survive the regimen in the camp. The first transport left on 31 March and arrived on the first of the month. It was organized by a Major Herzog, working from a list thought to have been drawn up by a Dr Hackl, an *Illegale* or Austrian Nazi who had fled the Corporate State and worked for the Gestapo in Berlin.[1] It contained 151 persons, the majority of them Gentiles who had loomed large in the Corporate State rather than Jews.[2]

After a shower and shave in their prison on the Rossauer Lände, they were transferred to five Black Marias. It slowly dawned on them they were being taken to Dachau. At the West Station there was a cry of 'Get out, you dogs!' Guards using rifle butts viciously beat them into the compartments of the train. Some were counselled by a more compassionate policeman: 'Take off your spectacles, look after your eyes.'[3] The train left at around midnight. The brutality was relentless. One man ran on to a guard's bayonet to put an end to it. From

Dachau railway station they were taken in cars to the camp. They arrived in the late forenoon and were received by the commandant with much mockery and disdain, a foretaste of what some would endure for seven years. They were led to the showers again and issued with their striped uniforms before having their heads shaved. When this was over, other, compassionate prisoners appeared with little presents of sausage, jam or butter, treasures extracted from their lockers. The Austrians proved a great attraction to the other prisoners, some of whom had been there since March 1933.[4]

Austrians formed over half of the 18,695 men admitted to Dachau in 1938. They were kept apart from the others and dismissed by the guards as 'lazy, Jew-infested, priest-ridden coffeehouse scum'.[5] At one point in the spring of 1938 they were put to work building a perimeter road around the camp. 'Amongst them were two ambassadors, three ministers, a state secretary, a senior judge, a state prosecutor, the mayor of Vienna, a general, a colonel and three majors, two university professors, some senior police officers, two prominent Viennese lawyers and a number of well-known journalists and authors.'[6] According to one of the deportees, this was the 'Austrian elite'.[7]

The extent of the Nazi purge was noticed by one Berliner in the camp: 'Looking at you one would almost be ashamed to be free.' There were several leaders of the Fatherland Front, such as the Corporate State's counterpart to Dr Goebbels, Colonel Walter Adam,[i] as well as Richard Alexander and Hans von Becker; other political grandees included propaganda man and later Vice-Chancellor of the Second Republic Fritz Bock; Eduard Ludwig, Minister for the Press, responsible for dealing with foreign journalists; Dr Viktor Matejka, who had run the cultural wing of the Christian trades union movement before converting to communism in Dachau; Ludwig Draxler, the former Minister of Finance; the later Chancellors Leopold Figl and Alfons Gorbach; and the future governor of Lower

---

[i] 'A repellent fellow! It will be good when he comes adrift.' Goebbels, *Tagebücher I*, V, 14 February 1938, p. 154.

Austria, Josef Reither. Johann Staud ran the Corporate State's trades unions (he died in Flossenbürg in 1939) and General Baron Karl Werkmann was the last secretary to the Emperor Charles. Baron Theodor Hornborstl was the Permanent Under-Secretary at the Austrian Foreign Office who had tried to drum up support from abroad at the moment the Nazis were gathering at the frontier. There was also the mayor of Vienna, Richard Schmitz.

Several people were there because of their earlier role in the persecution and suppression of National Socialism. The later minister of justice, Josef Gerö, as public prosecutor had imprisoned Nazis at Wöllersdorf. Dr Robert Hecht was the Secretary of State in the Ministry of Justice who had found the legal apparatus needed to wind up democracy and ban the Nazis. He was also a Jew and committed suicide in Dachau. Dr Eduard Streitmann, who had been an anti-Nazi police commissioner, was sent to Dachau with his son. There was also the head of security in Styria, Colonel Franz Zelburg; the Police General Rudolf Manda; Dr Alois Osio, who had been head of the high court, and naturally handed down impressive sentences to Nazis; and Major Baron Emmanuel Stillfried, who had been the camp commandant at Wöllersdorf.

There were also the socialists Robert Danneberg and Major Alexander von Eifler, Chief of Staff of the Republican Schutzbund.[ii] The highest-ranking socialist caught by the Nazis, Danneberg had tried to flee on the night train to Prague on 11 March, but was one of the unlucky ones who were packed off back to Vienna. A Jew, he was killed in Auschwitz in 1942. The socialist leaders Otto Bauer and Karl Seitz got away, but Bauer died in Paris in July. There was also the political informer Theodor Krisshaber, and a communist called Josef Händler who had been in and out of Wöllersdorf for four years and had little fear of Dachau. They joined General Archduke Josef Ferdinand of Habsburg-Lothringen and the two Hohenberg brothers,

[ii] He had previously seen the inside of a Corporate State cell, having been sent there by General Vaugoin, Minister of War. They were reunited in Dachau. Eifler was to die there in January 1945.

Max and Ernst, the children of the Archduke Francis Ferdinand, who had made no secret of their revulsion for Hitler, and had reached Dachau the day before.

There was a total of sixty full Jews among the 151, including Friedmann, Ehrlich[iii] and Stricker from the IKG; four members of the Schiffman family, whose premises had been so rigorously plundered on 11 March; and Willy Kurtz, who had been prominent in street combats between the Fatherland Front and the Nazis. The Nazis took particular pleasure in beating him now that he could not hit back. His size made him dangerously noticeable, as did his clothes: his trousers reached to his calves, while his tunic could only be buttoned at the top. He was finished off in Auschwitz in 1942.

Six of the eight Burstyn brothers were there, who owned a well-known bath-house as well as the Viennese taxis; Dr Wilhelm Blitz, a millionaire prominent in the Pan-German movement; Ludwig Klausner, who ran the Delka chain of shoe shops; the hatter Robert Korff; and the spice-merchant Johann Kotanyi, who hanged himself in the camp.[8] Pictures of their 'healthy' life in Dachau were shown in *Völkische Beobachter* to coincide with the opening of the Eternal Jew exhibition in August.[9] What the 'elite' thought of the inclusion of the Jews has not come down to us but within the camp, we are assured, there was no antisemitism. Others dispute this, and say the greens (criminals) and blacks (antisocials) were as antisemitic as the SS.[10]

The socialist bookseller Josef Kende joined newspaper magnates such as Alexander Geller, Ernst Buchbinder and Paul Kolisch, and journalists like Bruno Heilig, Markus Siegelberg, Bela Felsenburg, Ernst Colbert, Rudolf Kalmar and Maximilian Reich. Raoul Auernheimer was the vice-president of Austrian PEN and a *Mischling*. Among the other Jews who had the honour of being among the first to go to Dachau was Franz Lehár's librettist Fritz Löhner-Beda, the

[iii] Ehrlich was kicked to death by a capo in Dachau. Stricker and Friedmann were killed in Auschwitz in 1944.

author of the lyrics for much of Hitler's favourite music. In Buchenwald he wrote the camp song that the miserable prisoners had to sing during their travails. It was set to music by another unfortunate victim who arrived on a later transport, the violin virtuoso Hermann Leopoldi.[iv] Lehár could not intercede for Löhner-Beda with Hitler as he was protecting his own Jewish wife. Löhner-Beda was beaten to death in Auschwitz in 1942.[v] There was also one Nazi on that first transport, the Burgenland peasant Paul Hutfless. He had betrayed secrets to the Fatherland Front.[11]

Huber's concern for elderly or infirm Jews was a sham. Bruno Heilig's book, *Men Crucified*, first published in 1941, makes it abundantly clear what they faced. Heilig was arrested on 15 March and had been locked up in four prisons before the day came to ship him to Dachau. His book is a chilling record of brutality. The newspaper magnate Kolisch weighed twenty-two stone when he came to Dachau and was the butt of much cruelty. By the time he reached Buchenwald his weight had halved. The guards also singled out the Hohenberg brothers, whose work involved emptying the latrines. Prince Ernst remained in the camp until 1943.

The work was literally backbreaking. Any answering back was rewarded with blows from horsewhips, kicks or beatings. The Jews were separated from the Aryans, having their own block. They were fairly treated by the old inmates. Their capo had been the public prosecutor in Stuttgart. They found Kurt Eisner, the son of the man who had led the Bolshevik revolution in Munich, Königsberger, a former minister in the Saxon government, and Scholem, quondam editor of the *Rote Fahne*.

[iv] '*O Buchenwald, Ich kann Dich nicht vergessen,/weil Du mein Schicksal bist./Wer Dich verliess, der kann es erst ermessen,/wie wundervoll die Freiheit ist!*' ('O Buchenwald, how can I forget you?/As you have been my lot./Whoever leaves you will know at once how true/That freedom hits the spot.')
[v] If that was not bad enough, after Löhner-Beda left for Dachau, his wife was pestered remorselessly for the details of his fortune. Tina Walzer and Stephan Templ, *Unser Wien: 'Arisierung' auf Österreichisch*, Berlin 2001, 29–30.

A few weeks after the first Austrian transport, the camp received a visit from Heinrich Himmler. He paid particular attention to the Austrians, whom he endeavoured to humiliate. 'You know that from now on you are in protective custody, that means I shall accord you my most special protection.' He paused so that his retinue might voice their appreciation of his joke. He told the prisoners that they fell into four categories: professional criminals – they were the nicest; political prisoners – who were much more dangerous and would be given less protection; Jews – who belonged to the scum of mankind; the worst, however, were the communists.[12] To Stillfried of Wöllersdorf he said: 'So you see what it is like!' Stillfried answered back: '*Herr Reichsführer*,I would truly love to say that we are treated here like your people were in Wöllersdorf!' The others expected a reprisal, but none was forthcoming. Stillfried survived.[13]

At Wöllersdorf political prisoners had been detained without trial, but the Austrian camp was not to be compared with Dachau, unless you accepted Eric Gedye's quip: 'There was one thing in common between Wöllersdorf and Dachau. The Nazis seemed thoroughly to enjoy both.'[14]

Despite the grim existence led by the prisoners, there was a semblance of cultural life in Dachau. Sunday afternoons were free. Viktor Matejka put on a play written by Rudolf Kalmar strewn with oblique references to Hitler, which remained undetected by the guards. Grünbaum continued to perform with Paul Morgen and Hermann Leopoldi, and the Berliner dancer Kurt Fuss joined in. Jura Soyfer wrote a poem, the *Dachauerlied* (Song of Dachau). The rest of the time the prisoners were subjected to the whim not only of the guards but even of the commandant's vicious dog and chimpanzee. In the middle of the brutality, there were flashes of mercy on the part of the guards, although these were few and far between. Maximilian Reich was occasionally protected by a young SS-man who had recognized him as the organizer of a football tournament.

It was just the beginning: ten days later some Salzburgers arrived at the camp. The delivery of 24 May brought the governors of

Burgenland and Upper Austria as well as the later president of the National Council, Felix Hurdes. On 31 May there were also a number of police officers from the Vorarlberg. The transports to Dachau aroused international condemnation, particularly in Britain. This motivated Weizsäcker to seek an interview with Heydrich on 5 July 1938. Heydrich admitted to having 3,900 Austrians in 'protective custody'. Weizsäcker sought to have all those released against whom no charges had been preferred. It transpired that most of the middle-class prisoners were indeed released before war broke out. Jews were let out if they could show that they had an entry visa for another country. The communists were often left to rot in the camps until the end of the war.[15]

Until the Jews arrived that April, Germany's concentration camps had been filled with Gentiles, chiefly political prisoners and habitual criminals. Certain inmates had caught the attention of Corder Catchpool, particularly Fritz Küster of the *Friedensgesellschaft* (Peace Society), Hans Litten, a half-Jewish solicitor, the well-known Social Democrats Ernst Heilmann, Carlo Mierendorff and Kurt Schumacher, and the communist Theodor Neubauer. Like Gildemeester, Catchpool had been cleverly working his way into the Nazi regime's good books by visiting German political prisoners in captivity in Lithuania and Czechoslovakia. There had been eighty in Lithuania, and there were still sixteen serving long sentences at the beginning of 1938.[16] In February that year he estimated the German prison population to be between 110,000 and 120,000; 'of these about a quarter are political cases, mostly undergoing long sentences'. Of course this did not include those in concentration camps, who had been neither tried nor sentenced.[17]

Himmler had been in Austria in March to scout around for a site for a new concentration camp, but they were still comparatively few in number. Sachsenhausen in the Berlin suburb of Oranienburg was as ancient as Dachau, having been created after the abolition of the 'wild' concentration camps that flourished after Hitler's accession to power. Since then Buchenwald had opened on the Ettersberg in

Weimar in 1937. Lichtenburg had been converted into a women's camp. Esterwege, on the Dutch border, had gone, but Sachsenburg and Fühlsbüttel appeared to be still functioning.[18]

There was an expansion in the number of categories of prisoners eligible for 'protective custody' in 1938. That was going to mean more concentration camps, and the enlargement of existing ones. In the course of 1938, the population of Dachau tripled.[19] Between 21 and 30 April, the Gestapo rounded up around 2,000 'workshy' and took them to camps. In the summer Heydrich turned his attention to the 'antisocial'. Each criminal department was to locate around two hundred gypsies, tramps, beggars, pimps, violent criminals and Jews with criminal tendencies. The arrests started on 13 June, with the police working their way through railway stations and dosshouses. Twenty-five years before, they might have arrested their own Führer. The bag totalled over 10,000. They were taken to a new generation of camps: Flossenbürg, Mauthausen and Neuengamme, located close to quarries, because the SS needed labour for their own stone business.[20]

The arrival of 'work shy' and antisocial elements altered the social structure, swamping the communists and socialists who had previously been the mainstay of Sachsenhausen. The antisocials wore black triangles, as opposed to green for criminals and red for political prisoners. They were an incohesive group, and, although some ascended to the level of the green aristocracy among the prisoners, others fell victim to the terrible physical strain imposed by the camps, perishing in the mud or crushed to death in the quarries.

WHITHER SHALL I FLEE?

The Jews – the assimilated Jews in particular – had nowhere to go. With the Anschluss would-be immigrants to the United States were added into the tally for Germany, fixed at a little over 27,000 a year; Canada and Australia did not want their wide-open spaces polluted by Jews. Peter Fröhlich, who would later achieve fame as the cultural historian 'Peter Gay',[vi] was thrown out of his *Gymnasium* (grammar school) in Berlin-Wilmersdorf. With a little flourish of Prussian decency, the boys were issued with proper leaving certificates, which recorded – fallaciously – that they had left to take up a profession.[21]

In July Fröhlich *père* had been fired from his job. The family then set to work applying for visas. That meant paying calls on consulates to pick up forms, typing out applications and applying for residences.

Since the Olympics, Berlin Jews had been enjoying a holiday from persecution, but after the Anschluss the authorities began to get rough. As the son of an Austrian Jew, Gerhard Beck and his family were obliged to quit their spacious flat in Weissensee and move into the Scheunenviertel – the nearest thing Berlin had to a ghetto. The only hope for them now was to join the endless queues that radiated from the offices of the *Jüdischer Hilfsverein* and enquire into the possibilities of emigration. Beck's family soon came to the conclusion that escape was possible only if you were rich or a 'Zionist zealot'. The Quakers offered Gerhard's twin sister a way out if she were prepared to enter domestic service in Britain.[22]

The harassed Jews were prey to rumours. At the beginning of the month a ripple of optimism went through the community. It appeared that Australia was going to open its gates to the Jews and issue 6,000 visas. The rumour created siege conditions outside the British consulate in Vienna. Eventually the Australian Prime Minister Lyons released a clarification that Jews would only be admitted under the normal constraints of emigration. Two weeks later Miss Stamper at the PCO was forced to issue a leaflet to explain the separate policies on emigration of the various British colonies and dominions, Cyprus, Palestine and Australia in particular. It warned against bogus organizations that claimed to be able to help and had 'sprung up like mushrooms, enriching themselves from Jewish misery'. At the

[vi] 'Gay' is the translation of the German word *fröhlich*, but, as the writer is quick to point out, 'merry' was the sole meaning current at the time he adopted it.

consulate, Consul-General Gainer, Consul Taylor and Kendrick (who was responsible for Palestine) all handled the Jews with understanding and sympathy. On one occasion the SA forced the Jews in the queues to wash cars. After that the Consul-General issued a formal protest and allowed them to queue in the 'neutral' courtyard.

Despite the formal closure of the Swiss borders with Austria on 12 March, 3,000 Austrian Jews had managed to make it. *Der Stürmer* ran a particularly pungent caricature showing a 'Kosher snack': Jews crammed into a Swiss sardine tin.[23] Dr Pifrader had demanded on 22 March and 27 April that passports be issued with identifying marks to show that the Jews had paid their taxes. Others crossed the border into Italy and obtained visas for Switzerland, until this loophole too was closed in August.[24] Jews were still managing to cross the frontiers into Czechoslovakia, Hungary, Jugoslavia, France, Holland, Luxembourg and Belgium, even though the only legal form was the Zionist solution as backed by Eichmann.

For Eichmann, Jews remaining on the premises, that is to say in Europe, formed *Greuelzentralen* or 'centres of atrocity'. He wanted an end to assimilation – Germany had no foreign political interests in Palestine. The quickest method was to obtain a tourist visa to Palestine and then sit it out. Zionist organizations could effect this in Palestine itself.[25] The British government was under fire: despite the rigidity of official policy there was an elasticity provided by the consular officials who took pity on individual cases. This meant that tens of thousands of Central European Jews did find a refuge in the Mandate.

THE PLEBISCITE

On the 10th a plebiscite was held throughout the Reich: Germans on both sides of the Inn were to voice their approbation for the Anschluss. Hitler concentrated on Austria in the days immediately

HAPPY FAMILIES

Hitler admires Edda Göring, a crown princess for the Third Reich.

Onkel Adolf with Joseph, Magda and three younger members of the Goebbels clan.

PALACES

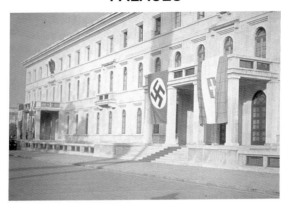

(*above*) The Führerbau in Munich, completed in 1938. It was to be the scene of the Munich Conference in September.

(*left*) The old Chancellery in Berlin was pulled down to accommodate Speer's magnificent new building, which opened its doors at the end of the year.

(*below*) Hitler's flat on the second floor of the Princeregentenplatz in Munich. It is now a police station.

ANSCHLUSS

(*top*) In Salzburg the Wehrmacht is received with enthusiasm.

(*above*) Not everyone was so happy: Jews queue for visas outside the Polish consulate in Vienna.

(*left*) In the former Austrian capital the shops were rapidly 'aryanized'.

OFF TO PALESTINE

Juden Raus ('Jews Out') was a popular board game. To win, the player had to round up six Jews from their shops and send them to Palestine.

THE ANGLICAN CHURCH AND
THE VIENNESE JEWS

(*top left*) Basil Staunton Batty, Bishop of Fulham, was responsible for the Anglican parishes of northern Europe. He secretly encouraged priests to help Jews.

(*top right*) The Reverend Hugh Grimes, chaplain in Vienna.

(*above*) The British Embassy chapel in Vienna, where 1,825 Jews converted to Anglicanism in the summer of 1938.

HOMMES FATALS

(*above left*) Herschel Grynszpan whose attack on the diplomat Ernst vom Rath on 7 November formed the pretext for the pogrom of 9–10 November.

(*above right*) On the left, Blomberg, Minister of War, whose marriage to a former prostitute provoked a national crisis in January. On the right, Fritsch. The army leader was the victim of trumped-up charges of homosexuality.

(*right*) Max Schmeling, German prizefighter who failed to clinch the world heavyweight title that year.

KINDERTRANSPORTE

(*top*) Jugendalija teenagers leaving the Anhalter Bahnhof in Berlin for Palestine.

(*above*) Jewish children prepare for a new life, leaving their parents behind.

(*left*) The half-Jewish dramatist Carl Zuckmayer escaped by the skin of his teeth in March.

CONCENTRATION CAMPS

(*above*) Goethe's oak at Buchenwald – a photograph taken by a French inmate in 1944. The tree was a source of solace for the prisoners.

(*left*) Political prisoners in Dachau. In 1938 Austria's governing elite were despatched to the camp.

before the poll. Spitzy travelled with him, staying in the Parkhotel in Graz and the renamed Österreichischer Hof in Salzburg – it was now the Salzburger Hof, as Austria was no more. On 7 April the Führer's party was in Innsbruck. At the same time Cardinal Innitzer had travelled to Rome for a private interview with the Pope. The Supreme Pontiff was none too pleased with the head of the Austrian Church. The Secretary of State, Eugenio Pacelli – the future Pius XII – ticked him off for the 'unfavourable impression' he had made by signing the bishops' letter condoning the Anschluss. On 6 April, Osservatore Romano published an explanation: the Pope did not approve of anything that went against the laws of God or the freedom and rights of the Catholic Church. A particular sticking point was the assault on youth organizations.[26]

Berlin's Bishop Preysing was more to the Pope's liking. His view was not shared by Goebbels, who called the bishop a 'clerical, un-German pig. This plague must be exterminated once and for all. They belong to Rome more than they do the commandment of the Fatherland.'[27] Innitzer had another audience with Hitler on 9 April. The Roman declaration had naturally angered the Führer,[28] but for the time being he forbore from punishing the Austrian Church, until the results of the plebiscite had come in.

Hitler's campaign ended in Vienna on the 9th. He addressed hundreds of thousands of his faithful from the Rathaus. Vienna was a pearl, and he would find it an appropriate setting within the German nation. His language was steeped in piety, presumably as a sop to the Catholic Viennese. When he spoke to them a second time that day in the North West Station, Goebbels said it was 'like Mass . . . at the end, it resembled a prayer'.

Even Goebbels enjoyed cult status. When Hitler appeared on the balcony of the Imperial, they called for him too: 'Lieber Führer, ach ich bitt', bring doch unseren Doktor mit.'[vii] Hitler and his Propaganda Minister travelled back to Berlin on the train on the 10th.[29] Over

vii 'Please our Führer, oh we pray,/Let the Doctor have his say!'

breakfast they discussed plans. 'The Führer wants to drive the Jews completely out of Germany, to Madagascar or whatever . . . a people smitten by God. Prague has also written them off.' From the Jews they progressed to the princes: 'They are worthless and must never be allowed back.' They were satisfied that the Hohenbergs were out of the way. The Habsburgs were the worst: 'Get rid of this rubbish.' Hitler and Goebbels had also placed the dispossession of the Austrian nobility high up on his agenda.[30]

The result of the poll on the 10th was a 99.08 per cent 'Ja' for the Führer. In Austria there were just 11,929 'no's. Goebbels feigned joyful surprise: 'Germany has conquered a whole country with the ballot-slip.' The plebiscite did, however, reflect the Führer's popularity. It showed that Hitler was exceedingly successful in Germany at the time and it marked the high-water mark of his stature in the land of his birth. The vote had obviously been manipulated and the electorate cowed into saying 'Ja', as was proved by the near unanimous assent from Dachau concentration camp, but Hitler's aims had struck a chord with national German aspirations; for the time being it was bloodless, and the plebiscite had been marginally fairer than that proposed by Schuschnigg:[31] all Germans and Austrians over the age of twenty were eligible to vote, with the exception of Jews and criminals and the many thousands of suspects in Hitler's gaols and camps. In Vienna some 300,000 voters had been deducted from the roll in this way.

The ballot was not exactly secret: a big circle contained the word 'Ja', a smaller one 'Nein'. The voter's name and address were printed on the back. Despite the pressure to conform, there were dissenters, like Friedrich Reck-Malleczewen:

I can now prove that the plebiscite to legitimize Hitler's takeover of Austria was falsified in the crudest possible way. Together with the other four adults of my house, I naturally voted 'No'. In addition, I know of at least twenty other reliable people in the town who did the same. Nevertheless, according to the official results, the town unanimously and without a single dissenting voice 'approved the actions of the Führer'.[32]

Klemperer confirmed that no one believed it had been a *secret* ballot. He wondered whether Hitler was going to have himself crowned Holy Roman Emperor. Facsimiles of the pusillanimous letter signed by Austria's bishops had been posted in prominent places throughout the Reich.[33]

Hitler's appeal for the Austrians was not to last. The appropriation of so much of Austria's wealth by the Reich and by Reich Germans; escalating prices; the failure to appoint Austrian Nazis to high office; the brutal treatment of the Church and its priests; the dastardly suppression of the old elite; the supercilious attitude which the Austrians liked to associate with the dreaded Piefke[viii] or Prussian – all contrived to make the honeymoon a short one.

The East Prussian writer Ernst Wiechert was arrested soon after the election and taken to a Gestapo prison to be interrogated. In the car from his home one of the secret policemen asked him if he had cast his vote. They knew that he had not. 'Half an hour after the closing of the ballots they were careful to beat anyone who had written "No" half dead.'[34] One of the very few who made his decision not to vote public was Bishop Sproll of Rottenburg. It was not that he disapproved of the merger, but he disliked the regime and did not wish to congratulate the Nazis. This led to a campaign against him by Gauleiter Murr that ended up with Sproll being banished from his diocese. Nazi thugs, led by Otto Sponer, the Kreisleiter of Reutlingen, wrecked his residence first. Goebbels approved these 'spontaneous' demonstrations: 'The Bishop of Rottenburg did not vote. Now the people have erupted and are rioting in front of his palace. He is looking for protection, so now

[viii] In practice, the *Piefke* is rarely a Prussian, but generally just a German from north of the River Main. Even Catholic South Germans are occasionally branded with the name, although Bavarians are thought to be honorary Austrians.

the state is good for something at least. He can protect himself. I shall not lift a finger.' Sproll's eviction established a precedent that would later be used in the cases of Cardinals Innitzer in Vienna and Faulhaber in Munich.[35]

The 'Prussian' Reck-Malleczewen was in Salzburg soon after the Anschluss and was able to witness the sort of scene that would put the Austrians off their new friends from the north:

> . . . these Berlin potato-faces fill the streets, together with their full-bosomed females. Thanks to the rate of exchange they are able to make off with everything for a song, including goods that are no longer available in Germany and the . . . shelves are empty. They are behaving like a horde of servants whose masters are away, who have found the keys to the wine cellars and are now having an orgy with their women . . .[36]

Some Germans mopped up the flood of Austrian Jewish property. One of these was Papen, who was destined for the embassy in Istanbul. He acquired the country place of the Eggers, industrialists in Styria.[37] Ribbentrop absorbed Schloss Fuschl, and added it to his burgeoning collection. The former owner, von Remnitz, was murdered in Dachau.[38] Goebbels threw a little confetti in the direction of the Austrians. He sponsored a lavish production of *Lohengrin* for the Salzburg Festival, but refused to allow Hans Tietjen to direct it.

On the same day as the poll, the new government in the Ostmark introduced the *Reichsfluchtsteuer*. It had actually been introduced in Germany on 31 January 1931, before Hitler came to power: any person (not just Jews) leaving the country had to pay the tax if they had an income of 20,000 RM (30,000 Austrian Schillings) in any year since 1931, or if they possessed a fortune of 50,000 RM (75,000 Austrian Schillings) at the time of applying to leave.[39] It is a measure of the success of the 'Viennese Model' that state income from the emigration tax more than quadrupled in 1938, from 81,354,000 RM to 342,621,000 RM. In 1939 it fell by a third to 216,189,000 RM.[40] Smuggling was rife, particularly of jewellery, which was small and potentially of great value. Aryans volunteered to carry jewellery for Jews. In one case in the summer of 1938, the smuggler was arrested by British customs. The case against the woman was dropped after representations from Jewish bodies.[41]

On 13 April, as Poland and Lithuania moved to the brink of war again, a law was passed requiring Austrian tradesmen to find Aryan owners for their businesses before 10 October. The Nazis had coined a new verb to dignify the process of robbery: *arisieren*.[42] Until their sale, Jewish businesses were to be placed in the hands of commissioners, who tended to be trusted Party members. The trust placed in them was seldom rewarded: they merely bled the businesses white and deposited a lifeless carcase on the market for sale. After the takeover of Jewish businesses, the only Jews left working were a 'very few' doctors who could treat Jews only and a similar number of lawyers who were allowed to act as consultants to Jewish clients. About 1,500 Jews were retained in industry where there was a shortage of labour. Between 3,000 and 4,000 were being retrained subject to the payment of certain taxes. Many elected to learn agriculture with a view to getting to Palestine. Artists and writers saw their publishers refuse to pay out royalties, even when those came in from abroad. Such was the case of Felix Salten, the author of Bambi, whose publishers were now able to absorb a huge income from his foreign sales. Another ripe plum was the royalty income of the film-score composer Erich Wolfgang Korngold.

At first some thought they would ride the storm. The dentist Hugo Schneider felt that now Jews could no longer go to Aryan dentists his business would expand. Within three months, however, his hopes were shattered by the appearance of a man in SA uniform at his door. He announced that he was also a dentist, and half the practice now belonged to him.[43]

There were 26,236 Jewish businesses in Austria: one for every 270 Austrians. This was a far greater concentration than in the old Reich, where the figure was one for every 1,693 Germans. They were mostly small businesses. The Aryan Austrians rushed to take over the firms. There were four times as many applications as there were businesses to acquire. Seyss-Inquart's excuse for the measure was to produce a legal framework for an orderly takeover. Some Austrians, however, were still not keen on the legal route. Parents encouraged their children to pilfer from defenceless Jews. Flats were stolen under the noses of their owners by maids with the assistance of their lovers. The victims could not go to the police; the only way to protect themselves was to offer the maids presents on their departure. Some companies were robbed over and over again, with fleets of lorries being brought up to take away the goods.[44]

There was a particularly high concentration of Jews in certain businesses. One in seven of Austria's pharmacies was Jewish owned, and in Vienna the figure was more than a third. The normal sale price for a business of this sort was two to two and a half times the yearly income. Now the official sales price was one-tenth of the pre-1938 value. The 25 per cent *Reichsfluchtsteuer* had to be subtracted from this. There was no recourse to the courts: if a Jew complained he was put in prison.[45]

The measures did not necessarily benefit the Austrian economy. The sacking of the Jewish textile workers, for example, caused a slump in the clothing industry, as there were no skilled workers to take their place.[46] The interpretation of the law was draconian, especially in a city like Vienna where many people had a dash of Jewish blood. The illegitimate children of Jews, even *Mischlinge* who had only one Jewish grandparent but could produce no baptismal certificate, forfeited their rights. If one of these had 25 per cent of the company, or a seat on the board, the company was defined as Jewish.[47]

As the authorities removed the Jews, the Viennese began to feel the loss. The central market in the Naschmarkt emptied out. The corn trade was 80 per cent Jewish, as well as 31 per cent of the leading wine companies. At the time of the harvest that year a cooperative had to be created to take the place of the old trade. The Hungarians complained that their firms were being closed down too and made a diplomatic protest.[48] When foreign trade began to suffer Göring started to sweat. On 29 October he told the Viennese authorities to slow down.

In the schools the Jewish children were made to feel increasingly unwelcome. The eleven-year-old Hans Schneider, the son of the dentist Hugo, was summoned out into the playground by his headmaster and told that it was impossible for true Germans to associate with Jews like him. His parents told him that the man in question had begun as a red (communist), had seen the advantage of becoming 'black' (a supporter of the Corporate State) and was now turning brown (Nazi). Hans Schneider took this to heart and stopped taking the chameleon headmaster seriously.[49]

HITLER'S BIRTHDAY

Hitler was forty-nine on Wednesday, 20 April. Easter had fallen the Sunday before but the Christian festival was upstaged by the antics of the Prussian boxer Max Schmeling, who was making a bid to regain the world championship he had lost to Jack Sharkey. On Easter Saturday he met the American Steve Dudas in the ring in Hamburg, and knocked him out in the fifth round. Goebbels called him a 'brave lad'.[50]

Two weeks before, the Hitler Youth leader, Baldur von Schirach, had decreed the Führer's birthplace, Braunau, to be a place of pilgrimage for young Germans.[51] His birthday was marked by the usual military parades, a laudatio from Göring and a special gift from Goebbels: a collection of recordings of his speeches on Austria. Leni Riefenstahl's *Olympia* was screened and universally admired. Goebbels noted that she would win the film prize that year and receive 100,000 RM. There was lunch for a small group of Hitler's intimates and Keitel came too.

Since the death of Paul Ludwig Troost, Albert Speer had become the Führer's favourite architect. He was able to bring Hitler a present of the plans for the first part of Berlin's intended great axis, four miles long and flanked by 400 street lamps. It was to house the principal ministries and part of a crossing of streets that would stretch thirty miles to the east and west and twenty-five to the north and south. Some of the designs – the great dome and the triumphal arch – had been sycophantically worked out from drawings supplied by the Führer himself.[52] For technical reasons, Hitler was in two minds about Berlin as a capital. The city was built on sand and there was a high watertable requiring the new Chancellery to be constructed on a concrete raft. Hitler had wanted to shift the capital to Lake Muritz. On the 24th his ministers had the chance to look over Speer's building, which was already impressively grandiose.

In the evening of Hitler's birthday there was a command performance: Furtwängler conducted Die Meistersinger. The Third Reich also celebrated by issuing a warrant for the arrest of Archduke Otto for high treason, while Der Stürmer revealed that the first Habsburg had actually been a Jew.[53] After the festivities, Hitler called Keitel to him and asked him to adapt the plans for Operation Green, a pre-emptive strike against Czechoslovakia.[54] Keitel was given the brief to study the Czech system of fortifications. The original blueprint had been drawn up to deal with the eventuality of a Soviet attack on Germany, using their Czech ally as a springboard. Hitler told Keitel there was to be a big opening in the east. The attack had to succeed in four days – the time the French needed to mobilize and come to their ally's aid.

The German Foreign Office had been sponsoring ethnic German resistance within Czechoslovakia for four years. Now with Ribbentrop in power in the Wilhelmstrasse there was an even greater desire to see the Czechs embarrassed by the complaints of the Sudetenländer. Göring, it seems, was not the prime mover, and he was one of the last to be won round to a Czech adventure: he had given Mastny his word, after all.[ix] He pointed out that the West Wall was not ready. It was Hitler who convinced him. On 23 April he was secretly named Hitler's successor. In Karlsbad on 24 April, Henlein outlined his new eight-point programme. Since the Anschluss, his hopes had been raised. On 28 March he had been up to Berlin to see Hitler and Ribbentrop and receive his orders. Hitler told him that a pretext would be found for a German invasion; in the meantime he was to continue making excessive demands. Ribbentrop told him to maintain the closest contact with him; he did not want to miss the party this time. The British and French response found an echo in Jochen Klepper's diary: they formed a military alliance. Once more Germans feared Hitler was driving them to world war.[55]

The Karlsbad Programme called for autonomy for the German regions and German-speaking regiments in the Czech Army. On 28 April Goebbels noted with interest that Prague was looking for security from London and Paris, and that Chamberlain did not appear keen.[56] The British put pressure on President Beneš to accommodate the Sudetenländer, but by honouring Henlein's requests he would have destroyed his state. Goebbels had been moved to see his Führer sitting and brooding over a map of Czechoslovakia.[57] Hitler had told Keitel that Czechoslovakia had to be destroyed because of a showdown with the Slavs, and not because of any injustice shown towards the Bohemian Germans. The timing for the attack would be to some degree dependent on progress in constructing his own defensive wall in the west, the answer to the French Maginot Line, designed to keep the French out if they chose that moment to honour their commitments to the Little Entente.

[ix] Not that it always counted for much: he told the blackmailer Otto Schmidt no harm would come to him, then authorized his execution. He could, on the other hand, be induced to save a well-heeled Jew, and even found a job for Schuschnigg's brother Arthur.

PASSOVER

In the days leading up to Passover, the spotlight fell on Berlin's Jews. Goebbels conferred with Helldorf. Their movement was to be curtailed: they were to have one swimming pool, and a few restaurants and cinemas, 'otherwise access forbidden. We are going to take away Berlin's character as a Jewish paradise.' 'The Führer wants to drive them out gradually. He is going to negotiate with the Poles and the Romanians. The best place for them would be Madagascar.'[58] Göring too was turning on the heat in his fight against Jewish capital. 'It won't be long before we floor them,' wrote Goebbels.[59]

Pessach was from 23 to 26 April, and over the weekend of 25–26 April prominent Jews were subjected to unspeakable acts of public degradation in the Prater park in Vienna. Kaltenbrunner had made attempts to rein in the SA but with little success. Near the Reichsbrücke over the Danube, Jews were forced to spit in one another's faces. One who refused died in a concentration camp soon after. In the Taborstrasse in the heavily Jewish Second District, orthodox Jewesses were obliged to remove their wigs and form a parade for the amusement of the Nazi thugs. Jews were strapped into the giant Ferris wheel and spun round at top speed.[60]

The Czech Consul-General in Vienna reported on the brutal scenes in the Prater on 24 April. Jews were forced to run around with their hands up. Others were stripped and beaten by SA-men. They had their beards shaved off and were obliged to lick human excrement. The sixty-six-year-old chief rabbi was beaten up. On the 26th and 27th twenty-eight Jews committed suicide, including five members of one family. The Jewish General Sommer appeared in uniform and was made to wash the pavement.[61] In the Aryan Johann-Strauss Café, opposite Gestapo HQ on the Morzinplatz, Jewish regulars were protected by the owner. When the SA came to make the customers clean the streets the proprietor replied, 'Over my dead body.' The café acted as a welfare centre.[62]

The violence culminated in a new edict from the Ministry of the

Interior: Jews and Jewish women married to Aryans had to reveal their fortunes of 5,000 RM or above by 30 June, whether in the Reich or abroad. In Austria the fortunes of a quarter of the Jews accounted for a sum of 2 milliard marks.[63] At the same time, the ministry decreed that its approval was required for all transfers of businesses from Jews to Aryans. Once again they were keen to close the stable door, even if some of the horses had bolted. The British Consul-General, Gainer, noted bitterly, 'It would almost seem as if the manner of their going, whether by the process of emigration to other countries, or by starvation in their own, was of little consequence to those in authority.'

The Zionist Leo Lauterbach wrote to the Central Bureau for the Settlement of German Jews on 27 April. Since the closing of the IKG, the process of emigration had come to a standstill. He had observed in Vienna that the authorities were 'bent upon an early evacuation of Austria by the Jews'. According to Lauterbach the message had gone home, and was voiced in the queues outside the British consulate. He was concerned that the maximum number should reach Palestine and that there were funds to help them. The preferred candidates were artisans – Chalutzim. Lauterbach also hoped for an extension of the Ha'avara scheme.[64]

Lauterbach arrived in Vienna with the former civil secretary to the Palestine Mandate, Sir Wyndham Deedes, on 18 April. The two left again on the 21st and proceeded to Berlin, where they stayed from 22 to 24 April. Deedes was equipped with letters of introduction to the appropriate bodies: the Foreign Office in Berlin and its Viennese branch. He was representing the Council for German Jewry and came with promises of financial support for those wishing to travel to Palestine. The message he transmitted to German official bodies was that it was important to reopen the offices of the Jewish congregation as quickly as possible so that organized emigration could proceed. They wanted the Jewish leaders to be released from Dachau to this end. The financial costs could not be entirely borne by foreign institutions and it was therefore necessary that the IKG raise money to fund emigration. The wild seizure of Jewish property would not help in the long run.

Deedes and Lauterbach met Gainer, Taylor and Passport Control Officer Kendrick, also the American chargé d'affaires, Wiley. Deedes paid similar calls in Berlin, as well as visiting officers of the German army, Quakers and 'non-Jewish non-Aryans'.[65] In Vienna they were fobbed off with minor officials from the Foreign Office and the Emigration Office. Attempts to see the governor, Seyss-Inquart, or members of the Gestapo came to nothing. They were able to visit the mayor, Neubacher, who expressed the desire to see emigration proceed in an orderly and humane manner. In Berlin they had a sympathetic meeting with Freiherr von Marschall at the Foreign Office, but he admitted to being powerless. He directed them to Himmler, who was not available. They saw some Gestapo officials including Dr Leo Lange, who was on his way to see Eichmann. He informed them that the problem of the Austrian Jews was being dealt with in Vienna. They did not receive the impression that the policy had been fully decided.

Visas were issued on a temporary basis. There was also the problem of finding transit visas. Switzerland and France were generally willing to grant these. Italy needed proof of baptism, and this led at least one Jewish family to visit Hugh Grimes at the Anglican chaplaincy. Lorli Rudov née Perger, then aged ten, remembered him 'totally unruffled . . . surrounded by a crowd of Jewish people . . . He was taking an enormous risk in offering help . . .' As in many other Jewish families, theory was stymied by practice: the Pergers needed to sell their house and pay the *Reichsfluchtsteuer*. By the time they had done so, the Italian window had closed.[66]

For many, business connections proved useful. That way money could be transferred without being taxed by the Nazi authorities. Connections also meant employment once the refugee entered Britain. Women could generally enter the country by agreeing to go into domestic service. A note in the files at Friends' House asks whether the dentist Dr Edith Mahler is 'capable of doing housework . . . We are trying to get her a permit, but have failed once.'[67] The equivalent for men was to enter full-time education. A remarkable number of Central European Jews, for example, applied to enter the Royal Agricultural College in Cirencester – one can only imagine because its entrance requirements were relatively undemanding. Zionist organizations also set much store by farming, and there was even some cooperation with the Gestapo in Austria, which ran a farm where non-Aryans trained Jews. Many went because it was seen as a means of leaving the country early.[68] The baptismal certificate might work, but it was no guarantee; an Anglican conversion was of more interest for someone hoping to go to Britain or the Dominions.[69]

The facts do not always bear this out, however. The British Empire let in a smattering of Jews: Southern Rhodesia was taking fifty a month by May 1939; Kenya admitted about 650 but were demanding a valid re-entry visa to Germany as a precondition of acceptance, something the Germans were not prepared to consider;[70] Mauritius let in 1,250, Cyprus 744, Jamaica 500, British Guiana 130, Hong Kong forty-two, Malta eighteen, British Honduras twelve, Ceylon six, Aden, North Borneo and Grenada five apiece, Fiji and Tanganyika, Barbados, Leeward Islands and Uganda two each and Sierra Leone one. St Helena allowed a solitary dentist.[71] The Dominions were all different: Australia admitted 10,000 'in spite of the government's best efforts';[72] South Africa took virtually none after passing the Aliens' Act of 1937; New Zealand took 1,100, including Karl Popper, who mentions a helpful man at the New Zealand High Commission in London.[73]

Many are now sceptical of the use of such conversions. One of these is the writer George Clare, who escaped from Vienna via Berlin and ended up in Ireland before joining the British Army. The problem he, like so many others, encountered was how to get to his chosen destination without the necessary transit visas. For some, the English Channel was an insurmountable obstacle: 'You would have got on the back of a crocodile if it was crossing the Channel.'[74]

5

MAY

As April blossomed into May, Salzburg enjoyed a copycat performance of the book-burning in Berlin. Special attention was given to the writings of Austrian Jews: Stefan Zweig, Arthur Schnitzler, Emil Ludwig and Franz Werfel. In the first week of May, Jews were banished from the cattle and meat markets, which had been a prominent area of activity in the past. Later that month Jews were excluded from the press and the arts. The First of May was National Labour Day. God withheld his blessing, and it was grey and wet. The flag-waving, marching columns and Arcadians on the village green went ahead as planned, combining tradition and the Party. The highlight was a gathering of 150,000 girls and boys at the Olympia Stadium in Berlin. At the Opera House on Unter den Linden, Goebbels awarded the cultural prizes for the year. As promised, Leni Riefenstahl was honoured for her *Olympia* film. Later there were speeches in the nearby Lustgarten by Hitler, Ley and Goebbels.[1] For those who had toadied to the Germans, an Austria Medal was to be struck for services to the Anschluss.

ROMAN HOLIDAY

Hitler made his first trip to Rome on 2 May. He was being treated to a state visit in return for that granted to Mussolini in Berlin the year before. The Duce declared a public holiday. It was a huge jamboree with three special trains filled with 500 officials thought worthy to accompany the Führer, together with their wives. The wags called it 'The Invasion of Italy'.

They were all got up in their 'admiral's uniform', a diplomatic costume dreamed up by Frau von Ribbentrop and the Nazi theatre designer Benno von Arendt, replacing the morning dress the Wilhelmstrasse had used in the past. Spitzy had to model the new kit, which came in various prototypes ranging from one of Lützow's riflemen from the Wars of Liberation to a Prussian musketeer or a hotel porter. The final version caused Göring to needle Ribbentrop, saying, 'You look just like the porter in the Rio-Rita-Bar.'[2] When the diplomats finally emerged from their offices into the Wilhelmstrasse, a Berlin street arab exclaimed, 'Oy! Look at that! A lot of admirals!'[3] The party travelled with a bewildering array of costumes ordained by the head of protocol, and were constantly being instructed to change their clothes.[4] Germany's leading clothes-horse, Göring, remained behind in Berlin as acting head of state. On 3 May he received the King of Sweden as he passed through Berlin.

The Italians accorded the uncouth Brownshirts an operatic reception. A special station had been constructed in Rome, where the Nazis were greeted by the governor, Prince Colonna. Carriages drawn by four horses conveyed the party to their lodgings. Hitler travelled with the king, as he was a guest at the Quirinal. Goebbels observed that the Italian sovereign was 'stiff'. There were baskets of fruit and bottles of grappa in every room at the Grand.[5] Goebbels revelled in the glory that was Rome, and regretted that Germany had nothing to match it. It would be up to the Nazis to provide durable monuments of this sort.[6] And there were pretty women wherever he looked – although Ciano thought they only had eyes for Hitler.[7] The only thing that marred the Germans' pleasure at being in the eternal city was the eternal rain.

Hitler was in raptures over all he saw, although he thought the monarch and his wife were looking down on him. The king was indeed perturbed by his house guest, who allegedly called for a woman at 1 a.m., because he needed to have his bed turned down (and this had to be done by a woman); the king also gained the impression that Hitler was injecting himself with stimulants and narcotics, which was possibly true. Even Mussolini told Ciano he was convinced the Führer had been wearing rouge to hide his pallor.[8]

Hitler found compensations: he was able to admire the beauties of Florence and Naples. At a banquet at the Palazzo Venezia, he put the Italians' minds at rest by stressing that he had no desire to reclaim the quarter of a million Germans stranded in the South Tyrol, whom the Italians had persecuted at least as aggressively as the Czech majority had ridden roughshod over the aspirations of the German minority in the Sudetenland. He understood the strength of the Duce's opposition to any border changes. Only recently Mussolini had decided to send the German *Tiroler* off to fight in the front line in Abyssinia, presumably in the hope that they would not return.[9] Hitler's abandonment of the German minority south of the Brenner was the price he was willing to pay for freedom of movement in Austria and Czechoslovakia.

This was not lost on intelligent Germans.[10] The poor Tyroleans had appeared like Banquo's ghost to watch the cortège pass. Goebbels looked out of the train window and felt pain in his heart.[11] Hess agreed. According to Paul Schmidt, the Tyroleans showed no enthusiasm: scarcely a single handkerchief was waved, and there were no fascist salutes.[12] There was no sympathy for them among the Blackshirts. They couldn't wait to see the back of them.[13] Some Nazis who had been agitating for the South Tyrol were arrested before the caravanserai set off.[14]

Ribbentrop was anxious to foist an outline treaty on Mussolini that would assure mutual assistance in the event of attack on either state. In his vision, the pact would bring Germany, Italy and Japan together against Britain. It was sprung on Ciano as they watched the fireworks over the Bay of Naples from the battleship Cavour. In their new uniforms the diplomats looked very much the part at the naval display. The Italian Fascists wanted to hang on to the Anglo-Italian Agreement they had signed the previous month, and Ciano knew how to face Ribbentrop's crassness with diplomatic persiflage: the solidarity between the two countries was so great that they hardly need put it in writing. Ribbentrop refused to be fobbed off, and on one occasion a heated argument broke out between the two men. Ciano thought such a pact would endanger his chances of having Chamberlain recognize Italy's new Mediterranean empire. Mussolini was not opposed to a treaty, but he was distinctly unimpressed by Germany's new Foreign Minister. He told his son-in-law Ciano – who didn't like Ribbentrop either – that this man who talked non-stop about making war was to be given a wide berth. 'He belongs to a category of Germans who are a disaster to their country.'[15] Even leading Nazis were pulling their hair out over Ribbentrop's idiocy. On 4 May Goebbels, Hess and Himmler had a discussion about the Foreign Minister's 'megalomania'. Hess agreed with Goebbels that he needed to be reined in soon.[16]

After the naval display there was a performance of *Aida* at the Teatro San Carlo. The Head of Protocol, Vicco von Bülow-Schwante, had slipped up badly. He had sent the Führer along bare-headed and dressed in tails to review the guard of honour, while the king was in full dress uniform. Hitler had felt like some 'despicable democratic leader'.[17] Goebbels thought they were being treated like shoeshine boys. Bülow-Schwante was sacked.[18]

Hitler expressed his anger at the court ceremonial in a letter to Winifred Wagner.[19] His gaffes caused chortling among his own men as well as the Italians.[20] The humiliations suffered by Hitler in Italy had the effect of hardening his resolve, firstly to resist any attempt to restore the monarchy and secondly to move against the nobility. Ciano was sympathetic, and relayed Ribbentrop's line that the one good thing the Social Democrats had done in Germany was to 'liquidate the monarchy for ever'.[21] As the nobility was still prominent in the army and the diplomatic service, Hitler planned to purge both. Naturally Goebbels egged him on: 'The nobility is international; it sees the nations only in terms of its own possessions. It should be banished.'[22]

One point of agreement struck between the two dictators was a greater coordination in internal affairs. In particular, Italy would finally adopt racial antisemitism. Over the next month Italian newspapers published articles by well-known professors showing that the Italians were racially 'nordic' and that the Jews were a peril. Many academics had to quit their posts, and senior army and naval officers were dismissed; Jews were banned from the professions. Mussolini had to find a new dentist.[23]

One important Roman refused to attend the festivities, however. In Paris Weisl voiced his admiration for the Supreme Pontiff, Pius XI, to the British Board of Deputies, citing '[the] *Osservatore Romano*, the mouthpiece of the Holy See, who [sic] ignored the presence of Kaiser Adolf in the eternal Rome. This policy of the Pope is not only dignified but also clever.'[24]

EICHMANN TIGHTENS HIS GRIP

On 7 May it was announced that Austrian civil servants would be required to furnish baptismal certificates going back to their grandparents. On the 20th the Viennese were warned that the Nuremberg Laws would take effect from 28 June. *Der Stürmer* celebrated the purification of blood in a brace of cartoons, which showed the appropriation of Moritz Kohn's dress shop by a proper Aryan, Fritz Schulz.[25] It was not as easy as that. All over the Reich, Jewish businesses were now proving hard to sell, because they were expensive, and they had run out of buyers. The German economy was suffering from Nazi mismanagement and there was not a lot of money about. The easiest method was to allow the firm to be bought out by a conglomerate. Buyers then dictated prices. That meant that they sold at between two-thirds and three-quarters of their market price. Some Jews were tempted to hang on and hope that the situation improved, often with disastrous results.[26]

The Jewish-owned papers in Vienna were now shut down. These included *Die Stimme*, *Die Neue Welt* (owned by Robert Stricker), *Die Wahrheit*, *Der Jude*, *Jüdische Front* and *Der Legitimist*. They were to be replaced by just one – the *Zionistische Rundschau* – edited by Emil Reich. Twenty-five issues appeared between 20 May and 4 November 1938, bringing welcome morale to humiliated and despairing people.[27] Eichmann was able to write to his old comrade Herbert Hagen on 8 May. He was on top of the work and looking forward to the first issue of the *Zionist Rundschau* which he had the 'boring' job of censoring. It was to be his paper. He was also getting on with the business of forcing Jews into emigration: he had told them that 20,000 indigent Jews had to go before May 1939. The physical pressure was to be exerted by the SD, while the Gauleiter was to deal with the economic issues.[28]

The institutions of the Jewish congregation had been re-created, but from now on they were ruled by Eichmann with a rod of iron. In agreement with his Berlin boss, Dr Six, Eichmann had authorized the relaunch of the IKG, the Zionist National Union and the Orthodox organization Agudas Jisroel. The IKG was reopened on 2 May and the Palestine Office the day after. After a hiatus of six weeks, Eichmann's desire to see the Jews go to Palestine could bear fruit. In theory, at least, this would be legal emigration. His first task was to see that 20,000 poor Jews would leave in the following year. The IKG was instructed to create a Central Emigration Office to deal with all other countries. For Palestine there was the Zionist National Union.[29]

His entire aim was to create a self-funding expulsion. To the end of his days Eichmann insisted that what he was doing was not personal: 'That I was no Jew-hater. I have never been an antisemite; I have never made any bones about that. I don't want to award myself laurels. I mean that the collaboration with the Central Office [for Jewish Emigration] was correct in all matters.'[30]

On 11 May Waldman in New York got wind of a bit of horsetrading at the British Passport Control Office in Vienna.

I learn from a reliable but indirect source that 300 young Jews will leave Vienna in the next few days secretly, in order to travel *without passports* by sea to Palestine.

. . . representatives of these Jews have approached the authorities in Berlin and got their consent for leaving the country and even for the export of the money necessary for the travelling expenses (some 700 Schillings per head). I am informed that the British Consulate of Vienna is aware of the illegal activity, but instead of hindering them the Consulate has so far rather been helpful, though of course not one of the Jews will get a regular visa.

If the attempt of those Jews should succeed another transport will follow immediately. I may add the leader of this adventurous enterprise is known to have already succeeded three times in bringing secret transports of young Jews from Austria to Palestine. The importance of this news would not consist in the fact of 300 Jews leaving a town of 160,000 but the silent encouragement of the Nazis as well as the British Consulate which should be obliged to hinder them.[31]

On 16 May Weisl reported tensions: 'Practically every European country [has] hastened to close its doors to Jews from Austria . . . especially *France*.' He pointed out that the French were considering new legislation that would affect up to 250,000 foreign Jews who were planning to enter the country. The Premier, Daladier, had already threatened to expel 10,000 Jews, including 2,000 Austrians.[32]

A note of *Schadenfreude* creeps into the correspondence between Weisl and Waldman in a document written at this time:

The Nuremberg Aryan Laws have been introduced formally in Austria, notwithstanding grave apprehensions due to the fact that practically the whole of the Viennese bourgeoisie and a good part of the Austrian aristocracy too, has Jewish blood. Exclusion from auctions means Jews can't sell property at a reasonable price. He has to give away whatever he owns, for a song – for the Horst Wessel Song . . .

Weisl gloated: 'Most of the victims are converted or even half-Jews. The sacrament of baptism did not save them.'[33]

The sacrament was not recognized anyhow. The Jews and the Nazis had that in common: as far as they were concerned the converts were still Jews.[34] Only the Christian churches had the power to change that, when there was a will. On 18 May Catchpool wrote to Alice Nike after a meeting with Sir Alan Holderness of the Aliens Department of the Home Office. There had been no deviation from official policy as far as the bureaucrat was concerned, and faked references by Jews were causing problems. 'The greatest difficulty of all, however, is that advice given in Vienna is not a guarantee that the individual who has received it will be allowed to enter this country. The last word is always the immigrant officer at the port of landing . . .' Miss Stamper of MI6 was out of the picture, having 'temporarily broken down'. She must have been an ally of Catchpool's. Catchpool had also been in touch with Gainer through a third party. He wanted to meet Bürckel, and he desired to have use of the diplomatic bag for particulars of individual cases.[35]

OPERATION GREEN

On 20 May Keitel finally sent Hitler an outline of Operation Green for the invasion of Czechoslovakia. The slowness might have been a reflection of the OKW's lukewarm feelings about it. After his success in Austria, Hitler was keener than ever to lay his hands on the western parts of Czechoslovakia. He wanted to achieve his 'mission' in his own lifetime.[36] His accomplice was the new Foreign Minister, Ribbentrop, who was lusting to prove himself. If possible, Hitler was going to wait for 'provocation' rather than risk naked aggression. This meant exploiting 'increasing diplomatic controversies and tension linked with military preparations so as to shift the war guilt on to the enemy' or by waiting for a 'serious incident which will subject Germany to unbearable provocation' and 'affording the moral justification for military measures'.[37]

Hitler was well aware that the Versailles settlement had given him two potential allies in the rape of Czechoslovakia. Hungary wanted to redeem the Magyars of Slovakia, while the Poles felt that they also had a right to Teschen in the north. Hitler realized that France would be unlikely to rescue Czechoslovakia if they were going to unleash a European war in the process. The only danger, Hitler felt, was from the Soviet Union. The pot came to the boil that very weekend of 19–20 May. The contents of Keitel's plan were possibly leaked, although this was probably no more than a sham used to make the Czechs tense. German troops were reported to be on the move near the Czech border. Local elections loomed and a worried President Beneš ordered a partial mobilization. Two Germans were killed and a hundred injured by Czech police during a disturbance in Eger. The British ambassador in Berlin, Sir Nevile Henderson, sent his military attachés to report on the situation and demanded assurances from Keitel, thereby further infuriating the already bitterly Anglophobic Ribbentrop.

In May, *Der Stürmer* launched its own offensive against the Czechs. Goebbels agreed with Ribbentrop for once, and revelled in the way the Czechs seemed to be hastening their own downfall. Ribbentrop made unseemly threats against the Czech people and during a stormy meeting with Henderson convinced him that Germany would fight. Henderson responded by telling his staff to start packing. The British and the French took the opportunity to warn Germany of the consequences of invading Czechoslovakia and the French and the Russians promised immediate military assistance.

Hitler was forced to back down, which did little for his mood. Ribbentrop's impotent rage continued. He ran to the Berghof to find his master yet more hardened in his desire to do away with the Czech state. Halifax was relieved to be communicating with the Under-Secretary of State, Weizsäcker, whom he warned of the consequences of precipitate action, which might put an end to European civilization. Germans felt certain that they were on the verge of war.[38] On 23 May the Czech ambassador in Berlin was informed that Germany had no designs on Czechoslovakia. The bubble burst on the 25th when Chamberlain made it clear to the Commons that, on the basis of the military attaché Colonel Mason-Macfarlane's report, there had been no cause for alarm.

In the aftermath of the crisis, on the 26th, Henlein gave a self-incriminating interview to the *Daily Mail* and Beneš lost a good deal of credibility in London and Paris for provoking Germany. Hitler spent a week sulking at the Berghof before returning to Berlin on 28 May and summoning a conference of the service chiefs in the Chancellery. Göring was still dragging his feet; his Research Bureau had tapped various reports that indicated that the French would not let this one pass. On the table was a map of the offending Czechoslovakia and they were to hear how it was to be eliminated. 'I am utterly determined that Czechoslovakia shall disappear from the map of Europe,' Hitler told them. On the 30th he voiced his intention to smash the Czechs in the immediate future. Keitel's plans needed to be effected by 1 October.

The Sudeten Party leader, Henlein, was still charged with the role of refusing any offer that might alleviate the position of the German minority. The German government was not officially involved. Hitler wanted the boil to get bigger so that he could lance it about the time of the Nuremberg Rally in September. The British were losing sympathy with the Czechs and sent the former President of the Board of Trade, Lord Runciman, to investigate. Beneš was urged to make concessions to the Sudetenländer on the basis of Henlein's Karlsbad Programme.

Hitler was also watching the Russians. He asked the Romanians to refuse them permission to cross their frontiers to intervene, and was pleased to hear from his ambassador in Warsaw that the Poles had no intention of accommodating the Soviet Union either; the Polish Foreign Minister, Colonel Jozef Beck, still had his eyes on Teschen. Hitler hoped that the British and the French would be reluctant to act in concert with the Soviet Union. He was unimpressed by the Hungarians dithering about committing themselves. 'He who wants to sit at table must at least help in the kitchen.'[39]

Hitler's plans alarmed his Chief of Staff, General Ludwig Beck, who feared an 'adventure' of this sort would lead to war with the Western powers. To the military planners, the idea of an attack on Czechoslovakia would result in a heavy risk that Germany would be dragged once again into world war. It was a view largely shared by Göring, who was now losing his kudos as a foreign policy advisor. Beck wrote a series of memoranda beginning on 5 May, in which he tried to bring Brauchitsch over to his way of thinking. The memoranda were written for Hitler too, but Brauchitsch did not even dare show him the more contentious parts. Hitler already believed the General Staff were sabotaging his plans.[40]

To delay the powerful French army, Hitler was building a counterpart to the Maginot Line along Germany's western border with bunkers and pillboxes to his own design. Annoyed by the military's vacillating attitude, he removed responsibility for the West Wall's construction from the army, assigning it to Fritz Todt's Nazi labour organization instead. He was fed up with the army getting in the way. Göring demonstrated that the Luftwaffe was made of sterner stuff by creating an Air Defence Zone behind the wall and arming it with anti-aircraft guns. Goebbels was authorized to launch a propaganda offensive to show how miserably treated the Sudetenländer were and fill the papers with atrocities carried out by the Czechs against ethnic Germans.

Beck's reaction to the service chiefs' meeting of the 28th was to pen two more memos on 29 May and 3 June. He was little concerned about legitimacy; he was worried that Germany would ultimately lose a war against the British and the French and was aware that the United States was prepared to back them. These doubts were shared by Göring, but despite this he was busy producing weapons at such a rate that he had set off an arms race with the Western powers. It was obvious to intelligence men in France and Britain that these countries were being seen as potential enemies in a future conflict caused by German aggression towards Czechoslovakia. Göring had ordered 7,000 Ju 88s, medium-range bombers capable of hitting targets in France and Britain. He had turned over half the workforce of the aeronautics industry to their manufacture, but progress was still slow. Germany also had an alarmingly low supply of explosives, with production at only half the total for 1918. On 12 July a New Military Economic Production Plan was launched, which placed the German economy on a war footing.[41]

Göring was in a quandary: on the one hand he wanted to prevent a war against France and Britain that in the long run Germany was likely to lose; on the other he was desirous of getting his hands on Czech goods that would be a considerable boon to the Four Year Plan. There was an added incentive in the massive Skoda arms firm, which was producing some of the most technically advanced weaponry in Europe, including the famous Bren gun beloved of the British Army. In the summer of that year all he could say was, 'Ways will be found', as it became increasingly clear that Germany was on the brink of economic collapse. Even the timing of Operation Green reflected this: the deadline allowed for the bringing in of the harvest, as food stocks were low too.[42] It was not for nothing that Göring was overjoyed later that year, when the West allowed Germany to make off with the Sudetenland without a fight: it was all he wanted, and without the war that he did not believe Germany could win.

Hitler rightly perceived that the British were unlikely to produce the only winning card they had and enlist the support of the Soviet Union. They detested it even more than Nazi Germany, but, together with France, it was a guarantor of Czechoslovakia's independence.

On 13 June the top army commanders had their own meeting at Barth in Pomerania. For the first time they were informed of Hitler's designs on Czechoslovakia. Hitler arrived late. He may have been less sure of his moves than he seemed to others in his camp, Goebbels in particular. He assuaged his generals by telling them the Fritsch business had been a mistake, that the general was innocent. Goebbels thought this would be a humilation for Himmler, since the Gauleiter of Berlin evidently did not know of Göring's involvement.[43] No one objected to Hitler's wider plans, agreeing they were not as unfeasible as some had suggested. Beck was absent from the meeting.

The Chief of the General Staff was not the only one who was fruitlessly badgering Hitler. No one seemed to be able to talk sense to him. The Minister of Finance, the former Rhodes Scholar Lutz Schwerin von Krosigk, asked for an audience with the Führer to alert him to the disastrous state of the economy. He had to content himself with writing him a memo. In the second quarter of the year the stock market went down 13 per cent. Beck's lamentations also went increasingly unheeded. On 16 July he made his famous call for the senior officers to resign *en masse*: 'Extraordinary times require extraordinary measures.' On 29 July he produced a formula for Brauchitsch:

> The Commander in Chief of the Army, together with the most senior commanding generals, regret that they cannot assume responsibility for the conduct of a war of this nature without carrying a share of the guilt for it in the face of the people and of history. Should the Führer, therefore, insist on the prosecution of this war, they hereby resign from their posts.[44]

Brauchitsch kept the memo back, and only had it read out at a meeting of the generals on 4 August. While many agreed that Germany could not win a war against the Western powers, no one heeded his call. The Nazi Reichenau suggested that such ideas would have a negative effect on Hitler, while another general thought that political decisions should be left to politicians. Gerd von Rundstedt drew attention to the February crisis, and thought a challenge to Hitler inopportune. Erich von Manstein thought Beck should stop worrying about politics and get on with his job. Beck went out into the wilderness on his own. Nor was Brauchitsch thanked for his work. When he passed on Beck's memorandum through a third party, Hitler summoned him to the Berghof and subjected him to a tongue-whipping in his study that was so loud that its contents were heard by those assembled on the terrace outside. He would not accept political advice from others: he alone knew what to do.

FURTHER TRANSPORTS TO DACHAU

On the 24th the second Dachau transport set off from Vienna. This time there were 120 on board of whom fifty were Jews. There were further arrests from 25 to 27 May. Intellectuals, doctors, engineers and lawyers were told to report to the Rossauer Lände or the Karajangasse and bring nothing with them. There were nasty scenes when their women turned up to bid farewell to their sons and husbands. There were four transports in all. A week later a purely Jewish cargo of 500 set off, followed by another on 2 June. Ninety per cent of Vienna's jewellers left on these transports, including Moritz Österreicher, whose family had served the emperors as court jewellers for generations. For those who had been in the camp since 1 April there was curiosity about the newcomers. The Viennese hangman Lang came, together with his assistant – he had killed Nazis, notably after the murder of Dollfuss. He hanged himself on the first night. In another account he was tortured to death before the eyes of the other prisoners.[45] The assistant refused to end his life, so they ended it for him.[46]

Dachau was getting seriously overcrowded. The summer's new arrivals sought support from the hardened men who had been there since April. 'Comrades around me were discussing the chances of release,' wrote Bruno Heilig.

These men were in a terrible state of mind, which I could well understand. A political prisoner accepts his punishment as one of the vicissitudes which one always risks in politics – and anyone involved in the fight against Nazism had to be prepared for [the] concentration camp – but these men had never thought of things in that light. They had simply gone about their own affairs, paid their taxes, played cards in cafés, slept with their wives and confined their political activity to reading the newspapers. And now they had suddenly become participants in a political struggle. Utterly disconcerted, they faced their fate without understanding, and the only defence they had was their hope of speedy liberation.[47]

Himmler had been inspecting the camps, and told Goebbels about them. 'There is only rabble. They need to be exterminated, in the interest and well-being of the nation.'[48] Naturally suicides in Austria rose that month: there were 143 in May and 144 in June.[49] In November many of the Jews in Dachau were transferred to Buchenwald above Weimar. The purpose of these shipments was to put pressure on Vienna's Jewish colony to emigrate as soon as possible.[50]

On 28 May Schuschnigg, who had been under house arrest, was finally taken into Gestapo custody at the Hotel Metropole. He was brought to a large room on the fifth floor with 'two heavily barred windows of opaque glass'. He was told he could smoke – for the time being. Any food he ordered was at his own expense. The hotel still seemed to function and the food was brought up from the kitchens by waiters. Sentries had orders to shoot him if he made trouble. He was denied books and newspapers. He was deprived of sleep: his light was left on and in the middle of the night there was an inspection of his belongings. Fortunately four years' service in the First World War had steeled his nerves.[51]

With his one towel he had to dust his room and clean the windows, then he had to go next door and do the same for the sentries: empty their buckets and basins and clean the lavatory after they had made a mess of it – again with his towel. Then the charwoman came to do the job all over again. One guard, known as 'the Stinker', used to amuse himself by aiming his gun at him. It appeared that these performances were revenge for the way that Nazis had been treated at Wöllersdorf and in the Corporate State's prisons. With time the guards relented and became reasonably friendly. They told him that he was to be tried for calling in the French and arming the communists; but if he was for the high jump, that was nothing to what was going to happen to 'the Jew' Louis Rothschild, who was occupying another room on that floor.[52]

Goebbels had been thinking about music. A Degenerate Music exhibition was planned to upstage the art exhibition of the year before. It struck him as too flat. He told Severus Ziegler to go away and redo it. He had to soothe Lehár's nerves, not least because Hitler's favourite composer was still worried about his Jewish wife. Meanwhile Germany was now rid of its Jewish plague, and Aryan composers could show how good they were, unencumbered by Jewish competition. He went off to see Nico Dostal's opera Extrablätter. On 28 May Düsseldorf's Music Week began. Richard Strauss opened it by conducting his Festival Overture and Leonora. 'He is happy when I address a few friendly words to him. He has been punished enough.' Goebbels felt proud to be German that night when he heard Hermann Abendroth conduct the Berlin Philharmonic in Beethoven's Ninth.[53]

6

JUNE

Central Europe was thawing out and swallows announced the summer. For Greater Germany's Jews, however, there was little or no relief from their dark lodgings. In Vienna they were now banned from public parks and gardens. The only area still open to them was the Jewish part of the Central Cemetery in Simmering. From his Swiss exile, Franz Werfel penned a little poem.

Volksgarten, Stadt- und Rathauspark,
Ihr Frühling war noch nie so stark.
Den Juden Wiens ist er verboten.
Ihr einziges Grün wächst bei den Toten.
Zur Stunde, da die Stadt erblasst
Von sonntäglicher Mittagslast,
Drückt es sich scheu in Strassenbahnen.
Hinaus zu halbervergessenen Ahnen.
Der Totenstadt von Simmering
Sind Christ und Jud das gleiche Ding,
Verschieden nur durch Zins und Kosten.

(City, People's and Town Hall Park,
Your spring was never quite so dark.
The Jews are banished and now it's said,
Their one patch of green lies among the dead.
The moment when the city slumps

Under the weight of Sunday lunch,
They shyly join the queues for trams
To pay respects to half-forgotten grans.
The Valhalla of Simmering, that is
Where Gentile and Jew share privileges
Distinguished only by rent and charges.)

On 1 June, Hitler officially launched the *Kraft-durch-Freude* car – the prototype for the Volkswagen 'Beetle' that he had had a hand in designing – by opening the new factory at Helmstedt. Every German was to have his car, at a price of 990 RM, a subscription of just five marks a week. At the end of the war, a lot of ordinary Germans had paid out to receive their Beetles, but no one had had a car delivered.

Some Jews had taken the decision to head for the big cities of the Altreich where they believed they would be safer, particularly Berlin, something that was particularly galling to Goebbels. The Gauleiter believed he had a firm ally in Helldorf, who had begun rounding up Jews at the end of May. By 1 June he had bagged 300 of them before taking temporary leave of the city. In his absence, an outraged Goebbels discovered that Schulenburg had taken it upon himself to behave like the Tailor of Gloucester and let all but six mice go, retaining only those who were suspected of criminal activity. 'You little bureaucrat!' Goebbels harangued him on the telephone. He was so angry that Schulenburg had to hold the receiver well away from his ear.[1] 'I was livid. I have never made such a fuss. Helldorf is to return at once and I will give him such a bollocking. You can't do anything with all these jurists in Police Headquarters.'[2]

On 10 June Goebbels lectured the Berlin police on why the Jews had to go. He did not want them spoiling his fun a second time. Helldorf still had the reputation of being a committed Nazi and an intimate friend of Goebbels. He was playing a double game, having moved over to the Opposition at the time of the Fritsch crisis.[i] He

[i] He was hanged after the failed plot of 20 July 1944.

later told the Gauleiter that he had purged the police, when he had done no such thing, as Schulenburg remained at his desk.[3]

Other 'old' Reich cities began to get tough too. The first synagogue was destroyed in Munich on 9 June. Hitler had decided that it was a blot on the landscape when he had visited the new *Deutsches Künstlerhaus* – The House of German Artists – a few days before. The Jewish congregation was given a few hours to empty the building. In Nuremberg, the Gauleiter Julius Streicher was anxious to destroy his synagogue. He ran a picture of it on the front page of *Der Stürmer* in July, calling synagogues 'dens of thieves' and 'Nuremberg's disgrace'. The 'eyesore' came down on 10 August.[4]

*

The Reich was jubilant on 2 June: its first lady, Emmy Göring, gave birth to a baby girl, who was named Edda.[ii] The actress was forty-five, and her husband had been shot in the groin during the Beer-Hall Putsch, so there was talk of immaculate conception. In Nuremberg Streicher put it about that Emmy Göring had been artificially inseminated.[5] There were naturally rumours that the Duce was the father, as Emmy had been in Italy with her husband nine months before.[6] Adolf Hitler sent several hundred roses to the mother. When Göring came to pick up his wife and child from the sanatorium ten days later, the streets were black with cheering crowds. They went directly to show the baby to the Führer, who volunteered to be her godfather.[7] He shared that office with Göring's old comrade-in-arms Pilli Körner. Tributes came in from all over the world including telegrams from Lords Halifax and Londonderry. Later that month a

---

[ii] Emmy Göring claimed that she was named after a friend, and not Mussolini's daughter and the wife of Count Ciano (Emmy Goering, *My Life with Goering*, London 1972, 76); Willi Frischauer (*Goering*, London n.d., 158–9) scoffs at this and says that she invented the story after Ciano's 'treachery'. She was originally named 'Ebba'; it was Göring who changed it to 'Edda'.

family gathering in Berlin to celebrate the birth mustered 200 Görings.

Little Edda had come two weeks late for Mothers' Day, a festival held on the second Sunday in May. That year the state had decided to honour motherhood, granting crosses of gold, silver or bronze to women 'rich in children'. Candidates were selected by Nazi block or cell leaders. The children had to be legitimate and have Aryan fathers. Childlessness was declared grounds for divorce. There had to be no history of mental illness, no dependence on alcohol and no known antisocial traits.[8] The crosses were to be worn on important occasions, but mothers were also provided with minuscule replicas for everyday use.[9]

Germany's model for motherhood was surely Magda Goebbels, who had a fifth child while her husband was away in Rome in May and was to go on to produce a sixth and last in 1940. That daughter was described as the 'reconciliation child', as it was produced after Hitler had forcibly patched up their marriage. For the time being the actress Emmy Göring would have to play the role. For the next few months Germans could purchase postcards of Emmy with little Edda.

EXIT STRATEGIES

Officially, no countries admitted Jews any more. A cartoon by 'Fips' showed a Jew marching past Polish, Swiss and Dutch doors marked 'Jews no longer welcome'.[10] In practice there were loopholes. On the day that saw the birth of Edda, Wolfgang Weisl told Waldman of the American Jewish Committee that he had run into an illegal immigrant from Austria in Paris. The man had told him that the smuggling of Jews across the border from Germany's best-known exit point, Aachen, to Eupen in Belgium was 'quasi-legal'. Jews with papers were often given a last kick in the backside to help them into their new world of freedom. For those who had none, smugglers charged them anything between 25 and 500 RM. The migrants assembled now in groups of twenty to thirty, whereas formerly the groups were smaller – five or six.

German border guards were very superficial in their examinations; and curiously Weisl was told they never removed jewels. People who wanted to avoid the German frontier posts, however, could do so by paying a little bit extra to the smugglers. Weisl's informer had marched forty-five kilometres on foot. Once they reached Eupen across the border they could take a bus or taxi to Liège, and then the train to Brussels. If they were caught by the Belgian police, they were handed back to the Germans at Aachen, where the Jewish Kultusgemeinde looked after them until they found a chance to try again. Two thousand Jews had been able to cross in this way since the Anschluss. 'Most of the Jews had no passport,' reported Weisl.[11] He was bitter about events in Vienna: 'Not one Christian . . . has interfered in favour of his Jewish friends.' Jews had been forced to urinate on the Torah.[12] This was less than the truth, but Weisl could be forgiven for believing it.

On 13 June the American Consul-General, John Wiley, expressed some of his frustrations in a report to the State Department. There had been a 'new wave' of Jew-baiting, with Jews being told they had between two and eight weeks to leave; otherwise they would face Dachau. He had also learned of the illicit transports.

> The authorities are encouraging clandestine emigration. I have received what I believe to be a conservative estimate from an authoritative source that over 1,000 have been obliged to cross the frontier at night into Belgium. A few days ago 350 were sent in sealed cars to Greece whence they will be shipped to Palestine without visas or permits of entry. It was explained to me that the competent British authorities are unofficially in the picture and not raising obstacles.[13]

Wiley had other complaints. One of these involved the treatment of Mischlinge. A distinguished composer had been refused admission to a Jewish hospital because he was not a Jew; yet he could not be treated by an Aryan hospital because as far as they were concerned he was defined as a Jew. Another bugbear was Gildemeester, whom he found highly suspicious: 'I am not in the position to cast any additional light on the nature of Mr Gildemeester's activities in Austria.' He had had a letter from Gildemeester complaining that the Americans had described him as a German agent, and that this was jeopardizing his work. He cited a list of Quakers as his friends. In his reply Wiley suggested the Dutchman write in German or French, as his English was not doing him any favours.[14]

Further repressive measures were introduced on 14 June, which were to lead the way for the compulsory transfer of all Jewish business to German hands. Branches of a business were Jewish if the branch was managed by a Jew. Moreover the measure was cunningly backdated to 1 January 1938, so that any shifting of positions after the Anschluss was null and void. That same day, Frick proposed compulsory Aryanization. A year before, Hitler had declared that the removal of Jewish doctors was even more important than the sacking of Jewish civil servants, because people regarded physicians as models.[15] The Führer had been slow to enact his will, because the removal of the Jews from medicine would have depleted the service by some 4,000 souls in the Altreich alone, some 8 per cent of the whole. In Austria it was much worse: nearly half of Austria's 7,000 doctors were Jews. Hitler nonetheless went ahead and signed the decree on 25 July.

The scales were slowly falling from the eyes of the damned. On the 17th, Jews were banned from practising dentistry. In response, the Viennese dentists Hugo and Bella Schneider, together with their eleven-year-old son Hans, decided to risk flight. They took a train to the Czech border and bribed a border guard to let them cross. They forfeited 'what had been a secure middle-class existence' and became 'refugees without resources, status or prospects'. They went to live in Karvina on the Polish border, where Hugo had come from and where his brothers still lived. After the Munich

Agreement it was ceded to the Poles, and they became illegal immigrants in Poland.[16]

The Schneiders' prospects were little better than those they had left behind. In the autumn, however, they found a place for Hans at a Quaker school in the Netherlands that had been established for German and Austrian refugees. Hans had to go to Warsaw to get a visa from the Dutch Consul. Then he had to fly to Prague, then to Amsterdam. The aircraft was cancelled owing to bad weather, which meant that Hans and his father had to hang about Warsaw without papers for ten days.

He asked the first reliable-looking man he saw in the street for help, who sent us to a member of the German embassy in whose apartment I then stayed. Equally amazing, the man who sent us there turned out to be a Polish policeman in the very department charged with deporting illegal aliens. I presume there was an anti-Nazi underground in both organizations . . . I was told to say that I was a relative from Vienna if anyone asked.[17]

Hans made it to safety in the Netherlands, but his parents were denounced in Karvina. The local police turned a blind eye while they disappeared into the Polish interior. They stayed with distant relatives while they waited for a British or American visa. In April 1939, Hugo Schneider became one of forty dentists allowed to enter Britain, travelling from Poland by boat. Hans rejoined them in August.

THE VIENNA THEATRE FESTIVAL AND HUGH GRIMES

Thwarted by his failure to rid his city of Jews, Goebbels was now being badgered by another group of pests. 'A large number of pastors have signed a petition for Niemöller. Wastepaper basket!'[18] More pleasant work took the form of the Vienna Theatre Festival. 'Vienna needs to become a fun city once again.' He flew in on 12 June, visiting the Cobenzl in the Vienna Woods with its magnificent views. The Festival opened with a performance of *Rosenkavalier* conducted by Böhm. That night Goebbels soothed the ruffled feathers of the Austrian comedian Hans Moser in a suburban wine tavern in Grinzing. There were violins, and Moser sang *Heurige* songs. It was 'indescribably romantic'. Dawn had risen before Goebbels made it back to his hotel.[19]

He stayed to see the performance of *Hamlet* starring Gründgens and Marianne Hoppe. The 'genius Shakespeare' was clearly an honorary German – 'how paltry others appear beside him'.[20] On 18 June Goebbels was back at the Festival with Magda and the following day drove up to the Kahlenberg that overlooks Vienna from the east. The Festival closed with a performance of *Lohengrin* given by the Berlin opera ensemble and directed by Tietjen.

On 14 June, while Goebbels was back persecuting Jews in Berlin, things began to accelerate in Vienna's Anglican Church. The incumbent, Hugh Grimes, initially decided to take matters in his own hands in a quiet way by marrying Jews in the Anglican rite, thereby conferring baptism at the same time. Grimes had been in Vienna since November 1934. In October 1935 he had paid a visit to Germany following the issue of the Nuremberg Laws and written to Bishop Bell, 'I may say that I myself am pro-Jew and have always been so.' He believed that Britain and the United States should tell the Germans to stop persecuting the Jews:

Obviously such declarations need to be conveyed to the government as wisely as possible, otherwise they will only strengthen the wild men on the left [of the Party] in their cry for the extermination of the Jews who are plotting against the Reich.[21]

That Grimes may have suggested baptism as a way out is implied by the next article in the file, which examines the use of baptism for humanitarian ends. It advises against, as under the new German law everything is based on race: 'Baptism alters nothing.'[22] Grimes knew better. He knew that he could not guarantee success but he could offer a glimmer of hope. There were the countries that accepted baptized Jews, at least in cases of transit, and there were the officials who were prepared to accept a baptismal certificate, even if it meant turning a blind eye to the physical appearance of the person trying to pass the frontier. The Germans were anxious to be rid of the Jews, after all. The only thing that held them back was the 'dough'.

Once Grimes had begun the process, word got round the assimilated Jews and they began to form a queue outside the chaplaincy. Grimes baptized eight Jews on 14 June; twelve on the 19th; sixteen on the 26th. He reached 103 on 10 July, beating that on 27 July with a mighty 129. The greatest number of baptisms he managed in a day was 229 on 25 July. After that he went on leave.[23] The entries in the Register provide evidence of the sort of Jews who were prepared to go through a 'political' baptism for the sake of acquiring papers of transit. The probable destination of such applicants was Britain, its colonies and Dominions, or the United States. Only in certain cases would Palestine have been meant: there were other ways of getting to Palestine that did not require this sort of compromise.

Most of the applicants were from Vienna itself, although there are Burgenländer among the entries, driven to Vienna by the move to 'purify' Austria's easternmost province. A few Germans figure in the books, but they are mostly married to Austrians. The rest come from the former lands of the Austro-Hungarian Monarchy: Viennese residents rather than fugitives. Many of them were hoping to go to Australia, but the contradictory policies of the Australian government proved a frustration. Some might have believed that baptism in the Anglican rite could have helped. This was probably the case with the distaff branch of the actor Paul Henried's family from Vienna. After a while they cut their losses and went to Paris, and from there to New York. His father found a sponsor in America at the last moment and left his mother behind. She was protected by a Christian family for a year, but the Gestapo found her and she perished in the camps.[24]

The Zeisl brothers collected as many visas as they could and rented a villa in Baden while they thought about what to do. The composer Erich Zeisl managed to get visas for Shanghai from a student called Hong Pan, who was a nephew of Madame Chiang Kai-shek. 'We bought somewhere a visa to Liberia where they said that when you arrive, somebody would come and stick a fork in you to see if you were good to eat.' Finally he went to the American consulate and looked at the New York telephone book for people called Zeisl. He found seven and wrote to them all.

Then one day they met a man in the coffeehouse who said he could obtain French visas for a price. They gave him the money and he handed over the visas, but they were from Cologne and not from Vienna. This presented new complications. They had to change their residence to Cologne and go to the embassy to activate the visas. They had applied for visas to Australia (and, although he doesn't say so, they had had themselves baptized by Grimes), but they were deterred by the fee of £1,500. Then a plumber called Zeisl in New York sent an affidavit. Eventually they chanced it and went to Cologne and by a miracle the visa worked.[25]

PALESTINE

Weisl had more news on 15 June: 300 Revisionists had been allowed to leave Vienna 'with the silent encouragement of both the Nazi authorities and the British Consulate in Vienna'. In fact a total of 480 had left on 9 June. This flatly contradicted British policy in Palestine, as it was Kendrick's duty to interpret it, and yet it is improbable that he allowed the Jews to leave without seeking advice from Whitehall first.

The British Consulate in Vienna seems to be aware of that illegal transport [wrote Weisl]. The secretary of the emigration depart-ment, a Miss Stamper, is told to have advised would-be emigrants not to wait for a certificate but to leave with that illegal transport. Incredible as that story seems to be I have heard it from different quarters, and I would be glad to be able to believe that not all of humanity has been lost even in consular offices.

Weisl was at a loss to understand the Janus-features of Nazism, which could encourage emigration at the same time as arresting young Jews and putting them to forced labour.[26] The policy seemed contradictory: on the one hand Jews were being told to go; on the other hand it could take weeks to obtain the necessary papers.[27] What he failed to appreciate was that the Third Reich not only wanted to be rid of the Jews, but needed slaves if they were to succeed: young German men were bound for the army.

BERLIN

Eichmann's work in Vienna pleased his masters: he was getting results, whereas in Germany the pace of emigration had been slow. George Clare remembered the particular kindness of the Berliners towards the Jews after his family's experience in their native Vienna.[28] Neither Hitler nor his Berlin Gauleiter was happy about this. Hitler had even managed to connect the Jews with another of his bugbears – the nobility. Nobles, he said, married Jews. On 16 June the police mounted a *razzia*: 'The persecutions were carried out exactly to the Viennese model.'[29] On 18 June the Gauleiter reported 'lots of arrests . . . we are going to make Berlin free of Jews'.[30] There was outrage in the foreign press.

The fact that so many Jews were emigrating to the capital of the Reich formed one theme for Goebbels' summer solstice speech that year. An audience of 120,000 gathered in the Olympia Stadium. The last movement of Beethoven's Ninth was played followed by fireworks. He reported that no fewer than 3,000 Jews had settled in

Berlin in the past few months. Together with Helldorf he made plans to step up the persecution and later came up with the idea of creating a proper ghetto in a largely Jewish district of Berlin, to be funded by the richer Jews.[31]

After the speech, Helldorf relayed the instructions to the Party. They were to daub slogans on Jewish shops. This upset Funk, who said it was illegal. When the *razzia* took place various unwanted elements joined in the looting, including gypsies. Goebbels had them taken to a concentration camp, but defended his notion of 'spontaneous demonstrations'. 'For the rest this sort of popular justice has certainly done some good once more. The Jews are terrified and they will certainly think twice before they see Berlin as their el dorado.' He was to use these methods again on a grander scale in November.[32]

On 22 June the German prizefighter Max Schmeling lost his bid to regain his title. He had beaten the black Joe Louis in 1936, which had resulted in rioting in Harlem. This time Louis cracked two of Schmeling's vertebrae two minutes into the fight and when he screamed with pain the German broadcasting authorities turned off the live link. Later Goebbels decided that the film of the fight would not be shown in Germany. Schmeling arrived back on a stretcher. Goebbels sent flowers to his wife, the Czech actress Anny Ondra. He had a weakness for Czech starlets.[33]

The defeat was a return to the embarrassing theme that had haunted the Berlin Olympics, when German sprinters had proved no match for black Americans.[iii] Not only was German defeat keenly felt in Nazi circles, but the Americans too saw it as an ideological victory. In the run-up to the fight, Jewish lobbies had tried to prevent the match from taking place. The fastidious Reck-Malleczewen naturally objected to being told that Germany had been subjected to national defeat.[34]

[iii] Only the sprinters: Germany won the 1936 Olympiad with a third more medals than its nearest rival, the United States.

There was another anti-Jewish *razzia* on 28 June in Berlin. The Jewish hostess Bella Fromm, who was protected by her contacts in various embassies and legations, went out with a friend to survey the damage. Jews were being roughed up by SA-men who had daubed various Jewish-owned shops in the Kurfürstendamm with slogans and cartoons. In the poorer Jewish areas shops had been looted or trashed. Even pint-sized Hitler Youth boys had joined in the sport. The mob had also attacked the Israel department store, owned by the eponymous family, who had joint German-British nationality.

The next day the municipality had to send people round to remove the graffiti.[35] After Funk, it was Göring who tried to queer Goebbels' pitch, but even if the action had been a failure this time, the latter would accept no criticism. 'For the rest, the fight against the Jews will go on, legally . . . They have to get out!'[36] On the 29th Jews had to sack their Jewish employees within two weeks. On the pretext of ascertaining the wealth of Vienna's remaining Jews, searches for gold, silver and jewels were carried out between 29 June and 3 July. Confiscations yielded 600,000 RM or the equivalent.[37]

7

JULY

Now the weather was warmer, Hitler was spending much of his time at the Berghof. The Chancellery was in chaos, as he had commissioned Speer to tear down the building and construct something in its place worthy of the Führer of the German Reich. A fire broke out at the site, causing fears that the Führer would not be able to move in on 1 August as desired. In fact, he did not have a chance to show it off to the world's press before the New Year.[1] Speer's architecture in general found favour with the bigwigs. Goebbels saw the great Berlin model on 7 July and thought it marvellous, its author a 'proper artist'.[2]

In Vienna the Nazi authorities had a problem when one of their weapons blew up in their faces: starved of advancement, Hitler's Austrian Legion mutinied.[3] In other areas, however, things were going to plan. It was reported that Louis Rothschild was still under arrest and all Rothschild property had been placed under the control of a commissioner. Governor Bürckel gloated. 'This is a revolution. The Jews may be glad that it is not of the French or Russian pattern.'[4] The next day he returned to the theme: Vienna was

> overfilled with Jews, who have obtained an overwhelming preponderance in industry and trade, the theatre and other branches of culture and in every branch of public life; a certain amount of time is necessary to clear them out, as we intend to do . . . I seize hold of the big offenders and lock them up.

Bürckel warned the world's press that the Jews would not be allowed to hang on to more than 4–5 per cent of their property after they had paid the *Reichsfluchtsteuer* and other taxes.[5]

Despite the uncompromising demands he made to Helldorf and the rest, Goebbels claimed that he was not happy with the physical maltreatment of the Jews – at least for the time being. On 4 July he heard that some Jews had been picked on in Sachsenhausen, which was part of his fiefdom as Gauleiter of Berlin. He sent word to stop it. On the 7th he despatched Helldorf to investigate these 'obscenities': 'I don't want this.'[6] Helldorf appeared to be doing his bidding, but a few days later Himmler – who had the means to find out – warned Goebbels of the police chief's questionable loyalty.[7] On 11 July Goebbels took the opportunity to tear Helldorf off a strip. 'He looked very small' when the Gauleiter had finished with him.[8]

On 2 July Malcolm Christie had reported to the Foreign Office in London that Hitler intended to attack Czechoslovakia in the autumn. The following day Chamberlain had delivered a speech at Kettering in which he had voiced his reluctance to go to war.[9] On 5 July, Goebbels had a long chat with Ribbentrop in the Kaiserhof Hotel. They spoke about the imminent strike against the Czechs, better relations with Britain (Germany would honour Austria's debts) and the Berlin–Rome Axis (they needed to forget about the South Tyrol for the time being). The German Foreign Minister also had cold feet about the savage treatment of the Jews. 'I promised him I would be a little gentler,' Goebbels confided to his diary. 'The principle, however, remains unchanged and Berlin must be cleaned up. For the rest we want to launch a great propaganda campaign about the Jewish problem all over the world, soon.'[10]

Himmler had no such reservations. Speaking to the boys of the NAPOLA[i] schools, he outlined the ideological fuel that was

[i] National Political Educational Institutes – the Nazi answer to the British public school.

generating the SS:

> We as a nation of seventy-five million are, despite our great
> numbers, a minority in the world. We have very, very many
> against us, as you yourselves as National Socialists know very
> well. All capital, the whole of Jewry, the whole of freemasonry,
> all the democrats and philistines of the world, all the
> Bolsheviks of the world, all the Jesuits of the world, and not
> least, all the peoples who regret not having completely killed
> us off in 1918, and who make only one vow: if we once get
> Germany in our hands again it won't be another 1918, it will
> be the end.[11]

Der Stürmer was naturally in agreement with Goebbels. The worry
was that powerful American Jews might spoil their plans. In issue 30,
the cartoonist 'Fips' showed Jews defiling the Stars and Stripes.
Another pair of cartoons presented a Jewish emigrant:

> *Als ich den Wanderer fragte: '*
> *Wo gehst Du hin?'*
> *Da sagte er: 'Ins Ausland,*
> *Weil ich ein Jude bin.'*

> (When I asked the wanderer:
> 'Where are you going to?'
> He said: 'I'm off to exile,
> Because I am a Jew.')

The flanking cartoon, however, showed the same Jew returned
to Germany. He was laughing: armed with a non-German
passport he was now a foreigner and enjoyed protection from foreign
powers.[12] Germany needed to know its enemy. That July,
Munich hosted a meeting of the Academic Society for Research
into Jewry.[13]

In July, *Der Stürmer* dedicated a special issue to Austria's Jews. It mocked the lawyers Hecht and Winterstein, who were already in Dachau, and the fact that 85 per cent of Vienna's advocates were Jews, followed by 80 per cent of cobblers and newspaper proprietors, 75 per cent of bankers, 73.6 per cent of the wine trade, 73.3 per cent of the rag trade, 70 per cent of dentists and 70 per cent of cinema proprietors. Of course none of this was true any more.[14]

There was more bad news for the Austrians. The regalia of the Holy Roman Empire were going to be moved to Nuremberg; in addition, increasing numbers of foreigners had cancelled their visits to the Salzburg Festival. In Vienna it was announced that the city was already one-third Aryanized, but the disadvantage of removing Jews from public life was plain in the hospitals, where there were already 147 positions vacant.[15] Jews were now being cleared out of their more luxurious homes in Sievering and Hietzing, on the Ringstrasse and the less salubrious Taborstrasse.[16]

On the 6th it was reported that there had been 800 Jewish suicide attempts over the past few days. There followed the final order removing Jews from their posts. Jews also had to leave flats with windows on to the streets and move into the courtyards, which were always of lesser value. 'Jews are hardly ever seen in the streets of the city, except in queues at the special passport offices.'[17] Gentiles could also justify not paying their rent if there were a Jew in the building.[18] The British press reported that Viennese businesses had to place a card in the windows saying that the premises were for sale to an Aryan buyer. Streicher's special Viennese issue of *Der Stürmer* pointed out – *inter alia* – that Jews still owned or controlled many Viennese papers. The official *Wiener Zeitung* published long lists every day of Jewish businesses going into liquidation. The *Reichspost* was culled in the second week of July, but the *Neue Freie Presse* and the *Wiener Journal* remained.

KENDRICK AND PALESTINE

On 5 July Weisl recorded that, contrary to pessimistic reports in the Jewish press, 381 illegal immigrants had arrived in Palestine.[ii] They were described as Revisionists but included nearly 100 Agudist sports club members. 'I learn that the Austrian authorities are ready to allow a new transport to leave Austria in July, under the same conditions, i.e. granting permits to £15 for transport fees per head of emigrant at the price of 12 RM per pound.' It transpired that the British would be prepared to turn a blind eye to 1,000 illegal migrants and that Eichmann had been brought round too.[19]

The coup had been brought off by Perl and his associates. Perl gathered around him the richer Jews who were ready to pay the costs of young Jews who wanted to go to Palestine, because they were unable to get their money out. On 9 July the young Jews left for Greece via Jugoslavia, the Greek Consul 'convinced' by a few banknotes. They were going to Palestine, theoretically to attend a sports camp. The Jugoslavs had even granted transit visas. Eichmann voiced his pleasure at seeing the back of them; quoting a line of the Revisionist Vladimir Jabotinsky, he told them, 'You need a Jewish state on both sides of the Jordan.'[20] At the South Station they sang the Zionist hymn *Hatikwah* in triumph.[21]

On 25 July Mosche Schapira wrote to Eliahu Dobkin to tell him that Kendrick had been asked by the British Foreign Office to give an account of illegal emigration to Palestine. Kendrick had not been satisfied by the answer Schapira had sent him from Jerusalem, 'but required positive steps to be taken against the Revisionists' or there would be disadvantages for legal emigrants. He showed understanding in a difficult situation but 'the law was the law.'[22] In fact, British policy was more liberal than it might have appeared. Rich Jews were

---

[ii] Weisl later gave this figure as 385, and the cost as £16. See Wolfgang von Weisl, 'Illegale Transporte', in Josef Fraenkel, ed., *The Jews of Austria*, London 1967, 166, 172.

the most welcome in Palestine, but there were quotas for artisans and workers too. In 1937 214 Austrian Jews went to Palestine, representing 28.1 per cent of legal immigrants. In 1938, that figure rose to 2,964, or 40.5 per cent of legal immigrants. Given that PCO officials could not handle more than twenty-five applications a day, Kendrick's office was evidently working flat out to process the applications. Austrians and Germans were always preferred to Poles.

If one of Kendrick's staff was more sympathetic than the rest to the activities of the Perl-Bureau, it was Miss Stamper.[23] She suffered a breakdown later, possibly brought on by stress. Mary Ormerod lodged a complaint against Miss Stamper, claiming she had been rude to applicants, told them that there were quite enough Jews in Britain, made antisemitic remarks and torn up a visa application in front of the petitioner. She resigned soon after but justified her conduct, saying she had gone out of her way to help Jews, which was undeniably true.[24] A report at the time describes the Passport Office staff as being 'so overwrought that they will burst into tears at the slightest provocation'. The Consul-General complained a few days later: 'We should need a staff of forty people and a building the size of the Albert Hall . . .'[25]

The Passport Office in Vienna had already been reinforced with extra staff from Sofia and Copenhagen, so that it could now handle between 150 and 175 applications a day. There were sometimes 600 waiting, preyed upon by black marketeers trading in tickets. Some pregnant women tried to go into labour in the queue, thereby having their babies on British territory; ushers were manhandled and occasionally struck by petitioners; and disappointed Jews hurled accusations at the officials. Benton, Kendrick's number two, admitted that the one and only time in his life when he had been reduced to tears was that summer. 'It gets under your skin, you see. In the end it just builds up.'[26]

Kendrick, however, remained adamant that there were to be no more exceptions, and he put pressure on the Jugoslav government to that effect. Transit visas for crossing Jugoslavia were annulled, together with entry visas for Greece. At the end of July the Greeks officially closed their borders to Jews.[27] The visas were already in the hands of the agent, who kept quiet about it, and tried to get the Jews to the Adriatic anyhow, without success. The Revisionists were stopped before they could reach the boat at Fiume. Some 850 despairing Jews went back to Vienna.[iii] Later that month the Royal Navy intercepted the *Attrato* with 100 Austrians on board. It was on its seventh journey to Palestine.[28]

Kendrick's forcing of the hands of both Jugoslavs and Greeks was a setback, closing two important doors simultaneously. At the Anglican Church in Vienna Grimes was just off on leave. His verger, Fred Richter, was without question bringing candidates for baptism from among the assimilated Jews of the city. They would have hoped to use one or other land route to escape from Austria. Richter was also Kendrick's office manager. Did Kendrick know about Grimes's activities? If he did, he must have taken no notice.

Perl was still hiring Greek boats and on 20 September 130 of the original party left Fiume on the *Draga* for Palestine. Now that Italy, Jugoslavia and Greece had closed their borders to the Jews, the only possible way out was down the Danube. No visas were required for the river steamers, but Romania would not let them leave from their ports without entry visas. The Liberian Consul in Vienna, however, was prepared to issue 1,000 visas for 10,000 RM on condition that none of the Jews turned up in Liberia. Perl not only had the use of the *Draga* but had two other ships, the *Gheppo* and the *Ely*. On the Danube route he was using the cruisers *Melk* and *Minerva*. On 31 October 1,100 people left Vienna on the two ships, successfully making it to Palestine.

[iii] In his later account, Weisl says there were only 750 Jews: see Fraenkel, ed., *The Jews of Austria*, 173.

JEWISH DESPAIR

The despair of the Jews struck many visitors to Vienna. Mosche Schapira of the Zionist organization Hechaluz Hamisrachi in Palestine reported on their terrible despondency at the beginning of July: 'I try to console them and give them courage, but this is all in vain if we cannot offer them real consolation in the form of certificates.'[29]

On 9 July the Quaker Ethel Houghton in Vienna wrote to Alice Nike in London:

The situation here has become infinitely more acute . . . Practically all Jews were dismissed from their employment on 1 July, without notice and given no compensation . . . All Jews are being given notice to leave their houses if they are living in municipal blocks of flats, and also those living in the better districts of Vienna are shortly to be moved out.

She added with a certain naivety, 'There is a rumour that even those entitled to pensions will not get them . . . the time has come when relief in some form is becoming an absolute necessity.' It appears that food parcels were suggested.[30]

The Gauleiter, Globocnik, made a speech on the 16th in which he asked disingenuously, 'Why are the borders closed to poor Jews? [. . .] No, comrades . . . we will solve the Jewish problem, and will not be dictated to by anybody else as to how.'[31] In London, *The Times* published a letter on 19 July, signed by – among many – the Archbishop of York and George Bell, the Bishop of Chichester. It related that there had been 7,000 Jewish suicides since the Anschluss. This is almost certainly a wild exaggeration. It called on Britain and the United States to act against this 'degrading reproach against our humanity'.[32] Bell made his maiden speech in the House of Lords on the 27th. He used the occasion to attack Nazi antisemitism. He chided Germans who had lowered themselves to 'dishonour and cowardice'. He reported that even ministers of state in Vienna had said openly that the place for the Jews was the Danube, or in one of the city's cemeteries.[33]

THE EVIAN CONFERENCE

The Evian Conference ran from 6 to 15 July. It was Roosevelt's appeal of 25 March that set the ball in motion. He created a Presidential Advisory Committee on Political Refugees while Secretary of State Cordell Hull invited the British, French, Belgians, Dutch, Danes and Swedes, together with twenty Latin American countries, to come to a conference to discuss the fate of the Jews. At first it seemed that America, Australia and South America could absorb a large number of them. In March the American Consul in Vienna had issued 25,000 forms, but this proved another false hope: the Jews had first to find backers in the United States, and the quota permitted from Austria was low – just 1,413.[34] Later that small tally was subsumed into a figure of 27,130 for the whole Reich, which was better than Ireland (17,853) but less than half the quota for Great Britain (65,721), where no one was being forced to emigrate.[35]

The League of Nations High Commissioner for Refugees, Sir Neill Malcolm, created difficulties too. He felt the Americans should not have convened the conference if they were unprepared to improve their quotas,[36] and he refused to accept that the League was responsible for Germany's Jews.[37] The Viennese-born Dr Henry I. Wachtel offered assistance to Jews, sending out copies of the New York telephone book and telling them to try their luck by contacting American Jews to secure affidavits.[38]

The delegates arrived on the 5th, and Roosevelt's Emissary to the Holy See, Myron C. Taylor, had dinner that night with Lord Winterton and Sir Charles Palairet, the former ambassador to Vienna. Although the meeting was called at Germany's behest, the delegates were there to discuss the fates not just of German and

Austrian Jews but of Jews from Poland, Romania and Hungary, countries that had also introduced racial laws and were anxious to see the backs of their Jewish populations. This was in response to the Romanians, who on 13 April had proposed an annual export equivalent to the number of Jews born every year. They also pointed out that 'Jewish problems' were not confined to Germany.[39] Jewish exiles were already causing internal problems in many countries. The big three closed ranks. The Americans did not want to change their quotas. There were 40,000 German exiles in France, and both France and Britain expressed their reluctance to take in any more. At Evian Lord Winterton excused the British record by pointing out that the Mandate had already absorbed 300,000 Jews, including 40,000 Germans.

Countries such as Britain were interested in creaming off the best. The United Kingdom only desired physicians with a worldwide reputation or younger ones with two years' practical experience. On the other hand Britain was open to Jews wanting to enter full-time higher education, although the money to pay for the courses had to be found first. Those taking medical degrees were not allowed to practise.[40] Other countries had more specific demands. In Central America they were against doctors and intellectuals; in Peru they wanted no lawyers. The Argentinians said they had done enough. San Domingo offered to take 100,000 Jews. A Belgian Catholic group agreed to help on condition that they submitted to baptism. Canada was not interested unless they brought riches with them; Denmark and Holland were fine for transit, but the Belgians required a visa, otherwise they would be sent back. China was still possible. Cuba wanted $500 a head.[41]

The idea of Madagascar was raised again in the French press. Later Taylor looked into the British suggestions for a Jewish homeland: their first choice of British Guiana was 'not ideal' as it would accommodate only 5,000 at the most. Northern Rhodesia could house 400–500 families.[42] The Jews in Palestine believed that the British should have removed all restrictions on emigration and that they could have fitted in 80–100,000 new arrivals every year. On the other hand peace between the Jews and the Arabs needed to be brought about first. The British agreed on a compromise limiting emigration to Palestine to 75,000 Jews spread over five years.

One of the greatest disappointments was the stance of the British Dominions, countries with huge unpopulated expanses that showed very great reluctance to allow significant numbers of Jews to settle. Kenya seemed particularly appropriate for Jewish settlement.[43] Northern Ireland was looking for industrious artisans.

As one Australian said at Evian, 'we have no real racial problem [and] we are not desirous of importing one'.[44] The Australians would not even allow Jews to land.

At the end of the conference the delegates had made provision for the inter-governmental committee to be opened in London 'to continue and develop the work of the Evian meeting'. This was a British idea. A director would be appointed whose job was to improve the 'conditions of exodus and to approach governments and countries of refuge'.[45] In short: nothing very much had happened at all.

The British government went back to sleep and left it to Sir Wyndham Deedes and Bentwich to put pressure on the Dominions. Lord Winterton agreed to chair the new committee and the American George Rublee became the director. Writing to his friend and collaborator Wilfred Israel at the end of the month, Catchpool called Evian 'a catastrophic setback'.[46]

Der Stürmer exulted. 'Fips' drew a picture of a Jew in black tie being pelted with eggs and fruit: the Jewish 'distortion' on Lake Geneva had come to nothing. The Jew was mocked for his cries of 'Oy Vey!'[47] Not all doors had closed, however. Writing on 27 August, an official at Friends' House in London said,

> I'm afraid we were too hopeful about the results of the conference. We frequently suggest Bolivia to people who have friends in London, who are prepared to help them to a small extent, because we understand that a visa can be obtained from

this end if a passport can be sent here . . . for an enterprising foreigner with some sort of technical training, prospects are good.[48]

Bolivia was considered 'the Rolls Royce of emigrations'. Entry cost £36 or £50 if travelling from Brazil. On the other hand the fee was waived if the immigrant had a job to go to. There were further complications from the point of view of transit to the landlocked state: Brazil was closed to non-baptized Jews and in theory even Christian Jews had to have been baptized as infants (Grimes's backdated certificates might have helped here). Argentina admitted Jews only if invited by a relative.[49] It had nonetheless been clear before the conference that South America was a rather more promising destination than the north, but at the meeting they created difficulties, and the conference closed more doors than it opened.[50] To some extent the Americans were to blame for this: they were worried that a large influx of German immigrants would upset their trading arrangements in Latin America, especially if something like the Ha'avara scheme were introduced.[51]

Some Austrian Jews had also been allowed to attend the conference: Arthur Kuffler was there from the Gildemeester Aktion, together with the ear specialist Heinrich von Neumann, who had a brief to sell the Jews to anyone who would buy them. There was also Berthold Storfer, who was negotiating with the American Jewish charities HICEM and JOINT. They were offering similar ideas to Gildemeester: a waiver on property rights and a lump sum payment into Nazi coffers.[52]

THE AUSTRIAN CHURCH

As Austrians began to grumble about Nazi rule, Berlin chose its moment to move against the Church. Innitzer had failed to continue his cooperation with the authorities and it was decided that the Nazis had no need to observe the Austrian Concordat by which the Church's role had been guaranteed under the Corporate State. The doubtful morality of a few monks in the past was used for propaganda purposes in justification.[53]

On 2 June Schuschnigg had been equally astonished and delighted to learn that he got married – by proxy. His brother had stood in for him. A package arrived containing a wedding ring. His pleasure was interrupted by the shouts of his tormenter informing him that he should have hanged Innitzer rather than Planetta, the man who killed his predecessor, Dollfuss. The Cardinal had failed to placate the Nazis. Schuschnigg cried out rather lamely, 'But Innitzer never killed anybody.'[54]

The temptation must have been strong: in the diocese of St Pölten alone, the bishop and eleven abbeys owned 35,439 hectares of land (some of it in Romania), and there were over a hundred well-endowed abbeys and convents. The first move was to secularize education on 19 July and move state schools into the vacant spaces. On 24 July Hitler's secretary Lammers informed Bürckel that there was no Concordat operating in Austria, and he could do what he liked.[55] On the 27th, the Nazi authorities began to take over the Cistercian abbey of Lilienfeld and majestic Melk on the Danube. With time these buildings would fill up with squaddies, POWs and injured soldiers. A Napola was established in the great Benedictine abbey of Göttweig.[56]

GÖRING BACK AT WORK

The Nazis boycotted Evian, but vainly hoped the conference would come up with the sort of offer they could not refuse, whether in cash or territory. Goebbels had been told that the 'hole' in Germany's western defences had been plugged and that there was foreign currency in the bank (which was doubtful) but that exports were down – bad news, as it meant no foreign currency was coming in.[57]

The man who should have been looking after all this was away. Göring was wallowing in fatherhood on his yacht *Carin II*. He went up to the island of Sylt, where Emmy was nursing little Edda, and then to Denmark, to buy pastries from the famous Christian Bach bakery. He travelled down Germany's waterways playing skat in remote villages and turning up the volume on his phonograph. In the morning he would regale the rustics with whole Wagner operas from the boat's loudspeakers.[58]

He went back to work on the 8th, when there was a conference at Carinhall at which the chief aircraft manufacturers were present. Göring informed them of the latest intelligence concerning the Western powers. Britain was opposed to war, and he did not think the French would fight on their own. Chamberlain was still making noises in the House about finding a solution to the Sudeten Question. America was unpredictable. The Jews were dismissed as trouble-makers. Claude Dornier, Ernst Heinkel and Willi Messerschmidt were told that the war with Czechoslovakia would begin with a provocation, but it would be no more than eyewash, and the world would see all too clearly that the Germans were to blame. The compensation was in the form of markets: Germany would control them, and the industrialists would be richer than ever.[59]

The next day he entertained the Italian Chief of Staff, Alberto Pariani, and repeated his claim that no one would go to the aid of the Czechs. General Pariani disagreed, and warned Göring that he needed to slay the enemy with one blow. On 11 July Göring held a conference on securing manpower for the air industry. The problem was acute in Germany, and in the end the country would draft in millions of slave labourers to leave the Germans free to fight. That day he conferred with a building contractor to find out if the new autobahns might be used as emergency runways. He discussed air-raid shelters and underground factories. He was back at the grindstone.[60]

As early as 16 June, Hitler had reiterated his intention of grasping Prague, but was isolated within his own entourage.[61] He had support from Goebbels, who worshipped his master, the bellicose Ribbentrop and, to a more limited degree, Himmler; but Göring was reluctant to commit Germany to war. He was behind the despatch of Hitler's former commanding officer and present adjutant, Captain Fritz Wiedemann, to London on 18 July. Wiedemann had played a number of roles, including prizefighter and roué.[62] Göring wanted to avail himself of the services of his lover, the remarkable Princess Stephanie zu Hohenlohe-Schillingfürst, a forty-seven-year-old Viennese Jewess who had charmed her way into Hitler's intimate circle and lived in London's Dorchester Hotel.

Princess Stephanie was well known to Halifax and was able to make the introduction. She was summoned to Carinhall to prepare the way for a visit by Göring or a possible state visit by Hitler. Hitler smiled on the plan, but Ribbentrop was naturally not to hear of it. Göring told Princess Stephanie that it was no bluff: Hitler was going to declare war soon. Halifax was worried about receiving Göring, who was rather too large to bring over discreetly. He met Wiedemann at his residence in Eaton Square on 18 July, with a nod and a wink from the Prime Minister. Wiedemann told him that Hitler would 'solve' the Sudeten problem by violence if Britain failed to mediate.

As he flew home, Wiedemann saw an article in the *Daily Herald* that alluded to his secret mission. The author was another Viennese Jew, Willi Frischauer, whose brother Eddie would eventually marry Stephanie's half-sister Gina Kaus. The article hit the Wilhelmstrasse like a sixteen-inch shell, making Ribbentrop predictably furious. It excited almost as much fury in Prague, and the minister in London, Jan Masaryk, penned an angry letter to Halifax claiming there was no decency in the world and that he was being manipulated by a Jewess. Wiedemann went to the Berghof to face the music. Hitler was walking with Unity Mitford when he arrived. Göring's London visit had already been ruled out. Ribbentrop forced Wiedemann to write an undertaking never to meddle in foreign affairs again. He was eventually banished to San Francisco, where he was appointed Consul-General. Princess Stephanie survived the storm for the time being.[63] She was awarded the theatre director Max Reinhardt's country seat, Schloss Leopoldskron, near Salzburg, where she entertained lavishly.

AFTER EVIAN

Italy's racial policy was falling into line with Germany's. On 13 July a manifesto was published against the Jews, provoking the Pope to speak out against fascist ideas on race. 'That is wonderful!' noted Goebbels, 'but how cheeky these priests are.' The Pope did not desist, and condemned racialism once again at the end of the month.[64]

With Italy closing its doors, the easiest path to safety for an Austrian Jew was still a quick dash across the green border at Bratislava. Sometimes the Gestapo simply pushed the Jews across, as in the case of some 800 reported by the Jewish Telegraphic Agency to be in Brno on 10 August.[65] From Brno there was a chance of getting on a Danube steamer. The first refugees to arrive in Greece were recorded in July. Here they waited until they could find someone to bribe to take them across the Mediterranean. It could be a long wait and risky too. In April 1939 the British fired on the *Aghios Nicolaos*, killing one Jew and wounding others. The ship sailed back to Athens. There were eighty-three former Austrians on board.[66]

The Dutch and Belgians were showing their teeth, evicting Jews without transit papers, even when they had visas for another country.[67] As the Jews had generally used up their money getting as far as they had, they had to reimburse the authorities for their repatriation. Sometimes the Gestapo or customs officers connived at pushing them back over the border in these circumstances, but only if they could prove they had paid all their taxes. Some even helped by changing their papers for them. In Aachen there was a Gestapo-man called Nägele who charged 100–200 RM to take Jews over the border. This sort of behaviour further incensed the Swiss police chief, Rothmund, and he insisted that Germany print the visas in the passports. The Italians now affirmed that they would take no more Jews with Portuguese visas, as the Portuguese had told them they were worthless without permission from the Portuguese Minister of the Interior. The Italians made it clear that these hopefuls could not stay in Italy either.

HITLER IN BAYREUTH

The Munich-based Festival of German Art opened on 8 July. This year there was a reception for the artists favoured by the regime, and a chance to see the Third Reich's latest monument, the Führerbau, which would come into its own at the Conference in September. Karl Krauss conducted a performance of *Lohengrin* at the Opera House the next day, when the Führer in person graced the Reichs Conference on the Arts, where the painter Adolf Ziegler presented his report on the artistic health of the nation. The solemn opening of the Great Art Exhibition occurred on the 10th, providing Hitler with the chance to make another speech. Despite early rain outside, a procession of floats, historical costumes and animals thronged the streets for the Day of German Art. Goebbels found the costumes very effective, and admired the pretty women.

The year before, Hitler had issued guidelines to German artists: they were not to use any colour other than those perceived by the human eye – a reference to the wilful pigmentation of Expressionists and Fauves. Goebbels must have winced. Not so long ago he had had to take down his Noldes, because the Führer had voiced his displeasure at seeing them on his walls.[68] In 1938 Hitler took aim at Jews, Dadaists and Cubists. The exhibition was revolutionary that year for containing a brace of industrial scenes among the Germanic landscapes, Nordic nudes and scenes of brave SA-men toiling for national glory. There were the usual works by Ziegler, displaying the full-frontal German womanhood which had led to his being dubbed the 'Master of German Pubic Hair', and sculptures by Josef Thorak, known as 'Professor Thorax' because of his obsession with the body-builder physique.[69]

Hitler also lent huge support to the exhibition, buying no fewer than 202 works for his own use or for various Party buildings at a cost of over half a million RM.[70] It transpired that the modern works went mostly into storage as Hitler favoured old German masters for his homes. Goebbels prudently followed suit, but there was no danger of him buying any Noldes any more: they were exhibited at the Degenerate Art show. In the evening there was a special performance at the opera and a number of concerts given by 'outstanding soloists'.[71]

Munich was the capital of 'German' art. The House of German Art played host every winter to an exhibition of architecture, arts and crafts. It had been designed by Hitler's quondam favourite architect, Troost, and officially opened the year before. The Munichois were quick to dub the building 'Athens Railway Shed' or the 'White Pudding Station'.[72] Troost had committed suicide in 1934, but his widow, Gerdy, remained a member of Hitler's circle. Despite the rigid limits imposed on the German artist's imagination, there were rich pickings for painters and other artists in the Third Reich. In 1938 alone there were 170 competitions with prizes totalling 150 million RM. The sculptor Arno Breker earned nearly 100,000 RM that year.[73]

After art, it was time for music. Following the success of the Degenerate Art exhibition the previous year, there was a Degenerate Music show in Düsseldorf. Jewish composers were pilloried along with those who founded their rhythms on jazz or adhered to the twelve-tone scale. The exhibition was mounted by Severus Ziegler, the manager of the Weimar Theatre and brother of Adolf, who had put on the Degenerate Art show. The Ziegler brothers had the full support of Goebbels. In May 1938 the Nazis tried to make a little money out of their *salon des refusés* and created a Commission for the Evaluation of Confiscated Works of Degenerate Art to sell them to foreign buyers or exchange them 'for good masters': 'We are hoping in this way to make a little money from this manure.'[74] What failed to sell was burned in March 1939.[75]

Richard Strauss was not considered degenerate, but Hitler did not care for his work. On 24 July his new opera *Der Friedenstag* was premiered as part of the Festival. It was possibly the last international cultural gathering in Germany before Allied soldiers arrived in 1945. *Der Friedenstag* was one of two one-act operas Strauss staged that year. Set during the Thirty Years War, it ended with a paean to peace, which was not exactly what Hitler had in mind. Even worse, the original idea had come from Stefan Zweig, who was not only a Jew but a pacifist.[iv] Hitler did not attend.[76, 77]

On the 17th Goebbels proceeded to his alma mater, Heidelberg, for the theatre festival. A performance of *Faust* was staged in the castle courtyard with Werner Krauss as Mephisto, Werner Hinz as Faust and Maria Wimmer as Gretchen. Goebbels was at the height of his popularity. In Innsbruck he was showered with flowers. He went on to Linz where he religiously took the trip to Leonding to see round his master's childhood home and the cemetery where his mother and father were buried: 'Eerie feeling that the parents of such a great historical genius rest here. I stayed standing by their graves for a long time.' In the village he met people who had been at school with Hitler: he had always been the leader.[78]

The Salzburg Festival had gone ahead, but without Max Reinhardt, Bruno Walter or Toscanini. Furtwängler, however, had come to the rescue and agreed to conduct four performances of *Die Meistersinger* – surely the most frequently aired opera of the Third Reich. Goebbels thought the Festival Theatre 'dreadful . . . proper Viennese kitsch . . . it should be pulled down'. The conductor merited praise, but the rest of the performance was awful. Hitler's favourite composer, Lehár, was still having a hard time. He had lost his favourite librettist to Buchenwald and was having problems keeping the police off his Jewish wife. Goebbels intervened.[79] The Führer may have preferred operetta but, as far as his public persona was concerned, Wagner captured the German soul. On the 23rd Hitler and Goebbels met up

[iv] The libretto was eventually written by Joseph Gregor.

at the Bayreuth Festival. The Führer was accompanied by a squad of his *Leibstandarte* as he felt that his proximity to the Czech frontier merited particular attention to his security. In fact 1,500 Sudeten Germans had crossed the border to cheer on their *real* Führer – Henlein was merely his stooge.

Hitler was in the best of moods. It was decided that Wagner was wrong for Salzburg, and that it should focus on Mozart. The talks between the two men were by no means restricted to musical matters. Wiedemann was in London buying time. The generals in Berlin were 'shitting themselves' because Hitler was going to lead them to war. He approved Goebbels' campaign against the Jews. In ten years he would have got rid of them. The princes were also giving him trouble, particularly Weimar and Dessau. On 30 July there was a wave of arrests as the Gestapo mopped up well-known monarchists.[80]

The Bayreuth programme that year contained guidelines on how Wagner's music was to be interpreted by National Socialists. *Lohengrin* taught Germans to be hard, while Hans Sachs in *Die Meistersinger* made it clear that they were to honour all things German. *The Ring* was naturally about the seriousness of the racial problem, while *Parsifal* was not about Christianity at all, rather 'the struggle towards a life made divine'.[81] Emil Preetorius had designed some radical sets for the production of *Tristan und Isolde*, which both Goebbels and the Führer disliked. Max Lorenz was a 'fat and ursine' Tristan, even if he sang magnificently. Goebbels thought the sets for *Parsifal* awful, and the sacred spear toppled over during the performance.[82]

Hitler, on the other hand, was always happy in Bayreuth; indeed, he was one of the few Nazi bigwigs to enjoy the music. Goebbels thought it useful propaganda; the others endured it, as did the proletarian rank and file.[83] Hitler was lodged in the splendour of Siegfried Wagner's home and for the performances he sat in King Ludwig's royal box. On Wagner's birthday that year he initiated the Richard Wagner Research Centre under Otto Strobel with the intention of purging any unwelcome Jews from the story of Wagner's life, and to banish the suggestion that Wagner's father Ludwig Geyer might have been a Jew.[v]

Furtwängler was being difficult about Nuremberg, as he thought it might harm his image abroad. Goebbels had no patience with his circumspection and vowed to put pressure on him.[84] Hitler would have been able to hear the more pedestrian Franz von Hoesslin conducting *Parsifal* again in 1938. Not only was Hoesslin a quarter Jewish, he was married to the singer Erna Liebenthal, who was completely so. Bormann was trying to have Hoesslin removed from the list of artists allowed to perform at Bayreuth, but Winifred was able to invoke Hitler's protecting aegis.[85] It was Hitler who insisted that the festival go ahead every year, rather than every second year.

At a small gathering in the new Führerbau the Czech situation was discussed with suitable outrage. According to one source Hitler merely laughed, and admitted quite shamelessly that it was he and not the Czechs who was 'the instigator of the violence'. He also boasted of the impregnability of the West Wall, which he was building so that Germans could sleep soundly.[86] Hitler had to miss *Siegfried*, as he and Goebbels travelled to Breslau to see the Gymnastics Festival on the 30th, taking Unity Mitford with them. She had suffered for her love of Hitler. In June she was allegedly insulted and stripped by the Czechs.[87] She had earned herself the name of Unity *Mitfahrt* ('Hitchhiker') by her travels with the Führer.

In Breslau Hitler and Goebbels endured a four-hour parade of 150,000 gymnasts, but the real purpose of the visit was talks with Henlein, who was instructed to step up the agitation.[88] Goebbels found Henlein ebullient: there was no chance of negotiation – 'The hatred between the Czechs and the Germans was insuperable.'[89] 'What are we going to do with six million Czechs when we have finally got the country? It is a difficult, almost insoluble question.'[90]

[v] *'Ein Geyer ist beinahe schon ein Adler'* ('A vulture' – *Geyer* – 'is almost an eagle' – *Adler*). The rumour was first put about by Nietzsche, who pointed out that Geyer was almost as Jewish a name as Adler: *Der Fall Wagner*, Taschen Ausgabe, Leipzig n.d., vol. II, 213.

They flew back to Bayreuth via Nuremberg the next day to see *Götterdämmerung* with Lorenz and Ludwig Hofmann playing Hagen. There was a reception that night to celebrate the fact that Winifred's son Wieland had joined the Party. It was a dull evening, despite a number of animal games with the soprano Germaine Lubin doing an imitation of the duck. Hitler indulged in one of his interminable monologues that lasted until 6 a.m.[91]

The 25th was party-time in Austria. It was the fourth anniversary of the assassination of Engelbert Dollfuss. The thirteen Nazi thugs who had left him to bleed to death in his study on the Ballhausplatz had been executed, but were now to be elected to the Valhalla of Nazi martyrs. By 28 July a third of Jewish property in Vienna had been transferred to Aryan hands. Göring's Office of the Four Year Plan had located 2.29 milliard RM in the hands of just 50,000 Jews, the vast majority of whom lived in Vienna. Forty per cent of Jews fitted into the lowest income group, those possessing between 5,000 and 20,000 RM. There were still 102 Jewish millionaires. The report also signalled that 16,000 had already left the city.[92] In Vienna they had been cleared out of their villas in plush Hietzing and moved into *Judenhäuser* in the Leopoldstadt. Their former homes were to be had for a pittance. Dressed in borrowed robes, horny-handed Nazis and their toadies moved into the refined elegance of the former elite. Dachau's Jews were also on the move. That month the bulk of them were transferred to Buchenwald to help expand the camp.

BUCHENWALD

Ernst Wiechert had been in Gestapo custody in Halle for weeks. Now he too was taken to Buchenwald. The train journey to Weimar was torture in itself. Then there were cars to take them to the camp:

> The doors slammed shut and the motors started up, and then they set off towards the Ettersberg, the same hill from which

Goethe and Charlotte von Stein had looked out over the
Thuringian Forest and where now, wrapped in electrified fences,
the camp now awaited them.[vi]

Wiechert was a Gentile. Jews had been sent to Buchenwald since
the round-ups in Berlin and other large cities in May and June.
Maximilian Reich was one of those who were transferred from
Dachau later that summer. He noted that Dachau was a kindergarten
beside Buchenwald, where brutality and sadism were coupled with a
degree of corruption he had yet to experience. One favourite method
of creating space in the camp was to toss the prisoners' caps into the
no-man's-land next to the wire. They were forbidden to approach the
fences. When guards ordered them to fetch their caps the machine
guns opened up from the towers. He estimated that 117 prisoners had
been killed in this way since the camp opened.[93]

The senior prisoner in Dachau saw them off with a stirring speech
about what good people the Jews were, something he had not known
before he had met them in the camp. Compared to the Bavarian
camp, Reich's new home was filthy and the huts only half built. The
food was even more paltry, and as a Jew Reich would have received
only half as much bread as the Gentiles, and nothing whatsoever on
Sunday. Prisoners were expected to work for thirteen hours a day in
gruelling summer heat, without a drop of water. The only liquid
provided was half a cup of warm broth at lunch. In July alone, 103
prisoners died.[94] A homosexual guard ('Johnny' Hartmann, thought
to have been the son of a Lutheran pastor[95]) wandered around the
buildings at night, hoping to find the prisoners indulging in illegal
sex – presumably with a view to punishing them. It was quite
prevalent, with the older, richer prisoners buying favours from the
younger men. Very few of those who indulged in homosexual sex were
incarcerated under article 175.[96]

The smell of corruption in Buchenwald went all the way down to

[vi] Wiechert tells his story in the third person.

the capos. In the beginning these had been members of the Communist and Social Democratic parties, who had been locked up after the Reichstag fire. In 1938, the reds were replaced by greens (criminals). They brought all their knowhow to bear and very soon anything could be obtained in the camp for those with money: food, alcohol, cigarettes. Money was pumped from the prisoners on all occasions. When the SS had something to celebrate, a 'contribution' was raised from the prisoners. The inadvertent killing of Commandant Rödl's pet wolf cost the inmates 8,000 RM. News of the corruption in the camp got out when production began to drop off. An investigation revealed large sums of money hidden in the capos' lockers.

The greens were then again replaced by reds. Conditions improved very briefly, but life was so bad that it was wise to develop a thick skin to deal with it. Wiechert was told: 'You must hear and see nothing. You have to get through everything like a stone . . . Anyone who feels pity here falls apart.' One way he found of dealing with the camp was to make for Goethe's oak.[97] Wiechert was suffering for having defied Goebbels, who described the distinguished novelist as a 'piece of dirt'. On 3 August the minister wrote, 'After three months in a concentration camp I shall win him over to my cause.'[98]

One cruelly tortured inmate was a Pastor Schneider, who could be heard occasionally from the punishment block shouting 'Jews, fear this devil not! Your God will deliver you . . .'[99] His speech turned to screams when the guards rushed round to deal with him. He spent a year in the bunker before yielding up his spirit.[100] Many became religious in the camps. Maximilian Reich learned later of an extraordinary phenomenon that occurred at Buchenwald at the Jewish New Year. A young Viennese rabbi had led prayers for an hour, undisturbed by the guards. Hundreds of Christians had come out of their huts to join the Jews in their orisons. There was a clear, starlit night sky. 'Jews and Christians, united in their great misery, were praying to the one immortal, the God of all men.'[101]

8

AUGUST

Goebbels had been using the garden pavilions at his houses in Lanke on the Schwanenwerder peninsula near Berlin to entertain 'Babkova', the Czech actress Lida Baarova, who lived round the corner in Schwanenwerder with the actor Gustav Fröhlich. Although Goebbels calls the summer 'the loveliest holidays of my life!'[1] his journal does not allude directly to the affair, but there are hints at problems within the Goebbels ménage. At the beginning of August he decided it was time to tell Magda. Rather than asking for a divorce or a separation, Goebbels proposed retaining both wife and mistress. At first Magda does not seem to have been too put out: 'It is so good to possess a person who is so totally dedicated to you,' he wrote.[2] On the 3rd he had an 'important discussion' with Magda. 'She is of great importance to me. I am happy that it is now out on the table.' Clearly there were arguments for all that. On the 9th he recorded unity with Magda: 'Let us hope it lasts.'[3]

For two weekends Lida lived in the house at Schwanenwerder. Magda tried to make both her husband and his lover see reason, but she also asked his second-in-command at the Ministry of Propaganda, Karl Hanke, to compile a dossier on his infidelities. When she learned how numerous they were she had him banned from the house. Goebbels then behaved in such an outrageous way that Magda took flight and poured her heart out to Emmy Göring. Hermann Göring naturally knew all about the affair from the *Braune Blätter* (Brown Sheets) – reports from his Research Office – that his manservant

Robert brought him with his morning coffee. He called Hitler and told him that Magda desired to see him urgently: she wanted a divorce.

On 15 August Hitler returned to Berlin. The Goebbelses, husband and wife, were summoned in turns. Magda informed the Führer that she wanted no more to do with her husband. Goebbels went to see Hitler next. Hitler told him that he was a public figure and could not give in to private scandal. He had a choice between dropping Lida or forfeiting his career. This was a *Führerbefehl*: an order from the Führer. He was not allowed to see the actress again. Goebbels' conversation with Hitler shook him to the marrow: 'The Führer is like a father to me. I am so grateful to him. At this difficult time I need something like this. I am taking very difficult decisions, but they are final.'[4]

Hitler was not only sentimentally attached to Magda but had a horror of scandals, as he had demonstrated at the time of the Blomberg–Fritsch Crisis. He was also preoccupied with his Czech project. It transpired that Goebbels' various conquests had been found work through the Ministry of Propaganda. When he discovered this Hitler was even angrier with Goebbels.[5] Goebbels rang Lida: ' . . . a very long and very sad telephone conversation. And now a new life begins. My youth is at an end,'[6] he concluded in his diary and wallowed in self-pity, pouring out his heart to Göring, his mother and his sister. In the end ambition got the better of him.

The actress, who was genuinely smitten with Goebbels, was summoned by Police President Helldorf and informed that she was forbidden to see her lover for at least six months. She reacted so hysterically that Helldorf was obliged to call Hitler for guidance. She insisted on speaking to Goebbels. He called her later that day. He was, he said, at the house of 'his friend' Hermann Göring. Hitler had allowed him to call only if there was a witness in the room. Magda was slow to forgive him. Goebbels was wasting away, refusing to eat: 'Humiliation . . . She is so hard and horrible . . . I have never seen her like this.' At the end of the month Hitler allowed him to come to the Berghof. He was still bitter about Magda: 'She is not nice and so hard-hearted.'[7]

THE ETERNAL JEW

The Nazis continued to heap repressive measure on repressive measure against the Jews. On the 1st Austrian Jews lost their servants as the Nuremberg Laws were fully enforced for the first time, although the measure was rescinded by Globocnik on the 3rd after complaints from the servants themselves, who had lost their jobs as a result. There was a spate of divorces after the Laws were applied, non-Jewish spouses dropping their wives and husbands to save themselves.

On the 8th Jewish doctors were banned from practising. In Vienna they represented 52 per cent of the profession. In Berlin, Goebbels was happy to report it was going according to plan. The next day Viennese Jews were obliged to leave Aryan flats and the streets were clogged with removal vans. As many Jews no longer possessed the means to pay off arrears of rent, their furniture was detained by their landlords. In Italy Mussolini also introduced new drastic measures against foreign Jews. On the 6th a *numerus clausus* came into force. The price of support for Germany over Czechoslovakia had been increasing the pressure on the Germans in Southern Tyrol where the place names were Italianized.

The *Ewige Jude* (Eternal Jew) exhibition opened in the empty hall of the North West Station in Vienna on the 3rd in the presence of the Reichsstatthalter Seyss-Inquart and Gauleiter Globocnik. The whole front of the building was covered by a poster of a 'Kaftan Jew' that could be clearly seen from the heavily Jewish Taborstrasse in the Second District. The aim of the exhibition was to demonstrate how German life had been weakened by Jewish influence.

There was an international dimension too. In London, the *Daily Telegraph* reported that it exhibited 'repulsive caricatures of Jewish individuals of all nations'.[8] The worst Jewish films were pilloried together with various prominent British Jews. The Rothschilds had a room to themselves. Space was given to the Goldschmidts, Charlie

Chaplin and Richard Tauber, the half-Jewish, Viennese-born tenor.[9] The show had been put on first in Munich, but new elements had been specially designed for Vienna by two local antisemitic businessmen: Dr Robert Körber, author of a literary spin-off, *Rassesieg in Wien* (*Racial Victory in Vienna*) that came out the following year, and one Zettl.[10]

Ten thousand people are reported to have visited the exhibition on its first day. For a time it attracted between seven and eight thousand visitors a day, but they rapidly declined and by September numbers had dropped to around two thousand. Yet it was claimed that 350,000 saw it before it was taken down at the end of September. The organizers asked Bürckel if they could keep it open, particularly as it was the start of the new school year.[11] From the capital of the *Ostmark*, the exhibition took off on its travels again. The Quaker Robert Yarnall saw it on his visit to Germany that winter. It was 'the same as in Vienna – a terrible display of demagoguery – one felt like taking a shower bath after coming out, in order to wash away the impressions. [There was] just enough truth in it to make it take hold of the people.'[12] The London *Times* claimed the exhibition was the inspiration behind attacks on Jews in Vienna's cafés[13] and could only add to their despair. Instead of making for Baden, as the Jews would normally do in summer, they continued to try to find a means of escaping. There were only four hotels in Baden open to them anyway.[14]

On 17 August the Party forced Jews to adopt the middle names of Israel (for men) and Sarah (for women). From then on, Jews would no longer be able to use Gentile names and Gentiles had to forgo the use of Jewish ones. The list was drawn up by Counsellor Globke in the Ministry of the Interior. There were certain exceptions such as Peter, Julius, Elisabeth, Marie or Charlotte, as they had been wholly assimilated – Julius was Streicher's name – while others, like Joseph and Jakob, were not mentioned; Joseph was Goebbels' Christian name and Jakob that of the Reichskommissar for Austria, Bürckel. Old Testament names were nonetheless discouraged and it was deemed that Sepp was better than Josef, Jutta preferable to Judith, and Jochen less questionable than Joachim.[15] Three days later, the various Jewish organizations became the Central Office for Jewish Emigration in the old Rothschild place in the Prinz-Eugen-Strasse.[16] The aim was to expedite the business at an even greater speed. The general director was to be Dr Stahlecker. The jumpy Swiss responded by once again closing their border.[17]

The Swiss action occasioned a limp British protest. The next day the British press reported that 30,000 now had permission to leave Austria but had no visas to enter another country. This was celebrated in a 'Fips' cartoon, which showed a Jew sitting in a wastepaper basket, where he offered comparison to the contents. Another showed a Jew being grabbed by a Brobdingnagian hand at the frontier: they could leave, but not without observing the formalities.[18]

On 12 August the Pope had spoken out in favour of tolerance for Jews and 'coloured' people. The following day Vienna thrilled to the news of the trial of a Dr Kurt Popper, who had tried to reach the Czech border with his wife and mother on the night of 11 March and had nearly run over a gendarme on the Prague road. It had been discovered that he was also concealing assets in a Zurich bank account. He was sent to prison for two months.[19]

GENERAL BECK RESIGNS

Hitler was aware of dissent within his army but he was determined not to let it stand in his way. His dissatisfaction with the army may have contributed to the decision, taken that August, to allow Himmler to upgrade the armed force within the SS organization. The Waffen-SS (SS in arms) were to be modern, political soldiers and under the ultimate control of Hitler himself. The army was to have no access to their command structure. Their aim was to eliminate the ideological enemies of the Reich: Jews, freemasons, Marxists and the Church.

On 9 August Goebbels found Hitler dividing Czechoslovakia up into Nazi *Gaue*. Hitler quarrelled with Brauchitsch, who was in broad agreement with Beck over Germany's readiness to engage in a major European war. Brauchitsch can have had little doubt by now of Hitler's expansionist dreams. Talking to him about the Balkans later that month, Hitler said, 'We don't want these people, we want their land.'[20] The next day he summoned a conference at the Berghof from which most of the senior generals were excluded. The younger men gave Hitler little solace. It appeared that some of them also sided with Beck and thought that Germany could not fight a long war yet. Hitler cursed his generals.

Five days after the Berghof meeting, artillery exercises on the old Prussian ranges at Juterbog were taken as another opportunity to show the generals that Hitler was right about the feasibility of invading Czechoslovakia, and they were wrong. Beck thought Brauchitsch might have seized the moment to drive home the army's point of view, but he lacked the courage. Instead Beck honoured his threat and resigned on the 18th. For reasons of state, Hitler required Beck to keep his resignation a secret until 31 October. The Opposition could gain nothing from the éclat. At the Foreign Office, Weizsäcker and the Kordt brothers thought Beck had played his last card too soon. The Bavarian general Franz Halder took his place from 1 September.

Hitler was also encountering resistance from another Bavarian general, Wilhelm Adam, who made no secret of his misgivings about the possibility of bringing France and Britain into a war over Czechoslovakia. Adam rode the storm for a while, even after an explosive meeting at the West Wall, which he was in charge of building as regional military commander. Hitler told him he was doing it all wrong and assaulted him with a barrage of statistics, some of which were correct, but only some. Adam pointed out that if Germany was so well prepared, and the Western allies so little of a threat, there was little point in building the wall in the first place. Meanwhile Germans became aware that war was in the offing as more and more people were despatched to help build the wall.[21] Adam was stripped of his command in November.

Göring was increasingly worried about Hitler's bellicose policy and it was rumoured that fatherhood had rendered the Luftwaffe chief dove-like. On the 18th he was given the job of pacifying the Gauleiters who had got wind of Hitler's plans, although his heart cannot have been in it. Hitler let it be known that he would negotiate if he had to. Goebbels was for a short war: the German people would not stand for more. 'We must aim for surprise victories.'[22]

Göring spent five hours alone with Hitler at the Berghof on the last day of the month. The upshot was a message sent in a roundabout way to the US State Department, transmitted via Göring's chief economic advisor, Helmut Wohltat, and Edgar Mowrer of the *Chicago Daily News*. A highly placed gentleman in Berlin wished to know whether, if Germany were to lose another war, Britain and America would combine to prevent France from imposing an even more draconian peace. It was Göring's first peace feeler: there would be more in 1939.[23]

The Czech crisis was now causing international concern. The French called the Czechs to order. In some circles in Britain the mood was shifting from appeasement to confrontation. In the Foreign Office, Sir Robert Vansittart felt that the moment had come to strike. On 7 August he wrote a memorandum calling for an emergency Cabinet meeting to discuss Czechoslovakia. Alternatively there could be a suggestion that Parliament was to be recalled. The intelligence he was receiving from Germany showed that an invasion was imminent. To prevent the mistakes committed by the British government in the weeks prior to the First World War, the Prime Minister needed to make a crystal-clear statement of intent, otherwise Europe would plunge into war. His plea fell on deaf ears.[24] In early August, Vansittart sent an emissary to the resister Goerdeler, who reported back that Hitler was mad and his successes had made him believe he was God. The only man with any influence on him was

Himmler. Meanwhile Germany was heading for bankruptcy, as they could no longer afford their rearmament programme.

Trouble was brewing elsewhere. Corder Catchpool had been in the former German town of Memel in Lithuania, and visited the German political prisoners in the gaols. Germany had been hoping to take Memel back when the bad relations between the Warsaw and Kovno govern-ments degenerated into war. Catchpool sent Vansittart a report, claiming that there had been an improvement in the position, but he thought that the German Memelländer might well want more: 'probably Anschluss', excited by the 'tireless propaganda of the Nazi Party, which here as elsewhere is determined to prevent the consolidation of any position won by a foreign country at Germany's expense as a result of the war'.[25]

Both before and after war broke out in September 1939, the British government was visited by a number of unaccredited emissaries: men and women generally representing the Opposition, who nevertheless left the British government in a state of perplexity as to what they actually wanted. Possibly the confusion resulted from a lack of desire to learn or listen. One of these emissaries was Kleist-Schmenzin, who had made no bones about his feelings about Hitler, and had seen the insides of the Führer's prisons. His usefulness to the Opposition was severely limited, as he was watched as soon as he left his Pomeranian estate. Already in May Canaris and Oster had made Kleist aware of the situation: Hitler was extremely vulnerable if he wanted to make war on the Czechs. A few hours later Kleist relayed this to Ian Colvin, the News Chronicle's man in Berlin. Colvin needed to tell the British that they had to stand firm and not waver when it came to German demands.[26]

Kleist met Beck at the beginning of August and reported Beck's message back to Colvin: 'Through yielding to Hitler . . . the British government will lose its two main allies here, the German General Staff and the German people. If you can bring me positive proof from London that the British will make war if we invade Czechoslovakia I will make an end of this regime.' Kleist wanted to know what the proof was. 'An open pledge to assist Czechoslovakia in the event of war.'[27]

On 16 August Henderson let Whitehall know that Kleist was coming to London. Detailed plans were drawn up and Kleist arrived the next day. He was armed with a false passport obtained for him by Canaris and had been escorted to his Ju 52 at Tempelhof Airport by his cousin, General Ewald von Kleist. The next day Beck resigned. In London Kleist met Halifax's friend Lord Lloyd, chairman of the British Council, and explained that Britain needed to take a firm stand and the Opposition would remove Hitler. Kleist told him that all the German generals were opposed to the invasion. Lloyd took the story to Halifax and Kleist then had a meeting with Vansittart.

Once again Vansittart missed the point: Kleist was in favour of a territorial link between Pomerania and East Prussia. This was not currently a Nazi cause, but it had always been a German national one, ever since the land between the two provinces was taken away at Versailles to give the Poles a path to the sea. Kleist had no truck with Hitler's claims to the Sudetenland, however, and thought that Prussia and Austria had nothing in common: Hitler was 'revenge for Königgrätz'.[i] Hitler was not asking for the Corridor, and that would take the wind out of his sails. Deny him Sudetenland, but make the much more popular move of altering the Polish frontier.[28] Goerdeler had burned his boats with Vansittart by supporting the cause of the Sudeten Germans who wanted to be part of the Reich. The Corridor was a cause close to Kleist's heart: he was a Pomeranian landowner after all.[ii]

Kleist's next appointment was with Churchill at Chartwell. Later Churchill forwarded an account of their talk to the Foreign Office. Kleist told Churchill the generals needed encouragement, but once again Kleist insisted on the Corridor. Churchill thought the idea of

[i] The battle of that name in 1866, when the Prussians defeated the Austrian army and established hegemony over north Germany.
[ii] Lloyd was to come into his own as Secretary for the Colonies under Churchill.

the restoration of pre-war German borders inopportune but none-theless wrote Kleist a letter of support to show his German friends, which went to Berlin in the diplomatic bag. Kleist passed it on to Canaris and the German Foreign Office edited it for internal use. It spoke of the inevitability of war, a war in which Germany would be 'utterly and terribly defeated'.[29]

Chamberlain obstinately maintained that there was no opposition in Germany. In a note handwritten to Halifax about Kleist he made his now infamous disparaging remark that compared the anti-Nazis with the Jacobites at the court of Louis XIV: 'We must discount a good deal of what he said.'[30] Kleist went back to Germany on 24 August and duly reported to Canaris.

Two days later Sir Nevile Henderson was summoned back to London for a meeting. He conferred with Chamberlain, Halifax, Sir Horace Wilson and Vansittart. It was now that Henderson suggested direct talks between Chamberlain and Hitler. Germany was to be admonished, but Chamberlain was for a softly-softly approach, the one he demonstrated at Berchtesgaden, Bad Godesberg and Munich.

The Opposition was increasingly worried. On the 27th the Sudeten leader Karl Hermann Frank told the General Staff officer Helmuth Groscurth what he had probably gleaned from Henlein: that Hitler was bent on war, and that he had heaped insult on Beneš, saying that he wanted to catch him alive and hang him in person.[31] Hitler boasted that Britain would stay neutral. Meanwhile the younger of the two Kordt brothers, Erich, had been working on the French journalist Pierre Maillaud in an attempt to influence French policy, while in Moscow he was in contact with the ambassador Werner von der Schulenburg's private secretary, Hans von Herwarth, who was leaking information to the diplomatic community in the Soviet capital. Wilhelmstrasse officials like Kordt, Albrecht von Kessel and Edward von Selzam did their best to influence foreign diplomats, but their efforts were dismissed by Sir Nevile Henderson – and probably many others – as 'a lot of treason'.[32] Many believed siding with this strange array of upper-class emissaries, many of whom were asking for large-scale territorial adjustments, was risky. Hitler was the bulwark against bolshevism, and the removal of the bulwark might mean civil war and a victory by the left.

THE KENDRICK AFFAIR

The Abwehr (military intelligence) had penetrated the British Secret Service and broken some of its ciphers. The journalist Ian Colvin heard it from Fabian von Schlabrendorff. One of Schlabrendorff's friends had suggested working with British intelligence to bring down Hitler. Canaris thought it unwise:

> I must warn you against the British Secret Service . . . for several reasons. Should you work for them it will probably be brought to my notice, as I think I have penetrated it here and there. They will want to send messages about you in cipher and from time to time we can break a cipher. Your names would appear in files and registers. That is bad, too. It would be difficult to overlook such activities in the long run. It has also been my experience that the Secret Service will requite you badly – if it is a matter of money, let me tell you, they do not reward services well, and if they have the least suspicion, they will not hesitate to betray you to me or to my colleagues of the Reich Security Service.[33]

On 17 August Thomas Kendrick, head of Vienna Station MI6, was arrested. A small diplomatic crisis ensued. The British ambassador in Berlin, Henderson, told the Foreign Office in London that Kendrick was a Passport Control Officer and not a diplomat, and therefore possessed no immunity from arrest.[34] It appears that Kendrick had been betrayed by Siegfried or 'Fred' Richter,[iii] his office manager, who had doubled up as the verger in the Anglican Church since 1924.

iii His own family called him 'Onkel Siegl'.

Richter was born in Vienna, but hailed from Rechnitz in Burgenland, which was Hungarian at the time. His father was a Jewish horsetrader, but his mother, Anna Schwach, may have been Catholic. He had gone to Britain as a stable lad in 1900, and met his Irish wife Maud Dollery there before returning to Vienna in 1912. He managed stables for the Schlesingers – rich Jews – and later for Graf Reventlow in Berlin.

British nationality acquired by his marriage had not prevented him from serving as a soldier-servant in the Imperial army in the Great War. He later possessed an Austrian passport as well, although the outgoing British ambassador, Selby, issued him with another British one in March 1938. Richter had had a chequered career since the war: he had been an interpreter and had an unsuccessful knitwear business. Soon after the Anschluss, he was formally engaged as a 'marshal' in the British Passport Office working for Kendrick. He had been casually employed by Kendrick for some time, running errands for the legation and the consulate. He earned 290 RM from both jobs and gave his wife 7 RM daily for the housekeeping. At the time of his arrest he owed the German state 600 RM in tax arrears.

Introduction fees greatly supplemented his income. The Gestapo estimated that he was earning anything up to 100 RM a day, probably by bringing in Jews for baptism. He may have had agents working for him too, such as Edmund Pollitzer. There was a considerable amount of money burning holes in the pockets of his various suits. Once, in a tram, he pressed a wad of cash on his sister-in-law, telling her that he did not wish to be caught with so much on him.[35]

During the Abyssinian War, Kendrick had asked Richter if he knew of anyone who could go to Italy to report on the Italian Navy. Richter knew of a Korvettenkapitän von Gatterer from his time in the Reparations Commission. Gatterer refused but suggested the secretary of the Navy League, Rudolf Koren. Koren went to Italy to spy for Kendrick with Richter acting as intermediary. Richter tried to introduce other potential agents to Kendrick, but he was not interested until Richter, in May 1937, met Karl Tucek, a Communist ex-foreman with Böhm, an engineering firm specializing in compressed-air and other machines. After being laid off he had turned inventor, fashioning a machine that he believed would be of interest to a foreign firm. Richter saw possibilities and asked for an introduction fee. He was even more interested when he learned that Tucek had been in the Austrian Navy and was terribly short of money. He told Tucek he could find him some if he would go to Italy and 'have a look around'.

In his testimony Tucek said he realized immediately that he was being asked to spy on the Italians and refused: it was too dangerous and his Italian was not good enough. Richter then suggested Germany. Tucek again refused. Richter found him a job with a German firm but he was still short of money and complained to Richter. In January 1938 he said he was ready to take up Richter's suggestion. Richter then went to Kendrick and described Tucek as a former naval engineer of great potential. Kendrick became interested when he saw some of Tucek's drawings. When Richter told Tucek that he was going to meet the head of the British Secret Service, Tucek provided him with his service record and asked him to tell Kendrick that he had a friend working in the Schicau Yard in Elbing who could employ him as a mechanic. Kendrick promptly asked for clearance from London.

Once this was granted, Kendrick arranged to meet Tucek in his flat with Richter. He said he would buy his patent for 1,000 Schillings if he would do a job for him. He then produced a questionnaire to be completed in Elbing. The answers he required concerned U-boat production, and the possible power and speeds of the submarines. Richter told Tucek he had to learn the questions and return the document to him. He then gave him a third-class train ticket. Tucek could explain his absence in Elbing by the need to sell his invention to the firm of Knorr-Bremse. He was also issued with a letter of credit and 500 Schillings in cash to add to the advance of 200 he had already received.

Tucek returned from Elbing on 20 March. Some big changes had taken place in Austria in his absence. Two days later Richter and Tucek met in the Mondl pub in the Favoritenstrasse where Tucek lived. It was agreed that he would deliver the questionnaire to the British consulate the following morning. Tucek countered that he was now a German citizen and that on German soil he could neither make the drawings nor hand over the material. He would only do that on neutral soil. He wanted to see an MI6 man in Switzerland. He refused to modify his stance despite Richter giving him another 100 Schillings. Richter asked him to meet him at the Anglican Church at four. When Tucek arrived Richter locked the door and took him into the vestry. Once again Tucek refused to hand over the plans, merely indicating which questions he could now answer: precise information about submarine production in Elbing, Königsberg and Danzig, where the submarines were built, in what number and their speeds. He proved obdurate, and added that 'he could give no details to a non-expert' and that he needed to talk to an expert in Switzerland.[36]

Kendrick once again asked London to advise. Meanwhile, Tucek took to dropping in to the consulate, as he was anxious to go to Switzerland. He told Richter that he had the chance of getting a job in Wilhelmshaven and wanted to know if this was of interest to British intelligence. Richter relayed this to Kendrick and on 4 April was able to inform Tucek that he was about to get a letter from England, from a firm that was interested in his invention. It would instruct him to visit an address in Switzerland. On receipt he was to visit the fiscal authorities and ask for permission to go, and then to come to the consulate to receive more money for the journey. From 11 to 27 April, Richter and Tucek were in almost daily contact. The letter was still not there on the 27th. Richter told Tucek that he would have several thousand Schillings if he were ready to spill the beans in Vienna. Tucek once again refused and asked to see Kendrick.

Finally Kendrick received a telegram. Tucek was to travel to the Berner Hof in Interlaken where a British agent would be waiting for him. He was to have 600 Schillings in expenses and hand over the information to an Englishman called Mr Brandon.[iv] Richter issued him with a third-class return ticket to Zurich. He had to buy his own to Interlaken because it was not to be clear what his ultimate destination was. Richter gave Tucek postal vouchers to the value of 150 Swiss Francs. He was told that Brandon would give him more in Interlaken.

Tucek's meeting with Brandon took place in Interlaken on 28 May. Tucek was as good as his word and told him everything he had learned in Elbing, Königsberg and Danzig. Tucek could answer all Brandon's prepared questions on the spot. Brandon therefore gave him 150 Swiss Francs and asked him what sort of expenses he might need for Wilhelmshaven for four to eight weeks. Tucek named a figure of 400 RM. Brandon thought there would be no problem obtaining that and told him he would have the money by 1 June at the latest.

Tucek returned to Vienna on 29 May and reported to the consulate on the 31st. There he told Richter that he was happy with the way things had gone in Switzerland. Kendrick gave Richter 600 RM to hand over to Tucek together with the message that the man in Switzerland was fully satisfied with the information provided. Tucek supposed that the real mission was to find out about the ships with tonnages in excess of 35,000. Kendrick said that 440 RM was for expenses, the rest for him, and there would be a bonus as soon as he had taken the new information to Switzerland after his return from Interlaken. Tucek found a job in Wilhelmshaven and left on 12 June. While he was away Richter took his wife 50 RM. From 9 to 31 July Tucek was on holiday in Vienna and had frequent meetings with Richter. Kendrick sent word that he would receive 600 RM monthly now, as an employee of SIS. Richter promptly deducted the 50 RM he had lent Frau Tucek.

Tucek told Richter of the things he had seen in Wilhelmshaven. He had a pass that allowed him access to the dockyards. He was working in the submarine and torpedo-boat yards as a technician. He

iv Captain Albert Ernest Acton Brandon, MI6 officer in Geneva.

said he wanted to see Brandon again in Switzerland, but Richter said he would need more information first, which meant going back to Wilhelmshaven. He was given another 800 RM in travel expenses and instructions, which he was to conceal immediately. They asked him to find out more about the battleship *Scharnhorst*. Tucek had to provide details of its capacity and speed as well as its fuel consumption at different speeds. He also needed to bring back similar information about the *Tirpitz*, which was under construction. British intelligence wanted to know how it was laid out, its horsepower, speed and fuel capacity, its strength and armour, both below and above deck, and the construction of the keel. Richter and Tucek met for the last time on 17 July, just before Tucek left for Wilhelmshaven.

It appears Tucek was a double agent working for the SD. Once he had mustered enough evidence to destroy the MI6 Vienna station he filed his report.

Richter might have had an inkling that things would not turn out well, and in August he made arrangements to leave for England. He was arrested on the 13th on the Elisabeth promenade together with Maud and his daughter Gretl. He had just locked up at the British consulate and had on him an envelope containing 1,000 RM. It was marked Capt. Kendrick, Brit. Passport Office. This was initially thought to be composed of Jewish bribes.

On 18 August Reuters announced Kendrick's arrest by the Gestapo. He had been going on leave to join his daughter in the company of his South African wife and been stopped at Freilassung near Salzburg on the 17th after skirting close to Wehrmacht manoeuvres. He had been taken by train from Salzburg to Vienna and then to their HQ at the Hotel Metropole. He was interned in one of the attic bedrooms next to Louis Rothschild and Schuschnigg. No reason had been given so far for his arrest.[37] On 22 August it was revealed that Kendrick was accused of espionage and had confessed.[38]

The shooting at Garrowby was interrupted to inform the Foreign Secretary, Halifax. Kendrick had been running the MI6 office for thirteen years.[39] It is to be assumed that both Henderson and Halifax were aware of his real role. Henderson believed that Richter's arrest had started the ball rolling, and that 'Kendrick's attempted departure on leave immediately after it will certainly be interpreted as a guilty conscience'.[40] Kendrick was interrogated for three days on end in eight-hour relays. The Foreign Office noted that these were 'practices usually observed in Moscow'.

Kendrick was released at midday on the 20th and went straight to his flat in Hietzing, to find his wife and members of the British consulate.[41] He had orders from Berlin to quit the German Reich within twenty-four hours. He left for Budapest after lunch, as he had no visa to enter any other country, and landed at Croydon Airport on Monday the 22nd.[42] The following day the *Daily Telegraph* ran a picture of his triumphant return. The German authorities maintained that he had been released only because they placed such importance on good relations between the two countries. It appeared that Ribbentrop was angry because he had been kept in the dark by the SD.[43] The spirit of Munich was already in the air. The Anglophobe Ribbentrop wanted to show off the panache that would earn him the title of 'the second Bismarck'.[44]

After Kendrick's departure the entire Vienna MI6 station had to be evacuated. His second-in-command, Kenneth Benton, and his wife Peggie were given twenty-four hours to leave and hot-footed it to Riga while the Gestapo sealed their flat.[45] Mary Holmes and Betty Hodgson, the two MI6 secretaries, left in his wake.[46] Eric Gedye, the *Morning Chronicle*'s man in Vienna, a thorn in the side of the Nazis and another suspected agent, was asked to leave. On 22 August he went to Prague, where his wife had established a *Daily Telegraph* bureau.[47, 48] The Vice Consul, Walker, who had been in Vienna for nine years, elected not to return after his leave.[49] In Berlin, Frank Foley and his entire staff were recalled.[50] It was the biggest disaster to befall the British Secret Service before the Venlo Incident of the Phoney War. As Halifax put it in a letter to Anthony Eden: 'It is altogether a most unfortunate case, and as I expect you know the Consulate General in Vienna have been put at a great disadvantage by the Kendrick Affair and its ramifications.'[51]

COLLARD AT THE METROPOLE

After a lapse of a week, on 3 August the baptisms of Jews had started up again at the Anglican Church. A temporary incumbent, the Rev. Fred Collard, took over from Hugh Grimes. Bishop Batty had been behind the appointment. As Collard wrote later: 'During my absence in Vienna in 1938 Dr B.S. Batty arranged for the chaplaincy [in Cologne].'[52] Collard was an unusual priest: sixty-eight years old, he was a decorated former stretcher-bearer who had risen through the ranks in the Medical Corps. He was gazetted major on his retirement from the Army on the Rhine in 1924 and stayed on in Cologne after demob. He had been instrumental in having the mayor, Konrad Adenauer, award the Rathaus chapel for use by the Anglicans. In the thirties he appears to have been examined for ordination without doing any formal course. From 1935 he was attached as a curate to the church of Saint Anne and Saint Agnes in the City of London – Batty's church. Possibly Batty ordained him in 1936, and, even if he did not, the bishop certainly knew all about him.[53] After his ordination he returned to Cologne to officiate in the former Rathauskapelle.

On the same day they let Kendrick go, the Gestapo burst into the flat of the chaplain to the British consulate, Grimes, at Lustig Preangasse 10. They found a large number of Jews receiving instruction in the Anglican rite in what was billed as a 'temporary chapel', since the church across the road was being redecorated. The Gestapo drove the crowd away and led off Grimes's *locum tenens*, Collard, as well as the forty-six-year-old Pollitzer and an unnamed woman.[54]

Collard was taken to the Metropole and interrogated at length until the Gestapo agent told him, 'You can go now.' He was badly shaken and asked for a police escort, as he feared for his life. The

Gestapo preferred no charges but they had ransacked the flat and impounded the baptismal register for a while and confiscated all the money that had been collected from the Jews by Richter and Pollitzer. The latter was demanding an introduction fee of 50 RM a head.[55]

Candidates for baptism were obliged to learn the Catechism and the Lord's Prayer by heart. In return they received an – often backdated – baptismal certificate and the Prayer Book. There was no attempt to convert them properly, and, controversially, there was no immersion in water. Neither Grimes nor Collard ever imagined they would become Anglicans. By the time the loophole closed in September that year, more than 1,800 Jews had become members of the Church of England in this way.

One likely path taken by Grimes and Collard's freshly baked Christians was Jugoslavia. Weisl recorded on 29 August that no anti-Jewish legislation had been enacted there yet, and that there were a 'few hundred refugees in Jugoslavia'.[56] That the Gestapo were also perfectly well aware of what was going on in the Anglican chaplaincy is clear from a report from Bovensiepen, the Gestapo chief in Eisenstadt, dated 11 August:

> In recent days the emigration has proceeded very slowly from here because Jugoslavia, Czechoslovakia and various other countries have either stopped transit or entry to their territories. They [the Jews] will try anything in order to receive an entry visa to a foreign country. A number of Jews have taken the decision to have themselves baptized according to the Anglican rite in order to obtain permission to cross Jugoslavia and enter Greece.[57]

In Vienna Collard was also working overtime after the Gestapo gave him back his register. Huge numbers of hopefuls lined the Lustig Preangasse. Latterly he had started baptizing only every second day, because he needed to drill the candidates in their Catechism. He was receiving more and more Hungarian Jews, possibly because they could no longer enter their own country without Christian credentials. Collard, and Grimes before him, baptized many babies, but they also converted several people in their eighties.

The converts were a mixed crowd: Melanie Adler, the daughter of the musicologist Guido; Margaret Bettelheim, the sister of the child psychiatrist Bruno; Oskar Bunzl from the leading paper manufacturer; the industrialist Willibald Duschnitz, whose villa had been designed by Adolf Loos; Kitty Fall, whose father Richard composed film scores in Hollywood; Joseph Kläger, an important figure in the IKG; the composers Arthur Kleiner and Erich Zeisl; the architects Oskar Neumann and Oskar Wlach; several members of the ennobled Pollack Parnau family; Lucie Rapoport von Porada and her husband, the parliamentarian Albrecht Freiherr Schey von Koromla; and Gertrude Rie, later Professor of Chemistry at Vassar.

The British Union of Fascists member George Lane-Fox Pitt-Rivers witnessed the scene.

Approaches to the British consulate in Vienna were blocked with thousands of Jews clamouring for British visas. A large quota were besieging the British chaplaincy, applying for baptismal certificates in order to qualify for the special benefits and assistance in registering for employment in England under the schemes of the 'Churches' Committee for Non-Aryan Christians' and other associated bodies. By the unflagging and persevering efforts of the temporary English chaplain, the permanent English chaplain being on leave, hundreds of Viennese Jews were weekly being baptized at the improvised font in the 'Office Chapel' at the English chaplain's residence, which is situated opposite the English church.

The church, unfortunately, was not then available owing to it being closed for the annual cleaning and redecorations. Through the courtesy of the temporary English chaplain I received personal assurance that the good work of 'conversion' was proceeding with the utmost possible despatch. I gladly undertook to testify to the work of this hard-pressed representative of the Church of England, who, without other clerical assistance, succeeded in converting, preparing for baptism, and baptizing so many hundreds of Jewish candidates for entry into the Anglican community, of whom not one in a hundred can speak a word of English. Qualifications for baptism were strictly laid down and complied with. Only those were accepted who were furnished with a) a British visa, b) an Ausweis or release from the Jüdischer Kultur Bund [sic], or Jewish congregation; and c) the German police permit to leave the country – and not return. Of course, in addition, converts paid the moderate baptismal fees.

I am informed it takes four days between application and baptism, during that time candidates are entitled to four hours of instruction in the tenets of the faith and in the Catechism. This, it must be admitted, is not too long a period for those who cannot speak a word of English. I am informed, also, that it is through the Anglican door of baptismal waters that alien Jews can most rapidly prepare for 'assimilation and absorption' in their new English homeland, flowing with milk – canned in Switzerland and imported under arrangements of the Milk Marketing Board, and honey – imported from Russia under arrangements of the Board of Trade.

Comments like those caused concern in Canterbury and Batty was called to account. Lang had already expressed concern about Batty's desire to send Grimes back to Vienna. They were worried that Grimes might be required to give evidence against Richter. Grimes was even prepared to forgo his £300 stipend. Batty must have lost heart.[58] On 15 September, as war loomed, he recalled Collard to Cologne. Six weeks later he made a pastoral visit to Vienna. Little or nothing is known about what he did there, but the conversions ceased.

Lane-Fox Pitt-Rivers was by no means alone in his jaundiced view of Jewish refugees. On 20 August the *Daily Express* reported that Herbert Metcalf, a magistrate in Old Street in London, had called the idea of Jews coming into Britain 'an outrage – I intend to enforce the law to the fullest'.[59]

Nor were Grimes and Collard alone in their work: 1,702 Jews converted to Catholicism between March and September that year, joining around 8,000 Jewish Christians in Vienna. Father Bichlmair reported to Cardinal Innitzer on non-Aryan Christians. His *Pauluswerk* charity was dissolved in August and Bichlmair was later deported to the east. In October 1938 two priests and a verger were arrested for falsifying baptismal certificates. Another was taken into custody in February 1939. He admitted to fifty counts.

The Swedish Church concentrated on Evangelical children of Jewish origin. The Swedish pastor, D. Göte Hedenquist, also admitted to baptizing thirty Jews.[60] In the Seegasse at number 16 was the Swedish Mission to Israel, which had been seeking Jewish converts since 1920. After 1938 the mission was turned over to helping the Jews with emigration and housing, as well as providing food and a refuge at lunchtime. In his autobiography Hedenquist claimed to have helped over 3,000 Jews and Jewish Christians to escape. Younger members of the mission were permanently in Eichmann's HQ obtaining the necessary papers.[61]

It was now clear that the consulate had been a nest of spies. An official called Richter 'a first class menace'. Sir Geoffrey Mander MP tabled one of his usual irate questions in the House, and 'Red Ellen' Wilkinson made noises until she received a visit from MI5 to warn her that it was not in the public interest to proceed.[62] When the storm broke, Grimes contacted the Foreign Office,[63] which was responsible for his appointment (he was officially chaplain to the ambassador who was no longer an ambassador since Austria had been subsumed into Germany). The Foreign Office advised him not to return.

On 25 August he went to see Gladwyn Jebb in Whitehall. He was asked about the various people involved in the scandal. Kendrick, said Grimes, was a Catholic. He had not had many dealings with him, although he admitted to asking for nine or ten passports: a clear allusion to a relief channel often to members of the embassy staff.

When Grimes was asked about Richter 'he registered no surprise and no great dismay . . . [Richter was] a slippery character, and though very useful had always been treated by him with considerable reserve.' Grimes very possibly objected to Richter's habit of feathering his nest.[64]

The state visit of the Hungarian Regent Admiral Horthy and his Prime Minister Imredy began on 22 August. The Hungarians were present for the launch of the battleship *Prinz Eugen* in Kiel, at which the honours were performed by the Admiral's wife and Seyss-Inquart. Prince Eugene of Savoy was an Austrian hero who drove the Turks from Hungary. After the festivities, there was a cruise on the Kaiser Wilhelms Canal. Goebbels was not feeling in the mood to join the party, and sulked in his cabin. The Hungarians were being pinned down about their role in the future Czech débâcle; they were supposed to march into Slovakia while the Germans made for Prague.

In Berlin Göring was indulging in a little psychological warfare, and with some success. He had invited the French General Vuillemin to Berlin on the 18th and taken him round the country to show off the pride of the new Luftwaffe. Vuillemin took fright. Bella Fromm saw General Milch driving past with him in a cavalcade and wondered what was going on.[65] Hitler was in Vienna on 26 August, staying at the Hotel Imperial. The following day the German bishops toed the Pope's line by condemning the campaign against the Jews.[66] Goebbels responded by impounding the pastoral and closing down the presses that printed it. Hitler returned to Vienna on the 28th, to go to the opera to see Hans Knappertsbusch conduct Eugen d'Albert's *Tiefland*.[67]

PUTSCH

With the Opposition hoping for a British declaration of war, its members were spurred into activity to make sure that Hitler could not wriggle free. Beck remained at the helm; in Berlin police headquarters Helldorf and Schulenburg were primed. Hans Oster ran between Halder at the General Staff and Weizsäcker in the Wilhelmstrasse. Schacht too was playing his part. The Chancellery was to be literally stormed by troops commanded by General Witzleben. Erich Kordt had access to the building and was to make sure that the doors to Hitler's study were kept open. The older men were anxious that Hitler should stand trial, whereas the younger ones were keener on the Nazi formula: shot trying to escape. It was important to make sure that Himmler's SS were disarmed immediately. Naturally the Gestapo needed to be taken out and the radio station occupied at the same time.

In London a meeting had been arranged between the diplomat Theo Kordt and Chamberlain's advisor Sir Horace Wilson on 23 August, in Conwell-Evans' flat in Cornwall Gardens. Sir Horace was told of the mood of the German Opposition and a report was drafted for the German Foreign Office in code. Sir Horace issued an assurance that Kordt's message would be given to the Prime Minister but there was no promise of support. Theo Kordt was already doctoring all his reports from London to make the British appear more bent on war than was the case. Hitler's information on whether the British would act had been supplied by Ribbentrop, who was more bellicose than his master. He insisted that the British would not move a muscle, and he was not wrong.[v]

As this did not produce the declaration the Opposition required, Weizsäcker and Erich Kordt decided to send another message to the British government. This time it was transmitted by the Kordts' cousin Susy Simonis, who committed the whole text to memory and took it to Theo Kordt in London on 5 September, who then wrote it down and conveyed it to Sir Horace Wilson in his office in Downing Street. The message provided exact details of Hitler's plans to go to war and his refusal to believe that the British and French would stand

[v] Ribbentrop's diplomacy has been rightly condemned for its crassness but in this evaluation he was correct.

in his way. Sir Horace promised to transmit the message to the Foreign Secretary, and told Cadogan of the visit. A secret meeting between Theo Kordt and Halifax was arranged at Downing Street for 7 September. He entered Number Ten by the garden. Once within, Kordt made it clear to Halifax that he had come as a representative of the Opposition and proceeded to repeat the need for a clear and unequivocal statement of intent on Britain's part. He then described what would happen if this were to happen: Hitler would be eliminated. Halifax promised to inform the Prime Minister.

Nothing ensued. Ciano summed the position up on 29 August when he said, 'The English [sic] will do anything to avoid a conflict.'[68] Weizsäcker sent for his friend, the Swiss High Commissioner in Danzig, Carl Burckhardt, and implored him to get in touch with the British. The only way forward, he said, was to send someone who could shout back at Hitler –

none of these all-too-polite Englishmen of the old school. If Chamberlain comes, these louts will triumph and proclaim that some Englishman has taken his cue and come to heel . . . they should send an energetic military man who, if necessary, can shout and hit the table with a riding crop; a marshal with many decorations and scars, a man without too much consideration.[69]

Burckhardt went hotfoot to Berne where he roused the British minister from his bed. He was able to tell him of Beck's resignation and its cause. He followed this up by calling R.A. Butler, Minister of State in the Foreign Office, and once again he presented Weizsäcker's views. In Geneva he consulted colleagues at the League of Nations about who was a suitable strong man to send to Hitler. The name suggested by Weizsäcker was General Ironside, a tough and powerfully built soldier who possessed the rare advantage of speaking fluent German.

9

SEPTEMBER

Chamberlain went north to declare war on the grouse, while Henderson returned to Berlin and entertained Weizsäcker at dinner on 2 September. It had been the ambassador's idea that Chamberlain should meet Hitler face to face; that way, he thought, Ribbentrop could be shouldered out.[1] Henderson appears to have informed the German of Chamberlain's ostensibly top-secret plans, because the premier didn't tell his Inner Cabinet until the 8th and the main British Cabinet did not learn of the idea of the visit to Hitler until the 14th.[2]

Weizsäcker clearly thought the audience a terrible idea, while Chamberlain for his part seemed to be reluctant to see the gravity of the situation. The impression given is of two ships passing in the night: the British had never had any serious intention of fighting for Czechoslovakia. This message either failed to get through or was not seriously entertained by the Germans in the Opposition who were so bent on ridding their country of Hitler. Beck was out of the picture, but continuity was to some extent assured by the new Chief of Staff, Halder, who agreed to depose Hitler on 2 September.

Hitler was in his mountain eyrie dreaming of Prague. At an emergency meeting of the British Cabinet on 30 August, it had been decided to make Beneš accept Henlein's Karlsbad Programme and accord virtual autonomy to the Germans. Responding to British pressure, Beneš tried making concessions: he was prepared to take in four Sudeten German ministers, declare three German autonomous districts, and make sure that a third of all civil servants were ethnic Germans from now on. His more reasoned tone received British backing but Hitler instructed Henlein to stay firm and make no concessions.[3]

On the 3rd Keitel and Brauchitsch arrived at the Berghof to run over the plans for the invasion of Czechoslovakia. The army was to be ready at the border on 28 September. Two days later, Beneš tried to spike Hitler's strategy by asking Henlein up to the Hradschin on the 5th and requesting that he write down his demands in full so that he might grant them – something he promptly did on the 7th, thereby removing the *casus belli*. All Henlein could do was point to the ill treatment of some ethnic Germans in Moravia and seek fresh instructions from Germany. Meanwhile his second-in-command, Karl Frank, was instructed to increase the number of such incidents.

It was said that the Czechs were prepared to give Henlein a ministry to shut him up. The ministry he wanted was the interior. The story gave rise to inevitable witticisms.[i] The premier, Hodza, had suggested that Henlein receive the portfolio for the colonies. At this Henlein countered, 'How come? That's impossible – Czechoslovakia has no colonies. 'What of it?' replied Hodza. 'Has not Italy a Minister of Finance and Germany a Minister of Justice?'[4]

NUREMBERG

On the evening of the 4th, the chief warmongers, Hitler, Goebbels and Ribbentrop, flew to Nuremberg. Goebbels was looking forward to a week of mounting pressure on the Czechs. He had also succeeded in bullying Furtwängler into conducting *Die Meistersinger* the next evening. That same day France called up its reserves and the Hungarians quietly introduced conscription. The Rally opened on the 6th with Hess delivering what Goebbels called 'a good sermon'.

---

[i] There are several contemporary versions of this joke.

The Tribune of Honour at the opening ceremony exhibited evidence that Hitler continued to exert a powerful erotic pull on the women of the world. At one end was Stephanie zu Hohenlohe and at the other Lord and Lady Redesdale, the parents of Unity Mitford. Princess Stephanie was wearing her gold Party badge. The rally kicked off with the Cultural Conference and Hitler made a portentous speech about art, as was his wont. It contained an unusually tolerant line about freemasons: Hitler said that 'only a man lacking in national respect' would allow them to get in the way of his enjoying Mozart's *Magic Flute*.[5]

The Brownshirts were treated to a performance of Bruckner's Seventh from the Berlin Philharmonic conducted by specialist Hans Weisbach. Once the cultural overture was out of the way, the Nazi leaders descended into their habitual rabble-rousing tirades and malicious squabbles. Rosenberg launched an attack on the Pope's pretensions to power. He would have had support from Goebbels, for a new *Kulturkampf* against the Church was never far from the Gauleiter's mind. Goebbels was pleased that he had succeeded in winding up the exemption from military service previously enjoyed by theological students. Now they had to serve in the front line as stretcher-bearers. Goebbels was seething because he had seen a 'frightful' telegram the Kaiser had sent the Abbot of Maria Laach. 'This simple-minded, cowardly former monarch finds it supremely necessary to open his gob again.'[6]

Backbiting was not confined to the leaders. Unity took the trouble to warn Hitler that his friend Stephanie was 100 per cent Jewish. She was also advising Hitler that Britain would not fight, thereby supporting Ribbentrop. The brief reconciliation between Hitler's two biggest hawks had ended. Goebbels now thought the Foreign Minister a 'vain, stupid primadonna'.[7] As usual, Hitler appeared to take no notice of the discord among his underlings. He was planning a positive cacophony of sabre-rattling for the last day, 12 September. The British ambassador, Henderson, was there, eating the local Bratwürste and disparaging the Czechs to his SS minder. Officially, he was meant to push the idea of holding a plebiscite in the disputed areas, which would hand the initiative to the Czechs. An article in *The Times* had advocated the cession of the Sudetenland to Germany. The leading Nazis believed this had been placed by the Cabinet. Henderson thought Hitler had been led astray by evil people in his entourage, and if the British were to say what a good boy he was, he would behave better. His view was not shared by Halifax, who was now of the opinion that Hitler was mad.

But Hitler was impervious to any form of pressure to desist, be it from his diplomats (Neurath[ii] thought no good would come of it), his own intelligence service, which brought him news of the Duce's unhappiness, or the army. Goebbels' admiration for his master knew no bounds: 'He faces danger with the surefootedness of a sleepwalker.' 'The Führer says and does what he knows to be right, and never lets himself be intimidated.' 'Now the most important things are nerves.'[8] Goebbels was utterly convinced that the Western powers would stay out of any conflict. Despite his outward resolve, Hitler was less certain.

The 7th was cold and wet. Goebbels noted, 'Things are ripening more and more into a crisis.' The British, Dutch and Belgian armies called up their reserves. The British offer was now insufficient: 'We have to have Prague.' He gloated, pleased to hear about a couple of German deaths in Mährisch Östrau. Now there could be a deafening chorus of outrage.[9] There was a reception that evening for the diplomatic corps in Nuremberg, and the doyen, the outgoing French ambassador, François-Poncet – whom Spitzy called an 'all-licensed fool'[10] – made a speech in which he said, 'The best of laurels are those gathered without reducing any mother to tears.' All eyes turned to Hitler.[11] In Berlin there was frenzied activity in resistance circles, where the plan was to seize Hitler and put him on trial before the People's Court or lock him up in a lunatic asylum. On 9 September, following the usual *son et lumière*,[12] Hitler held an all-night conference in Nuremberg attended by Halder, Brauchitsch and Keitel. He was

[ii] The future 'Protector' of Bohemia and Moravia.

contemptuous of the army's plans and demanded there be an uprising in the Sudetenland.

On the 9th, refreshed from his shooting, Chamberlain met his Inner Cabinet. He rejected Halifax's proposal of sending a final warning to Germany, and revealed his desire to go to Hitler. He nonetheless set about mobilizing the fleet. He also issued a warning to Hitler on the 10th that France would be duty bound to honour its obligations to the Czechs, and that Great Britain could not stand aside from any general conflict, but Henderson had qualms about delivering this ultimatum and it remained in his baggage. He had difficulty meeting Hitler anyway and had been frightened that any tough talk – or even a toughly worded note – might upset the German leader. He didn't even attempt to speak to Ribbentrop, thereby causing exasperation in some quarters.[13] The message the Germans received was that Britain would agree to the cession of the German areas but would not permit a strike against Prague. 'That would be disappointing, as it is only the half-measure,' wrote Goebbels, who showed that he was well aware of Chamberlain's message despite Henderson's refusal to deliver it.[14] Canaris was also concerned about Hitler. He told Groscurth, 'He is already on to the next step; thinking about Romania, Ukraine etc.'[15]

On the 12th Henderson signed as many as 150 autographs in the Rally's diplomatic stand, now fragrant from the presence of so many Austrian girls in dirndls. Goebbels noticed them too: 'I greet a hundred delicious Austrian girls, who can hardly contain their excitement.'[16] Goebbels adorned the cards with his signature, and Henderson was happy to hand them out to Sudeten Germans too.[17]

Hitler's final speech had an 'indescribable' effect on its audience.[18] Göring too delivered a particularly stirring piece of invective, then took to his bed, leaving Hitler in the company of Ribbentrop, who wanted war and as soon as possible. When four of his most senior ambassadors clubbed together to tell him this was a mistake, he banished them from Nuremberg and sent them on leave for the rest of the month. The effect of the Rally was immediate: Hitler and

Göring's oratory inspired civil disobedience in the ethnic Bohemian German towns of Eger and Karlsbad. Czech and Jewish property was attacked. The Czechs responded by firing on the crowds and declaring martial law.

In Prague the people went to work carrying gas masks. Henlein fled to Bavaria to organize a Freikorps to fight in his native land. The Czechs seemed to be in control of the situation. It was at that moment that French resolve collapsed: their Cabinet vote was badly split with six calling for war and four against. Their leader, Daladier, asked Chamberlain to see Hitler and try to make the best deal he could that would forestall the need for France to honour its obligations to the Little Entente. Hitler's liaison with the Wilhelmstrasse, Walther Hewel, said that Chamberlain himself had been alarmed by the tone of Hitler's speech at the Rally.[19]

In reality the ground for Chamberlain's mission had been prepared by Göring and Henderson on 8 September. The Luftwaffe chief had invited Henderson up to his home at nearby Veldenstein, where the suggestion was aired that the Sudeten question be settled by direct talks. Göring dropped hints about a hunting party at Rominten[iii] at the end of the month, and said he hoped that the Czechs were not going to disrupt it, meaning that peace could be maintained. He even promised Halifax the four best stags in Germany if Britain were to disclaim any interest in Czechoslovakia. Henderson filed a report and had it taken to London on a private plane. On 13 September Chamberlain proposed flying to Germany for a meeting.

As there was no doubt about Hitler's invasion plans, Halder conveyed the message to General Witzleben on the 13th. The Opposition had to act fast. While the two men were talking, news came in that Henderson had told Ribbentrop of Chamberlain's intention to visit Hitler at the Berghof. The note was passed to Schmidt to translate:

[iii] The hunting lodge in East Prussia that Göring had bought from the former Kaiser.

Having regard to the increasingly critical situation, I propose to visit you immediately in order to make an attempt to find a peaceful solution. I could come to you by air and am ready to leave tomorrow. Please inform me of the earliest time you can receive me, and tell me the place of the meeting. I should be grateful for a very early reply. Neville Chamberlain.

The carpet had been pulled out from under the feet of the plotters. They could not proceed while Hitler was talking peace. It also showed that Ribbentrop had been right all along: the British and the French would not fight. The interpreter Schmidt set off for Munich. He was fully aware of the plot. Weizsäcker's final piece of advice was: 'Keep your mind quite clear . . . Tomorrow at Berchtesgaden it will be a matter of war and peace.'[20]

BERCHTESGADEN

On the 15th 'peace-envoy Chamberlain' (as the Germans called him), together with Sir Horace Wilson and Sir William Strang, flew to Munich, where he was met by Ribbentrop and Schmidt. They travelled to Berchtesgaden on Hitler's train. It took the British Prime Minister seven hours to reach him. Not only had he taken his first aeroplane, there had been turbulence. Dressed in Nazi uniform, Hitler received him on the steps of his home. In reply to Hitler's 'German Greeting' Chamberlain waved his hat. He had the inevitable umbrella hanging from his left arm.[21] After tea the two men went to Hitler's study, accompanied only by the interpreter Schmidt. By divesting themselves of advisors, they were able to rid themselves of Ribbentrop.

The Poles had thrown a potential spanner in the works, which may have rendered Hitler keener to negotiate. The Sejm had been dissolved and new elections in November threatened to bring in Germany's enemies. The German–Polish cooperation that had been

Jozef Beck's policy was hanging in the balance: the Poles were expected to lend a hand in carving up Czechoslovakia by snatching the Teschen pocket in Czech Silesia.[22] Many Poles thought Beck's policy brought Poland too close to Germany and they feared finding the country on the same side as Germany in a war.[23] Leading Nazis also believed the British were being cunning by offloading increasing amounts of guilt on to Germany should war break out.

The Berghof discussions lasted three hours. Outside the rain pelted down and the wind howled. Chamberlain wanted to know if Hitler would be satisfied by the cession of the Sudeten areas. Hitler mentioned the Hungarians and Poles but he was not interested in the rest. He exclaimed that he was ready to risk world war to settle the matter. Chamberlain rejoindered, 'If that is so, why did you let me come to Berchtesgaden? Under the circumstances it is best for me to return at once. Anything else now seems pointless.'[24] At this Hitler conceded that if Chamberlain were to accept the principle of self-determination then there could be room for talk, and promised not to attack the Czechs before they met again – unless, that is, the Czechs did something particularly atrocious. Chamberlain told Hitler he needed to consult his colleagues. He spent the night in the Grand Hotel Berchtesgadenerhof before travelling back to London with the news. He took with him the impression that Hitler was a man who would stick to his word – not that he had that word: he had not brought an interpreter, and left without a copy of the minutes, because Ribbentrop had churlishly denied him one, an act of 'private revenge'.[25]

After the Berchtesgaden talks Schmidt was able to keep Erich Kordt informed of the conversations between the two men. Kordt took the record to Oster to show that Hitler had not abandoned his war plans. He wanted the terms imposed on the Czechs to be so humiliating that they would refuse to accept; then he could strike. The Opposition was now fired up again and waiting for Hitler's return to Berlin. At dinner on the 15th, Eva Braun's friends mocked the old-fashioned Englishman who had seemed so wedded to his umbrella.

Hitler was gratified that 'the old man took an aeroplane for the first time in his life in order to come and see me'.[26] Hitler had made a half-hearted offer to go to London, but had expressed the fear that he would be heckled by Jews.[27] Chamberlain had to some extent got the measure of Hitler too: he told the Cabinet that he was 'the commonest little dog he had ever seen'.[28]

Chamberlain's visit had been a small success. His great achievement, if it might be expressed that way, was to get Beneš to agree to detach the Sudeten areas from Czechoslovakia and hand them over to Germany. This obliged Hitler to drop his plans to swallow up the rest of Bohemia and Moravia – for the time being. The Czechs vented their frustration in what they believed to be privacy. Masaryk got wind of the talks on the 14th and referred to Chamberlain's right-hand man Sir Horace Wilson as 'the Sow'.[29] Goebbels consoled himself that even if their spoils were limited to the Sudeten areas, they would still have put themselves in a better position strategically to take Prague the next time round.[30]

Hitler summoned Goebbels and a small staff to the Berghof. He was going to need his propaganda machine.[iv] Alarmed both by Czech violence towards ethnic Germans and German scaremongering, streams of refugees were seeking refuge in Silesia. Goebbels had foreign journalists sent into their camps to witness their despair. Ward Price was brought up to Berchtesgaden to interview Hitler. They were very happy with the results. In the meantime Hitler and his little pressman distracted themselves by watching popular films and reading the minutes of Beneš' conversations with Jan Masaryk in London. They would have been amused to hear the British envoy Runciman dismissed as 'the Lord who wrote the mad book', and Goebbels in particular would have liked the references to the 'fat Field Marshal' – Göring.[31]

Beneš, they concluded, was the problem: he was 'dangerous, mendacious, sly and scheming'.[32] They were not wide of the mark:

[iv] Goebbels was the original spin-doctor.

Beneš and his ministers were trying to find friends who would baulk
at negotiations and press for war. The former Foreign Secretary Eden
was one of these.[33] The Germans were later able to show the British
that the Czechs were conniving at the overthrow of the Cabinet. On
19 September they had a meeting with the Labour Party leader
Attlee. Churchill had been sounded out and had apparently expressed
his hope that they 'would not put up with it'. On the afternoon of
the 22nd there was an optimistic report that Chamberlain's Cabinet
was on the point of resigning. The Czechs also hoped for a change of
government in France and referred to the foreign minister Bonnet as
'the Swine'.[34] When the Poles offered to find a solution to the Danzig
problem, Hitler was triumphant: in ten years he would reverse not
only the punitive clauses of the Treaty of Versailles, but also those of
the Treaty of Münster that closed the Thirty Years War.[35]

Cadogan was detailed to tell Beneš to cede the Sudetenland on the
18th. The Soviet Union was exerting pressure by massing troops at its
border (it had no common border with Czechoslovakia) but Hitler
was still undeterred and continued his military preparations. The state
the Allies created at Versailles was falling apart. Encouraged by
Henlein, the Slovak People's Party demanded autonomy for their half
of the country. This was granted after the débâcle at Munich. On the
19th London and Paris agreed to waive the plebiscite, but at the same
time refused to grant concessions to Poland and Hungary. Hitler was
furious with Horthy for dragging his heels. The Polish ambassador,
Józef Lipski, was conjured up and told to make a gesture. Goebbels
thought they had it in the bag, and the Führer 'a genius'.[36] Urged on
by Göring, the Poles and Hungarians began to rally on 21 September.
The Poles demanded a plebiscite in Teschen, and on the 22nd the
Hungarians finally made a similar appeal for the Magyar areas of
Slovakia.

In Berlin the Opposition was gritting its teeth. Something of
Germany's desperate economic problems became clear from a
meeting between Ulrich von Hassell and Schacht on the day of
Chamberlain's talks with Hitler. Schacht was bitter about the Führer

and referred to him as a 'swindler'. He did not think that the talks with Chamberlain would do anything to prevent war. Schacht made it clear that Hitler needed more than just the border areas if he were to stave off economic disaster: all his secret funds and all Austria's stolen reserves had been used up. He thought Germany was already in the red. When Hassell cautiously alluded to Schacht's own responsibility in this, Schacht denied it: even as a cabinet minister he was informed of nothing. He did not know how they could get out of the mess unless they started printing money, and when that happened he would resign.[37]

On the same day the Sudeten Freikorps seized the towns of Eger and Asch. More and more Sudeten Germans were crossing the border into Germany to avoid the conflict they imagined would break out any day now. A camp was built for them in Hirschberg in the Riesengebirge.[38] Klemperer saw members of the Freikorps in Dresden on the 20th, poised to strike. He had no doubt as to the outcome: the Reich would win in the long run, either by force or by bluff. Nor did Hitler have any doubts, for the time being.[39]

The raiding party that was to attack the Chancellery had been supplied with weapons by the Abwehr and lodged in safe houses and flats all over Berlin. The chief fear was that the putsch would be thwarted by the SS.[40] In Munich, General Hoepner's armoured division was ready to move against the SS, should there be an attempt to intervene. The Opposition had reason to believe that Hitler's end was approaching. When Schulenburg saw streams of military vehicles heading towards Berlin from Mecklenburg on the 17th, he said, 'Look, in a few days these troops will liberate us from the nightmare of Hitler.' On 22 September he hurriedly despatched his growing family to the country estate of a friend to get them out of the way in the event of an uprising.[41]

BAD GODESBERG

At 8.50 on the night of the 20th, Masaryk reported to Beneš that 'the Old Man will soon be on his travels again'.[42] At 11 p.m. on 21 September, Hitler, Goebbels and Ribbentrop flew from Bavaria to Bad Godesberg near Bonn on the Rhine to meet Chamberlain. Hitler told the others that he wanted the Poles and Hungarians to attack so that he could push all the way to Prague. He was going to grant autonomy to Slovakia, but not to Bohemia or Moravia. The generals had plied him with memos, but he refused to be shaken from his path.[43] A few hours later, Chamberlain took to the skies for the third time in his life. Hitler lodged at one of his favourite haunts, the Hotel Dreesen, which had been refurbished for the occasion, and Chamberlain was put up with his party in the Hotel Petersberg on the other side of the river. The British Prime Minister had been able to win round the French, and, after refusing at first, the Czechs had also given in. There was to be no plebiscite; a commission would settle the areas of mixed population and decree where transfers of population were to take place. Czechoslovakia's current alliances would be dissolved. Instead Britain would form part of an international body to guarantee Czech independence and neutrality.

Chamberlain had been receiving reassurances from Henderson, who had been speaking to a Göring anxious to minimize the risk of war. Sadly it was not Göring who was tugging at Hitler's sleeve now but Ribbentrop. Göring had been lured away by the stags of Rominten, taking his old Richthofen Squadron cronies and Tsar Boris of Bulgaria with him, and was excelling himself at ridding the forests of East Prussia of horned beasts. Chamberlain was having no such luck. First, he was faced by a map, on which the Germans had carved out a very large slice of the Czech cake for themselves;[v] then, to his

---

[v] Chamberlain had been prepared for the cession of all areas with more than 50 per cent Germans, but Hitler wanted to remove the votes of Czechs planted in German-speaking areas after 1918, while any German who had left after that date would be allowed to make his views known.

astonishment and dismay, Hitler said it was too late anyway. Events of the past few days had made his offer unacceptable.

He mentioned the Poles and the Hungarians, and the grievances of the Sudetenländer, and said the matter needed to be settled by 1 October. The Czechs had to withdraw from the areas he had marked on a map, and allow these to be occupied by German armies. The immediate German occupation of the Sudetenland was the essential condition. It may have been that Hitler had received word that Beneš had no more intention of honouring his word than Hitler, although this was vigorously denied by Masaryk on the 28th.[44] Göring's Research Bureau had intercepted some revealing conversations between him, Mastny and Osusky, the Czech ambassador in Paris, spiced up with rude references to members of the British and French governments. Göring had presented the file to Henderson with obvious delight. They were not calculated to make the Czech case any more sympathetic.[45] After three hours' discussion Hitler took his guest out on the terrace. 'Oh, Mr Prime Minister, I am so sorry: I had looked forward to showing you this beautiful view of the Rhine . . . but now it is hidden by the mist.'[46]

Both parties withdrew to their hotels. All night a motorboat plied the Rhine taking messages from one to the other. Chamberlain had failed to understand that Hitler intended to destroy the Czech state and was simply using the German minority as a pretext. Hitler for his part had realized that he could safely ask for more, as Chamberlain was bound to concede. When Hitler refused to budge the following morning, Chamberlain sent word that there was nothing more for him to do, and he would return to London. Hitler entrusted his reply to Schmidt. It was in German, and his interpreter was to read it to Chamberlain, translating it as he went along. It took about an hour; then Schmidt, fortified with 'the right stuff', fled through the lines of journalists back to the ferry and the Rhine.[47]

There was a final discussion between the heads of state at 10.30 p.m. on the 23rd. The British Prime Minister insisted that

Sudeten Germans control the evacuation of the Czechs, rather than German troops. The Nazis thought this was another of Beneš' tricks. In response Hitler insisted that the Czechs start to vacate the border areas on the 26th and complete them in forty-eight hours. Chamberlain threw up his arms in outrage, while Henderson, who liked to toss in a word or two of German, called it 'Ein Diktat'.[vi] At this moment of deadlock, the door opened and an official brought Hitler a note. He read it and asked Schmidt to translate it for the British. It was Beneš' order to mobilize. There was some question as to whether the Czechs had intended to wreck the talks by summoning their men to the colours; alternatively it might have been an Anglo-French ploy to force Hitler to compromise.[48]

Hitler made his final 'concession': he took a pencil and changed the date for the Czech withdrawal to 1 October, the date set down long before for the attack on Czechoslovakia. Chamberlain brightened and Hitler told him that this would be the last territorial demand he would make in Europe. Chamberlain was to relay this pledge to the House of Commons. Before Chamberlain returned to Britain, Hitler's official photographer, the drunkard Hoffmann,[vii] was able to snap the two leaders standing beside the 'palm of peace' in the hotel lobby.

Halifax thought things had gone far enough. To Chamberlain's dismay, the British Cabinet, which met on Sunday, 25 September, refused to accept Hitler's demands and pledged support to France should they wish to launch military action. By all reports, however, the French were woefully unprepared for war.[49] On behalf of the Czechs, Jan Masaryk handed over a memorandum rejecting the Bad Godesberg proposals. Daladier and Bonnet arrived in London to see Chamberlain and Halifax. As Goebbels had noted, Beneš was tougher than Schuschnigg and he thought the Czech ambassador to London superior to Dirksen, who was 'shitting himself'.[50]

[vi] A reference to the hated 'dictated peace' of Versailles.
[vii] The father-in-law of Baldur von Schirach and the discoverer of Eva Braun.

Britain began to lumber into war. The French got tough, manned the Maginot Line and mobilized 500,000 men; the Russians voiced their readiness to move too. Hitler was now convinced that Beneš would brazen it out. He was worried about the Poles, and wondered whether they would give him the backing he craved. In fact they made a small move and partially mobilized their armies while the Italians called up three years of reserves. Hitler's other ally, Hungary, did nothing whatsoever, much to his fury. Göring had been sent on a special mission to Horthy, but returned empty-handed.

Chamberlain had another card: he sent his closest advisor, Sir Horace Wilson, to Berlin with a letter asking Hitler to negotiate with the Czech government directly, with the British present as a third party. He was also to warn Hitler that France would honour its commitments to the Czechs, and Britain its to France. When Hitler heard from Wilson that the Czechs had rejected his demands, he became over-excited, jumped out of his seat and began to shout: 'The Germans are being treated like niggers; one would not dare treat even the Turks like that.'[viii] Hitler stopped short of biting the carpet. He was pleased with his performance, a sign that these tantrums were a sham. He told Goebbels all about it.[51]

Jochen Klepper was in Krummhübel, a resort near the Czech border in the Riesengebirge. He could hear shooting in the distance; a Czech frontier post had been attacked with grenades. 'Now we have arrived at the last consequence of the "Peace" of Versailles. Eight million Czechs against three million Sudeten Germans; seventy-five million Germans against eight million Czechs! Twenty years ago the seed of all this was planted.'[52]

The reckless Silesian noblewoman Gräfin Maria von Maltzan was in the Sudetenland that summer undergoing a cure. She noted that

[viii] The Czech language was apparently remarkably similar. Officials at the Czech Foreign Office told Eric Gedye, 'The Chamberlain government . . . is treating our head of state as though he were a nigger chieftain ruling some troublesome colonial tribe.' G.E.D. Gedye, *Fallen Bastions*, London 1939, 410.

many of the nurses were Jewish, and they were frightened about what
would happen to them when the Nazis walked in. She managed to get
herself into trouble with some Henlein men, and thought she could
wangle her way out of it by mentioning her brother-in-law, General
von Reichenau, whose corps was across the border waiting for orders
to march. For a while she was in custody, but managed to escape to
Berlin.[53]

BERLIN

Goebbels may have been thinking wishfully when he described the
mood of 'his' Berliners that autumn as 'half war mania and half
determination'. It was his idea that Hitler should address them at the
Sportpalast on the 26th.[54] Despite the apparent enthusiasm of the
Berlin crowd, Goebbels was not taking any chances. The 'audience
should represent the people only', which meant he was going to rig
it.[55] On the night, the Führer reiterated his mendacious claim that
this venture was his last territorial demand. He found easy meat in
the Allied principle of self-determination: the Czech state was a lie,
there was no Czechoslovakia, there were just Czechs and Slovaks and
the Slovaks did not like the Czechs. A catalogue of untruths and
exaggerations followed. The decision lay with Beneš: peace or war.
Either he gave the Czech Germans their freedom or the Germans
would snatch it for them. 'Now let Herr Beneš make his choice.'[56]
Groscurth called it 'a horrible, undignified rant'.[57]

War seemed unavoidable. In Washington, President Roosevelt was
alarmed enough to make an appeal for peace and to tell Chamberlain
to negotiate to the last moment.[58] The threat was keenly felt in the
concentration camps too. In Dachau they realized that, if the conflict
broke out, it would be curtains for them. They were perfectly aware
that any lip service to international opinion or law would be
jettisoned at that point.[59] They noted with trepidation the dis-
appearance of their guards: the younger SS-men were sent to the

Czech border and were replaced by older men of a more kindly disposition than the usual eighteen-year-old sadists. The bubble burst when Chamberlain flew to Munich at the end of the month and the young men returned and resumed their brutal ways.

On the morning of the 27th, Sir Horace Wilson found Hitler obdurate. Not even the mention of Britain's need to support France's mobilization had any effect. Hitler claimed to be wholly indifferent about whether there was a European war or not. 'So – next week we'll all find ourselves at war with each other.'[60] After Wilson left he assembled yet more elements of the Wehrmacht to go into action on the 30th. The gambler Hitler had been more impressed with British moves than he appeared, however, and was prepared to lend an ear to the doves who made up the majority of his entourage. Once again the only other warmonger was Ribbentrop. Another intimate member of Hitler's circle who had increasing reservations about war was Goebbels. He was still keeping his head down because of the fallout from his affair with Lida.

That day Hassell lunched with a number of conservative Germans at the Continental in Berlin. One of those present was Popitz, the Prussian Minister of Finance. Popitz told him that speeches like that which the Führer had just delivered at the Sportspalast gave him physical nausea. There were also fears that Hitler's next move would be to proceed against the 'upper stratum', as he called it. Before lunch Hassell had had a meeting with Emil Georg von Strauss, President of the Deutsche Bank. He was 'one of the first business leaders to go over to Hitler. He is now filled with the greatest anxiety and disgust.'[61] It seemed certain that Hitler would go to war.[62]

The German Army was on the point of mutiny. There were desperate worries about the weakness of Germany's western defences. France could bring sixty-five divisions to bear against, at the most, a dozen German. Meanwhile the Czechs had called a million men to arms. The German people were not enthusiastic. In some cities open criticism was heard in public places.[63] When an armed division rumbled through the streets of Berlin for an hour and a half on the evening of 27 September, the Berliners observed them with 'frigid silence'.[64] At the Foreign Office Spitzy told Kordt: 'Look at the people's faces, filled with pale horror at the prospect of war.'[65] At the beginning Hitler stood on his balcony to watch the parade, but when he saw how things were going, he went inside and hid behind a curtain.[66] He had hoped that it would concentrate the minds of the foreign journalists and diplomats in the capital. He was amazed and infuriated by the apathy of the Berliners, which struck the journalists far more than the show of firepower on the roads.[ix]

The hawks paid no heed to the reservations expressed by the military men. Himmler – who hoped to be able to replace the army by his own Waffen-SS – 'complained about the generals. The Führer added his sharpest verdict on the old, senile generals. They should be laid off as soon as possible.'[67] Not all of Himmler's men agreed with Himmler, or with Goebbels' optimistic view of the Berliners. SS-Gruppenführer Lorenz told Ribbentrop, 'If the Berliners knew how much you have been beating the drum for war, I'd have to position the entire *Leibstandarte* along the Wilhelmstrasse to protect you.' For the first time since Hitler came to power, it was clear that the Germans were ready for change.[68]

The last thing the people wanted was war. There was a bad harvest, which was compounded by an outbreak of foot and mouth disease.[69] That same day Chamberlain made his notorious speech on the wireless about a 'faraway country', reiterating his reluctance to fight. The broadcast was not seen in the bad light it enjoys today, when it is perceived as an admission of indifference to the fate of Czechoslovakia. Groscurth thought that, in contrast to Hitler, the British Prime Minister had been 'calm and dignified'.[70] Later Admiral Raeder brought Hitler the news that the Royal Navy had been mobilized. The planned declaration of war against the Czechs was

---

[ix] Goebbels either failed to notice, or was taken in by his own propaganda. He observed, 'Everywhere the most profound impression was made.' *Tagebücher, I, VI,* 117.

hurriedly retracted. Hitler fired off a letter to Chamberlain, leaving it up to him to make the Czech government see reason.

Göring was still at Carinhall near Berlin on the 27th. He had been informed that the power of his present airfleet was insufficient to destroy London as planned. In panic he ordered that the experimental Junkers Ju 88 be put into production immediately. He reappeared in Berlin the next day, when his credentials as a peacemonger were most needed.

The 28th of September has gone down as Black Wednesday, the gloom of impending war hung like a pall over the capitals of Western and Central Europe. The French were the first to attempt to dispel it. François-Poncet arrived in the Chancellery at 11 a.m. to find tables set for lunch for commanders designated to invade Czechoslovakia.[71] He brought Hitler an offer that would allow partial occupation by the 1st and complete evacuation of the areas in question by the 10th. 'Why should you take the risk when your essential demands can be met without war?'[72]

Hitler was visibly moved by what the Frenchman told him but a little more pressure was required to make him desist. The British had decided to bring in Mussolini, who was as alarmed as anyone at the prospect of a European war. Hitler had kept the Duce in the dark as the proposed meeting between the two dictators at the Brenner had not taken place. Mussolini saw Chamberlain's policy as the 'liquidation of English prestige' but both he and his son-in-law Ciano were convinced there would be war.[73] Chamberlain also offered to fly for a fifth time, this time to Berlin.[74]

At 10 a.m. the British ambassador in Rome, Lord Perth, showed Ciano a telegram from Chamberlain: with four hours to go before the German armies went into Bohemia, Italian mediation was the last chance to save Europe. Mussolini despatched his ambassador, the highly experienced, anti-Nazi Bernardo Attolico, who arrived on the heels of François-Poncet.[75] Attolico was also a friend and confidant of Weizsäcker. The Italian asked for a twenty-four-hour stay of execution. Hitler was not impressed by the sight of the Italian diplomat, who arrived flushed and breathless, and told Linge, 'He's shitting himself! If we took his advice we'd never see the end of this business.' He listened for all that.

Göring and Neurath were also working on Hitler, while the Finance Minister Schwerin-Krosigk submitted his views in writing. Hitler dismissed Göring's qualms, calling him an old woman. Schwerin-Krosigk's line echoed that of Schacht: Germany did not have enough money to go to war. The country was already 'done for'.[76] Next Henderson arrived bringing Chamberlain's reply to his letter. The Prime Minister wanted an international conference. Hitler said he would talk it over with Mussolini. Attolico had a message from the Duce that he supported Chamberlain's plan. In his 'dazzling hatred' for Britain, Ribbentrop was alone in egging Hitler on. Göring took the RAM to one side and angrily berated him as a 'criminal fool'. Göring said he knew the meaning of war and that it was not to be undertaken lightly. If it were to break out, Ribbentrop should sit beside him in the first bomber. There was never any love lost between the two.[77] It was a Madhatter's Tea Party only to be compared to that which followed the abortive 20 July Plot in 1944.

Hitler, who had been wandering around the Chancellery ranting, agreed to Chamberlain's suggestion shortly before noon. The Italian leader had managed to sugar the pill. It temporarily dampened Hitler's ambitions. 'We'll carry on fortifying ourselves for a future opportunity,' wrote Goebbels.[78] Hitler decided that the conference should take place in Munich. Only the French and the British would be invited; the Soviet Union and Czechoslovakia would learn of the decisions later. Neither was a great power in Hitler's eyes. The information was carried back to London, where Chamberlain was addressing a House of Commons expecting to hear a declaration of war. The news was greeted with 'indescribable enthusiasm'.[79]

The Opposition was still hoping to strike on the 29th. On the morning of the 28th Kordt gave the text of Chamberlain's letter to Hitler to Oster. It was circulated to Witzleben and Halder. They interpreted it to mean that Hitler was bent on war. Halder went to

Brauchitsch, who was finally convinced to act. Kordt wanted it to happen at once, not even waiting for the morrow. It was then that the Opposition learned of the Italian démarche, which would preserve Hitler at the expense of Czechoslovakia. 'Colombo'[x] Brücklmeier, who was on duty in the Chancellery, took the news to Kordt. Hitler postponed mobilization for twenty-four hours.

MUNICH

On 28 September European war still seemed unavoidable. Hitler met Mussolini off his train on the platform at Kufstein on the old Austrian border and they travelled together to Munich. Hitler thought he was briefing the Italian leader, but Mussolini was keener to calm Hitler down and prevent him from dragging Europe into war, all the time reassuring him that, if the conference did break down, Italy would be behind him. Mussolini was in two minds. Half of him was saying that there was a chance of eliminating France and Britain for ever. On the way to Munich, Hitler told him of his long-term plans: he had to knock out Czechoslovakia to leave his hands free to fight Britain and France. They needed to go to war soon, while they were 'young and full of vigour'.[80] Mussolini was to be the focus of the conference, largely because, unlike Hitler, he could speak the languages of the other attendees.[81] Ciano accompanied his father-in-law.

Chamberlain was met by Ribbentrop and Bavarian State Councillor Christian Weber at the airport in Oberwiesenfeld. The RAM was still shouting for war,[82] behaving 'like a petulant child' and wanting to wreck the conference.[83] He was particularly furious at the presence of his predecessor, Neurath.[84] Chamberlain was lodged in the Hotel Regina on the Maximiliansplatz in Munich together with the Czech 'observers' Mastny and Masaryk, who were present to receive whatever scraps were handed down from the top table. The

---

[x] So called because he had been German consul in Ceylon.

French delegation stopped at the Vier Jahreszeiten. Outside in the streets of Munich people were on tenterhooks, hoping that peace would be preserved. Even Winifred Wagner thought that was what her 'Wolf' really wanted.[85]

The talks began at 12.30 p.m. in Hitler's study in the Führerbau. The seating had been managed so that Hitler had his back to the window and his face in shadow. Chamberlain was on his left. Daladier and Mussolini sat together on a sofa. The basis for the Munich Agreement was the document drawn up by Neurath and Weizsäcker together with Göring that stemmed from the British note. It had then been given to Attolico to send to Rome. Mussolini had passed it off as his, to mislead Ribbentrop.

There was little opposition to Hitler's diktat: a General Staff map was brought in and, although the talks lasted thirteen hours, the conference took the form of a 'border commission'. The international treaties that guaranteed the Czech state had been effectively torn up. There was occasional rearguard action from Daladier, on the advice of Alexis Léger, the head of the Quai d'Orsay, who expressed concern for the future existence of Czechoslovakia.[86] Hitler seemed to take this well, and later expressed his liking of the French premier,[87] who impressed the Germans much more than the frigid, vulpine Chamberlain.[88] The draft was signed at around 2.30 a.m. on 30 October. The Poles and Hungarians had to lodge their claims to territory within three months. Hitler could still march in on the first of the month, and appeared so pleased with the result that he ordered the guest book to be brought over from the Brown House so that the leaders could enter their signatures.

The Agreement gave Hitler pretty well everything he had craved at Bad Godesberg, and the German armies went in on 1 October as planned. The new borders were drawn on strategic lines, thereby leaving a quarter of a million Germans in Czechoslovakia and bringing 800,000 Czechs into the Reich. The Czech version of the Maginot Line was absorbed into German territory. Czechs who did not wish to remain in the new German Zone (including ethnic

Germans for whom Nazi rule would have been unpalatable, and some 30,000 Jews) were to leave before 10 October, in the clothes they were standing up in; everything else was to be left behind. The Germans would pay no compensation. Chamberlain's attempts to win some sort of deal for the Czechs had caused the only disagreement between him and Hitler at the conference. In the end he had not even been able to save a few head of Czech cattle.[89]

On 20 November, an 'international commission' allotted 11,000 square miles to the Germans. These contained 66 per cent of Czech coal, 80 per cent of lignite, 70 per cent of iron and steel, and the same amount of the nation's electric power, as well as 40 per cent of its timber. Göring rubbed his thighs in glee and a humiliated Beneš went into bitter exile. On 10 October the Czechs conceded that the Teschen pocket belonged to the Poles and on 2 November Ribbentrop and Ciano redrew the Czech–Hungarian border. Czechoslovakia was now defenceless against Germany's next blow, which would not be long in coming.

Hitler could be said to have won hands down, but he was still cross. He cared little for the Sudeteners – he wanted Prague. He was especially angry when Chamberlain was cheered by the Munich crowd as he travelled in an open-topped car after his visit to his 'modest apartment'[90] on the Prinzregentenplatz. Without informing Daladier, Chamberlain had gone to seek a further assurance of Hitler's peaceable intentions.[91] The Anglo-German agreement was to create machinery for constant maintenance of peaceful relations. Hitler seemed sullen and distracted. Schmidt (who was present once again) believed he appended his signature only to placate the Englishman. That night the Munichois celebrated with double measures of beer.[92] Even *Die Stürmer* congratulated Chamberlain on standing up to the (Jewish) mob and working for peace.[93] Hitler did not join them: he thought the British Prime Minister had spoiled his triumphal entry into Prague.[94]

Chamberlain must have felt relieved, but he went home and told the relevant bodies to rearm, quickly. He had bought some time, and he was right about one thing: Hitler wanted war, and that had only been delayed. There had never been any intention of going to Czechoslovakia's aid anyhow. Back on 18 March, shortly after the Anschluss, Vansittart's successor at the Foreign Office, Sir Alexander Cadogan, had written in his diary, 'Foreign Policy Committee unanimous that Czechoslovakia is not worth the bones of a single Grenadier. And they're quite right too!'[95] Among the leading Nazis, Göring was also in the doghouse for spoiling Hitler's fun. Ribbentrop now moved into the ascendant and the corpulent former air ace would never have Hitler's ear again when it came to foreign policy. Hitler may have been obliged to shelve his plans to absorb Bohemia and Moravia, but only until the next opportunity arose.

In Berlin, Klepper's mind was put at rest that war had been avoided. There was, however, no mention of the fate of the Czechs. He noted that the feeling of happiness was universal; even voices on the telephone sounded different. Everyone was 'exhausted and happy'; Hitler's 'magic was shattered'. In the church in Berlin-Mariendorf that Sunday, people cried as they sang the *Leuthen Chorale*[xi] – '*Nun danket alle Gott!*'[96] Goebbels retired to bed 'as happy as a child'. Germany's prestige 'had grown monstrously, now we are really a world power and that means arm! Arm! Arm!'[97] The 'old woman' Göring was naturally as pleased as Punch at his success. He had got the resources he wanted and he had managed to avert a conflict: 'he fought bravely for the sake of peace'.[98] He woke Emmy at the conclusion of the conference and told her, 'We've pulled it off . . . it's peace.' He was delighted at all that he had acquired for his Four Year Plan. Taking Ciano to the station the next morning, he told the Italian: 'Now, there's going to be rearmament the likes of which the world has never seen.'[99]

Far away in China, the German Rhodes Scholar Adam von Trott zu Solz, who was later to perish for his part in the 20th July Plot, wrote

[xi] So called because the wounded soldiers sang it spontaneously on the battlefield at Leuthen on 5 December 1757, once Frederick the Great's victory was assured.

to his friend Shiela Grant Duff on 1 October. He felt the one advantage of what had taken place was that it had been a European decision, and not merely a Germano-Czech one, 'but I agree with you in your present apprehensions'.

He wrote again on the 6th:

I confess that I failed to realize the intrinsic turning point which came about with the Anschluss and which opened up a path for a coercive settlement of the Central European problem – which I had never considered possible with the power, prestige and commitments of the Western Democracies in that area. Though I did realize there was in England a large body of opinion that favoured a negotiated settlement of the Sudeten question in Germany's favour, I believed that France and Russia would remain intransigent on the matter and that your country would back [them] up . . .[100]

Trott's father's death that month ended his Asian idyll. When he got home he learned of the opposition in the army and the Wilhelmstrasse. They would have to shelve their plans too. There was a furious reaction against Canaris and Kleist-Schmenzin and all those who had implied that Britain would fight. For generals like Gerd von Rundstedt, who had been initiated into the plot by his friend Kleist, the whole thing now felt like a hoax.

Brauchitsch would hear no more talk of a revolt; the servile Keitel had been kept out of the picture from the start; Halder, who had been found slumped at his desk by Hitler's adjutant, Engel, had despondently told General von Witzleben, the most eager of the rebels, that he could not be answerable for military action against Hitler if Mr Chamberlain found a peaceable solution to the Czechoslovak dispute. Kleist went back to his estates in Pomerania, utterly disillusioned.[101]

There was not to be another coordinated attempt to remove the Führer until 20 July 1944.

DOORS CLOSING

On 7 September Italy slammed a door shut: Jews were now to be defined racially and not religiously. Up until then, Italy had still been on the escape route for many baptized Jews. Now, foreign Jews who had settled in Italy after 1919 were to be expelled. The measure affected as many as 40,000 people, including an estimated 6,000 Austrian and German Jews. There were around 70,000 Jews living in Italy, defined as full Jews, with two Jewish parents. From 3 September they were no longer permitted to enter Italian schools and universities.[102] In Rome, Pius XI quietly made his views clear to a group of Belgian pilgrims on the 6th after delivering a reading about Abraham, 'our father, our ancestor'. He said, 'Antisemitism is not compatible with the sublime thought and reality which are expressed in this text. It is not possible for Christians to participate in antisemitism. Spiritually, we are Semites.'[103]

Collard performed his last nineteen baptisms on 15 September before returning to Cologne. Following his departure there were developments in Britain. Appeasement was in the air. An initiative from Sir Wyndham Deedes led to the creation of a Christian Council to assist Jews from Germany and Austria. The new body joined the others in Bloomsbury House, which had campaigned for non-Aryan Christians, children and students, as well as the Quakers' own operation. It would put pressure on the Dominions to accept the Jews.[104] Collard's departure came at a time when the first large-scale releases were being made from Dachau. Some were not so lucky: Bruno Heilig was transferred to Buchenwald on the 22nd, and if anything the camp was even grimmer,[105] although one of the capos turned out to be a relatively sympathetic Prussian Junker whose grandmother was a Jew.

On 17 September Fred Richter appeared before an examining magistrate at the *Landgericht* (state court) in Vienna and denied any involvement in espionage. He maintained he had only expressed an interest in Tucek's invention.

The Jews showed little sympathy for the Czechs. President Beneš created the problem for himself by his attempts to prevent a Habsburg restoration in 1934 and 1935: 'Better Hitler than Habsburg,' he is supposed to have said. Weisl predicted that six million Jewish lives would now be lost between the Rhine and the Dniester.[106]

Nazi methods in Austria were not always crowned with success. In Mistelbach, near the Czech border, the Jews were refusing to sell out. The Gestapo suggested they should be pushed across the frontier as their closeness to Czechoslovakia caused a danger of communist infiltration. The huge taxes levied on Jews leaving the country were also a disincentive. Eichmann was up against Göring. The latter wanted to fill the coffers of the state at the expense of the Jews, while Eichmann desired the fastest emigration possible.[107] The number of Jews marooned in a hostile Central Europe was causing alarm in Jewish circles: there were 20,000 in the Sudetenland, which would soon be prey to Hitler's racial policies; a further 385,000 were in rump Czechoslovakia, which was about to pass racial laws of its own; there were 410,000 in Hungary, which had already promulgated racial laws; and 78,000 in Jugoslavia, where the government had decreed measures against the Jews. Romania had 800,000 with 50,000 Christian converts. Poland had another 3.3 million. If you included 170,000 in Austria and 350,000 remaining in Germany, that made a European total of 4.1 million, not including Russia.[108] Latvia was now the sole European country that remained open to Jews.[109]

In the autumn of 1938 there were an estimated 200 Austrian Jews stranded in Jugoslavia.[110] At the beginning of October, however, the Jugoslav government finally ruled that it intended to expel all foreign Jews in three months.[111] The Dutch too were showing frustration at the number of illegal immigrants, and on 20 September the Jewish Telegraphic Agency reported that forty-four Austrian Jews had been sent home from Rotterdam.[112] The British were flexing their muscles again over Palestine. Cyprus, with its proximity to the Mandate territory, was an obvious magnet. The numbers of Jews landing was causing concern, with thirty to forty fresh refugees arriving every week.[113] On 21 September it was reported that an 800-man transport from Vienna had been sent back. Weisl had promises of £1,000 to grease palms, but he needed twice that.

In the wake of Evian he noted that Nicaragua was prepared to take in 3,000 Jews, but they had to hand over $100 on landing.[114]

The news from Vienna was not all doom and gloom: there was a small sprinkling of that frivolity for which the city is famous. While the leaders of the Western world met to assign Hitler the German-speaking parts of Czechoslovakia, a court convened in the former Austrian capital to decide who possessed the right to sell the 'original' *Sachertorte* (chocolate cake), Sacher's Hotel or the café Demel. The court ruled in Sacher's favour: the 'original' had to come from their kitchens.[115]

10

OCTOBER

The German Army officially took control of the Czech borderlands on 1 October. The Poles wasted no time either in occupying Teschen and Freistadt, east of Mährisch Östrau. They went in the following day. In Germany's new *Gaue* the Jews were now at great risk. There were 27,000 Jews and non-Aryan Christians in the Sudetenland. In the summer there had been antisemitic riots in Eger, Asch and Karlsbad, and Jewish shops had been ransacked. Famous spas like Carlsbad and Marienbad had been immensely popular with rich Jews. *Der Stürmer* reckoned that 80 per cent of Carlsbad's customers were Jewish, noting maliciously that although Jews had lost the choice to regain their health at Carlsbad, they could keep fit by running.[1] The doctors who treated them were also likely to be Jews. There were other powerful Jewish clans in the region: the hop merchants of Saaz, for example, were largely Jewish. The message was clear, and thousands fled.

The Czech government was heartless towards its citizens, reneged on stipulations made at Munich that accorded a 'choice of residence' to the Sudetenländer, and forcibly returned as many as it could find to the German occupied areas.[2] Although the Munich Agreement had laid down a provision for citizens to 'opt' for Germany or Czechoslovakia, the Czechs refused protection to Jews who feared for their safety under the Nazis.[3] Many eluded them. By May 1939 only a tenth of that number remained in the new German Gaue. It was not only the Jews the Czechs were reluctant to accept: there were thousands of ethnic German Social Democrats too. The Nazis said they had no right to opt for Czechoslovakia. There were also 5–6,000 Germans who had taken refuge in Prague and other parts of Czechoslovakia after Hitler's assumption of power. There was discrimination against Sudeten Jews, who were denied access to the funds they had been able to bring out, and the others who had crossed the demarcation lines penniless. The British donated £10 million to help alleviate the situation. This failed to prevent the Czechs from putting pressure on a quarter of a million Jews in the country to emigrate.[4] Sopade, the organization of German socialists in exile, also decided it was prudent to run. They set up their new home in Paris.

The new Czech government under President Emil Hàcha sought a rapprochement with Germany and aligned its policies accordingly. The French were to wind up their alliance with the country – which had done the Czechs little good – and the Czechs themselves decided to abandon their flirtation with the Soviet Union. German-style restrictions on the movement and employment of Jews were also introduced. On 11 October Mastny assured Göring that the Czechs would 'seriously tackle the Jewish problem'.[5] To some extent the attitude of the new Czech Second Republic was dictated by weakness. Stripped of their fortifications, they now had no means of holding the Germans back. As it was, the settlement had been clumsy: 478,589 ethnic Germans remained in rump Czechoslovakia, while 676,478 Czechs were now living in Germany. Those half a million Germans were hardly popular either.[6] Hitler was still straining at the leash. As he told Goebbels on the evening of the 2nd, it was his unshakable decision to smash Czecho. 'And he will make it happen too: this dead, amorphous, artificial state must go.'[7]

Groscurth accompanied Admiral Canaris on his tour of inspection of the new German Gaue. Canaris was anxious to avoid the Gestapo, who had made as many as 200 arrests by the 3rd of the month. He did not wish to be seen shaking hands with either Himmler or Heydrich.[8] In the regular army there was resentment against the SS too. General

Bock complained about Heydrich but Groscurth noted that they confined themselves to grumbling: 'No general dares show this criminal the door.'[9] Groscurth nonetheless noted the excitement of the Sudetenländer: 'There is a marked contrast with Austria. The people there were more or less drunk; here, however, you note a real liberation and a sigh of relief from people who have been freed of a heavy load.'[10]

Hitler went on a tour of the Czech defences on the 3rd and 4th. SS bands played his favourite *Badenweiler March*. He recognized Canaris and stopped his car to greet him. In his cavalcade of thirty-odd cars there were just three Wehrmacht men; the rest were SS or Sudetenländer. The RAM was with him, in the grey diplomatic uniform with 'lots of gold'.[11] Groscurth discovered a boorish Reichenau knocking back *Sekt*, infatuated with Hitler. He repeated some of his hero's remarks on Chamberlain and Daladier. The latter he called a 'master baker'. Groscurth remarked that this was a case of the pot calling the kettle black.[12] Rundstedt had a different view: 'Canaris, how long do we have to put up with this foolish performance?'[13]

Groscurth was sent on a second tour of duty, this time on Henlein's staff. Contrary to the rumours running riot in the SS, the Sudeten leader revealed himself as a family man with a fondness for burgundy. He had set up his HQ in a deserted Jewish villa. While Groscurth explored the new *Gaue* he noted the misery of the 40,000 or so Czech coalminers around Dux and Brux, who had now become German citizens. In a fish factory he was greeted with shouts of '*Heil Hitler*' by the 500 chiefly women staff but was told that a few days before they would have cried, '*Heil Moskau!*'[14] Elsewhere Hitler observed the Czech fortresses were built in the same style as France's Maginot Line. He then turned them over to the Wehrmacht for gunnery practice. He was still sulking.[15] Armed with his experiences of the Czech defences, he toured his own West Wall before returning to Munich on 14 October. He saw the new Czech Foreign Minister, Frantisek Chvalkovsky, and uttered furious threats about how quickly he could crush them were they ever to transgress. On 21 October Hitler issued plans to take the port of Memel.

The Slovaks declared themselves an autonomous region on the 7th just as Göring took off for a tour of the new German *Gaue* centred on the town of Reichenberg, where Henlein had established his headquarters. Göring was convinced that the rest of Bohemia and Moravia would fall like ripe fruit into German hands. There were drawbacks for the Nazis: eventually Germany would acquire all those Czech Jews who had failed to flee, just as they had gained a further 200,000 Jews in Austria. These disadvantages would become all the greater when Germany invaded Poland a year later. It was relatively easy to find homes for lawyers and doctors from the sophisticated assimilated Jews of Vienna and Prague, who had contacts abroad who could issue them with guarantees. There would be few if any takers for the *shtetl* Jews. As Germany mopped up more and more land to the east, the likelihood of a 'radical' solution to the 'Jewish problem' became all the greater.

Yet more doors were closing. On 1 October Argentina threatened to revoke 600 visas it had granted to Jews from the Reich. This would also affect those travelling through Argentina to the landlocked South American states. George Rublee, the director of the committee concerned with Jewish emigration, quickly made them reconsider.[16] On 5 October the Swiss Police President, Dr Rothmund, finally succeeded in putting pressure on the German authorities to stamp Jewish passports with a large red J, the better to identify would-be Jewish immigrants and turn them back at the frontier. Otherwise they would interpret the passport as invalid. This was the final stage of a long process of trying to make Jewish passports distinct from those of Gentiles.[17] The Swiss authorities had clearly had enough: 7,000 Jews had settled in the country since 1933, 2,000 of them arriving illegally from Austria.[18] The Polish government adopted the same policy the very next day.[19]

On the 6th a letter went out from the SS-man Peworezky to the SD in Vienna: an operation was planned in the suburb of Wieden for the

10th which would encourage as many Jews as possible to hurry up and leave. The first to be evicted were Czech Jews. Any Jews who did not possess the requisite papers would simply be pushed over the Czech frontier. If they were penniless they were to be given 40 RM. It was to be dressed up to look like a 'spontaneous demonstration', as the Party was not meant to be behind it. Force would combat resistance. Jews were cleared from houses in the prosperous areas of Ottakring, Hernals, Währing and Döbling and boarded on trains. No passports were required. The next day Jews in the suburbs of Mauer, Atzgersdorf, Liesing, Percholdsdorf and Mödling were accorded the same treatment. They had to hand over their keys.[20]

On the 7th the Nazis celebrated their victory in the Sudetenland by intimidating Jews in the plush Viennese suburb of Döbling, threatening them with 'Dachau or worse'. *The Times* actually reported that Jews were being released from Dachau and alluded to the interest in baptism among the assimilated Jews of the city:

> It is reliably reported that besides Mr Frederick Richter, the verger of the Anglican Church in Vienna (who is a British subject of Austrian birth), eighteen sextons, registrars, and other officials of various Roman Catholic churches in Vienna have been arrested during the past three months on charges of forging or falsification of baptismal certificates for Jews.[21]

The Nazis were also closing the Catholic associations, bringing them into line with their own and taking away their flags and banners. Religious instruction in schools was being discontinued, and schools closed while the regime helped itself to the treasures of Austria's monasteries. Hundreds of priests had been packed off to Dachau. Religious symbols and holidays came under fire too.[22] The Nazis had enjoyed some success in luring Austrians away from the Church, but for many the Anschluss was not looking as attractive to pious Austrians or south Germans as it had done in March. It was high time for Cardinal Innitzer to make a stand. On 7 October he addressed some 6–8,000 young Catholics in the cathedral in what Goebbels called a 'cheeky homily': 'My beloved Catholic youth of Vienna, we will affirm our faith from now on and in these times, with yet more strength and resolution . . . Christ is our Führer and king!' he told them. 'Guard your belief and stand firm! For only belief can bring happiness!'[23]

The homily resulted in a demonstration of support outside the Archbishop's palace: '*Lieber Bischof, sei so nett: zeige Dich am Fensterbrett.*'[i] The youths also cried, 'Innitzer command, we will obey!' – mocking the Nazi formula – and 'Christ is our Führer!'[24] A crowd of 200 Hitler Youths tried unsuccessfully to disperse them and were scattered in their turn. Some of the demonstrators were arrested. The storming of the Archbishop's palace the next day poured cold water on any remaining enthusiasm for Hitler there might have been among the Austrian clergy.[25] Around fifty members of the Hitler Youth aged between fourteen and twenty-five spent forty minutes breaking and burning everything they could, including 1,245 window-panes. What they did not break they stole. They also defenestrated Father Johann Krawarik, breaking his thigh-bone.[26] Goebbels did not want the foreign press to make too much of the story, and played it down.

Goebbels might have hoped to conceal the new persecution of the Church in Austria but Bürckel answered Innitzer in his speech on the Heldenplatz in Vienna on the 13th. He denounced the Church, and the crowd carried banners with the legend 'String up the priests!'[27] At 10 p.m. that day a mob of twenty or thirty people attacked the Cistercians in Lilienfeld, breaking 487 panes of glass while they claimed to be searching for weapons. One of the men told the monks: 'You have Innitzer to thank for this.'[28] On 17 October all religious schools were closed, including Austria's oldest academy, the monastic Gymnasium in Kremsmünster. In rural Württemberg there was still confusion as to the level of participation in business life allowed to the Jews. Since February it had been unclear as to whether the Jews were

---

[i] 'Dear Bishop, if you will, show your face at the windowsill.'

allowed to trade in local markets. As far as farmers were concerned, as long as they came to market, they were happy to carry on doing business with them. A formal prohibition was only issued in October.[29]

SAARBRÜCKEN

Hitler's anger over Munich had not abated. Prompted by the opening of the Westmark *Gau*'s new theatre, he made what Hassell called an 'incomprehensibly rude' speech in Saarbrücken on the 9th. He attacked Duff Cooper, who had resigned from the Cabinet over Munich, and Eden and Churchill as warmongers and expressed his resentment at Munich and foreign interference in the question of the German Jews. He accused his British critics of behaving like 'governesses' and revelled in their problems in Palestine.[30] After the speech there was a performance of *The Flying Dutchman*.

Outside Germany it was thought that the speech was a signal he would soon be on the march again. Goebbels had been present and found the reaction to the speech in the foreign press hard to understand: 'It wasn't at all aggressive and most of it was given off the cuff.'[31] He reported that his master had arrived 'tired and weary' and full of his impressions of the Sudetenland. Hitler told his minister that having seen the Czech bunkers, he now realized that they would have cost much blood, and he believed he had done the right thing, 'and we will swallow this Czecho one day. We have to free the road to the Balkans.'[32]

The one consolation for Hitler was the new theatre, a representative Nazi-style building designed by Paul Baumgarten. He promptly decided that Baumgarten should draw up the designs for the theatre in his city of Linz. Hitler retired to Bad Godesberg, where he met up with the RAM on the 12th. The German Foreign Office was to issue a statement that the country had no further territorial demands in Bohemia and Moravia. Hitler declined to help the

Hungarians over Pressburg, as the Hungarians had not helped him over the Sudetenland.[33]

He travelled from there to the Berghof. Goebbels was still in the doghouse and Hitler was arbitrating between him and Magda. On the 23rd Goebbels was summoned to his master, where the couple's heads were knocked together. He resigned himself to his fate like a chastened cur: '. . . I submit and arrange my personal wellbeing and happiness in the interests of the state and the people.'[34] It was the Führer who 'remade the marriage' and the Führer, not his humiliated propaganda chief, who ordered photographs to be taken for the press of the happy reconciliation. A picture on the front page of the *Berliner Illustrierte Zeitung* showed the three of them together. Only Hitler was smiling.[35]

When he wasn't too cross with Goebbels, he spoke to him about future plans. 'In the distant future he sees a really difficult fight ahead, probably with England [sic].'[36] At a birthday party Hitler told guests that all Germans were behind him. 'Only the ten thousand in the upper stratum have any doubts.'[37] The French ambassador François-Poncet went to Berchtesgaden to say farewell to Hitler on the 17th. The French had been alarmed by the Saarbrücken speech and were now seeking a Franco-German declaration that would tie Hitler's hands. There must have been a worry in the Quai d'Orsay that Hitler would snatch Alsace-Lorraine. From the German side, it was thought that the moment might be ripe to split the French from the British. Saarbrücken had been rude about the latter: the French had been let off the hook. François-Poncet was very impressed by the setting, and the amazing piece of engineering that was the so-called 'Eagle's Nest': Hitler's tearoom 1,900 metres up, which put the Frenchman in mind of Knights of the Holy Grail at Monsalvat. François-Poncet was struck by what a baffling person Hitler was. Goebbels held the diplomat in high esteem, and regretted his going to Rome.[38]

Hitler returned to Austria, slipping back across the old border on 20 October into his new Moravian territories, where Groscurth listened to a speech he made to a small circle. He described it as 'dangerous': 'it was peppered with attacks on the English [sic], French, and above all the Hungarians, whom he characterized as cowards and wet rags'. He did imitations of the Hungarian minister and heaped praise on the Poles and Jugoslavs. The Polish were 'a great people', ambassador Lipski 'a statesman and towering intellect'. Stojadinovich was also acclaimed.[39] Hitler was back on form.

NEW PLANS FOR THE JEWS

Maximilian Reich was released from Dachau on 12 October after more than six months of servitude. His wife in Vienna had learned that six was standard for Jewish journalists with exit papers. As a Gentile reminded him before he left, there was no such hope for the many communists; they were there until the end. A guard showed him the way to Weimar and respectfully called him 'Sie'. He had time to kill at the station, but was not prepared to be seduced into the buffet by well-wishers who recognized him as a former inmate. One man enquired whether he had money; another called him Kumpel (mate) and wondered whether he needed help. He realized that it was true what they said in the camp: there were human beings out there.[40] He arrived at the East Station in Vienna. The family had been alerted by telegram, but his wife failed to recognize her husband: he was wearing a worn-out suit that had been lent to him; his head had been shaved, and he had lost his moustache; he was also emaciated. The second time she entered the station she spotted him. She had a shirt and a suit in a case for him to change into; they had to buy a hat in the Mariahilferstrasse on the way home.[41] Some, at least, of his dignity had been restored.

On 14 October there was a significant meeting chaired by Reichsmarschall Göring at the Air Ministry in Berlin, in the course of which the minister intimated that Hitler had big plans. He almost certainly meant war. The economy was in a parlous state; foreign currency reserves had been used up, and work performance had dwindled; he, Göring, was now going to produce some radical solutions. Once again it was Henry VIII's technique he was suggesting: rob the richest part of the community. In good King Harry's time it had been the Church, but Göring was going to get the money from the Jews by 'eliminating them from the German economy'. The next day all Jewish passports were rescinded in the Altreich. This meant that they had to apply anew. It was a further measure to prevent their money from leaving the country. It also provided an opportunity for the police to make a little money on the side.

There were also changes in the administration of the Ostmark. Vienna was to be reduced to a purely administrative entity. New areas to the south were made part of a 'Greater Vienna', a city of two million souls. A minor pogrom also took place on 14 October, and the windows of seven synagogues were broken. The next day seven more were profaned in the Jewish Second District. On the 16th a synagogue was torched in the Tempelgasse, and on the 17th two prayer houses were destroyed in the Second District. The destruction continued until the 19th.[42]

Later that year, the IKG in Vienna produced figures for emigration up to 15 October. Of the 165,000 members before 11 March, 40,000 or so had already left. The largest number (2,000) had reached the US, followed by Palestine (1,384) and Britain (1,321); 681 had gone to Switzerland and 480 to Czechoslovakia. A total of 444 had reached Argentina, 155 Australia, 136 Greece, 88 Cyprus (these last two were stage-posts for Palestine), 47 Bolivia and nine Canada.[43] On 22 October *The Times* reported that there were 5,000 illegal Jewish immigrants in Belgium without visible means of support. The Belgian government had decided to intern 1,400, rather than expelling them.[44] The British were having considerable problems with Palestine at the time, with the Arabs rioting and striking against the increasing numbers of Jews. Not only were many of Germany and Austria's Jews knocking on the door but measures against them introduced by the Second Republic in Czechoslovakia meant that Czech Jews were also looking for asylum.

It wasn't only the Jews who were suffering as outlaws; Germany was now doing away with most vestiges of the rule of law. On 22 October Hitler spoke to proclaim that '. . . every means adopted for carrying out the will of the Leader is considered legal, even though it may conflict with existing statutes and precedents'.[45] In June that year all security police – the Gestapo and the Kripo (criminal police) – were enrolled in the SS, and therefore became subservient to the Party through the SD. It was a process that reached its inevitable end when the police were taken away from the Ministry of the Interior and placed under the control of the SS. There were now no legal controls on the police and divergent political opinion was *ipso facto* a crime.

Meanwhile other parts of Central Europe were playing games with their Jewish citizens. Responding to the pressure exerted by their neighbours, the Germans made moves to expel all their *Ostjuden* – generally Russian Jews who had settled as a result of the pogroms and the Russian Revolution.

At the beginning of 1938 they were given weeks to get out or face imprisonment and the confiscation of their belongings. The next move was against the Romanian Jews. After the Germans moved into Austria and the Sudetenland it was the moment to oust Czech and Slovak Jews. Camps were established for them in no-man's-land, as their countries of origin were very reluctant to take them back.[46]

POLAND

A shared antipathy to Jews led to the end of the 'benevolent neutrality' that existed between Germany and Poland.[47] There were around 3.3 million Jews in Poland: just under 10 per cent of the population. Their movements were restricted and antisemitism was endemic. Earlier that year Ciano had defined the relationship between the two countries, which managed to coexist despite the fact that Poland had been re-created out of the rib of Prussia: 'The Polish Corridor is accepted for an indefinite period by Germany, which actually desires to see the power of Poland increased as a means of strengthening the anti-Bolshevik barrier.'[48] The sticking point was the very large number of Polish Jews living in Germany and smaller groups in Austria. Despite Polish citizenship, the Poles refused to readmit them; nor did they want to return, as many of them had fled to Germany in the first place to escape from pogroms and persecution in Poland or the Ukraine. In 1936 the Poles had produced plans to make all Jews emigrate and on 31 March 1938 they rescinded the citizenship of all Polish Jews who had lived abroad for more than five years. Nearly 40 per cent of these expatriate Polish Jews had been born in Germany.

Such policies found favour in Poland, where successive governments had been trying to steal a march on the National Democratic or Endek Party, with its antisemitic policies and calls for ghettoes and boycotts of Jewish businesses. There was a certain rapport between Göring and Jozef Beck, the Polish Foreign Minister. Beck had served in the German cavalry in the First World War and liked the Germans, but disliked both the French and the Russians. His policy was anti-Bolshevik, intending to maintain an equal distance between Soviet Russia and Nazi Germany. The timing of the Polish move was clumsy, however, as Göring was still trying to woo the Poles into approving an alliance directed against Russia, where Germany later intended to create its empire, and was dangling the Ukraine at Poland as compensation for border changes in the west.

The acquisition of the Teschen pocket with its quarter of a million Poles and the railway knot at Oderberg made the Germans more popular in Poland too. Indeed, there had been cries of 'Long live Hitler!' in Warsaw after the Polish incursion.[49] Ribbentrop stormed in and held talks with the Polish ambassador, Lipski. On the 24th Lipski was invited to Berchtesgaden. In return for a railway line or motorway to link Germany with its estranged province of East Prussia, and possibly some border changes around Posen-Poznan, Germany was prepared to create a free port for Poland somewhere near Danzig. There would also be a sweetener of a non-aggression treaty lasting twenty-five years guaranteeing the present frontiers. Danzig itself would naturally return to Germany under the same arrangements.

While such treaties were not worth the paper they were printed on, it is an indication that the Germans were not seeking radical border changes in Poland for the time being; but Ribbentrop was unable to sell the deal. Under his tenure at the Wilhemstrasse, the Poles changed from friends to enemies. They took no interest in the offer, which betrayed a certain degree of pragmatism on the part of the Germans, as any revision of the Polish–German border was bound to be popular with the German people and the Wehrmacht. As far as Memel was concerned, things were coming to a head with mass protests against Lithuanian rule.

Meanwhile, the official Foreign Minister of the Third Reich, Ribbentrop, was in Rome at Hitler's behest, trying once again to make the Italians sign a tripartite military pact with Germany and Japan. The Japanese alliance was meant to deter America from coming to the aid of Britain and France, his enemies in the West. He told Mussolini that Germany would be ready for war with Britain and France from the beginning of 1939. Neither Mussolini nor his son-in-law Ciano appreciated the visit. Mussolini told Ciano, 'You only have to look at his head to see that he has a very small brain.'[50] Ciano, for his part, thought Ribbentrop 'vain, lightweight, loquacious . . . He has fixed in his head the idea of war, he wants war, his war.'[51] Whether Mussolini and Ciano despised Ribbentrop or not, they signed on 6 November.

THE EXPULSION OF THE POLISH JEWS

German–Polish relations were declining ever further. On the 6th the Polish government had announced that 30 October was the last date for the renewal of passports for Polish Jews. On 24 October

Ribbentrop demanded the return of the city of Danzig and free access to East Prussia through the Polish Corridor. On the 27th and the 28th the Gestapo, working with the German Foreign Office, took the decision to expel the *Ostjuden* and some 17,000 Polish Jews were pushed over the Polish border. A memo from Best dated the 29th justified the policy, saying that the Poles were foisting 70,000 Jews on Germany.[52] Those selected for expulsion came from Germany, Austria and the Sudetenland. The Gestapo entered schools in Berlin and dragged Jewish children away from their lessons.[53] One of those expelled at the time was the later literary critic Marcel Reich-Ranicki, who had just finished school in Berlin. On the morning of the 28th he was woken by a policeman bringing him a document telling him to leave Germany within a fortnight. When Reich-Ranicki objected that he had two weeks, the policeman said, 'No, come along at once.'

He was allowed to take five marks and a briefcase. He put in a Balzac novella and a handkerchief. Everything else had to be left behind. Reich-Ranicki had no idea why he was receiving this treatment, and felt someone must have borne false witness. It became clearer at the police station.

> Here I immediately found myself among ten or perhaps twenty fellow victims. They were Jews, all of them older than me . . . They were speaking perfect German and not a word of Polish. They had either been born in Germany, or had come to Germany as small children and attended school there. But like me they all, as I soon discovered, had Polish passports.

Only men were expelled from Berlin, although other cities had sent the women away too. When it was dark later that afternoon, they were transferred to a siding at the Schlesischer Bahnhof where a train was waiting. Everything was done quietly and mostly by night. No one was supposed to see. At the frontier they had to form up in columns. There were shouts and shots fired. Then they were driven into a Polish train, where the doors were sealed from the outside. It was packed, and many of the women were wearing nightgowns under their coats: they had not been given time to dress.[54]

The German plan was to get rid of the Jews before they finally ceased to be Poles and became their responsibility. As the Poles were not willing to take them back, around 8,000 of them sat in gypsy camps in no-man's-land from November 1938 until August 1939, while Polish Christians and Jews administered aid. Of the 4,000 who arrived in Gdynia by ship from Danzig, only 1,500 were allowed to land. The rest had to remain on board. In revenge the Poles expelled Germans from the former German areas of Poznan and Pommerelen. Later the expulsions were limited to German Jews.[55] The German expulsions, and the brutal way they were carried out, provided the Gestapo with what was for them valuable experience in rapid deportation. The Polish Jews were allowed to take the very minimum with them, and often had to put up with nights of imprisonment before they were taken to the border. At the beginning of November 'Fips' wallowed in the Jews' despair in *Der Stürmer*: 'Three simple questions for Hebrews – What can I do against the Nazis? How do I get my money out of the country? Where oh where can I – a proper Talmud Jew – settle in peace?'[56]

The tug of war over the Jews had been a bad omen for future good relations between the two countries. When Canaris met Weizsäcker on 12 December, the diplomat thought war with Poland unavoidable, despite Ribbentrop's best efforts to maintain the strongest ties with the Poles, while pursuing his war against the West.[57]

11

NOVEMBER

More frontiers were being redrawn. On 2 November the German and Italian Foreign Ministers met in Vienna to arbitrate between the Czechs and the Hungarians over the Slovakian border. Ciano ran into Göring in the Imperial. He was wearing a flashy grey suit, a ruby tie-pin and more large rubies on his fingers. In his buttonhole was a large Nazi eagle with diamonds. The Italian found 'a slight suggestion of Al Capone'.[1] Ribbentrop surprised Ciano by being pro-Czech, which he found inconsistent with the attitude towards the country he had espoused just a month before. Ciano thought Hàcha should give Ribbentrop a medal. Largely as a result of Ciano's superior preparation, the Hungarians recouped 12,000 square kilometres of territory but failed to regain their city of Pressburg (Bratislava). It spelled more bad news for the Jews, as the newly autonomous Slovak government also wanted to see the back of them. Klepper quoted a distressing report from Pressburg: 'Without interruption, entire goods trains filled with Jews are rolling through Pressburg and into the area ceded to Hungary.' The number of Jews was estimated at between 3,000 and 4,000, but it was thought the number from all over Slovakia was far higher. They had all been ejected from Czechoslovakia without a penny 'in compensation for the damage that Jews had wrought in Slovakia'.[2]

There was a lull in the impending storm on 4 November, when Edda Göring was christened by Reich Bishop Müller. She received some fine presents: a Cranach from Milch, and another from the city of Cologne.

The Luftwaffe subscribed to build a miniature copy of Frederick the Great's palace at Sanssouci in an orchard at Carinhall, where she might play with her dolls. There was shock and horror when it was discovered that Edda Göring's nanny was not a Party member. Emmy confessed that she wasn't one either. Hitler put the matter right at Christmas by sending her a gold Party badge and investing her with the number of a member who had conveniently expired.[3] Göring's star was in the ascendant again. Goebbels wrote, 'He goes his own way, and does not allow himself to be waylaid by the hyper-radicals in the Party.'[4] The Propaganda Minister was still down in the dumps. Despite Hitler's ukase at Berchtesgaden, he was finding Magda hard to take. He went to the theatre with her on 26 October. Three days later it was his birthday, the saddest of his life. It was not helped by a telegram from Hitler that was 'short and frosty'. He needed to find a way back into his master's favour.[5]

Hitler was also enjoying Berlin's cultural life. He went to see Werner Egk's new opera based on the tale of Peer Gynt. Critics found a good deal of the degenerate composer Kurt Weill in the music, but either Hitler didn't notice or he didn't care. He invited Egk to his box and gave him a commission worth 10,000 RM. *Peer Gynt* became standard repertory for the opera houses of the Third Reich. It was almost certainly superior to some of the new music composed that year, such as Cesar Bresgen and Heinrich Spitha's three-movement cantata *SA Lives for Ever*, which was based on the *Horst-Wessel-Lied*.[6]

HERSCHEL GRYNSZPAN

Two of the Polish Jews expelled from Germany were Sendel and Ryfka Grynszpan. They had been herded into a barracks in the town of Zbaszyn with 500 others. Twenty Jews died on the first day alone. Their seventeen-year-old son Herschel was living illegally in Paris helping his uncle Abraham, a tailor. Here he received word of their situation on 3 November. After an argument with his uncle on the 6th, he left his flat and spent the night in the Hôtel de Suez. He had been told that his request to remain in France had been declined. The next day he purchased a revolver for 245 FF and loaded it at 'Tout va bien', a homosexual bar. He went to the German embassy, where he told reception he had a document to give to a 'secretary'. A Frau Mathes showed him the door to the office of the Secretary to the Legation, Ernst vom Rath, while an embassy servant called Nagorka asked if he could have the document to take to Rath. Grynszpan, however, insisted on seeing Rath in person. The latter, hearing Grynszpan's name, ordered him shown in. Nagorka heard screams: Grynszpan had fired five bullets, two of which inflicted serious wounds. He was later arrested by the French police. Rath was operated on at once, the surgeons removing his pancreas. Hitler sent his personal surgeon Karl Brandt assisted by Georg Magnus and there was hope for a while, but his injuries turned out to be too grave. Grynszpan later admitted killing Rath to avenge his family.[7]

The official version still leaves many questions unanswered, especially as the evidence was falsified in 1942 and a story inserted that Grynszpan had originally intended to kill the ambassador, Graf Welczek. The Nazis caught Grynszpan after the fall of France and put him in Sachsenhausen concentration camp while they concocted a show trial for treason (he was not a German and could not have committed such a crime). He was said to have confessed to having had a passionate affair with Rath and that he had been able to afford his lifestyle – the hotel, the revolver – from the money he earned as a homosexual prostitute. Rath was a prominent homosexual who frequented louche bars such as 'Le Boeuf sur le toit' and was known in their circles as 'Madame Ambassadeur' or 'Notre Dame de Paris'. He had just returned from the German consulate in Calcutta with a dose of anal gonorrhoea. One of the men who claimed to have been aware of the relationship was André Gide.[8] Grynszpan is supposed to have shot Rath because he had failed to secure papers for him allowing him to remain in France – hence the 'document'. The revelation of the relationship led to the indefinite postponement of the trial. Grynszpan's ultimate fate is uncertain. He was officially declared dead in 1960 but some people believe that he survived the war and was living in Paris in the sixties, working as a car mechanic.[9]

Was it a Nazi plot intended to be used as a pretext to launch a pogrom against the Jews? An attack on a German diplomat abroad, as a pretext for some action within the Reich, was one of the Nazis' standard tricks. Heydrich had planned to sacrifice Papen in Vienna and Eisenlöhr in Prague in just this way. On the other hand, not all putative assassinations of Germans by Jews were Nazi fakes. In 1936 Wilhelm Gustloff, head of the Swiss Nazi Party, was gunned down in Davos by David Frankfurter, a Jewish student; no one has suggested that Frankfurter was an unwitting Nazi agent. The Gustloff case had been frustrating to the Nazis, as any attempt to punish the Jews might have resulted in an international boycott of the Olympic Games.

There were reports that the hue and cry over Rath's attempted assassination extended as far as the non-Czech areas of Czechoslovakia.[10] All the German newspapers had to cover the story. The *Völkischer Beobachter* was supposed to voice the attitudes of right-thinking Germans:

> It is clear that the German people will draw their own conclusions from this new deed. It is an impossible situation, that within our borders hundreds and thousands rule over whole streets of shops, occupy places of pleasure and as 'foreign' householders pocket the money paid to them by German tenants, while the racial comrades abroad call for war against Germany and gun down German public servants . . . These shots fired in Paris will not just mean the beginning of a new attitude to the Jewish question, we hope that they will be a signal for those foreigners who up to now have failed to understand the

only person who stands in the way of a closer cooperation between peoples is the international Jew.[11]

On the 8th the first outrages took place against the Jews. Two synagogues were set on fire and Jewish shops attacked in Vienna. That same day Himmler gave one of his pithiest definitions of the nature of political and ideological antisemitism. He noted with appreciation that increasing numbers of people were opposed to the Jews:

We must be clear that in the next ten years we face unprecedented conflicts of a critical nature. It is not only the battle of the nations . . . it is the ideological battle against all Jews, freemasons, Marxists and the churches of the world. These forces, behind which I assume to be the Jews . . . are clear that if Germany and Italy are not destroyed, it will be them that are eliminated. That is elementary. In Germany the Jew cannot hold out. It is a matter of time. We will drive them more and more by unrivalled ruthlessness. Italy is going the same way and Poland does not want its Jews . . .

The other states, Sweden, Norway, Denmark, Holland and Belgium, are not naturally antisemitic today but they will go that way with time. We are sending our best propagandists in there. The moment Jewish emigrants to Switzerland and Holland etcetera begin to go about their usual business, patriotic antisemitism will suddenly begin. If three out of ten barristers in a Swiss town are Jews the Swiss ones will have nothing left to eat, and when his purse begins to pinch he will have reason to become an antisemite.

Furthermore, Czechoslovakia has become antisemitic, all the Balkan states are antisemitic, all Palestine is engaged in a desperate struggle against the Jew, so that some day there will be no place left in the world for the Jew. [The Jew] will come to the conclusion that the danger can only be removed if the country that originated antisemitism [sic], Germany is turned to scorched earth and eliminated.

You mark my words, in the decisive battle to come, if we are defeated we will be given no quarter, they will be allowed to starve to death or butchered. That will be the fate of every man, whether he be an enthusiastic supporter or not, it will be enough that German is his mother tongue.[12]

Himmler fairly accurately predicted the first weeks of the Allied occupation in 1945.[13]

Himmler's ideology was inspired by the need to preserve his *Volk*. It was a dispassionate view. People needed to be kind and decent but when it came to preserving a race, there was to be no pity. Himmler would kill a hundred people in a town, and he would expect his men to do so without qualms.

THE POGROM

One reason to dismiss the idea of Rath's death as an SD plot is the fact that the pogrom that occurred on the night of 9–10 November was almost entirely the brainchild of Joseph Goebbels, and Goebbels was not connected to the Heydrich–Himmler machine. This magnificent opportunity to worm his way back into his master's affections dawned slowly on the Gauleiter of Berlin. His diary does not allude to the expulsion of the Polish Jews and it is only in his entry for the 8th that he finally records the wounding of Rath, together with sporadic outbreaks of violence against the Jews, notably in Hessen. It was then that the penny dropped: this was the chance to expand the largely unsuccessful programme he had conceived for Berlin to cover the whole Reich. 'Now we want to be blunt. In Hessen big antisemitic projects. The synagogues are going to be burned down. If we could only let rip with the fury of the people once and for all!'[14]

ITALY

(*above*) Hitler's 'Roman Holiday' in May: the Nazi leaders assemble with Mussolini on the steps of the monument to Victor Emmanuel II.

(*left*) Hitler felt certain Italians were looking down on him. After an incident at the opera in Naples, he sacked his chief of protocol.

DER STÜRMER

(*above*) *Der Stürmer*. Germans read cases containing copies of the magazine that was the unofficial organ of Nazi antisemitism.

(*left*) 'Jewish Advertising Revenue: the so-called pressure of public opinion is the weight of Jewish sacks of gold.'

ANTISEMITIC PROPAGANDA

Legion der Schande

*Unaufgeklärt, verlockt vom Gold – Stehn sie, geschändet, in Judasfold
Die Seelen vergiftet, verseucht das Blut – In ihrem Schoße das Unheil ruht*

Antisemitic propaganda cartoons from *Der Stürmer*.
(*above*) Aryan women defiled by Jewish gold.
(*below*) Corrupt Jewish businessmen.

Barmat

*Als Jude war der Barmat groß,
Nun ging er ein in Abrahams Schoß.
Er hat, wie's einem Juden ziemt,
Den Talmudhimmel sich verdient.*

LIVING IT UP

(*above*) The people of Steyr in Upper Austria greet their new Führer and Dr Goebbels. Hitler had spent a miserable year as a schoolboy in the town.

(*right*) Vienna's best restaurant, Zu den Drei Husaren, was aryanized and placed in the hands of Otto Horcher, the Restaurant-Tsar of the Third Reich.

NAZI ART

(*above*) Göring's birthday in January: he receives a painting by Austrian artist Hans Makart from his master.

(*left*) Albert Speer's model for a new Berlin.

(*below*) The Munich art parade in July.

KRISTALLNACHT

(*right*) A wrecked synagogue after Goebbels' pogrom of 9–10 November.

(*below*) Jewish men from Baden-Baden are led off to a concentration camp.

(*bottom*) Jewish women are singled out for humiliation.

CONFERENCES

The Evian Conference in July failed utterly in its attempt to find a refuge for Germany's Jews.

In September the Munich Conference sealed Czechoslovakia's fate.

THE RAPE OF CZECHOSLOVAKIA

(*above*) Hitler visits his new domain, the Sudetenland.

(*left*) Ethnic Germans prepare to celebrate their return to the Reich.

(*below*) Poles and Hungarians were rewarded with a share of the spoils – here Hungarian troops enter Slovakia.

Goebbels needed to bend Hitler's ear first. That evening was the annual re-enactment of the 1923 Putsch that began on 8 November in the Bürgerbräukeller in Munich. Hitler returned to the theme of attacking his British enemies, Churchill, Eden and Duff Cooper. After the speech, the leading Nazis went to the Führerbau where Bormann addressed them on the plans for celebrating Hitler's fiftieth birthday on 20 April 1939. They proceeded to the 'Café Heck', where Goebbels and Hitler sat until 3 a.m. He may have had a chance to talk over his plans, but nothing is recorded in the diary.

The main action of what has come to be known as *Reichskristallnacht*, or Night of the Broken Glass, occurred after the celebrations for the fifteenth anniversary, which began with a traditional march to the Feldherrnhalle on the 9th. There was the usual backbiting among Hitler's men. Lutze poured his scorn for the SS into Goebbels' ear. His SA was to do the spadework later. Göring took his place among the marchers on what was a grey November day but at 7.30 that evening he boarded a train and returned to Berlin. Goebbels had by now begun to take a keen interest in Rath's deteriorating condition. In Kassel in Hessen the 'spontaneous demonstrations' continued as well as in Dessau in Anhalt; some Jews were attacked by a hostile crowd outside the French tourist office in Berlin.

Hitler was talking war in his Munich flat when Rath expired at 4.30 that afternoon but registered very little interest. Two minutes' silence was observed when the wireless announced the diplomat's death, instructions that must have been issued by the Minister for Propaganda. Goebbels seized his moment.

Now the dish is cooked [he wrote in his diary]. I go to the Party reception in the Old Town Hall. A huge crowd. I brief the Führer on the matter. He decides to let the demonstrations go on. The Jews should feel the wrath of the people once and for all. That is right. I immediately hand out fitting instructions to the

Party and the police . . . The Führer has ordered that 25–30,000 Jews should be arrested at once.[15]

Goebbels informed the Party leaders that they must not appear involved in the pogrom. It was to be the 'demonstration' that they had been unable to enact at the time of Gustloff's death. At 10 p.m. Goebbels called for hate and revenge. It has been suggested that *Reichskristallnacht* was a test of Hitler's ability as an actor, and that he passed the audition with flying colours.[16] He successfully kept his own role a secret, even going so far as to voice his condemnation of the excesses. Hitler was sensitive to the effect that association with the actions might have on his international image. German goods had been boycotted since March 1933 and that meant an ever-worsening balance of payments. Goebbels had been told to postpone his campaign against the Jews in Berlin until after the Rome trip in early May. Again, in mid-June, the special mini-pogrom organized by Goebbels in Berlin was called off because Hitler was worried about opinion abroad.

As was often the case, he was candid with his friend Winifred Wagner. He confirmed to her that getting the Jews to emigrate had been the point of *Kristallnacht*, and that justified the extreme violence. When her children asked him about it, he changed his tune and blamed it all on Goebbels.[17] In September Hitler insisted that the laws passed removing Jewish lawyers from practice should be kept quiet until the storm over the Sudetenland had passed. Goebbels was a more than willing mouthpiece for his master and was anxious to accelerate the persecution of the Jews with the usual objective: to encourage them to go more speedily.

Goebbels' pogrom caught everyone off guard: neither of the SS leaders Wolff and Heydrich had been informed. At midnight Heydrich was drinking in the Nobel Hotel in the Maximilianstrasse when Gestapo Müller called to tell him that in Berlin Jewish businesses were being destroyed by roving gangs. Heydrich decided to call on Himmler, who was in Hitler's flat in the Prinzregentenstrasse preparing to swear in a detachment of SS-officers at the Feldherrnhalle. Wolff was to take Himmler there after the session with Hitler. They discovered Himmler had not been told either. When Hitler heard what was going on he appeared beside himself with rage. 'Unbelievable . . . I completely disapprove.' Wolff believed to the end of his life that Hitler had not ordered the pogrom.[18]

Hitler turned to Himmler and told him: 'Find out immediately who issued the orders. I don't want my SS involved in any of these actions under any circumstances.'[19] The times the orders were issued also give a further idea of how pluralistic the command structure of the Third Reich was: the Party (Goebbels) was told to move at 10.30 p.m.; the SA (Lutze) at 11; the police (Himmler) at midnight, and the SS at 1.30 a.m. The SS were told they were to wear mufti. Himmler made no bones about his disapproval:

The order comes from the Reich's propaganda leadership, and I suppose that Goebbels in his empty-headedness and in his hunger for power – something that struck me long ago – has launched this campaign in what is, foreign politically speaking, the most difficult time.[20]

Heydrich's instructions to the police and SD that night make curious reading. It was to be a well-mannered pogrom: German lives and property were not to be endangered and where a synagogue abutted on to an Aryan property it was to be left unmolested; there was to be no looting – any pilfering would be answered with arrest; care was to be taken to make sure no damage was caused to non-Jewish commercial properties; foreigners were to be left in peace – even foreign Jews. Heydrich also gave instructions that historical documents found in the synagogues were to be preserved and handed over to the SD. On the other hand, in keeping with Hitler's wishes, Heydrich ordered his men to arrest male Jews, especially wealthy ones, and to hold them in police cells prior to transferring them to concentration camps. They were only to arrest 'healthy male Jews'. 'Particular care must be taken that Jews arrested on the basis of this directive are not mistreated.' Now was the moment to put some of Eichmann's methods into practice in the old Reich.

The first acts of hooliganism occurred in Munich itself, where a drunken band of members of the *Stosstrupp Hitler* went on the rampage and wrecked the synagogue in the Herzog-Rudolf-Strasse. Goebbels claimed that he tried to stop it going up in smoke, but that he had not succeeded.[21] The city's Gauleiter, Adolf Wagner, had to be goaded, as his heart was not in it and Goebbels was obliged to transmit the order personally to destroy the synagogue in the Fasanenstrasse in Berlin. He smugly noted the 'blood red sky' in Munich. 'In the future, the dear Jews will think twice before they go about shooting German diplomats.' Before he turned in that night he parodied *Hamlet* in his diary: 'Continue to wield our arms, or bring it to a halt? That is the question.'[22]

The 9th was the most important feast day in the Nazi calendar; many of the men were drunk. The SA-men had a job starting fires and no one had laid down stocks of incendiary material. In Rüdesheim the SA-men managed to set fire to themselves rather than the synagogue.[23] Some were mere boys, big on destruction but often small in courage. In Feldafing on the Starnberg Lake, the youths were armed with bricks.[24]

It did not all happen as Heydrich had foreseen. There were accounts to settle too. In Erfurt, the baptized lawyer Flesch was tortured, because he had appeared against an SA-man in a divorce case.[25] In Aschaffenburg the killing of Jewish businessmen had all the hallmarks of settling scores.[26] Heydrich was not heeded in Frankfurt either, where rioters tore up the old books in a Jewish library. In Vienna they arrested all the Jews queuing for visas outside the British consulate.[27] They demolished the Jewish hospital in Nuremberg and the Jewish children's home in Caputh, near Potsdam. Five Jews were shot in Bremen (Goebbels called them 'unlovely excesses'[28]).

In Munich the 'demonstrators' made straight for Schloss Planegg, the home of the Jewish Baron von Hirsch, and destroyed it.[29] Five hundred Jews were arrested in the city, and the banker Emil Kraemer apparently committed suicide by hurling himself out of the window of his flat, although he had been unable to walk for two years. The archbishop, Cardinal Faulhaber, lent the Rabbi Leo Baerwald a lorry so that he might rescue the contents of his synagogue.

The destruction was generally the work of the SA, occasionally encouraged by local Party officials and carried out by local boys who knew the Jews they were attacking. In some rural parts of Germany the purge was half-hearted. The Jews were too well known and the locals did not want to be seen joining in the destruction. It was often necessary to bus the thugs in from elsewhere. Although Jew-baiting was a long-established custom in the German countryside, the disparities between religious and racial antisemitism were shown in stark relief. You were supposed to love your neighbour. There was also a fear that the Catholics would be the next victims, and in some instances thugs destroyed Church property when nothing Jewish was to hand.[30]

In Buttenhausen in Württemberg the synagogue was torched by boys from nearby Münsingen, but the local fire brigade put the blaze out and rescued the contents of the building. The Münsingen thugs came again the next day and set the building alight again. This time they locked the mayor in his office to stop him getting in the way. The wreckers who came to Oberdorf issued from Ellwangen. When they told the local SA chief, Böss, to set fire to the synagogue he refused: 'I can't do this in Oberdorf, because I've grown up with these people, gone to school with them and seen active service with them on the battlefield.' The Ellwangen SA returned the next day, but Böss was adamant. He was stripped of his command, but later restored to it because they could find no one else prepared to do the job. When the Ellwangen SA finally got the fire going, local people arrived to put it out. The SA nonetheless managed to take some Jews away and kill one.

In Würzburg the caretaker of a Jewish teachers' training college came to tell the girls to flee. He appeared in a full brown Party uniform for the first time. The synagogue in Bayreuth was spared because it was next to the lovely baroque opera house. Both the police and the fire chief stood by to protect it, but could not prevent the SA from wrecking the interior.[31] In Fulda the Jews were put in prison to protect them from being sent to a concentration camp, and released when the coast was clear.[32] A uniform also came in handy in Schirwindt in East Prussia. The *Landrat*, Wichard von Bredow, was informed that he had to issue the order to burn down the synagogue. Bredow put on his army fatigues and went to the place where the Nazis were awaiting his orders. He stood before the building and loaded his revolver. The Nazis fled. He was not punished.[33]

It is easy to exaggerate the efficiency of the operation: the orders had been quickly issued and often only half understood. There is also a danger in believing the many accounts of self-glorification in which righteous Gentiles chase away Nazi thugs who are terrorizing Jewish citizens; but they cannot all be dismissed out of hand. The German journalist Bernt Engelmann remembered the events in Düsseldorf. He had just finished his labour service and was due to join the Luftwaffe. On the night of 9–10 November he was summoned from his bed by the din coming from downstairs where some Jews lived. The Nazis were playing the song *Bei der blonden Kathrein* at full blast to cover up the noise of their handiwork as they smashed glass and lanced paintings. Apparently one was a Chagall.

He told a neighbour to call the police, but she informed him the police were right outside. His mother finally incited him to act. Like Zuckmayer, Engelmann found the most effective way was to shout at the boys in his best *Komissdeutsch* or parade-ground German. The destruction ceased while one of the thugs called for his superior. Engelmann continued in a commanding tone, implying that his underlings were indulging in theft. He gave the SA-man the impression that he was a bigger Nazi than he was. The squad dispersed and went on its way. Later he witnessed the killing of a Jewish ophthalmologist who had put up a fight against the vandals. He seems to have taken one of the thugs with him.[34]

In Berlin children looted a Jewish toyshop. When Gentile women remonstrated with them they were spat upon and manhandled by the mob.[35] Over thirty synagogues were wrecked. The author Erich Kästner witnessed the destruction of the city's best-known shops on the Tauenzienstrasse. He could see the looters' SS jackboots under their 'civilian' clothes. They went about their work systematically and he reckoned that they had each been allotted five shops. Each time he tried to get out of his taxi to remonstrate with them, a man came up and said 'Criminal Police!' and slammed the door shut. On the last occasion the driver verbally restrained him: 'What's the point? . . . and apart from everything else it constitutes resistance to the power of the state!'[36]

The fifteen-year-old Peter Fröhlich rode that way too a few hours later. Façades on the Tauenzienstrasse had 'been effectively reduced to rubble, their huge display windows shattered, their mannequins and merchandise scattered on the pavement. Evidently more Jewish-owned shops had survived the government's efforts to "Aryanize" them than I had imagined.' Much worse was to follow: the shop of his uncle, Fröhlich, the milliner on the Olivaer Platz, had been similarly trashed.[37] For Gerhard Beck the destruction was revelatory: he had not always known which shops in the Badstrasse were Jewish-owned – now it was clear. When he went to work on the 10th, the façades of Hemdenmatz,[i] Bata, Etam and Salamander had been wrecked. He was working for a furrier in the same street. All the furs had been smeared with excrement. As one Jewish shop assistant exclaimed in disgust, 'What did the SA eat to shit like that?'[38]

It was not rare for Gentiles to deplore what was happening. There is even an instance of a member of the Gestapo saving a Jew, and the Nazi authorities placed sentries outside a Jewish seminary run by a

---

[i] He was possibly wrong about Hemdenmatz, or else the owners were cunning, for they advertised in Der Stürmer.

rabbi who had rendered Germany valuable service in the Great War.[39] Klepper went through the Bayrischer Viertel in Schöneberg and noted that the population had not supported the action. His Jewish wife received gestures of support from virtually everyone. The philosemitic Maria von Maltzan said the same. She was driving around that night with friends, upset by the burning synagogues and the sight of laughing SA-men throwing the Talmud scrolls on to bonfires and beating up rabbis. 'The actual private citizen was not involved in it at all.'[40] Most of the synagogues went up in flames, but the SA merely wrecked the one in the Heidereutergasse, as it had recently rented space to the post office.[41] It carried on holding services until 1940. The city's most famous synagogue in the Oranienburgerstrasse was saved by the timely intervention of the head of the local police, who informed the arsonists it was an historic building.[42]

The pogrom in Vienna was predictably the most savage of all. It was organized on the ground by the head of the Jewish department of the Gestapo, Dr Lange. Skorzeny was commissioned to destroy the remaining synagogues, tasting blood for the first time. Despite the damage inflicted in October a further forty-two prayer houses were burned to the ground or blown up with hand-grenades, together with the halls in the Central and New Cemeteries. The efficiency of the operation is clear from the report of the fire brigade, which had to be present in case the flames spread to Aryan properties. The action started at 8 a.m. on the 10th. By 9.30 they had destroyed the synagogue at Neue Weltgasse 7 in Hietzing, inflicting 100,000 RM worth of damage, but they ensured that the neighbouring buildings were safe.[ii] Half an hour later the fire brigade was in the Jewish Leopoldstadt. The damage at the synagogue was only half as great. Half an hour later, in the Untere Viakduktgasse, a mere 3,000 RM; a minute later, another synagogue in the Sixth District, 10,000 RM;

[ii] Incidentally, opposite was the family house where the author's mother was born in 1927.

half an hour later in the Fifth, 150,000 RM, the biggest prize to date. It was still burning although it had been made safe. Fifteen minutes later it was the turn of the Grosse Schiffgasse in the Second – 100,000 RM – and similar damage was done to the synagogue in the Fifteenth half an hour later. It took the fire brigade nearly an hour to reach the Eighteenth, and by that time the arsonists had notched up 80,000 RM worth of damage. The synagogue in the Seitenstettengasse in the First District was not to be torched: the Gestapo feared for the valuable archive material housed in the neighbouring buildings of the IKG.[43]

The Sophiensäle concert halls were turned into a temporary prison. The violence was followed by 680 suicides on 10 November or later.[44] There was dancing on the Torah rolls, and in prisons like the Karajangasse eighty-eight Jews were badly hurt and twenty-seven killed. For the first time women were the targets of violence. They were locked in cells with whores and forced to perform orgiastic acts. In Brigitenau 200 Jewish women were obliged to perform a goose-step march in the nude. One who refused was strapped to a table and the others had to spit in her face.

Using violence to accelerate the tempo of emigration was not particularly popular in Vienna either. From Styria the SD reports showed that the people preferred the 'legal' persecution. The same report showed how counterproductive the destruction had been. Papers had been incinerated that would now have to be reissued, and that meant that the targets for emigration would not be met. In at least one instance the thugs destroyed a restaurant that had already been transferred to the ownership of a Party member.[45] In Innsbruck four prominent Jews were murdered, three of them in front of their families. The anti-Jewish measures had been popular up to now, but in the wake of the pogrom citizens openly expressed their sympathy for the Jews. Similar sentiments were expressed in Vienna.[46] The jails were filled with Jews. Eichmann addressed the prisoners in the Karajangasse, issuing dark warnings: if the emigration could not be speeded up he would find other means.[47] The pogrom was followed by a wave of confiscations: nearly two thousand Jewish homes were seized, and their inhabitants forced to find shelter either in *Judenhäuser* or with their relatives.

AFTERMATH

Hitler and Goebbels had met for lunch on the 10th at the Führer's favourite restaurant, the 'Osteria Bavaria' in Munich's Schellingstrasse.[iii] Goebbels gave Hitler a report on the night: 'He approves of everything. His views are wholly radical and aggressive. The measure itself went off without a hitch.'[48] Hitler now wanted the Jewish businesses appropriated. There was no question of their claiming for the damage on their insurance policies. Hitler continued to keep his role a secret, but some people realized that he was involved. When the Prussian Minister of Finance, Popitz, complained to Göring, he told him the perpetrators should be punished and tried to resign. Göring replied, 'My dear Popitz, do you wish to punish the Führer?'[49]

Hitler and Goebbels were alone in seeing the pogrom as a universal success. The Finance Minister Funk was one of the angriest of his critics, calling the riots *Schweinereien*, a shambles.[50] Ribbentrop called the Propaganda Minister a 'little beast': 'Goebbels smashes the windows and I have to mend the foreign situation.'[51] Hefty criticism from all round moved Goebbels to make an announcement at 5 p.m. on the 10th, calling the party to an end.[iv] Exhausted looters and arsonists went home, often carrying baskets filled with food, wine and valuables. Goebbels was disappointed at the outcome and thought the number of people who had participated in the vandalism had been miserably small.[52]

[iii] It is still there and looks much the same, except that it is now called the 'Osteria Italiana'.

[iv] Some say this was Göring: see Martin Gilbert, *Kristallnacht: Prelude to Destruction*, London 2006, 46.

Göring didn't like Goebbels and he was furious about the destruction. Hitler nonetheless mediated between his two princes. In a telephone conversation with Hitler, Göring was won round with the idea of a fine: 1 milliard marks for his Four Year Plan. Göring was strapped for cash and it may well have been he who suggested it. Besides a huge armaments programme and no money to pay his civil service, there was a near total lack of reserves of foreign currency. Even if he could make some money from it, the effect on foreign trade was disastrous – this would not make international Jewry call off its boycott. Göring managed to win an assurance from Hitler that such methods would not be used again.[53]

Of the 7,800 Jews arrested in Vienna, 1,226 were already in the process of effecting their departure through the Central Office for Jewish Emigration. There were 4,083 businesses closed down and 1,950 buildings confiscated. Jews who were still in the possession of their flats and houses were obliged to hand over the keys. They were given no time to pack up their belongings. Their remaining valuables were predictably stolen. It provided another chance for some informal plunder, and the police had to step in again to dampen the ardour of the Viennese Gentiles.[54]

Across the Reich, official figures listed seventy-six synagogues destroyed and a further 191 set on fire. Twenty-nine Jewish-owned department stores had also been demolished, including the provocatively named Nathan Israel in Berlin, which had been protected until then. At a conservative estimate, the thugs had also destroyed a further 815 shops and 117 private houses. The real figure is probably far higher.[55] Even the Party condemned the action, calling it destructive, expensive and misguided.[56] The SD reports spoke of Party members saying, 'This is no longer anything to do with culture or decency.'[57] They wanted to know if the perpetrators of the destruction were to be punished too. That Sunday there was a tellingly small amount contributed to the boxes that collected money for the Nazi *Winterhilfe* (Winter Aid) charity. No one seems to have been too concerned for the Jews themselves, although 200 of them were beaten up, and officially thirty-five were killed, though the tally is more likely to have been between 100 and 200. The approximately 30,000 who had been rounded up were taken to Dachau, Buchenwald and Sachsenhausen, where they were encouraged to think about emigration.

The SS promulgated new measures as soon as Rath's death was announced. In Buchenwald the prisoners were deprived of food, and there was no more talk of early release. The *Manchester Guardian* said that as many as seventy Jewish prisoners had been executed. Bruno Heilig, who was there at the time, reported a number of deaths from savage punishment.[58] Some of the Aryan prisoners saved their food and hid it in the woods for the Jews. Buchenwald was so full that there was no more room and the transports had to be stopped. Himmler gave orders for the release of all Jews over the age of fifty, to accommodate new arrivals. On 14 November more places were secured by Heydrich's order releasing all Jews having papers allowing them to emigrate. They were to leave within three weeks.

On the night of 9–10 November Eichmann received a summons to Berlin by telegram. The Nazi leadership took stock of what they had achieved or destroyed through Goebbels' 'spontaneous' demonstrations. Heydrich insisted on Eichmann being there to 'communicate his experiences of practical procedure'. Eichmann was to tell them how things *should* be done. This was the background to the conference on the progress of the 'Jewish Question' that took place in the Air Ministry in Berlin on 12 November.[59] There were over a hundred persons present including Göring, Goebbels and Heydrich. Himmler was absent: he had taken himself to Italy for a five-week break.

Hitler had requested a coordinated solution to the Jewish question. As such, this was a forerunner of the better-known Wannsee Conference. The host, Göring, was unimpressed by the weekend's demonstration. He feared for his own credibility, as he had exhorted the German people to hang on to every scrap of material for the Four Year Plan, and now this wanton destruction had come. He wanted to know who was going to pay for the damage, particularly insurance bills of between six and ten million RM for the 7,500 businesses destroyed. The Berlin jeweller Margraf in Unter den Linden was presenting a reckoning for 1.7 million RM;[v] the bill for the glass alone came to 6 million RM. The replacements had to be brought in from Belgium, meaning a payout of 3 million RM in foreign exchange; the loss amounted to half of Belgium's annual production in plate glass. The total bill was estimated at 220 million RM.[60] 'I have had enough of these demonstrations,' Göring told the meeting. 'In the end they don't damage the Jews, they damage me, as in the last resort, I am the economy . . . I would be happier if you had beaten 200 Jews to death and not destroyed so much of value.'[61] Göring issued orders to catch the pillagers and some 800 others. No charges were brought against the men who murdered Jews that night, but four who assaulted women were expelled from the Party and handed over to the courts.[62]

Instead of 'spontaneous demonstrations', Eichmann's Viennese model was recommended for the Altreich, 'where they had yet to achieve so much' and where emigration had stagnated to 20,000 Jews a year. The Reich could not afford to finance the transfer of Jewish assets, and the taxes they had imposed on the Jews were failing to bring in enough money. Heydrich argued that the most important thing was to get rid of the Jews and drew the others' attention to Eichmann's success. Heydrich then had a brainwave: the insurers should pay the Jews and at that point the money would be confiscated. There was discussion as to what to do with the damaged synagogues. Goebbels suggested that the Jews should demolish them themselves. He seemed much exercised by the question of Jews sharing cinemas, theatres and circuses with Gentiles, or even breathing the same open air in public parks and woods. Jews had been seen freely walking around the Grunewald in Berlin. The Reich's

[v] Goebbels later had a brilliant idea: he was going to issue a statement that the jeweller had been plundered by a Jew. Hitler was delighted. *Tagebücher* I, VI, 199.

Master of Hunts, Göring, clearly saw it as a matter of little importance and made light of it: he would have reservations made for the Jews and all those animals that resembled them – for example elks, which had similarly hooked noses – could come and join them there.[63]

In his diary, Goebbels interpreted his role in a heroic light, and failed to mention Göring's ribbing. (On 22 November he claimed that he and Göring were wholly of the same mind when it came to the Jews.[64]) 'A hot debate over the solution,' he wrote. 'I represent the radical point of view.' He dismissed Funk as 'soft' and claimed, 'I work splendidly with Göring', and 'the radical opinion won the day'.[65] He did not mention the fact that he had Hitler's blessing and they did not.

In six months Eichmann had produced a tally of emigration that was two and a half times as great as that of the Altreich. The method was explained: the rich Jews had to pay for the poor. 'The problem was not getting the rich out, but the Jewish mob.' Göring expressed his fear that they would take their money with them. Heydrich was able to reassure him: 'In Vienna the Gerstl [dough] stayed in the country.'[66] In reality Goebbels' pogrom had actually slowed down the process of emigration and Heydrich had every reason to be angry with the propaganda chief. Once Göring had been shown the colour of the money he could hope to receive, he conferred with the Austrian Economics Minister, Fischböck, about the fate of 17,000 Jewish businesses in Vienna. It was decided that only between 3,000 and 3,500 would stay open, and the rest would be either closed or taken over by the state and awarded to trustees.[67]

In the aftermath of the pogrom in Vienna, the police had instructions to arrest the richest Jews, and a total of 6,547 were taken into custody and 3,700 were shipped out to Dachau. At the end of the year the Gestapo totted up their figures and estimated that they had packed 20,793 Austrians off to concentration camp since 13 March.[68] When the Jews arrived in Dachau, the guards were delighted to find that they had a number of rabbis under their roofs and singled them out for special punishments.[69] Urns filled with ashes began to arrive a few days later: 350 of the Jews detained after *Reichskristallnacht* died in Buchenwald that winter, and the combined total for the three camps – Buchenwald, Sachsenhausen and Dachau – exceeded 5,000, of whom nearly 3,000 were Austrian.[70] Sachsenhausen had the reputation of being the mildest of the three, Buchenwald the worst.[71] After the *Rath-Aktion* the oldest inmate was ninety, the youngest twelve.[72]

Many of the Jews in Dachau and Buchenwald were released before June 1939. The former frontline soldiers were the first to be liberated. A large number of those were allowed to go as a celebration of Hitler's fiftieth birthday on 20 April. The condition imposed on all of them was that they should leave the Reich and never return. They had also to promise that they would say nothing of their experiences in the camps.[73] Even Jews who had not been through this mill were advised to keep quiet about what they had seen and heard. When Arnold Schoenberg's son-in-law, Felix Greissle, arrived in the United States, the composer told him:

> Don't say anything you don't have to say about your experiences of the last few weeks. Especially not to newspapermen or to people who might pass it on to them. You know the Nazis take revenge on relatives and friends still in their power. So be very reserved and don't get mixed up in politics. I have kept to this strictly, always refusing to tell any stories, out of consideration for my friends and relatives in Germany. And people completely understand this.[74]

In Dresden, Victor Klemperer was lucky. On 11 November two gendarmes appeared at his door to search his house for weapons. He had the impression that the search was pure torture to one of them. They eventually found the sabre he carried as an officer in the First World War. They took him down to the police station but he was quickly released. Stubborn though he was, he decided it was high time to emigrate and on 28 November he visited the Advice Bureau for

Emigration in the Pragerstrasse. A very humane Major Stübel told him he could be as frank as he liked. Stübel made it clear that if he sold his house he would be able to leave Germany naked, with 7.5 per cent of its value. Even then he would have had to obtain a berth on a ship and all the places were taken. Klemperer decided to stay put.[75]

Following the pogrom there were audible rumbles from abroad. The former Kaiser in Dutch Doorn echoed the feelings of many members of the old military caste: 'What is going on at home is certainly a scandal. It is now high time that the army showed its hand; they have let a lot of things happen . . . all the older officers and all decent Germans must protest.' Of course he was hoping that an army coup would place him back on his throne. His son, August Wilhelm, or 'Auwi', who had been an early and enthusiastic member of the SA, took the opposite line, incensing his father with his support for the pogrom. 'When I told him that any decent man would describe these actions as gangsterism,' wrote the former Kaiser, 'he appeared totally indifferent.'[76]

The pogrom took away the regime's last vestiges of credibility. Hitler and Goebbels had 'unconditional' support from the Duce, who worked himself up into a lather against the Jews, but elsewhere they found little sympathy.[77] In many places the embargo on German goods was reinforced and doors were shut to German trade. The Manchester Guardian in England was not taken in by Goebbels' 'spontaneous demonstrations' and attributed the action to Hitler's 'old guard'. Goebbels' own newspaper, Angriff, riposted by making out that the assassination of Rath had been instigated by Churchill and Attlee.[78] Der Stürmer presented a gallery of 'Jewlovers': Mayor [sic] Attlee, Anthony Eden (who, they had already pointed out, had Jewish cousins), Winston Churchill, Lloyd George, Duff Cooper, Stalin and Roosevelt.[79] The weekly left it to 'Fips' to celebrate the actions that night. In one cartoon a Jew is complaining of the cold draught; in another he runs into the arms of the Church, the Nazis' other bugbear.[80]

The United States was particularly virulent in its condemnation. Hitler and his men saw all too quickly that it was not the 20 million German Americans who led public opinion. There were formal protests in Britain and France, and in Rome the Pope spoke out against racialism and the destruction of lives and property. This led to a demonstration against Jews *and* Catholics in Munich when the Gauleiter, Adolf Wagner, warned His Holiness that his utterances constituted an incitement to the Jews to agitate against the Germans. On the 10th the Cardinal's palace was wrecked as a response to his kindness towards the rabbi.[81] Pius XI was not to be put off and continued to attack the Nazis, challenging their claim to racial superiority. There was, he said, just one human race. He wanted to break diplomatic ties with Germany but was dissuaded by Eugenio Pacelli, the former German nuncio, and the man who would succeed him as Pius XII three months later.[82] Archbishop Lang wrote to *The Times* to express his disgust:

> Whatever provocation may have been given by the deplorable act of a single irresponsible Jewish youth, reprisals on such a scale, so fierce, cruel, and vindictive, cannot possibly be justified. A sinister significance is added to them by the fact that the police seem either to have acquiesced in them or to have been powerless to restrain them.[83]

The letter annoyed Goebbels so much that he had *The Times* withdrawn from sale. The pogrom proved a watershed: the Church of England would now be united in its desire for the British government to assert itself in Germany.

Even within Germany the pogrom marked a change of course. It is said that among the conservative elite there was a fear that the left were now back in the saddle with the end of Goebbels' disgrace, and that they could now expect an attack on the churches as well as on the capitalists, not to mention the nobility.[84] Certainly Hitler appeared to have forgiven Goebbels. On 16 November the Gauleiter was proud to note, 'The Führer wholly approves my and our policies.' Hitler showed his solidarity by coming to stay with the Goebbels family in Schwanenwerder after a performance of Schiller's *Kabale und Liebe*. The next day Uncle Adolf played with the children before heading off to Düsseldorf for Rath's state funeral.[85]

There were numerous small acts of personal courage in which Germans showed their sympathy for the Jews. The industrialist Robert Bosch in Stuttgart put half a million RM in a Dutch bank to help out Jews lacking funds to continue their journeys to freedom.[86] For Peter and Christabel Bielenberg in Hamburg, it made up their minds for them that they were going to leave Germany and go and live in Ireland. It was only their friend Adam von Trott who held them back: he argued that the evil needed to be fought from within.[87]

For many Germans there was an all-pervading sense of shame. Major Groscurth said, 'You have to feel ashamed to remain German,' but thought Göring and Hitler innocent of the outrage.[88] Another who disapproved was Heydrich, who believed it had been 'the heaviest blow against the state and Party since 1934'.[89] Klepper noted there was a desire among rich Gentiles to emigrate, and that both churches were muzzled by flagrant attacks on them in the Nazi organs: they were not to speak out for non-Aryan Christians.[90] Eleanor von Trott, the widow of a former imperial minister and mother of Adam, went into Bebra, where one of the 'spontaneous' demonstrations had occurred before those unleashed by Goebbels. Leaving her driver at a safe distance she went into each Jewish shop in turn and personally apologized for the damage to their property.[91] Smallbones, the British consul in Frankfurt, talked of 'passionate resentment' among Christian Germans and in the army and civil service, while Vansittart's informant, Group Captain Christie, overheard similar views expressed in Berlin and Essen, talking of 'universal horror' and 'general abhorrence'.[92]

In Württemberg, responses to the action ranged from 'childish' to 'inhumane'. In Stuttgart glaziers sold glass at a reduced rate 'because it was not the Jews who had caused the damage'. A Party member sent flowers to a Jew to show his support. Another Nazi in Creglingen helped an arrested Jew to escape with the support of the local leader of the Nazi War Veterans' Association. The ordinary clergy were highly vocal in their condemnation, particularly the Protestants. The Catholics tended to be more cowed after the expulsion of Bishop Sproll.[93]

In Nuremberg the public outcry was so great that Julius Streicher had to make a speech to protest against sympathy being shown for the Jews. Pity for the Jews might have induced relative silence from *Der Stürmer*, which did not formally celebrate the pogrom until issue 48 came out at the end of the month. On the other hand, the more likely cause was Goebbels, who had once again gagged the press.[94] Ernst Hiemer wrote *Der Stürmer*'s cover story, entitled 'Has the Jewish Question been solved?' The previous issue, number 47, however, did include a poignant image by 'Fips' entitled 'November Storms' and showing a Jew being levelled by a huge fist.

The rounding up of the Jews had proved an excellent source of wealth for corrupt German officials. Göring did not see all of it by any means. In Streicher's Nuremberg the Jews had to sign away the rights to their property before they went into concentration camps. The taxable value of the estate was calibrated at 10 per cent of its real worth. In Vienna the corruption was so flagrant that Bürckel was obliged to pack a number of Aryan administrators off to Dachau to join their victims.[95] In response Jews north of the Inn laid siege to the consulates to obtain visas to leave. Few found what they wanted. Of 300 who queued at the Argentinian and Paraguayan consulates in Berlin only two were able to proceed to making a formal application.[96] On the 19th it was decreed that no one could leave until the milliard-mark fine or Atonement Contribution had been paid.

The Contribution was based on the data accumulated since the enforced registration of Jewish property after 26 April. The sum total for Jewish property was set at 7,538,500,000 RM, of which nearly two-thirds was estimated to be in the form of liquid assets. Every Jew liable had to make over 20 per cent of his property in four instalments: the first on 15 December, and thereafter at intervals of three months.[97] Together with the Emigration Tax, the Atonement Contribution yielded 2 milliard RM. Using the Jews as a cash cow to fund rearmament and other projects was short-sighted, because they had already given away so much, and their milk was soon to dry up altogether: income from the beleaguered Jews amounted to some 5 per cent of tax revenue.[98] Even the takeover of Jewish businesses only altered German economic life in small areas such as textiles and department stores. There was still no alleviation of the Reich's finances, which continued to cause grave concern.

On 18 November Göring met members of the Defence Council and explained the parlous state of the nation's coffers and that there was a fear of renewed inflation.[99] The rearmament programme was in itself inflationary as it failed to expand consumer sales. In the New Year the Reichsbank sent Hitler a letter requesting restraint in government spending. Hitler's response was to sack Schacht, although there may have been other reasons. The national debt had increased threefold since Hitler's takeover. Autarky prevented Germany from indulging in conventional foreign trade.

Göring was aware that he was not getting his hands on all the money and that he still lacked buying power abroad. On 14 November Fischböck came to him with the first of several schemes to make the Jews sponsor German exports, an idea that had been aired before *Kristallnacht*. It came about as a result of a meeting between George Rublee's wife and the German Air Attaché in London, Wenninger. Wenninger had introduced her to Theo Kordt, which had eventually resulted in a direct channel opening up between Göring and Rublee.[100] Once again it was necessary to keep Ribbentrop in the dark, especially as the RAM had got it into his head that Rublee was a Jew. The international boycott was starving Germany of foreign currency.[101] The chemical giant IG Farben's foreign orders were down by 40 per cent, for example. Göring wanted the Jews to be allowed to remain in the export trade: 'the business point of view must prevail . . . every concession involving ideological principles is possible'.[102] Under the scheme, Germany would relieve the richer Jews of 200 million RM and allow them to emigrate; in return, after thirty years Germany would pay 3 per cent to the governments participating in the scheme.[103]

The Opposition had a new straw to grasp at. Goerdeler relayed the contents of a speech made by the Minister of State and Vice-President of the Reichsbank, Dr Brinckmann, to an audience of industrialists in Cologne. The news was bleak: all the money sucked out of Austria since the Anschluss was now spent. The luxury and high cost of Party functions and the state were to blame. There was no foreign currency and a dearth of raw materials. The annual state budget needed to be reduced by 6,000 million RM straight away. There was only a short time before Germany suffered complete economic collapse.[104] Brinckmann later went insane, although it is not clear whether this resulted from the shambles in the Nazi economy or some other cause.

Within Germany it was clear that the Nazi state was anything but efficient. A further report by Goerdeler showed that the railway system had broken down because it was being bled in the interests of free transport for Party members, road building, and compulsory contributions to various Party funds. They were short of 3,000 locomotives and 30,000 coaches. Goods from Hamburg to Vienna had to go via Trieste to make use of Italian trains.[105] The opportunities for working in the arms industries and in other related trades had led to a huge desertion of the land with drastic results in food production. There had been a 16 per cent drop in the number of farm labourers, which would eventually require migrant labour, chiefly from Poland. It was not just the farms that lacked workers: in the mines of the Ruhr, they were 30,000 men short. Overall Germany needed another million men. The temptation to grab them from elsewhere was obvious.

On that same 7 November that witnessed Rath's death, the *Daily Express* in London ran a story under the headline 'Wife Appeals for Briton': 'Somewhere in a German jail lies a forgotten prisoner – 56-year-old Fred Richter.' The article alluded to Richter's past as a jockey. His wife Maud had been imprisoned too, but she had been released after a week. There had been no news of Richter since 13 September.[106]

KINDERTRANSPORTE

Even before *Reichskristallnacht* there was a growing awareness of the urgency of finding homes for the Jews. At the beginning of November one of the busiest of the Quakers, Howard Elkington, was prepared to stump up £100 'to help suitable people to emigrate to Australia'. A month later he was obtaining visas in bulk from the Foreign Office in London.[107] Norman Bentwich, too, was keen to explore the chances of upping the quotas for Australia. He also looked into the possibility of sending some to Ceylon. Four hundred Austrian Jews were on the water, ostensibly on their way to Liberia. They had left from Galata in Romania on the steamship *Minerva*.[108]

After the pogrom, parents understood that even if they could not make it themselves, it was imperative to let their children go. On 15 November the leading Zionist Chaim Weizmann[vi] went to see Neville Chamberlain and asked for action to save them. Weizmann set a figure of 10,000 to be found homes in Britain. Pressure was also put on Malcolm MacDonald, the Minister for the Colonies. It was agreed that a further 5,000 Jews could enter Britain providing they left again within three years.[109] The idea of the *Kindertransporte* had been an informal one at first. It was believed that they should be allowed to recover in lands like Switzerland and Norway before returning to their parents. Jews in Britain were particularly active in arranging the transports. One of these was Wilfred Israel, the model for Gustav Landauer in Christopher Isherwood's novel *Goodbye to Berlin*. Israel's colleague in 'Youth Aliya' was Lola Hahn-Warburg. The pro-Zionist MP Josiah Wedgwood also sponsored 222 refugees.[110]

[vi] First President of the State of Israel.

One of those who worked for Lola Hahn-Warburg was Diana Hopkinson, another former lover of Adam von Trott. She was attached to the Movement for the Care of Children from Germany. In her book *The Incense Tree* she describes how the 'steady stream of Jews who had been trying to leave Germany' became

> a torrent which almost overwhelmed the organizations who were working for them. In the large blocks of Bloomsbury offices we were invaded by a throng of bewildered and anguished people. We were busy not only interviewing those who had arrived but with correspondence about those who still hoped to escape. We battled with the Home Office for the necessary permits and sought financial guarantors; interviewed English relations and friends. They wrung their hands and wept and offered bribes or threats in their efforts to free those still in Germany or Austria. If one became a little hardened it was only in the attempt to keep one's balance and help more effectively. One could not forget that the case numbers concealed suffering human beings, but they themselves hated those 'case' numbers. None of us knew that a number on their file might save them from a number branded on their body in an extermination camp later.[111]

Diana's office had been issued with a block permit for 10,000 Jewish children, but that was not enough. She and her colleagues could only take twelve from every thirty applicants. 'I was in despair over the hopeless task of assessing those whose claims were the strongest, trying not to choose the most attractive or the most pathetic looking. I was haunted by the thought of what would happen to those left behind.'[112]

Once the children arrived in Britain, Jews were concerned about their retaining their faith. Of the 9,000 children who arrived unaccompanied in Britain between 1933 and 1939, only 1,000 were placed with Jewish foster parents. The British Board of Deputies was at pains to stress that even non-religious children were Jews and that *konfessionslos* did not generally mean Christian, but rather 'the parents were not members of the Jewish *Kultus Gemeinde*, for political reasons or because they wish to avoid paying the taxes of the KG'. As it was, only a small percentage submitted to baptism while in the care of Christian foster parents.[113]

In Germany, measures against the Jews were redoubled. On 11 November they were banned from possessing weapons. By the end of the year they were to be excluded from economic and social life, theatres, German schools (15 November) and universities (8 December). The *Zionistische Rundschau* was closed, and very briefly replaced by the Jüdisches Nachrichtenblatt. On 16 November they lost the right to serve or wear military uniform. Their driving licences were revoked and their assets, property and jewellery, with the exception of wedding rings, had to be handed in. All Jewish businesses were to close down on 23 November. At the end of the month Victor Klemperer found that he was banned from the library and effectively cut off from new literature.

In Franconia the Gauleiter, Streicher, decided that the time had come to relieve the Jews of all their property. In Fürth the Jews filed in one by one, ceding their rights for a few peppercorns. Some court officers refused to enter the compulsory sales in the land register.[114] Jews were now banned from cafés and restaurants. One victim was the writer and former ladies' man John Höxter, who was wont to cadge money in the 'Romanisches Café' in Berlin. When his friends offered him a coffee, he said he would rather have the 50 Pfennigs. They usually gave him that and more, in the understanding that he could not earn a living any more. After *Reichskristallnacht* he could no longer enter the building. Realizing he would now starve, he hanged himself from a tree in the Grunewald.[115]

One or two things improved. With the winding up of the Gildemeester charity for non-religious Jews in Vienna, the whole machinery for emigration was brought under the roof of the Palais Rothschild. Jews no longer had to look for passports in their own districts. The seriousness of the situation was now clear. In

Württemberg the number of Jews dropped from around 7,000 to nearer 6,000 by March.[116] In Britain a total of £250,000 was raised for non-Aryan Christians by means of a whip-round in the parishes; more substantial contributions were made by Jewish peers, such as Rothschild and Bearsted, as well as Simon Marks of Marks & Spencer.[117] On 29 November the British Consul-General in Vienna was moved to complain about the confiscation of Alfred Piccaver's villa on the river at Klosterneuburg. A Party member called Rafaelsberger made off with it. The singer was British-born, but he had been principal tenor at the State Opera from 1910 to 1937.[118]

Some of the Jews in Dachau, Sachsenhausen and Buchenwald, who had papers for Palestine, were out by the end of the month. Others would have to apply to the Jewish agencies or find places on the Perl-transports. After the British had closed the Greek door, Italy was the most promising alternative, despite the racial laws. Long queues of women gathered outside Passport Control Officer Foley's office in Berlin, seeking to have their menfolk released from concentration camps. Foley had requested fresh supplies of blank visas for Palestine as well as 'Youth Aliya' certificates that allowed young Jews to go to Palestine without their parents. He also asked for more staff to deal with the workload.[119]

Sworn to secrecy about their treatment in the camps, for the most part Jews did not wish to talk about it anyway. Bernt Engelmann came across a man who simply had to get it off his chest when he visited an hotelier relative. His aunt had hidden a Jew who was waiting for a passport to take him to Sweden. It was no longer legal for Jews to share hotels with Gentiles. She had put him in the hunting lodge where no one would see him. Engelmann noted that the man, Herr Kahn, had evidently lost a good deal of weight, as his clothes no longer fitted him. He had been in Buchenwald and told Engelmann of the treatment that had been meted out to the Jews who had arrived after *Kristallnacht*. Kahn had been released after twenty days.

He had been shaved and inspected by a doctor. He had to swear that any cuts and bruises had been inflicted prior to his arrest. A

lecture was given by a superior SS-officer who told them they had
been rehabilitated, and encouraged them to make a donation to the
Nazi Winter Aid. They were then led past the boxes and another
myrmidon made sure they contributed. Next they had to pay for the
use of their eating utensils. There was another levy, and anyone who
had no money to pay had to be covered by those who did. It was a
five-mile walk to the railway station in Weimar. Another SS-man
was collecting money for taxis because the old and infirm would not
have made it.

Engelmann and Kahn shared a room in the hunting lodge, and
several times he was woken in the night by the other man's groans.
Once he shouted, 'Don't hit me!' When in the morning a motor car
drove up, Kahn became agitated and asked where he might hide. It
was a false alarm: it was Engelmann's aunt with his passport
emblazoned with a J.[120]

On 27 October Bishop Batty had left England on a pastoral
mission to Austria.[121] He needed to appoint someone to take over
from Grimes, and make sure that the baptismal business had been
properly halted. A month after his trip to Vienna to clear up after
Grimes and Collard, he was hauled over the coals by his fellow
bishops. The first to take a shot at him was none other than Bishop
Bell of Chichester. He wrote to Alan Don on 30 November: 'I am
really very much perturbed at getting the enclosed letter from Mrs
Baker about the baptism of Jews in Vienna! I thought from what
the Bishop of Fulham told me at the moment on relations with
foreign churches that, though there had been a great scandal, it was
now over. You see, however, that this complaint is dated 22
November, and baptizing at the rate of some fifty a day is really
shocking!'[122]

Mrs Baker was not the only one to blow the whistle. Less than a
week later Alan Don wrote to Batty himself:

> I think you ought to know that it has come to the knowledge of
> the Archbishop that a Church of Scotland chaplain at Budapest,

the Rev. G.A. Knighton by name, states in a letter dated November 22nd that trouble is being caused in Hungary by the action of the Anglican chaplain in Vienna, who, it is stated, is continuing to baptize a large number of Jews. The actual words are as follows: 'All summer the chaplain has accepted Jews and baptized them, without any preparation whatsoever, and baptized them in batches of fifty a day. Several eyewitnesses told me as much.' Seeing as you have recently been in Vienna, you may be able to judge as to whether this statement is in accordance with facts or not. If it is you will doubtless consider what action should be taken as this practice, if continued, is likely to cause a good deal of scandal.[123]

Don had forwarded the correspondence to the archbishop. Batty replied the following day:

The matter to which you refer was first brought to my notice by an article in a German paper which attacks all Christian institutions and leaders. It appeared to me to be a matter for investigation on the spot and I went out to Vienna.
The position is as follows –

1) We have our mission to the Jews and it is difficult for a priest to refuse to deal with a Jew who wishes to become a Christian, but at the moment on political grounds the greatest care is necessary and instructions were issued to the chaplain at Vienna to this effect.
2) It is a fact that a number of Jews were baptized but the statement that they were baptized without any preparation is *absolutely untrue*. The preparation given was carefully thought out and I was assured that it covered all that was essential.
3) The chaplain responsible in the summer when this occurred was the Revd. C.H.D. Grimes, a scholar and a gentleman in whom I have confidence. I think it must be admitted that his

intense sympathy with these poor people in their terrible suffering led him to a greater belief in their sincerity than an outsider would have done.

4) Mr Grimes resigned the chaplaincy and left over three months ago. He has been succeeded temporarily by the Revd. F.A. Evelyn who is an experienced priest. He has been instructed that the greatest care must be taken in these cases and long preparation given. Also that if there is the slightest ground for believing that baptism is wanted on political grounds, it must be refused.

The situation has therefore been dealt with directly it was brought to my notice, but I must protest against the statement of the Scotch minister that no preparation was given.

Don was satisfied with Batty's letter and also wrote to assuage Bell on 7 December.[124]

Batty may have felt he had successfully concealed Collard's and his own role in the conversions, but he still had not heard the last of it. On 12 January 1939 a Mrs Elsie Ludovici of Upper Norwood in the south London suburbs – almost certainly a converted Jew herself – wrote to Lang:

I was . . . horrified to hear that mass baptisms had been taking place in Vienna, that they were being admitted at the rate of as many as 900 a day into the Anglican Church, that the whole process of conversion was carried out in four days, and that the Jewesses who knew a little English were present to prompt the converts to say 'yes' and 'no' at the right moments in reply to the questions put to them during the ceremony because the converts did not know English or understand what they were being asked. You may imagine my confusion with such allegations which amount to charging the refugees with being converted to the Anglican communion merely for the purpose of benefiting from the charities organized for the help of Christians.

Lang asked Don what he knew about this, and Don assured the archbishop that it was 'grotesquely untrue'. Mrs Ludovici seems to have heard about the mass conversions from the Mosleyite Lane-Fox Pitt-Rivers.[125]

12

DECEMBER

The Philadelphia-based industrialist Robert Yarnall was in Vienna in December looking specifically to help non-Aryans and *Mischlinge* who counted as Jews under the Nuremberg Laws. The IKG was still in funds and continuing the work of getting Jews out. Engel told him that 55,000 Jews had left to date out of the total of 165,000, and 20,000 of a supposed figure of 120,000 non-confessional Jews. Yarnall paid a call on Gildemeester, 'the mystery man of Vienna': 'He has a Gestapo man at his side all the time to check his work.' Yarnall acknowledged, however, that Gildemeester was good at getting children out and Jews released from Dachau and other camps. Yarnall saw some of Heydrich's staff in Berlin and was granted authority to continue in his own task.[1]

The first *Kindertransport* left on 2 December, and another was despatched from Vienna on the 10th. There were 700 children under fourteen on the train, including a third non-Aryan Christians who had been assembled by the Quakers and Gildemeester. The children had been tested, medically examined and issued with passports. Their luggage had been examined. Eichmann bent the rules to allow collective passports for children under the age of eighteen. They left Vienna from Hütteldorf railway station. The scene was predictably tearful. In general only the mothers were there to see them off, as the fathers were often already in concentration camps.[i] That month the

[i] Gertrude Scholz says that no parents were present. She was there. See Elfriede Schmidt, *1938 . . . und was dann?*, Thaur bei Innsbruck 1988, 201.

Quakers in Vienna successfully despatched 300 non-Aryan children as part of a 1,000-strong transport, and 900 more were to follow. Of these 711 went straight to London and fifty-five to Sweden. Another eighty-three stopped in Holland and thirty-three remained in Belgium. Priority was given to those with parents who were already dead or in concentration camps, or who were manifestly in danger themselves. When war broke out there were still 650 cases that had yet to be placed on transports.[2] The children were looked after in Britain by the Movement for the Care of Children from Germany run by Lola Hahn-Warburg. The honorary president was Bentwich. A 'children's market' was established in London. Gentile foster parents mopped them up with alacrity.[3]

For non-IKG Jews, one-third of the places on the trains were assigned by the Quakers and another by Gildemeester. The last third was divided in two and managed by the Swedes and Caritas. Jewish emigration had been self-funding from the first. This had been Eichmann's aim all along. When the Quakers Ethel Houghton and David Hodgkin went to see Engel at the IKG in February 1939, he explained:

> Since the money obtained from the sale of foreign currency was used either for emigrating Jews or for giving them material relief, the government benefited in the first instance by getting rid of some undesirables and in the second by being saved from having itself to give relief to starving people since it is by law bound to relieve even Jews when they are absolutely destitute.[4]

The 4th was the Day of German Solidarity and a curfew was imposed on the Jews between midday and eight that evening. The leading Nazis were out on the streets shaking their *Winterhilfe* boxes. Goebbels and some of his children took up position in front of the Adlon Hotel on Unter den Linden. There was another campaign occupying their minds: elections in the Sudetenland. Hitler had been in the region on the 2nd. Maybe the incorporation of many pious

Catholics led Hitler to issue instructions to postpone the attack on the Churches until after a solution had been found for the Jews. By the end of the day they had collected 15 million RM. Later, results came in from the Sudetenland: 99 per cent were in favour of joining the Reich.

A last nail was driven into the coffin when all Jewish firms were to be taken over by trustees prior to sale. The trustees in these cases were named by the Ministry of Economics. The decree also allowed the government to force the sale of Jewish property. All stocks, bonds and securities had to be deposited at the regional offices of the Ministry. It was the culmination of the 'economic solution' to the Jewish problem. By the end of the year the Jews had been removed from business life throughout the Reich.[5] There were still exceptions: the decree was not yet applicable in Bohemia and Moravia, nor did it apply to foreign nationals. When an attempt had been made to register the fortunes of foreign Jews on 26 April, it led to a storm of protest from abroad and the government was forced to step down. Now every acquisition was to be made to enrich the state, rather than the purchaser. A tax was levelled on buyers equal to the difference between the price paid and the value of the business. The Jewish names and trademarks were also to be removed – a considerable disincentive to the purchaser. One Aryanized company that complained vigorously was Rosenthal porcelain, which had a significant export business. The Justice Ministry was prepared to make an exception, as there were no Jews left in the business.

Nazi diplomacy was still sending out contradictory signals. On 6 December Ribbentrop went to Paris to sign the Franco-German Declaration guaranteeing their present frontiers. The French were ready to massage the Germans for the time being, as there was no knowing where they would spring next. Ribbentrop, for his part, was pursuing his own dream of driving a wedge between the hated British and the French.[6] There was a comic scene in the Gare des Invalides when Ribbentrop stuck his nose so high in the air that he all but fell backwards on to the tracks.[7] On 9 December the RAM and Bonnet had another meeting at which Bonnet brought up the question of the Jews. France did not want any more. They were about to promulgate measures to keep them out and had plans to shift 10,000 of them to Madagascar. Ribbentrop conceded that no one wanted the Jews.[8]

At the beginning of December the Nazi leaders were forced to admit that, although they wanted the Jews to go, they could find nowhere that would take them. Extreme violence between Jews and Arabs made Palestine less and less tempting and the other doors were shut and bolted. In mid-November the German Foreign Office had decided to arrange a meeting with Rublee to work on the idea of creating a fund that would promote German exports. In exchange a degree more protection was to be accorded to the Jews. Under direct orders from Hitler, Hjalmar Schacht arrived in Britain as the guest of Montagu Norman, the Governor of the Bank of England. He met George Rublee, Lord Winterton and Sir Frederick Leith-Ross in London on the 14th.[9] The following day he saw Halifax and also had a meeting with Chamberlain. Schacht rightly saw that his days were numbered. In the event of his losing his plenipotentiary powers, he urged them to make contact with Funk.[10]

Schacht's scheme provided for the export of 150,000 Jews over the next three years. In exchange German Jews would create a fund amounting to 1.5 milliard RM to be matched by the same sum invested by Jews outside the Reich. This was to be used as credit for the purchase of German exports. The Germans would pay an annual interest of 4 per cent and amortize the sum at 2 per cent annually. The persecution of the Jews would cease during that period. Schacht was still prepared to run errands for Hitler to find a way back into his favour. Both Hitler and Göring had endorsed this scheme, the so-called Warburg Plan. Schacht reported back to Hitler on 2 January 1939.

The project did not find much favour among the Jews themselves, particularly in America. The Secretary of State Cordell Hull, pointed out that the boycott was not official and the Jews preferred the idea of a loan that was not linked to German exports. Rublee still hoped to be able to do a deal, and for that reason he went to Berlin on 13 January. A week later Schacht was relieved of his duties. It seems that a jealous Ribbentrop had finally had his way. Rublee was able to see Göring, who thought it would be possible to continue negotiations through his economic advisor Helmut Wohltat. German acceptance of the scheme remained conditional on a relaxation of the boycott.[11]

On 14 December local elections in the Memelland showed as many as 87.1 per cent had voted for Germany. In Britain, a debate in the House of Lords revealed the extent of immigration to date. There was concern about the transit of refugees and children in particular. Tallies were limited by the number of voluntary workers prepared to deal with them. Some 15–16,000 had landed in Britain, but 4–5,000 had left again. There were around a thousand children under eighteen who were granted right of asylum. Equally, people over the age of sixty were allowed to stay. There was evidence of a softer attitude: refugees were allowed to apply for visas in Britain and remain there for two years without papers provided they had some means of support. Those aged between sixteen and thirty-five could submit to further training with a view to finding work in another country. Employment was only to be granted in the case of no Briton wanting to do the work.[12]

The United States had already taken in 40,000, and there were 45,000 German refugees in France, 25,000 in Holland (8,000 had already moved on) and 100,000 in Czechoslovakia. It was not apparent at the time, but all those remaining on the Continent were at great risk.[13] There were ninety-four Austrian refugees in Albania.

The British government was exerting pressure on the colonies. The Australian government was still claiming it would take 15,000. One S.C. Leslie of the Gas, Light and Coke Co. was to go to Austria to interview candidates to work in Australia on 28 December.[14] Tanganyika and British Guiana were seen as good bets.[15]

The heat was being turned up in Italy: on 7 December Jewish refugees were told they had until 12 March to leave or face imprisonment.[16] The Dutch closed their borders to Jews on 17

December, but sent no children back if they had been placed in the carriages by their parents.[17] The Swiss too were being increasingly pettifogging in their attitude to the tide of refugees, many of whom had made their way over the green border from the Austrian Vorarlberg. On 17 December the Swiss tally was estimated to be between 10,000 and 12,000. 'Permission to enter Switzerland will be given to near relatives of Swiss if in danger and if their onward journey is certain within a reasonable time. Elderly persons will be admitted and arrangements are being made to take about 300 children temporarily.'[18] That very day Hitler issued a Führerbefehl: rump Czechoslovakia was to be liquidated as quickly as possible.

The British Legation in Berne reported directly to Halifax. Jews required visas to enter Switzerland, in direct response to the Austrians: 'In the course of July there was a great influx of Austrian Jews, mainly from Vienna.' The German attitude was largely one of 'good riddance': 'German frontier authorities . . . facilitated this illegal crossing of the Swiss frontier. This had, however, been stopped, on diplomatic representations being made to the German government.' The policy now was to send back Jews who had entered illegally. Germans had no need of visas to cross the frontier: 'The federal government has entered into communication with the German government. The latter announce that all passports would in future bear a special sign (a large J).' Since 4 October, German non-Aryans had to possess a visa too,[19] so only racially pure Germans were allowed to enter Switzerland freely.

It was not just the Jews that were feeling the heat. On 8 December Himmler decided he would clamp down on gypsies, issuing a 'Decree for the Struggle against the Gypsy Plague'. Henceforth gypsies were to be issued with papers for easier identification: brown for pure-bred, light-blue for *Mischlinge* and grey for Aryan nomads. The aim was to prevent any congress between gypsies and Aryan folk.[20] The text darkly hints at the 'final solution of the gypsy problem'.[21]

The knives were also out for the Church. A cartoon in Der Stürmer showed a priest pelting the regime with muck, but succeeding only in fouling the Cross.[22] For extreme Nazis, the SS and members of Himmler's circle, Christmas was already a dead letter anyway. *Stürmer* mocked the idea of Christmas in the ruins of Bethlehem and showed Father Christmas with a sack of Jews that no one wanted in their stockings. Germans celebrated the Winter Solstice on the 21st instead. On 10 December the Nazis once again showed their fangs towards the Christian churches. The singing of carols and school Christmas concerts were banned that year. The Christmas tree, being German, was permissible, but shorn of its Christian associations. Klemperer noted that the newspapers had been muzzled for the first time. Christ had been banished from Christmas. The feast celebrated the Great German soul, the rebirth of the light and the reawakening of the German Reich. 'The Jew Jesus, everything spiritual as well as anything generally human has been thrown out.'[23] All traditions were under attack, and that included the conservative-minded among the Germans. On 21 December Keitel emitted an ukase that no officers might congratulate the ex-Kaiser on his eightieth birthday. 'This was signed by a former Imperial officer,' wrote Groscurth. 'God forbid! And my, how little certain of itself this regime is.'[24]

The execution laid on in Buchenwald that Yuletide was not just a warning – it was a gift. Peter Forster had managed the unimaginable: he had escaped from the camp, killed a guard and crossed the Czech border; but the Czechs had handed him back. His execution was to be a lesson to them all. The executioner was none other than the senior prisoner. The entire camp was assembled by night. Spotlights lit up the scaffold, as well as the prisoners. No one was allowed to avert his sight. The senior appeared before the prisoner, twisting the rope – to what end, they couldn't say.

Then Forster was strung up, but when this happened, the senior jumped up and grasped him by the knees. The extra weight broke Forster's neck. The senior jumped down, and it was then that they realized why the rope had been twisted: the corpse proceeded to spin faster and faster on the rope lit up by the spotlights. It was a grotesque scene. Only then were the men allowed to return to their huts. A few days later it was discovered that alcohol had been smuggled into the camp for a New Year's party. Fifty men were made an example. They were stripped and tied to wooden horses and beaten until the flesh hung from their backs. A drunken Commandant Rödl meandered around, and the Buchenwald band was on hand to play the camp song.[25]

On Christmas Day Kurt von Schuschnigg was still in the Metropole, but he had the solace of a small radio furnished after Himmler's visit on 11 December. He could listen to the Coronation Mass from the Steffl, and took solace in the *Agnus Dei*.[26] On 31 December 1938 Austrian passports became invalid. Now Austrians had to seek new papers, and fresh humiliations along the way. On 30 December Helmuth Groscurth recorded a story about Goebbels, who had attempted to rape a young actress in Schwanenwerder. She was able to flee with the help of her fiancé. The Gestapo had learned of the incident and sent the girl a bunch of flowers with the message 'for the brave little lady'.[27] This may have explained the minister's mood as he donned his pyjamas that night. 'And so to bed. A new year! It is spine-chilling! The best thing to do would be to hang myself.'[28]

CONCLUSION

By the end of the year the national conservatives and the Nazis had parted ways. National government had been abandoned in favour of an ideologically correct Nazi one. At first Hitler's causes had also been theirs, but there were clear indications in 1938 that this was no longer so. Hitler had already dropped the nationalists from his ranks with the January crisis. The Prussian generals were no longer leading the army; the old-school diplomats no longer controlled the Wilhelmstrasse; the voices for a sensibly managed economy had been thrust out into the cold. Göring, a Nazi with national credentials, was increasingly sidelined as the year went on.

Apart from a few diehard Prussians like Kleist-Schmenzin, no one objected much to the merger with Austria or the redemption of the Sudetenländer: they were national causes that signified the end of the Versailles settlement and Germany's return to glory. A liberal German like Peter Bielenberg affirmed this:[1] Czech security, the maintenance of their efficient chains of forts – such arguments meant very little: the Sudetenländer had been given a rough deal and they were better off in the bosom of the Reich. People at the time did not possess the benefit of hindsight, and did not know what we know now: that Chamberlain's choosing not to fight – although utterly practical – was a disaster for the world.

Many of Hitler's decisions in 1938 were purely pragmatic and neglected to take stock of the national view, like the abandonment of 250,000 German South Tyroleans to Italy to gain Italian support, or the failure to come to a deal with the Poles to revise the border in return for a common stance against Bolshevik Russia. The fact that Vansittart was suspicious of Goerdeler's demand for the return of Danzig and the Polish Corridor is a sign that the diplomat was also incapable of telling the difference between Nazism and Nationalism.

On the domestic side, the *Reichskristallnacht* was no crowd-puller, and for many Germans it was either an embarrassment or a reason for distancing themselves from a regime they had tolerated up to then. The conspiracy around Goerdeler, Weizsäcker, Canaris, Witzleben and Halder is the clearest indication that Hitler had now gone too far, but the Opposition was increasingly distant from the source of power, and had problems removing him.

It had lost its chance after the failure of the putsch in September but there was a new generation in the wings that would eventually join forces with the older men and get the ball rolling again. Adam von Trott went to Berlin in November and stayed with Wilfred Israel in his flat in the Bendlerstrasse. He learned of the attempt to remove Hitler from Schacht. Schacht would keep him and others informed of moves within the Nazi elite. Through mutual friends, Trott was also able to meet some of the military leaders of the Opposition: Beck, whom he encountered at the house of the former chief of staff, Hammerstein-Equord, Alexander von Falkenhausen and Fritsch.[2]

During the year the balance of power within the Party and its organizations shifted. Himmler and Heydrich gained influence, touting a state based on a racial model too radical for nationalists. Eichmann's 'Viennese model' was copied to the Altreich, as Heydrich intended when Eichmann went to Berlin in February 1939 to accelerate the emigration of the Jews there. His solution was increasingly restricted by the decreasing number of countries ready to take in Jews. When the war started in September, most of these lands were no longer an option. When America joined the Allies in 1941 the last haven disappeared. By that time the Nazis had adopted the 'final solution'.

Palestine was closing the door to new immigrants and the Zionists took matters into their own hands. In Vienna Mossad was run by Mosche Averbruch or Agami. He worked with the Gestapo agent and wine merchant Giuseppe Matossiani and a Nazi 'old-fighter' called Wilhelm Karthaus to ship Jews to Palestine. They produced 20,000 Jugoslav visas to be used from Susak or Fiume. The Mexican consul had issued visas to imply that they were heading his way. This was the standard method of disguising the fact that the final destination was Palestine. Mexico, San Domingo, Liberia and China were the most common target destinations given. A Greek captain sailed under Panamanian colours. Nearly 2,000 Jews escaped from Constanza in Romania to Palestine before February 1940.[3] The hundreds of thousands of German and Austrian Jews who either stayed put or escaped to countries on the Continent were mopped up and despatched to the murder machines in the east.

Many of the men and women mentioned in these pages died violent deaths. The Nazis were killed in action, committed suicide or were hanged after the war. Many of those who resisted their power suffered a similar fate in the last stages of the conflict. Those Jews who failed to leave mainland Europe mostly perished.

Fred Richter's later history makes sad reading. He appeared before a magistrate at the Landgericht on 20 January 1939. He seems to have successfully retailed the argument that he was only a messenger and had no idea of what he was involved in. He later complained that the magistrate had been rough with him, and recanted everything he said. He had no idea that espionage was involved. On 15 September 1939 he was tried before the notorious Peoples' Court in Berlin. Tucek was naturally a model witness. *Kriminalrat* Preiss appeared for the prosecution: he had interrogated Kendrick, and was able to produce his testimony. Preiss informed the court that Richter had tried on several occasions to interest Kendrick in agents. The court concluded that Richter had been lying. Kendrick's testimony was in keeping with Tucek's. Richter was therefore convicted of acting as an accomplice to Kendrick. He was sentenced to twelve years' imprisonment and to pay a fine of 1,000 RM for wasting the court's time. He was released into captivity in Austria. He remained in Stein prison until 15 June 1942. He wrote his last letter to Maud from there in May that year before he was moved to Marburg in present-day

Slovenia; in September that year he was translated to Graz. He left Graz in February 1943 for Auschwitz, dying at 8.22 a.m. the day after his arrival, allegedly from heart disease: he had not survived the ramp.[4]

Tucek appears to have been working for the Gestapo. A man of that name was active in tracking down and torturing Austrian communists in Paris during the war and the French requested his extradition once he had been spotted on the streets of Vienna. He was sentenced to five years' imprisonment by a military court in Paris.[5]

The pogrom of 9 November had destroyed Chamberlain's policy of appeasement in Germany. The shock felt by many Britons after the events of the *Reichskristallnacht* made it untenable. It was now quite clear that Hitler would push for war, and that dangling trifles at him such as the return of the German colonies would not satisfy him in the long run. Although Chamberlain was unaware of it then, Hitler had already given instructions to OKH on 21 October to draw up plans for the invasion both of rump Czechoslovakia and Memelland.

Foreign boycotts of German goods were slowly strangling the regime. The new enemy was the 'Jewish State' – the United States, which for Hitler meant 'world Jewry'. If the United States was to stop importing German goods, then Germany would institute a policy of expansion to the east: it would mean the conquest of *Lebensraum*.[6] That the die was cast is evident from Hitler's speech in the Reichstag of 30 January 1939:

> I want today to be a prophet again: if international finance Jewry inside and outside Europe should succeed in plunging the nations once more into a world war, the result will not be the bolshevization of the earth and thereby the victory of Jewry, but the annihilation of the Jewish race in Europe.

In Goebbels' interpretation, the two-and-a-half-hour speech was a 'tough polemic against America'.[7] Others have seen the 'prophecy' as a green light to his hardline supporters who would begin to implement the 'final solution' in the last weeks of 1941.[8]

Hitler's style of despotism had become increasingly oriental. He rose at lunchtime and spent much of the day reading thrillers, watching films and delivering rambling monologues to his secretaries and adjutants. Cabinet meetings had ended in February 1938 and now only the closest members of his clique had the right of access to their Führer. His satraps were there to interpret the All Highest's will.

At the end of the year, Hitler's new Chancellery was well enough advanced for him to invite the press to revel in his glory. It was as if Hitler was now Wotan in the final bars of *Das Rheingold* inviting his gods into the new Valhalla. The man who had made the dream come true was Albert Speer, who had been appointed General Inspector for the Reich Capital on 30 January 1937. He had been given a mere nine months to build the Führer's new palace. In November he had summoned the sculptor Breker to the Prussian Academy on the Pariser Platz and told him to make two three-metre-high heroic figures to flank the entrance from the courtyard: 'The subject is up to you, we'll meet again in a week.' The meeting had taken all of five minutes.

Money was no object: he later commissioned five bronzes and two life-sized reliefs for the circular saloon that was created by the slight bend in the Vossstrasse. The Mosaic [sic] Saloon was decorated with work by Hermann Kaspar.[9] As Hitler told one of his adjutants, 'When these gentlemen [the press] enter the Mosaic Hall they must immediately sense the whole sublime nature of the Greater German Reich. The long corridors will reduce my visitors to humility.'[10] Beyond the granite hall with its cupola there stretched a hall of mirrors lined with red marble modelled on that of Louis XIV at Versailles, except that at 146 metres it was a little under twice as long. The goal of the visitor was Hitler's study. Its proportions were just as generous: 27 metres by 14.5, and nearly 10 metres high. At one end a portrait of Bismarck hung over a massive fireplace, while on the white marble table rode a statue of Frederick the Great on horseback. The whole edifice had cost just under ninety million marks. The wraps came off the new palace on 12 January 1939, Göring's birthday.

EPILOGUE

The history of Central Europe in 1938 is, to some extent, the history of my own family. That year my maternal grandfather's family scattered to the four winds. The Zirners and the Zwiebacks had come to Vienna from Baja and Bonyhad in Hungary two generations before, when, following defeat in the Austro-Prussian War, the emperor finally allowed Jews to settle in the capital. The cloth merchant Ludwig Zwieback promptly bought the stock exchange building housed in the old Palais Arnstein-Pereira in the Weihburggasse and opened a department store round the corner in the Kärntnerstrasse. His brothers opened a more downmarket version in the Mariahilferstrasse. When Ludwig died at his home on the Morzinplatz in 1906, he left each of his three daughters a third share in a fortune of some 2.2 million gold crowns, at a time when a genteel retirement might have been eked out on 3,000 a year.

The daughters were my great-grandmother Gisela, Ella, who inherited the business, and Malwine, who married the lawyer Siegmund Kranz. My great-grandmother married Marton Zirner, who had succeeded his father Max as court jeweller. They had four children: Josef, Katharina, Walther and Felix, my grandfather. Josef died an 'aspirant' in the K & K dragoons in the Bukovina in 1915. In civilian life he had been co-répétiteur in the opera houses in Hamburg and Breslau, having abandoned the law for music. He was hoping to become a conductor.

On 11 March 1938 great-uncle Josef's wife, the feminist novelist and later screenwriter Gina Kaus, was the first of my relatives to take the decision to run. She was another sparkling example of old Viennese Jewry, and the half-sister of Princess Stephanie zu

Hohenlohe, Hitler's Jewish spy.[i] Her books had been burned in Berlin in 1933 and she had made her way home to Vienna. Referring in her autobiography to the flames that engulfed the works of Heine, Thomas Mann and Sigmund Freud, she said, 'Never have I been in such good company.'[1]

After Josef's death great-aunt Gina married the Trieste-born Gentile Otto Kaus,[ii] but that marriage ended in separation. She left Vienna in 1938 with her latest lover and third and last husband, Eddy Frischauer, the brother of the journalist and writer Willi, who was already based in Britain. As Kaus's wife she had an Italian passport. When they were detained in Feldkirch in the Vorarlberg and asked to show their papers, Frischauer flourished his baptismal certificate, prudently issued to him shortly after his birth by his Catholic, assimilated-Jewish parents. It worked. They found safety in Switzerland. His parents were gassed. Gina eventually started a new career in Hollywood. She wrote no more novels, however: she had lost her language and her audience in Germany. She died in Los Angeles aged ninety-two.

Great-aunt Kathi died in Kasauli near Simla in 1927, shortly after giving birth to a boy called Martin. Martin was born premature and suffered from cerebral palsy. Kathi's husband, the Latvian Jew Dr Rudolf Rapaport, demanded my aunt's dowry, and my great-grandmother had to sell her last properties – the villa in Hietzing and country house on the Mondsee near Salzburg and the heavily mortgaged shop in the Graben – to pay him off. After escaping the Nazis from the south of France, Rapaport achieved fame as the painter Rudolf Ray in Mexico and the United States. Kathi may have had a second child called Bonifacius, the fruit of a liaison in Paris during her student years. He was secretly lodged in an orphanage in Klosterneuburg. The fate of Bonifacius is unknown.

---

[i] Stephanie was the result of a liaison between Gina's father and Stephanie's mother. Stephanie's father was in prison at the time.
[ii] Killed in an air-raid on Berlin.

My grandfather Felix and great-uncle Walther had started up a small business after the *déroute* caused by Rudolf Rapaport demanding my great-aunt's portion.[2] They naturally had no future in Vienna after March 1938. Walther was arrested in June, along with all the Viennese jewellers. He was sent to Dachau before being transferred to Buchenwald, but was eventually released. His Protestant Bavarian wife had divorced him. Whether she had bought him out or he was released for Hitler's fiftieth birthday, no one seems to know now. He died a broken man in 1963 in Central America, where he ran a coffee plantation.

My grandfather Felix Zirner had married Katharine Bacon. She was an English Catholic, the daughter of the Royal Academician John Henry Bacon. They had a daughter, my mother. The marriage broke up soon after and Katharine Zirner returned to England, where she died of TB in a nursing home in Haselmere, Surrey, in 1937. Felix was refused entry into Britain, where he might have joined his daughter. He left for Argentina from Genoa in September. His admission was presumably engineered by the pressure exerted by Rublee on the backtracking Argentinians. He made his way to Bolivia – 'the Rolls Royce of emigrations'[iii] – and established a small firm restoring churches. It is not known how he financed the journey and visa. A member of his wife's family probably obtained the latter for him in London or Washington. He died of heart failure in 1943 at the age of just thirty-eight.

Gisela Zirner died in 1930. Her sister Ella was still running the family department store in the Kärntnerstrasse with her son Ludwig as managing director. Ella was one of the most prominent women in Vienna. She led a fabulous life, took many lovers and had an estate across the Jugoslav border where guests were collected from the station by a carriage drawn by a team of white horses. In 1933 the Zirners rented out the former canteen of the department store to three Hungarian noblemen who turned it into the famous restaurant 'Zu

[iii] The phrase belongs to the late cabaret artist Gerhard Bronner.

den drei Husaren'. In 1938 the owner, Count Paul Pallfy, decided that he no longer wished to operate a restaurant in a Nazi Vienna and sold the lease to Otto Horcher, the restaurant-tsar of the Third Reich. During the war years its banquettes groaned under the weight of Hermann Göring and other Nazi luminaries.[3]

Ella had married my great-grandfather's brother, Alexander, who sat on the board of the Jewish congregation with my great-grandfather and was not only a pillar of the community but also one of the most prominent 'industrialists' in the city. Ella and Alexander went their separate ways before the First World War, and Alexander lived in a suite in the Imperial Hotel. When he died in 1924, several hundred people accompanied his coffin to the Central Cemetery.[4]

Ella had three children: Renée, who married the scion of a Hungarian magnate's family with the sonorous name of Erös von Bethlenfalva, and another, Erich, who fled to Monaco when the Germans attacked France and was still there in the fifties. The third child, Ludwig, however, was not Alexander's son but the result of a long-standing affair between Ella and the composer Franz Schmidt, the disciple of Bruckner. He had known her since her time at the Academy of Music, where Ella had won first prize for piano. Schmidt had wanted to marry Ella, but my great-great-grandfather felt the impecunious musician lacked prospects. Schmidt dedicated his First Symphony to Ella, and later made a present to her of the score of his opera Notre Dame, which was also inscribed to her. At around the time he was writing Notre Dame, Schmidt was a constant presence in Ella's flat next to the Bristol Hotel on the Ring. Schmidt and Ella used to play duets together. A form of synthesis was achieved when Ludwig was born in February 1906.[iv] Ludwig also studied privately and at the Academy under his natural father, but his mother refused to allow him to become a professional musician. The Nazis greatly

[iv] To celebrate Schmidt's Second Symphony Ella had the painter Adalbert Franz Seligmann decorate her music room with eight panels of various bacchanalia.

revered Schmidt and were presumably unaware that he had a Jewish son.

They commissioned a new work from him: *Eine Deutsche Auferstehung* (*German Resurrection*), which he was half-hearted about and failed to finish before he died in February 1939. Shortly before Ludwig left Vienna, a Gestapo-man came to see him and confiscated the score of *Notre Dame*. He never learned for certain who had informed them that he had it in his possession, but he suspected that it was Schmidt's pupil, the pianist Friedrich Wührer. Wührer was the first to tell Ludwig that he was Schmidt's son.[v] That was in America after the war. His mother had never discussed his paternity.

On 6 April 1938 Horcher became the owner of the walls of the restaurant as well, when Ella's property was Aryanized. The Nazis swiped one half of her wealth, her creditors the other: principally the *Zentrals-parkasse der Stadt Wien*. A large sum was paid into a closed account, of which Ella and her son Ludwig naturally saw nothing.[5] After Ella and Ludwig were forced to relinquish their property they made their ways via Cherbourg to New York, Ella on the arm of her new beau, the painter Viktor Krausz.[vi] Ella died in 1970. She had wanted to return to Vienna and become involved with the department store again, but Ludwig would not hear of it. Having been given a part of her property back in 1951, she sold it again in 1957. When Krausz died she took a younger lover who ran off with all that remained of the family fortune.

Ludwig was free at last. After serving as a musician in the American army, he cast off the fetters of commerce, sat numerous exams and submitted a doctoral dissertation on American piano music. He finally achieved complete metamorphosis, becoming Professor of Piano at the State University of Illinois. Assisted by his

[v] 'Do I thank him or punch him?' Ludwig asked his wife Laura at the revelation.
[vi] Krausz's rich Jewish wife Marianne had committed suicide in 1938. The Krausz collection passed into the hands of the Nazi authorities. The old masters must have pleased them, Krausz's own paintings rather less.

Viennese-born wife Laura, he began the opera courses that were later to distinguish the school of music at Urbana. He also prepared and translated scores and conducted a wide range of operas, and was the life and soul of the famous Tanglewood Music Festival. As Schmidt's son, he was the heir to the purest Viennese musical tradition.

At his invitation Stravinsky, Britten, Milhaud, Kubelik, Hindemith and Beecham all visited Urbana. He was so successful that he was invited to take over the opera school at the Academy of Music in Berlin. He eventually realized his dream of building a proper opera house in Urbana, and, although already a very sick man, shortly before his death he put on a performance of *Rheingold* there, with Wagner's great-grandson, Wolf Siegfried 'Wummi' Wagner, at his side. After he died in 1971, his wife Laura returned to Vienna to join their teenage son August, who was training to be an actor. August is now an Austrian citizen and celebrated for his theatre and cinema performances in the German-speaking world.

The Zirners and the Zwiebacks were lucky. They were rich and well connected, and were able to escape from Austria before it was too late. Two of my close relatives perished: the painter Rudolf Rapaport abandoned his mentally retarded son when he fled to America. Martin Ray perished awaiting transport to Auschwitz in November 1944; his first cousin Otto Kranz was gassed at Hartheim in 1940.

NOTES

MANUSCRIPT SOURCES

FLA   Friends Library Archive, London.
BBD   British Board of Deputies Archive, London.
PRO   Public Record Office, London.
LMA   London Metropolitan Archive.
DGFP   Documents in German Foreign Policy.

INTRODUCTION

[1] Richard Grunberger, A Social History of the Third Reich, London 1974, 269.

PROLOGUE

[1] Hermann Foertsch, Schuld und Verhängnis: Die Fritsch-Krise im Früehjahr 1938 als Wendepunkt in der Geschichte der national-sozialistischen Zeit, Stuttgart 1951, 75–6.

[2] Ian Kershaw, Hitler 1936–1945: Nemesis, London 2001, 47.

[3] Foertsch, Schuld und Verhängnis, 77–9.

[4] Fröhlich, Elke, Die Tagebücher von Joseph Goebbels I, V, 29.

[5] See Adam Tooze, The Wages of Destruction: The Making and Breaking of the Nazi Economy, London 2006, xxiii–xxiv, 239–43.

[6] Goebbels, Tagebücher I, V, 95, 96.

[7] Andrew Roberts, 'The Holy Fox': The Life of Lord Halifax, London 1997, 71.

[8] Michael Bloch, Ribbentrop, revised edition, London 1992, 159–60.

[9] Henrik Eberle and Matthias Uhl, eds, The Hitler Book: The Secret Dossier Prepared for Stalin, trans. Giles MacDonogh, London 2005, 25.

CHAPTER 1: JANUARY

[1] Walther Nowojski and Hadwig Klemperer, eds, Victor Klemperer, Ich will Zeugnis ablegen bis zum letzten – Tagebücher 1933–1941, Berlin 1995, 391; Goebbels, Tagebücher I, V, 82.

[2] Goebbels, Tagebücher I, V, 97.

[3] Der Stürmer 3, January 1938.

[4] Der Stürmer 1, January 1938.

[5] Klemperer, Tagebücher, 395.

[6] Goebbels, Tagebücher I, V, 96.

[7] David Irving, Göring, London 1989, 194.

[8] Irving, Göring, 196.

[9] R.J. Overy, Goering – The Iron Man, London 1984, 69.

[10] Jochen von Lang, Der Adjutant: Karl Wolff – der Mann zwischen Hitler und Himmler, Munich and Berlin 1985, 80.

[11] Goebbels, Tagebücher I, V, 54.

[12] André Brissaud, Canaris – Le 'petit amiral', prince de l'espionage allemand (1887–1945), Paris 1970, 161; Goebbels, Tagebücher I, V, 117.

[13] T.P. Conwell-Evans, None So Blind, Based on the Private Papers of Group Captain M.G. Christie, London 1947, 115.

[14] Foertsch, Schuld und Verhängnis, 86.

[15] Peter Padfield, Himmler – Reichsführer SS, London 1990, 212.

[16] Goebbels, Tagebücher I, V, 103, 105.

[17] Anthony Read, The Devil's Disciples: The Lives and Times of

Hitler's Inner Circle, London 2003, 449.

[18] Lang, *Wolff*, 80.

[19] Thomas Mang, *'Gestapo-Leitstelle Wien – Mein Name ist Huber'*: *Wer trug die locale Verantwortung für den Mord an der Wiener Juden*, Münster 2004, 118.

[20] Wilhelm Keitel, *Mein Leben: Pflichterfüllung bis zum Untergang*, Berlin 1998, 201–204.

[21] Lang, *Wolff*, 81–2.

[22] Mang, *Mein Name ist Huber*, 119; Lang, *Wolff*, 82.

[23] Foertsch, *Schuld und Verhängnis*, 94.

[24] Lang, *Wolff*, 82.

[25] Foertsch, *Schuld und Verhängnis*, 88.

[26] Lang, *Wolff*, 82.

[27] Goebbels, *Tagebücher I*, V, 117; Read, *Devil's Disciples*, 450.

[28] Goebbels, *Tagebücher I*, V, 115.

[29] Overy, *Goering*, 70.

[30] Keitel, *Mein Leben*, 207.

[31] Keitel, *Mein Leben*, 207.

[32] General Baron Geyr von Schweppenburg, *The Critical Years*, London 1952, 171–2.

[33] Overy, *Goering*, 70.

[34] Padfield, *Himmler*, 217, who does not disclose his source, which was probably Lang, *Wolff*, 84.

[35] Foertsch, *Schuld und Verhängnis*, 91.

[36] Foertsch, *Schuld und Verhängnis*, 93.

[37] Goebbels, *Tagebücher I*, V, 124.

[38] Jodl, diary, quoted in Foertsch, *Schuld und Verhängnis*, 89.

[39] Goebbels, *Tagebücher I*, V, 117–18.

[40] Mang, *Mein Name ist Huber*, 120.

[41] Brissaud, *Canaris*, 160.

[42] Goebbels, *Tagebücher I*, V, 132.

[43] Goebbels, *Tagebücher I*, V, 122.

[44] Lang, *Wolff*, 83.

[45] Foertsch, *Schuld und Verhängnis*, 95.

[46] André François-Poncet, *Souvenirs d'une ambassade à Berlin*, Paris 1946, 285.

[47] Goebbels, *Tagebücher I*, V, 119.

[48] Detlef Graf von Schwerin, *'Dann sind's die besten Köpfe, die man henkt.' Die junge Generation im deutschen Widerstand*, Munich 1994, 139.

[49] Franz von Papen, *Memoirs*, translated by Brian Connell, London 1952, 404.

[50] Foertsch, *Schuld und Verhängnis*, 94.

[51] Foertsch, *Schuld und Verhängnis*, 102.

[52] Reinhard Spitzy, *So haben wir das Reich verspielt – Bekenntnisse eines Illegalen*, 2nd edn, Munich 1987, 218.

[53] Bloch, *Ribbentrop*, 165–6; Goebbels, *Tagebücher I*, V, 127.

[54] Eberle and Uhl, *Hitler Book*, 24.

[55] Elke Fröhlich, ed., *Die Tagebücher von Joseph Goebbels*, Teil 1, Band 5, December 1937–July 1938, Munich 2000, 65, 122.

[56] Stefan Kley, *Hitler, Ribbentrop und die Entfesselung des Zweiten Weltkriegs*, Paderborn 1996, 46.

[57] Willi Frischauer, *Twilight Vienna*, translated by E.O. Lorimer, London 1938, 291.

[58] Ray Moseley, *Mussolini's Shadow: The Double Life of Count Galeazzo Ciano*, New Haven and Yale 1999, 41.

CHAPTER 2: FEBRUARY

[1] Goebbels, *Tagebücher I*, V, 131.

[2] François-Poncet, *Souvenirs*, 184, 285.

[3] Goebbels, *Tagebücher I*, V, 132.

[4] Kershaw, *Nemesis*, 58.

[5] Foertsch, *Schuld und Verhängnis*, 103.

[6] Keitel, *Mein Leben*, 209.

[7] Jochen Klepper, *Unter dem Schatten deiner Flügel: aus den Tagebüchern der Jahre 1932–1942*, Stuttgart 1955, 553.

[8] Bloch, *Ribbentrop*, 161–2.

[9] François-Poncet, *Souvenirs*, 291.

[10] Erich Kordt, *Nicht aus den Akten . . . Die Wilhelmstrasse in Frieden und Krieg. Erlebnisse, Begegnungen und Eindrücke 1928–1945*, Stuttgart 1950, 172.

[11] Kley, *Hitler, Ribbentrop*, 10; Spitzy, *So haben wir das Reich verspielt*, 228.

[12] Bloch, *Ribbentrop*, 171.

[13] Spitzy, *So haben wir das Reich verspielt*, 219.

[14] Malcolm Muggeridge, ed., *Ciano's Diary 1937–1938*, trans. Andreas Mayor, London 1952, 61, 62, 81.

[15] Kershaw, *Nemesis*, 59.

[16] Klepper, *Tagebücher*, 551.

[17] *Der Stürmer* 1, January 1938.

[18] Conwell-Evans, *None So Blind*, 124.

[19] Tooze, *Wages*, 243–6.

[20] Bloch, *Ribbentrop*, 176.

[21] Papen, *Memoirs*, 406–8.

[22] G.E.R. Gedye, *Fallen Bastions: The Central European Tragedy*, London 1939, 224; George E. Berkley, *Vienna and Its Jews: The Tragedy of Success 1880s–1980s*, Cambridge, Mass. 1987, 249.

[23] Eberle and Uhl, *Hitler Book*, 26.

[24] *Ciano's Diary*, 82.

[25] Kurt von Schuschnigg, *Austrian Requiem*, trans. Franz von Hildebrand, New York 1946, 13.

[26] Hubert Wingelbauer, 'Das Österreichische Bundesheer', in Verein für Geschichte der Stadt Wien [afterwards Stadt Wien], *Wien 1938*, Vienna 1978, 39.

[27] Spitzy, *So haben wir das Reich verspielt*, 226.

[28] Bloch, *Ribbentrop*, 178.

[29] *The Ribbentrop Memoirs*, with an introduction by Alan Bullock, London 1954, 84.

[30] Kley, *Hitler, Ribbentrop*, 49.

[31] Papen, *Memoirs*, 415–17.

[32] Keitel, *Mein Leben*, 218.

[33] Papen, *Memoirs*, 417. This may well have been his sole appearance as the God of War.

[34] Eberle and Uhl, *Hitler Book*, 26.

[35] Schuschnigg, *Requiem*, 25.

[36] Schuschnigg, *Requiem*, 26.

[37] Hanns Haas, 'Der Anschluss', in Emmerich Talos, Ernst Hanisch, Wolfgang Neugebauer, Reinhard Sieder et al., *NS-Herrschaft in Österreich, Ein Handbuch*, Vienna 2001, 40–1.

[38] Papen, *Memoirs*, 420.

[39] Bloch, *Ribbentrop*, 172.

[40] Kershaw, *Nemesis*, 71 quoting Papen, *Memoirs*, 420.

[41] Brissaud, *Canaris*, 185.

[42] Jodl diary, also quoted in Ian Colvin, *Chief of Intelligence*, London 1951, 47.

[43] Haas in Talos et al., *NS-Herrschaft*, 40.

[44] *Ciano's Diary*, 74, 77.

[45] Goebbels, *Tagebücher I*, V, 159, 161.

[46] Rudolf Aschenauer, ed., *Ich Adolf Eichmann*, Starnbergersee 1980, 84–5.

[47] Padfield, *Himmler*, 219.

[48] Mang, *Mein Name ist Huber*, 57.

[49] Hans Safrian, *Die Eichmann Männer*, Vienna and Zurich 1993, 27; Theodor Venus and Alexandra-Eileen Wenck, *Die Entziehung jüdischen Vermögens im Rahmen der Aktion Gildemeester*, Vienna and Munich 2004, 89; David Cesarani, *Eichmann: His Life and Crimes*, London 2004, 54.

[50] John Mendelsohn and Donald S. Detwiler, eds, *The Holocaust – Selected Documents in Eighteen Volumes*, VI, New York and London 1982, 69.

[51] Klemperer, *Tagebücher*, 397.

[52] Hans Roos, *Polen und Europa: Studien zur polnischen Aussenpolitik 1931–1939*, Tübingen 1957, 300.

[53] Schuschnigg, *Requiem*, 32.

[54] Goebbels, *Tagebücher I*, V, 168, 155, 174, 100.

[55] Klepper, *Tagebücher*, 559.

[56] Klemperer, *Tagebücher*, 397.

[57] Goebbels, *Tagebücher I*, V, 178.

[58] Roberts, *Holy Fox*, 87.

[59] Goebbels, *Tagebücher I*, V, 169, 188, 194.

[60] Goebbels, *Tagebücher I*, V, 166.

[61] Goebbels, *Tagebücher I*, V, 181.

[62] Berta Geismar, *The Baton and the Jackboot, Recollections of Musical Life*, London 1944, 325.

[63] Goebbels, *Tagebücher I*, V, 172

[64] Goebbels, *Tagebücher I*, V, 181–2.

[65] Goebbels, *Tagebücher I*, V, 143, 146.

[66] Schwerin, *junge Generation*, 140.

CHAPTER 3: MARCH

[1] Klemperer, *Tagebücher*, 398.

[2] Goebbels, *Tagebücher I*, V, 183.

[3] Goebbels, *Tagebücher I*, V, 183, 192.

[4] Schwerin, *junge Generation*, 141.

[5] Schwerin, *junge Generation*, 141.

[6] Lang, *Wolff*, 85.

[7] Goebbels, *Tagebücher I*, V, 241.

[8] Schuschnigg, *Requiem*, 33.

[9] *Ciano's Diary*, 84.

[10] Ernst Lothar, *Das Wunder des Überlebens: Erinnerungen und Ergebnisse*, Hamburg and Vienna 1960, 103.

[11] Lothar, *Erinnerungen*, 104.

[12] Kordt, *Nicht aus den Akten*, 192–3.

[13] *Ciano's Diary*, 79.

[14] Roberts, *Holy Fox*, 89.

[15] Kordt, *Nicht aus den Akten*, 195.

[16] Goebbels, *Tagebücher I*, V, 198–9.

[17] Spitzy, *So haben wir das Reich verspielt*, 234.

[18] Jodl, *Diary*, quoted in Foertsch, *Schuld und Verhängnis*.

[19] *Ciano's Diary*, 87.

[20] Papen, *Memoirs*, 424.

[21] See Richard Lamb, *The Ghosts of Peace*, London 1987, 56; Goebbels, *Tagebücher I*, V, 199.

[22] See Isabella Ackerl, 'Die Propaganda der Vaterländischen Front für die geplante Volksfragung vom 13 März 1938', in Stadt Wien, *Wien 1938*, 18–23.

[23] See Haas in Talos et al., *NS-Herrschaft*, 42.

[24] Spitzy, *So haben wir das Reich verspielt*, 231.

[25] Georg Stefan Troller, *Das fidele Grab an der Donau – mein Wien 1918–1938*, Düsseldorf and Zurich 2004, 239–40.

[26] Goebbels, *Tagebücher I*, V, 200.

[27] Lothar, *Erinnerungen*, 105.

[28] Bloch, *Ribbentrop*, 194–5.

[29] Viscount Templewood, *Nine Troubled Years*, London 1954, 282.

[30] Jonny Moser, 'Das Schicksal der Wiener Juden in März-und Apriltagen 1938', in Stadt Wien, *Wien 1938*, 173.

[31] Gina Kaus, *Und was für ein Leben – mit Liebe und Literatur, Theater und Film*, Hamburg 1979, 198.

[32] *Ciano's Diary*, 87.

[33] Eberle and Uhl, *Hitler Book*, 27.

[34] Schuschnigg, *Requiem*, 46.

[35] Goebbels, *Tagebücher I*, V, 203.

[36] Wingelbauer in Stadt Wien, *Wien 1938*, 41.

[37] Haas in Talos et al., *NS-Herrschaft*, 43; Wingelbauer in Stadt Wien, *Wien 1938*, 42.

[38] Lothar, *Erinnerungen*, 108–9.

[39] Kershaw, *Nemesis*, 77.

[40] *Ciano's Diary*, 87.

[41] Schuschnigg, *Requiem*, 48.

[42] Kordt, *Nicht aus den Akten*, 191.

[43] Maximilian Liebmann, *Theodor Innitzer und der Anschluss – Österreichs Kirche 1938*, Graz, Venna, Cologne 1988, 65.

[44] Troller, *fidele Grab*, 242.

[45] Troller, *fidele Grab*, 242.

[46] Kaus, *Und was für ein Leben*, 200.

[47] Haas, 'Anschluss', in Talos et al., *NS-Herrschaft*, 45.

[48] Gerhart Botz, *Nationalsozialismus in Wien: Machtübernahme, Herrschafts-sicherung, Radikalisierung 1938–1939*, Vienna 2008, 62–3.

[49] Irving, Göring, 209.

[50] Geismar, *Jackboot*, 327.

[51] Goebbels, *Tagebücher I*, V, 203; *Der Stürmer* 12, March 1938.

[52] Golden book of 'Zu den drei Husaren', communicated by the owner, Uwe Kohl; see also Giles MacDonogh, 'Otto Horcher, Caterer to the Third Reich', in *Gastronomica*, Volume 7, Number 1, Winter 2007.

[53] Willi Frischauer, *Goering* [sic], London n.d., 153.

[54] Rosenkranz, *Verfolgung*, 9.

[55] Andrew Chandler, 'Lambeth Palace, the Church of England and the Jews of Germany and Austria in 1938', in the *Leo Baeck Institute Yearbook*, 1995, 227.

[56] Sylvia Maderegger, *Die Juden im österreichischen Ständestaat 1934–1938*, Salzburg 1973, 47–8, 56.

[57] Alexander A. Bankier, '"... auch nicht von der Frau Hinterhuber." Zu den ökonomischen Aspekten des November-pogroms in Wien', in Historisches Museum der Stadt Wien [afterwards Historisches Museum], *Der Novemberpogrom 1938*, Vienna 1988, 71.

[58] Troller, *fidele Grab*, 66–7.

[59] Herbert Rosenkranz, *Verfolgung und Selbstbehauptung: die Juden in Österreich 1938–1945*, Vienna and Munich 1978, 32.

[60] Nina Scholz and Heiko Heinisch, '... alles werden sich die Christen nicht gefallen lassen': *Wiener Pfarrer und die Juden in der Zwischenkriegszeit*, Vienna 2001, 56–7.

[61] E-mail from Henry Wellisch of Toronto, 22 November 2007.

[62] Lambeth Palace, Bell Papers 35.

[63] Sheila Spielhofer, *Stemming the Dark Tide, the Quakers in Vienna 1919–1942*, York 2001, 111; Freund and Safrian in Talos et al., *NS-Herrschaft*, 789.

[64] Karl Popper, *Unended Quest*, Glasgow 1982, 105.

[65] Sylvia Maderegger, *Ständestaat*, 60.

[66] Georg Fischer in Elfriede Schmidt, *1938 . . . und was dann? Fragen und Reaktionen*, Thaur bei Innsbruck 1988, 31.

[67] Bruno Heilig, *Men Crucified*, London 1941, 94.

[68] Lambeth Palace, LR 1CC21 report by Hugh Grimes, 1 February 1937.

[69] See Gerhard Botz, *Wien vom Anschluss zum Weltkrieg*, Vienna 1978.

[70] Maximilian and Emilie Reich, *Zweier Zeugen Mund: verschollene Manuskripte aus 1938. Wien – Dachau – Buchenwald*, with an introduction by Henriette Mandl, Vienna 2007, 200.

[71] BBD, C11/8/1/1.

[72] Reich, *Zweier Zeugen Mund*, 36.

[73] FLA, Germany Files, GE9, Emma Cadbury to Alice Nike, 11 March 1938.

[74] Gedye, *Fallen Bastions*, 18.

[75] George Clare, *The Last Waltz in Vienna*, London 1994, 200.

[76] Botz, *Nationalsozialismus*, 71.

[77] François-Poncet, *Souvenirs*, 317.

[78] Rosenkranz, *Verfolgung*, 31.

[79] Gedye, *Fallen Bastions*, 363.

[80] Carl Zuckmayer, *Als wär's ein Stück von mir*, Frankfurt/Main 2006, 83.

[81] Zuckmayer, *Stück von Mir*, 84.

[82] Zuckmayer, *Stück von Mir*, 90.

[83] Lothar, *Erinnerungen*, 110–12.

[84] Lothar, *Erinnerungen*, 120–6.

[85] Kaus, *Und was für ein Leben*, 205–8.

[86] Troller, *fidele Grab*, 226.

87 Goebbels, *Tagebücher I*, V, 214, 219, 222, 238, 240.

88 Geismar, *Jackboot*, 329–31.

89 Rosenkranz, *Verfolgung*, 23.

90 Troller, *fidele Grab*, 245.

91 Reichsgesetzblatt, I, 1938, 237.

92 Michael Smith, *Foley, the Spy Who Saved 10,000 Jews*, London 1999, 107.

93 Interview with the late Sir Dudley Forwood, 12 June 2000.

94 Wingelbauer in Stadt Wien, *Wien 1938*, 46.

95 Rosenkranz, *Verfolgung*, 33.

96 Safrian, *Eichmann*, 31; Lauterbach in BBD, Acc 3121/c11/12/2/1938.

97 Elisabeth Klamper, 'Der schlechte Ort zu Wien. Zur Situation der Wiener Juden vom "Anschluss" bis zum Novemberpogrom 1938', in Historisches Museum, *Novemberpogrom*, 34–5.

98 Emilie Reich in Reich, *Zweier Zeugen Mund*, 268.

99 Botz, *Nationalsozialismus*, 74.

100 Hans Witek, 'Arisieren' in 'Wien: Aspekte national-sozialistischer Enteignungspolitik 1938–1940', in Talos et al., *NS–Herrschaft*, 795.

101 Safrian, *Eichmann*, 34.

102 Rosenkranz, *Verfolgung*, 30.

103 Rosenkranz, *Verfolgung*, 28.

104 Sophie Lillie, *Was einmal war: Handbuch der enteigneten Kunstsammlungen Wiens*, Vienna 2003, 429–30.

105 Elfriede Schmidt, *1938 . . . und was dann? Fragen und Reaktionen*, Thaur bei Innsbruck 1988, 2.

106 Schmidt, *1938 . . . und was dann?*, 18.

107 Reich, *Zweier Zeugen Mund*, 61.

108 Troller, *fidele Grab*, 253.

109 Berkley, *Vienna and Its Jews*, 274.

110 Lydia Marinelli, ed., *Freuds verschwundener Nachbarn* (Exhibition Catalogue), Vienna 2003, 28.

111 Schwerin, *junge Generation*, 145.

[112] Emilie Reich, in Reich, *Zweier Zeugen Mund*, 262–3, 267.

[113] Robert Young, *A Young Man Looks at Europe*, Kingswood, Surrey 1938, 327.

[114] Zuckmayer, *Stück von mir*, 94–107.

[115] Zuckmayer, *Stück von mir*, 90.

[116] Gedye, *Fallen Bastions*, 54.

[117] Herta Maria von Kubinzky in Schmidt, *1938 . . . und was dann?*, 120–1.

[118] Rosenkranz, *Verfolgung*, 13.

[119] BBD, C11A/7, 6 April 1938.

[120] BBD, Acc 3121/c11/12/2/1938; Rosenkranz, *Verfolgung*, 45.

[121] Chandler, 'Church of England', 230.

[122] http://oesterreich-2005.at/projekte/1143303416/1143309027.

[123] Rosenkranz, *Verfolgung*, 153; private information.

[124] Ludwig Reichhold, 'Die Liquidierung der Vaterländischen Front', in Stadt Wien, *1938*, 25; Wolfgang Neugebauer, introduction to Reich, *Zweier Zeugen Mund*, 14; Lang, *Wolff*, 87.

[125] Jonny Moser, *Die Juden Verfolgung in Österreich 1938–1945*, Vienna, Frankfurt and Munich 1966, 5; Marianne Engel, 'Archive des Grauens', in *Profil*, 23 July 2001.

[126] Engel, 'Archive des Grauens'.

[127] Padfield, *Himmler*, 222, from Lang, *Wolff*, 89–90.

[128] Lang, *Wolff*, 91.

[129] Safrian, *Eichmann*, 27.

[130] Safrian, *Eichmann*, 27.

[131] Venus and Wenck, *Die Entziehung jüdischen Vermögens*, 21.

[132] Keitel, *Mein Leben*, 219.

[133] Frischauer, *Goering*, 154.

[134] Klepper, *Tagebücher*, 564.

[135] *Der Stürmer* 12, March 1938.

[136] Kershaw, *Nemesis*, 80.

[137] Haas, 'Anschluss', in Talos et al., *NS-Herrschaft*, 47.

[138] Emmerich Talos, 'Die Etablierung der Reichsgaue der "Ostmark"', in Talos et al., *NS-Herrschaft*, 59.

[139] Jagschitz in Talos et al., *NS-Herrschaft*, 98.

[140] Helene Maimann, 'Die Reaktionen der Auslandspresse auf den "Anschluss" Österreichs an das Deutsche Reich', in Stadt Wien, *Wien 1938*, 116–17.

[141] Maimann in Stadt Wien, *Wien 1938*, 118.

[142] Irving, *Göring*, 217.

[143] Lang, *Wolff*, 88.

[144] Young, *A Young Man*, 336.

[145] Frischauer, *Goering*, 154.

[146] Sebastian Bock, *Österreichs Stifte unter dem Hackenkreuz. Zeugnisse und Dokumente aus der Zeit des Nationalsozialismus 1938–1945*, Vienna, 1995, 54.

[147] Liebmann, *Innitzer*, 66–7.

[148] Rosenkranz, *Verfolgung*, 23–4.

[149] Papen, *Memoirs*, 432.

[150] Spitzy, *So haben wir das Reich verspielt*, 248.

[151] Erika Weinzierl, 'Kirche und Nationalsozialismus in Wien im März 1938', in Stadt Wien, *Wien 1938*, 168–9.

[152] Liebmann, *Innitzer*, 71 and 264 n156. Hitler's adjutant, Gerhard Engel, was witness to the blessing.

[153] Goebbels, *Tagebücher I*, V, 242.

[154] Walter Sauer, 'Loyalität, Konkurrenz oder Widerstand?', in Talos et al., *NS-Herrschaft*, 162–3.

[155] Goebbels, *Tagebücher I*, V, 209.

[156] Botz, *Nationalsozialismus*, 95.

[157] Spitzy, *So haben wir das Reich verspielt*, 249.

[158] Patricia Meehan, *The Unnecessary War: Whitehall and the German Resistance to Hitler*, London 1992, 51.

[159] Safrian, *Eichmann*, 31.

[160] Klamper in Historisches Museum, *Novemberpogrom*, 37.

[161] Reichsgesetzblatt, I, 1938, 262.

[162] Safrian, *Eichmann*, 32.

[163] Gerhard Jagschitz, 'Von der "Bewegung" zum Apparat', in Talos et al., *NS-Herrschaft*, 94.

164 Botz, *Nationalsozialismus*, 133.

165 Goebbels, *Tagebücher I*, V, 216.

166 Goebbels, *Tagebücher I*, V, 228.

167 Roos, *Polen und Europa*, 301, 305, 307–8.

168 Roos, *Polen und Europa*, 319.

169 Goebbels, *Tagebücher I*, V, 222.

170 Printed in Schmidt, *1938 . . . und was dann?*, 296.

171 Haas, 'Anschluss', in Talos et al., *NS-Herrschaft*, 46.

172 Liebmann, *Innitzer*, 76, 78, 93–4.

173 Cesarani, *Eichmann*, 63.

174 Rosenkranz, *Verfolgung*, 34, 37.

175 Safrian, *Eichmann*, 37.

176 Engel, 'Archive des Grauens'.

177 Mang, *Mein Name ist Huber*, 21.

178 Tina Walzer and Stephan Templ, *Unser Wien: 'Arisierung' auf Oesterreichisch*, Berlin 2001, 30.

179 Wolfgang Neugebauer, 'Der NS-Terrorapparat', in Talos et al., *NS-Herrschaft*, 730.

180 Troller, *fidele Grab*, 224.

181 Engel, 'Archive des Grauens'.

182 Botz, *Nationalsozialismus*, 316.

183 Tooze, *Wages*, 246.

184 Walzer and Templ, *Unser Wien*, 38.

185 Irving, *Göring*, 218.

186 Raul Hilberg, *The Destruction of the European Jews*, 3rd edn, I, 10–1.

187 Hilberg, *Destruction*, 3rd edn, I, 118–19.

188 Walzer and Templ, *Unser Wien*, 39–40.

189 Walzer and Templ, *Unser Wien*, 40.

190 Rosenkranz, *Verfolgung*, 40–1.

191 Reich, *Zweier Zeugen Mund*, 201.

192 Gerhard Botz, 'Beseitigung der Arbeitslosigkeit in Wien 1938/1939', in Stadt Wien, *Wien 1938*, 190.

193 Botz, *Nationalsozialismus*, 172.

[194] Goebbels, *Tagebücher I*, V, 254.

[195] Schuschnigg, *Requiem*, 62–3.

[196] Goebbels, *Tagebücher I*, V, 238.

[197] Goebbels, *Tagebücher I*, V, 159.

[198] Kley, *Hitler, Ribbentrop*, 72, 79.

[199] Roberts, *Holy Fox*, 93.

[200] Lang, *Wolff*, 101.

[201] Kordt, *Nicht aus den Akten*, 207.

[202] Conwell-Evans, *None So Blind*, 135.

[203] Goebbels, *Tagebücher I*, V, 221, 237.

[204] Quoted in Roger Moorhouse, *Killing Hitler: The Third Reich and the Plots against the Führer*, London 2006, 68.

[205] Klemens von Klemperer, *German Resistance against Hitler: The Search for Allies Abroad 1938–1945*, Oxford 1992, 24–5.

[206] Meehan, *The Unnecessary War*, 36.

[207] Klemperer, *German Resistance*, 20.

[208] Meehan, *Unnecessary War*, 121–2.

[209] Schwerin, *junge Generation*, 147.

[210] Bella Fromm, *Blood and Banquets: A Berlin Diary 1930–1938*, New York 1990, 267.

[211] Bodo Scheurig, *Ewald von Kleist-Schmenzin, ein Konservativer gegen Hitler*, Frankfurt am Main 1994, 153.

[212] Klemperer, *German Resistance*, 97–8.

[213] Ian Kershaw, *Hitler, the Germans, and the Final Solution*, New Haven and London 2008, 55.

[214] Hilberg, *Destruction*, I, 138–42.

[215] Reichsgesetzblatt, I, 1938, 338.

[216] BBD, C11A/7, 6 April 1938.

[217] Clare, *Last Waltz*, 199.

[218] PRO TI 5833 580 14 December 1938 607–9.

[219] Clare, *Last Waltz*, 206.

[220] Clare, *Last Waltz*, 205.

[221] Safrian, *Eichmann*, 35.

[222] Clare, *Last Waltz*, 211.

[223] Safrian, *Eichmann*, 44–5.

[224] Louise London, *Whitehall and the Jews 1933–1948: British Immigration Policy and the Holocaust*, Cambridge 2000, 60.

[225] London, *Whitehall*, 66.

[226] PRO T1 5833 580, 17 December, 624–5.

[227] Safrian, *Eichmann*, 15.

[228] Venus and Wenck, *Die Entziehung jüdischen Vermögens*, 16.

[229] Safrian, *Eichmann*, 24–5.

[230] Florian Freund and Hans Safrian, 'Die Verfolgung der österreichischen Juden', in Talos et al., *NS-Herrschaft*, 769.

[231] Rosenkranz, *Verfolgung*, 108–9.

[232] Wolfgang von Weisl, 'Illegale Transporte', in Josef Fraenkel, ed., *The Jews of Austria*, London 1967, 169–70.

[233] BBD, Acc 3121 C11/12/2, Norman Bentwich, Report 17 August 1939.

[234] BBD, Acc 3121 C11/12/2, Norman Bentwich, Report 17 August 1939.

[235] B4/I/34 BBD, Acc/3121/CO2/01/006, 23 March, 3 May, 4 July 1938.

[236] BBD, Acc 3121/c11/12/2/1938.

[237] PRO W1 6579/3 Extracts from the House of Lords Debate, 14 December 1938, 40–1.

[238] Smith, *Foley*, 106, quoting an interview with Benton made shortly before his death. Interview generously communicated to the author by Michael Smith.

[239] PRO FO 371 329, 335–6.

[240] Paul Bartop, *False Havens: The British Empire and the Holocaust*, London 1995, 7–8, 13.

[241] Professor Lucian Meysels, note to Christopher Wentworth-Stanley, 2 March 2003.

[242] Smith, *Foley*, 108.

[243] Damien McElroy, 'Family Fights to Clear Stigma that Haunted China's "Schindler"', *Sunday Telegraph*, 10 April 2001.

[244] BBD, LMA, B4/1/5; BBD, C11/7/1/4, 21 June 1939.

[245] Walter Gardner in Schmidt, *1938 . . . und was dann?*, 41.

[246] BBD, Acc/3121/BO4/WE/24.

[247] BBD, LMA, B4/1/5.

[248] BBD, Acc 3121/12/2/1938.

[249] Paul Bartop, *Australia and the Holocaust 1933–45*, 1992, 44, 56, 85.

[250] PRO FO 336.

[251] PRO FO 371 323, 14 December 1938.

[252] Lambeth Palace, Bell Papers 35/144–5.

[253] Lambeth Palace, Bell Papers, Church of England Committee for Non-Aryan Christians, Annual Report 1937–38.

[254] Lambeth Palace, Headlam Papers 58, to Dowson, 27 October 1933.

[255] Lambeth Palace, Headlam Papers 60, 29 October 1935.

[256] Lambeth Palace, Lang Papers, 38/1, 12 March 1933.

[257] Lambeth Palace, Lang Papers 38, 14–15, 31 March 1933.

[258] Quoted in Klemperer, *German Resistance*, 40.

[259] Lambeth Palace, Headlam Papers, Batty to Headlam, 27 November 1935.

[260] Lambeth Palace, Lang Papers, 38, 152, 22 March 1938.

[261] Quoted in Chandler, 'Church of England', 228.

[262] Goebbels, *Tagebücher I*, V, 239.

[263] Chandler, 'Church of England', 228–9.

[264] Chandler, 'Church of England', 233; Lambeth Palace, Lang Papers, 38, 178, Batty to Lang, 21 July 1938.

[265] *Der Stürmer* 52, December 1938.

[266] Sheila Spielhofer, *Dark Tide*, 115–16.

[267] Lawrence Darton, *An Account of the Work of the Friends' Committee for Refugees and Aliens, First Known as the Germany Committee of the Society of Friends*, London (?) 1954, 46–7; FLA, Germany Files, GE9.

[268] Catchpool Papers, letter to Sir Robert Vansittart, 16 May 1938.

[269] HNN to Emma Cadbury, FLA, Germany Files GE9.

[270] Venus and Wenck, *Die Entziehung jüdischen Vermögens*, 122–3.

[271] Catchpool Papers, letter to Lotte Leonhardt, 26 August 1938.

[272] Peter Berger, 'The Gildemeester Organisation for Assistance to Emigrants and the Expulsion of the Jews from Vienna, 1938–1942', in Terry Gourvish, ed., *Business and Politics in Europe: Essays in Honour of Alice Teichova*, Cambridge 2003, 215.

[273] Venus and Wenck, *Die Entziehung jüdischen Vermögens*, 124–5.

[274] William R. Perl, *Operation Action*, New York 1983, 45.

[275] BBD, C11/12/2 Letter from Prof. Dr D. Cohen, 31 May 1938.

[276] Henry Friedlander and Sybil Milton, eds, *Archives of the Holocaust*, New York and London 1990, 300, 346.

[277] Norman Bentwich, 'The Destruction of the Jewish Community in Austria', in Josef Fraenkel, ed., *The Jews of Austria*, London 1967, 469.

[278] Gertrude Scholz in 'Schmidt, *1938 . . . und was dann?*, 199.

[279] FLA, Germany Files, GE9, Friends' House; idem, B.G. Lawson to Alec Marsh in Vienna, 14 December 1938. See also Berger in Gourvish, *Business and Politics*, 217.

[280] Perl, *Operation Action*, 43.

[281] Berger in Gouvish, *Business and Politics*, 225.

[282] Berger in Gouvish, *Business and Politics*, 221.

[283] Berger in Gouvish, *Business and Politics*, 227–8, 230–1.

[284] Moseley, *Mussolini's Shadow*, 46.

[285] Douglas Reed, *Disgrace Abounding*, London 1939, 228–9.

[286] Reed, *Disgrace*, 234–5.

[287] *Der Stürmer* 7, February 1938.

[288] Scholz and Heinisch, *Wiener Pfarrer*, 65.

[289] Reed, *Disgrace*, 235–6.

[290] Rosenkranz, *Verfolgung*, 51–2.

[291] Burleigh, *Third Reich*, 276–7.

[292] See, for example, Bernt Engelmann, *In Hitler's Germany – Everyday Life in the Third Reich*, trans. Krishna Winton, London 1988, 109.

[293] Botz, *Nationalsozialismus*, 186–7.

[294] Goebbels, *Tagebücher I, V*, 245.

CHAPTER 4: APRIL

[1] Neugebauer in Reich, *Zweier Zeugen Mund*, 16.

[2] The full list is printed in Stadt Wien, *Wien 1938*, 16–17.

[3] Reich, *Zweier Zeugen Mund*, 66.

[4] Fritz Bock in Stadt Wien, *1938*, 12–13.

[5] Neugebauer in Reich, *Zweier Zeugen Mund*, 21.

[6] Heilig, *Men Crucified*, 78.

[7] Fritz Bock in Stadt Wien, *1938*, 12.

[8] Moser, *Juden Verfolgung*, 6.

[9] Neugebauer in Reich, *Zweier Zeugen Mund*, 20.

[10] Kautsky, *Teufel und Verdamte*, 193.

[11] Neugebauer in Reich, *Zweier Zeugen Mund*, 20.

[12] Reich, *Zweier Zeugen Mund*, 96.

[13] Neugebauer in Reich, *Zweier Zeugen Mund*, 24.

[14] Gedye, *Fallen Bastions*, 169.

[15] Wolfgang Neugebauer, 'Der NS-Terrorapparat', in Talos et al., *NS-Herrschaft*, 725.

[16] Catchpool Papers, to W. Arnold Foster, 1 January 1938.

[17] Catchpool Papers, to Dr Margery Fry, 7 February 1938.

[18] Catchpool Papers, to Dr Margery Fry, 7 February 1938.

[19] Benedikt Kautsky, *Teufel und Verdamte: Erfahrungen und Erkenntnisse aus sieben Jahren in deutschen Konzentrationslagern*, Zurich 1946, 27.

[20] Burleigh, *Third Reich*, 375–6.

[21] Peter Gay, *My German Question: Growing Up in Nazi Berlin*, New Haven and London 1998, 120–1.

[22] Gad Beck with Frank Heibert, *An Underground Life*, trans. Allison Brown, Madison and London 1999, 32.

[23] *Der Stürmer* 13, April 1938.

[24] Rosenkranz, *Verfolgung*, 56–7.

[25] Rosenkranz, *Verfolgung*, 59.

[26] Liebmann, *Innitzer*, 136, 139.

[27] Goebbels, *Tagebücher I*, V, 248.

[28] Liebmann, *Innitzer*, 142.

[29] Goebbels, *Tagebücher I*, V, 254–6.

[30] Goebbels, *Tagebücher I*, V, 258.

[31] Botz, *Nationalsozialismus*, 236.

[32] Friedrich Reck-Malleczewen, *Diary of a Man in Despair*, London 2000, 76.

[33] Klemperer, *Tagebücher*, 401, 403.

[34] Ernst Wiechert, *Der Totenwald*, Erlangen 1946, 23.

[35] Goebbels, *Tagebücher I*, V, 280; Jill Stephenson, *Hitler's Home Front – Württemberg under the Nazis*, London and New York 2006, 60–1.

[36] Reck-Malleczewen, *Diary*, 67.

[37] Lillie, *Was einmal war*, 292.

[38] John Weitz, *Hitler's Diplomat*, with an introduction by Tom Wolfe, London 1992, 152.

[39] BBD, Acc/3121/BO4/WE/24, Weisl to Waldman, 2 June 1938.

[40] Hilberg, *Destruction*, I, 133.

[41] London, *Whitehall*, 80–1.

[42] Walzer and Templ, *Unser Wien*, 11.

[43] Communication from Professor Hans Schneider, 11 September 2003.

[44] Rosenkranz, *Verfolgung*, 65.

[45] Rosenkranz, *Verfolgung*, 66.

[46] Rosenkranz, *Verfolgung*, 30.

[47] Rosenkranz, *Verfolgung*, 128.

[48] Rosenkranz, *Verfolgung*, 130–1.

[49] Communication from Professor Hans Schneider, 11 September 2003.

[50] Goebbels, *Tagebücher I*, V, 260.

[51] Klemperer, *Tagebücher*, 401.

[52] Peter Adam, *The Arts of the Third Reich*, London 1992, 263.

[53] Geismar, *Jackboot*, 331; Klepper, *Tagebücher*, 583; *Der Stürmer* 16, April 1938.

[54] Keitel, *Mein Leben*, 222.

[55] Klepper, *Tagebücher*, 585.

[56] Goebbels, *Tagebücher I*, V, 276.

[57] Kershaw, *Nemesis*, 83.

[58] Goebbels, *Tagebücher I*, V, 269–70.

[59] Goebbels, *Tagebücher I*, V, 277.

[60] Rosenkranz, *Verfolgung*, 43; Berkley, *Vienna and Its Jews*, 260.

[61] Lambeth Palace, LR 1, reports from Czech Consul-General and 'The Sack of Vienna'.

[62] Rosenkranz, *Verfolgung*, 86.

[63] Erika Weinzierl, *Zu wenig Gerechte: Österreich und Judenverfolgung 1938–1945*, Graz, Vienna, Cologne 1969, 34.

[64] BBD, Acc 3121/c11/12/2/1938.

[65] Leo Lauterbach, 'The Jewish Situation in Austria', BBD, Acc 3121/c11/12/2/1938.

[66] Letter from Lorli Rudov to the author, 20 October 2001.

[67] 8 July 1938, FLA Germany Files, GE9.

[68] Darton, *Friends' Committee*, 48.

[69] E-mail from and telephone conversation with George Clare, 16 January 2001.

[70] PRO T15833 580 of 14 December 1938.

[71] Bartop, *False Havens*, 5–6.

[72] Bartop, *False Havens*, xi.

[73] Bartop, *False Havens*, 189; see also Anne Beaglehole, *Jewish Refugee Immigration to New Zealand 1933–52*; Karl Popper, *Unended Quest*, 105.

[74] Conversation with George Clare, 16 January 2001.

CHAPTER 5: MAY

[1] Goebbels, *Tagebücher I*, V, 282–3.

[2] Spitzy, *So haben wir das Reich verspielt*, 260.

[3] Kordt, *Nicht aus den Akten*, 210.

[4] Paul Schmidt, *Hitler's Interpreter*, London 1950, 80.

[5] Schmidt, *Interpreter*, 82.

[6] Goebbels, *Tagebücher I*, V, 286.

[7] *Ciano's Diary*, 113.

[8] Moseley, *Mussolini's Shadow*, 42; *Ciano's Diary*, 113.

[9] Klemperer, *Tagebücher*, 412.

[10] See Klepper, *Tagebücher*, 589.

[11] Goebbels, *Tagebücher I*, V, 285.

[12] Schmidt, *Interpreter*, 81.

[13] *Ciano's Diary*, 96.

[14] Kordt, *Nicht aus den Akten*, 211.

[15] *Ciano's Diary*, 112.

[16] Goebbels, *Tagebücher I*, V, 287.

[17] Kordt, *Nicht aus den Akten*, 218.

[18] Schmidt, *Interpreter*, 82.

[19] Brigitte Hamann, *Winifred Wagner: A Life at the Heart of Hitler's Bayreuth*, London 2005, 284.

[20] Spitzy, *So haben wir das Reich verspielt*, 271.

[21] *Ciano's Diary*, 112.

[22] Goebbels, *Tagebücher I*, V, 288–91.

[23] Denis Mack Smith, *Modern Italy – A Political History*, New Haven and London 1997, 396.

[24] BBD, B4/WE/24 May 11 1938.

[25] *Der Stürmer* 18, May 1938.

[26] Hilberg, *Destruction*, I, 98–100.

[27] Rosenkranz, *Verfolgung*, 75.

[28] The Attorney-General of the Government of Israel v. Adolf Eichmann, Minutes of Session No. 18, Jerusalem 1961.

[29] Rosenkranz, *Verfolgung*, 71.

[30] Safrian, *Eichmann*, 44.

[31] BBD, Acc/3121/BO4/WE/24.

[32] BBD, Acc/3121/BO4/WE/24.

[33] 'News from Austria and Germany', in BBD, Acc/3121/BO4/WE/24.

[34] Office of the Chief Rabbi, report March 1944, BBD, 3121 C2/2/4/1.

[35] FLA, Germany Files, GE9, Corder Catchpool to Alice Nike, 18 May 1938.

[36] Kershaw, *Nemesis*, 92.

[37] Quoted in Alan Bullock, *Hitler, A Study in Tyranny*, Harmondsworth 1962, 446.

[38] Klemperer, *Tagebücher*, 409.

[39] Quoted in Bullock, *Hitler*, 449.

[40] Kershaw, *Nemesis*, 98.

[41] Tooze, *Wages*, 249–53.

[42] Tooze, *Wages*, 264.

[43] Goebbels, *Tagebücher I, V*, 345; *I, VI*, 41.

[44] Peter Hoffmann, *The History of the German Resistance 1939–45*, 77.

[45] Reich, *Zweier Zeugen Mund*, 91–2.

[46] Heilig, *Men Crucified*, 90.

[47] Heilig, *Men Crucified*, 93.

[48] Goebbels, *Tagebücher I, V*, 323.

[49] Rosenkranz, *Verfolgung*, 87.

[50] Moser, *Juden Verfolgung*, 7–8.

[51] Schuschnigg, *Requiem*, 77.

[52] Schuschnigg, *Requiem*, 75.

[53] Goebbels, *Tagebücher I, V*, 305, 308, 323.

CHAPTER 6: JUNE

[1] Schwerin, *junge Generation*, 166; information from Angela Bohrer, Schulenburg's daughter. Her mother witnessed the telephone call.

[2] Goebbels, *Tagebücher I, V*, 329.

[3] Goebbels, *Tagebücher I, V*, 331.

[4] Klemperer, *Tagebücher*, 417; *Der Stürmer* 29, July 1938.

[5] Overy, *Goering*, 73.

[6] Fromm, *Diary*, 272.

[7] Emmy Goering [sic], *My Life with Goering*, London 1972, 81.

[8] Michael Burleigh, *The Third Reich, A New History*, London 2000, 230–1.

[9] Grunberger, *Social History*, 108.

[10] *Der Stürmer* 20, June 1938.

[11] BBD, Acc/3121/BO4/WE/24, Weisl to Waldman, 2 June 1938.

[12] BBD, Acc/3121/BO4/WE/24, Weisl to Waldman, 2 June 1938.

[13] Perl, *Operation Action*, 75.

[14] Mendelsohn and Detwiler, *Holocaust*, V, 222–5.

[15] Hilberg, *Destruction*, I, 123.

[16] Communication from Professor Hans Schneider, 11 September 2003.

[17] Communication from Professor Hans Schneider, 11 September 2003.

[18] Goebbels, *Tagebücher I*, V, 339.

[19] Goebbels, *Tagebücher I*, V, 337, 342–3.

[20] Goebbels, *Tagebücher I*, V, 344.

[21] Lambeth Palace, Bell Papers, 428/27 of 22 October 1935.

[22] Lambeth Palace, Bell Papers, 428/118.

[23] Baptismal Register in the Anglican Chaplaincy in Vienna.

[24] E-mail from Peter Henried, 14 October 2002.

[25] E-mail to Celia Male from E. Randol Schoenberg, 18 June 2002. Zeisl had recorded a tape of the escape story in 1975.

[26] BBD, Acc/3121/BO4/WE/24, Weisl to Waldman, 15 June 1938.

[27] BBD, C11A/8.

[28] Clare, *Last Waltz*, 230.

[29] BBD, Acc/3121/BO4/WE/24, Unsigned undated document in German.

[30] Goebbels, *Tagebücher I*, V, 352.

[31] Goebbels, *Tagebücher I*, V, 366.

[32] Goebbels, *Tagebücher I*, V, 333, 335.

[33] John Exshaw, obituary for Max Schmeling, *Independent*, 5 February 2005; Goebbels, *Tagebücher I*, V, 306, 358.

[34] Reck-Malleczewen, *Diary*, 72.

[35] Fromm, *Diary*, 274–5.

[36] Goebbels, *Tagebücher I*, V, 358.

[37] Rosenkranz, *Verfolgung*, 67.

CHAPTER 7: JULY

[1] *Prager Presse*, 22 July 1938.

[2] Goebbels, *Tagebücher I*, V, 372.

[3] Goebbels, *Tagebücher I*, V, 366.

[4] *Daily Telegraph*, 1 July 1938.

[5] *Daily Telegraph*, 2 July 1938.

[6] Goebbels, *Tagebücher I*, V, 372.

[7] Goebbels, *Tagebücher I*, V, 375.

[8] Goebbels, *Tagebücher I*, V, 377.

[9] Conwell-Evans, *None So Blind*, 135.

[10] Goebbels, *Tagebücher I*, V, 369–70.

[11] Quoted in Padfield, *Himmler*, 224. [12] *Der Stürmer* 30, July 1938.

[13] Klemperer, *Tagebücher*, 415.

[14] *Der Stürmer, Sondernummer – der Jude in Oesterreich*, July 1938.

[15] *Prager Presse*, 22 July 1938.

[16] Rosenkranz, *Verfolgung*, 154.

[17] *Daily Telegraph*, 6 July 1938.

[18] *The Times*, 6 July 1938.

[19] Wolfgang von Weisl, 'Illegale Transporte', in Josef Fraenkel, ed., *The Jews of Austria*, London 1967, 172.

[20] Geoffrey Wheatcroft, 'No Fairy Tale: The History of Zionism: Vladimir Jabotinsky's Difficult Legacy, and Its Powerful Supporters and Opponents', in *TLS*, 22 February 2008.

[21] Rosenkranz, *Verfolgung*, 111.

[22] Rosenkranz, *Verfolgung*, 112–13.

[23] Conversation with Eric Sanders, the former Ignaz Erich Schwarz, 8 November 2001. Sanders remembered a kindly woman at

the PCO who suggested the best means of getting to Britain. In his case it was to apply for a full-time course in higher education.

[24] London, *Whitehall*, 68.

[25] Christopher Andrew, *Secret Service*, London 1986, 535–6, quoting Sherman, *Island Refuge*.

[26] Smith, *Foley*, 148.

[27] Klepper, *Tagebücher*, 619.

[28] Rosenkranz, *Verfolgung*, 170.

[29] Rosenkranz, *Verfolgung*, 94.

[30] FLA, Germany Files, GE9, Ethel Houghton to Alice Nike, 9 July 1938.

[31] *Daily Telegraph*, 16 July 1938.

[32] Quoted in Gedye, *Fallen Bastions*, 350.

[33] Chandler, 'Church of England', 234.

[34] Rosenkranz, *Verfolgung*, 97.

[35] Mendelsohn and Detwiler, *Holocaust*, V, 242–3.

[36] Mendelsohn and Detwiler, *Holocaust*, V, 242–3, 250–2, 258. [37] Marc Eric McClure, *Earnest Endeavors: The Life and Public Work of George Rublee*, Westport and London 2003, 248.

[38] Rosenkranz, *Verfolgung*, 104.

[39] McClure, *Rublee*, 248–9.

[40] Rosenkranz, *Verfolgung*, 98, 102.

[41] Rosenkranz, *Verfolgung*, 101.

[42] Mendelsohn and Detwiler, *Holocaust*, V, 152–6.

[43] Rosenkranz, *Verfolgung*, 102. A Jewish acquaintance told the author recently that he had spent his early years in Kenya, where his father had a farm after training in Britain. His parents had emigrated from western Germany.

[44] Amy Zahl Gottlieb, *Men of Vision – Anglo-Jewry's Aid to Victims of the Nazi Regime 1933–45*, London 1998, 86.

[45] T120/3183/E523535-E523542 in Mendelsohn and Detwiler, *Holocaust*, V.

[46] FLA, Germany Files, GE9. Corder Catchpool to Wilfred Israel, 31 August 1938.

[47] *Der Stürmer* 30, July 1938.

[48] FLA Germany Files, GE9.HNN/IB to Emma Cadbury, 27 August 1938.

[49] Author's conversation with the late Gerhard Bronner in Vienna; FLA, Germany Files, GE9, Emma Cadbury to Hermia Neild, 27 August 1938.

[50] McClure, *Rublee*, 249.

[51] McClure, *Rublee*, 253–4.

[52] Berger in Gouvish, *Business and Politics*, 220.

[53] Stefan Spevak, *NS Vermögensentzug, Restitution und Entschädigung in der Diözese St Pölten*, Vienna and Munich 2004, 15.

[54] Schuschnigg, *Requiem*, 69.

[55] Bock, *Österreichs Stifte*, 12.

[56] Spevak, *St Pölten*, 31–2, 35.

[57] Goebbels, *Tagebücher I*, V, 365.

[58] Irving, *Göring*, 221.

[59] Irving, *Göring*, 222.

[60] Irving, *Göring*, 223.

[61] Goebbels, *Tagebücher I*, V, 349.

[62] Martha Schad, *Hitlers Spionin*, Munich 2002, 96.

[63] Schad, *Hitlers Spionin*, 98–102.

[64] Goebbels, *Tagebücher I*, V, 385.

[65] BBD, E3/282.

[66] BBD, C11/7/1/4.

[67] Rosenkranz, *Verfolgung*, 106.

[68] Lang, *Wolff*, 96.

[69] Grunberger, *Social History*, 537–8.

[70] Adam, *The Arts of the Third Reich*, 115.

[71] Breker, *Strahlungsfeld*, 109.

[72] Hellmut Lehmann-Haupt, *Art Under a Dictatorship*, Oxford and New York 1954, 114.

[73] Grunberger, *Social History*, 540, 543.

[74] Goebbels, *Tagebücher I*, V, 97, 399.

[75] Hildegard Brenner, *Die Kunstpolitik des Nationalsozialismus*, Munich 1963–95.

[76] Grunberger, *Social History*, 522.

[77] Michael Kennedy, *Richard Strauss*, Oxford 1995, 95–7.

[78] Goebbels, *Tagebücher I*, V, 390.

[79] Goebbels, *Tagebücher I*, V, 366.

[80] Goebbels, *Tagebücher I*, V, 393.

[81] Grunberger, *Social History*, 519.

[82] Goebbels, *Tagebücher I*, V, 394–5.

[83] Frederick S. Potts, *Bayreuth: A History of the Wagner Festival*, New Haven and London 1994, 165.

[84] Goebbels, *Tagebücher I*, V, 366.

[85] Hamann, *Winifred Wagner*, 289.

[86] Hamann, *Winifred Wagner*, 291–2.

[87] Goebbels, *Tagebücher I*, V, 331.

[88] Lang, *Wolff*, 99.

[89] Goebbels, *Tagebücher I*, V, 401.

[90] Elke Fröhlich, ed., Joseph Goebbels, *Tagebücher, Teil 1, Band VI – August 1938 – Juni 1939*, Bearbeitet von Jana Richter, Munich 1998, 29–30.

[91] Hamann, *Winifred Wagner*, 293.

[92] Rosenkranz, *Verfolgung*, 67.

[93] Reich, *Zweier Zeugen Mund*, 209.

[94] Wiechert, *Totenwald*, 108–9, 114.

[95] Wiechert, *Totenwald*, 108.

[96] Kautsky, *Teufel und Verdamte*, 146, 196.

[97] Wiechert, *Totenwald*, 119.

[98] Goebbels, *Tagebücher I*, VI, 32.

[99] Reich, *Zweier Zeugen Mund*, 224.

[100] Kautsky, *Teufel und Verdamte*, 137.

[101] Reich, *Zweier Zeugen Mund*, 185.

CHAPTER 8: AUGUST

[1] Goebbels, *Tagebücher I*, V, 367.

[2] Goebbels, *Tagebücher I*, VI, 32.

[3] Goebbels, *Tagebücher I*, VI, 34, 38.

[4] Goebbels, *Tagebücher I*, VI, 44.

[5] Hassell, *Diary*, 11.

[6] Goebbels, *Tagebücher I*, VI, 44.

[7] Goebbels, *Tagebücher I*, VI, 47, 51, 67.

[8] *Daily Telegraph*, 3 August 1938.

[9] *Daily Telegraph*, 6 August 1938.

[10] *Neue Freie Presse*, 3 August 1938.

[11] Rosenkranz, *Verfolgung*, 153.

[12] FLA, Germany Files, FSC/GE/5, Factual Notes on a German Trip by D. Robert Yarnall, 7 December 1938.

[13] *The Times*, 5 August 1938.

[14] *Daily Telegraph*, 15 August 1938.

[15] *Prager Presse*, 26 August 1938; Hilberg, *Destruction*, 175–6.

[16] *Neue Wiener Presse*, 22 August 1938.

[17] *Wiener Zeitung*, 19 August 1938.

[18] *Daily Telegraph*, 6, 8, 9 August; *Der Stürmer* 34, August 1938.

[19] *Daily Telegraph*, 13 August.

[20] Goebbels, *Tagebücher I*, VI, 54.

[21] Klepper, *Tagebücher*, 627.

[22] Goebbels, *Tagebücher I*, VI, 48.

[23] Irving, *Göring*, 224–5.

[24] Meehan, *Unnecessary War*, 140.

[25] Catchpool Papers, letter from Sir Robert Vansittart, 8 August 1938.

[26] Colvin, *Intelligence*, 55.

[27] Colvin, *Intelligence*, 62.

[28] Scheurig, *Kleist-Schmenzin*, 154, 158, 164–5.

[29] Colvin, *Intelligence*, 67. Colvin was a friend and confidant of Kleist's.

[30] Meehan, *Unnecessary War*, 144.

[31] Helmuth Groscurth, *Tagebücher eines Abwehroffiziers 1938–1940*, Stuttgart 1970, 104.

[32] Klemperer, *German Resistance*, 103–4.

[33] Colvin, *Intelligence*, 54.

[34] PRO FO C3401 254.

[35] Conversation with Mrs Chapman, Richter's niece, 13 September 2000.

[36] All these details in Richter's trial before the *Volksgerichthof*: 1 J 172/38g 3 L 46/39.

[37] *Daily Express*, 13, 15, 17, 19, 20 August 1938; *Daily Telegraph*, 20 August 1938.

[38] *Neue Freie Presse*, 23 August 1938; *Daily Telegraph*, 22 August 1938.

[39] *Prager Presse*, 19 August 1938.

[40] PRO FO C8453/261.

[41] *The Times*, 22 August 1938.

[42] PRO FO C8533/270.

[43] PRO FO C8454 263.

[44] *Prager Presse*, 21 August 1938.

[45] Peggie Benton, *Baltic Countdown*, London 1984, 11.

[46] Nigel West, *MI6*, London 1983, 58.

[47] Conversation with Mrs Gedye, 14 June 2000.

[48] West, *MI6*, 115.

[49] PRO FO 8564/274.

[50] Smith, *Foley*, 116.

[51] PRO FO C8982/241/18.

[52] Guildhall Library, Uncatalogued, Cologne Chaplaincy, File 1936, 1950–7, Rev F.E. Collard letter to Mr Williams of 7 April 1950.

[53] Fred Collard's daughter-in-law remembers attending his ordination in Saint Paul's Cathedral. Telephone conversation, 15 August 2000.

[54] PRO FO C85264/309–310; PRO FO C8756.

[55] Conversation with Mrs Collard, Fred Collard's daughter-in-law,

15 August 2000. She said he was proud of what he had done for the
Jews, and while he remained in Cologne, he used to tell them, 'Get
out and go as far as you can.'

[56] BBD, Acc/3121/BO4/WE24, Weisl to Waldman, 29 August
1938.

[57] Rosenkranz, *Verfolgung*, 89.

[58] PRO FO C8673 321–323.

[59] *Daily Express*, 20 August 1938.

[60] Erika Weinzierl, *Zu wenig Gerechte*, 103, 111.

[61] Ulrich Trinks, 'Die schwedische Mission in der Seegasse', in
Dialog-Du Siach 43, June 2001.

[62] Communicated by Professor Munro Price.

[63] PRO FO C8564 274.

[64] PRO FO C8673 286.

[65] Fromm, *Diary*, 278.

[66] Goebbels, *Tagebücher I*, VI, 61.

[67] *Neue Wiener Presse*, 26, 28 August 1938.

[68] *Ciano's Diary*, 148.

[69] Meehan, *Unnecessary War*, 154.

CHAPTER 9: SEPTEMBER

[1] Kley, *Hitler, Ribbentrop*, 122.

[2] Meehan, *Unnecessary War*, 156.

[3] Goebbels, *Tagebücher I*, VI, 61, 66, 70.

[4] Gedye, *Fallen Bastions*, 440.

[5] Quoted in Grunberger, *Social History*, 515.

[6] Goebbels, *Tagebücher I*, VI, 76, 79.

[7] Schad, *Hitlers Spionin*, 89–92; Goebbels, *Tagebücher I*, VI, 80.

[8] Goebbels, *Tagebücher I*, VI, 75.

[9] Goebbels, *Tagebücher I*, VI, 78.

[10] Spitzy, *So haben wir das Reich verspielt*, 305.

[11] François-Poncet, *Souvenirs*, 322.

12 Goebbels, *Tagebücher I*, VI, 81.

13 Conwell-Evans, *None So Blind*, 141.

14 Goebbels, *Tagebücher I*, VI, 84

15 Groscurth, *Tagebücher*, 117.

16 Goebbels, *Tagebücher I*, VI, 85.

17 Meehan, *Unnecessary War*, 167.

18 Goebbels, *Tagebücher I*, VI, 88.

19 Eberle and Uhl, *Hitler Book*, 29.

20 Schmidt, *Interpreter*, 90.

21 Eberle and Uhl, *Hitler Book*, 29.

22 Goebbels, *Tagebücher I*, VI, 90.

23 Roos, *Polen und Europa*, 33–9.

24 Schmidt, *Interpreter*, 93.

25 Spitzy, *So haben wir das Reich verspielt*, 307.

26 Eberle and Uhl, *Hitler Book*, 30.

27 Groscurth, *Tagebücher*, 120.

28 Lamb, *Ghosts*, 80.

29 PRO FO C11001.

30 Goebbels, *Tagebücher I*, VI, 97.

31 PRO FO C11001.

32 Goebbels, *Tagebücher I*, VI, 103.

33 PRO FO C10929.

34 PRO FO C11001.

35 Goebbels, *Tagebücher I*, VI, 98.

36 Goebbels, *Tagebücher I*, VI, 102.

37 Ulrich von Hassell, *The von Hassell Diaries 1938–1944*, London 1948, 11.

38 Klepper, *Tagebücher*, 645.

39 Klemperer, *Tagebücher*, 424.

40 Groscurth, *Tagebücher*, 124.

41 Schwerin, *junge Generation*, 158.

42 PRO FO C11001.

43 Goebbels, *Tagebücher I*, VI, 105–6.

44 PRO FO C11001.

[45] Kordt, *Nicht aus den Akten*, 261.

[46] Bullock, *Hitler*, 458.

[47] Schmidt, *Interpreter*, 99.

[48] PRO FO C11001.

[49] Roberts, *Holy Fox*, 115.

[50] Goebbels, *Tagebücher, I, VI*, 111.

[51] Goebbels, *Tagebücher I, VI*, 117.

[52] Klepper, *Tagebücher*, 653.

[53] Gräfin Maria von Maltzan, *Memoirs*, unpublished MS translated and communicated to the author by Peter Ede, 55.

[54] Goebbels, *Tagebücher I, VI*, 111.

[55] Goebbels, *Tagebücher I, VI*, 113.

[56] Bullock, *Hitler*, 463.

[57] Groscurth, *Tagebücher*, 124.

[58] PRO FO C10931.

[59] Reich, *Zweier Zeugen Mund*, 211.

[60] Schmidt, *Interpreter*, 105.

[61] Hassell, *Diaries*, 13.

[62] Schwerin, *junge Generation*, 160.

[63] Meehan, *Unnecessary War*, 52–3.

[64] Klepper, *Tagebücher*, 656; Conwell-Evans, *None So Blind*, 148; Spitzy, *So haben wir das Reich verspielt*, 313.

[65] Kordt, *Nicht aus den Akten*, 267.

[66] Conwell-Evans, *None So Blind*, 148.

[67] Goebbels, *Tagebücher I, VI*, 115.

[68] Schwerin, *junge Generation*, 162.

[69] Stephenson, *Home Front*, 62.

[70] Groscurth, *Tagebücher*, 125.

[71] François-Poncet, *Souvenirs*, 327.

[72] Schmidt, *Interpreter*, 106.

[73] *Ciano's Diary*, 154, 156, 162.

[74] PRO FO C10883/1941/18.

[75] Moseley, *Mussolini's Shadow*, 37.

[76] Hassell, *Diaries*, 15.

[77] Goebbels, *Tagebücher I*, VI, 119; Spitzy, *So haben wir das Reich verspielt*, 316.

[78] Goebbels, *Tagebücher I*, VI, 120.

[79] Kershaw, *Nemesis*, 121.

[80] *Ciano's Diary*, 166.

[81] Bullock, *Hitler*, 468.

[82] Groscurth, *Tagebücher*, 128.

[83] Bloch, *Ribbentrop*, 213–14.

[84] Kley, *Hitler, Ribbentrop*, 140.

[85] Hamann, *Winifred Wagner*, 295.

[86] François-Poncet, *Souvenirs*, 331.

[87] Schmidt, *Interpreter*, 109.

[88] Goebbels, *Tagebücher I*, VI, 125–6.

[89] Schmidt, *Interpreter*, 110.

[90] *Ciano's Diary*, 167.

[91] François-Poncet, *Souvenirs*, 334.

[92] Schmidt, *Interpreter*, 114.

[93] *Der Stürmer* 44, November 1938.

[94] Bullock, *Hitler*, 471.

[95] Meehan, *Unnecessary War*, 132.

[96] Klepper, *Tagebücher*, 657, 658.

[97] Goebbels, *Tagebücher I*, VI, 121.

[98] Goebbels, *Tagebücher I*, VI, 124.

[99] Irving, *Göring*, 229.

[100] Klemens von Klemperer, ed., *A Noble Combat: The Letters of Shiela Grant Duff and Adam von Trott zu Solz 1932–1939*, Oxford, 1988, 327, 329–30; quoted in Giles MacDonogh, *A Good German: Adam von Trott zu Solz*, London 1990, 118.

[101] Colvin, *Intelligence*, 70.

[102] *Prager Presse*, 2 September 1938; Andrew McFadyean, Report on Italy, 25 January 1939, BBD, C2/2/2.

[103] Quoted in Martin Gilbert, *Kristallnacht: Prelude to Destruction*, London 2005, 136.

[104] Chandler, 'Church of England', 234–5.

[105] Heilig, *Men Crucified*, 113.

[106] BBD, Acc/3121/B04/WE24, Wolfgang von Weisl to Mr Waldman, 21 September 1938.

[107] Rosenkranz, *Verfolgung*, 94, 96.

[108] BBD, Acc/3121/BO4/WE24, Weisl to Waldman, 20 September 1938.

[109] Clare, *Last Waltz*, 213.

[110] BBD, C11/2/33, Joint Foreign Committee.

[111] BBD, E3/282, N. Laski to George Rublee 4 October 1938.

[112] BBDF, E3/282.

[113] BBD, E1/37, Philip Vos KC, 7 September 1938.

[114] BBD, Acc/3121/BO4/WE24, Weisl to Waldman, 21 September 1938.

[115] Leo Mazakarini and Andreas Augustin, *Hotel Sacher Wien*, Singapore 1994, 72–4; A.A. Löwenthal, *Sammtliche Schriften*, Band VII, Stuttgart und Tübingen, 1959, 56–9.

CHAPTER 10: OCTOBER

[1] *Der Stürmer* 47, November 1938.

[2] Livia Rothkirchen, *The Jews of Bohemia and Moravia: Facing the Holocaust*, Lincoln 2006, 79.

[3] London, *Whitehall*, 143; Gedye, *Fallen Bastions*, 489.

[4] London, *Whitehall*, 146–7.

[5] See, for example, Melissa Müller and Reinhard Piechocki, *A Garden of Eden in Hell*, trans. Giles MacDonogh, London 2007, 106–7, for the plight of a Jewish doctor from the Sudetenland; Irving, *Göring*, 241.

[6] *Documents on German Foreign Policy 1918–1945*, D IV Washington 195182, 152, 183.

[7] Goebbels, *Tagebücher I*, VI, 127.

[8] Groscurth, *Tagebücher*, 135.

[9] Groscurth, *Tagebücher*, 130.

[10] Groscurth, *Tagebücher*, 131.

[11] Groscurth, *Tagebücher*, 132.

[12] Groscurth, *Tagebücher*, 134.

[13] Groscurth, *Tagebücher*, 135.

[14] Groscurth, *Tagebücher*, 146.

[15] Donald Cameron Watt, *How War Came: The Immediate Origins of the Second World War*, London 1989, 30.

[16] McClure, *Rublee*, 256.

[17] Klepper, *Tagebücher*, 660.

[18] BBD, E3/282, Letter from Saly Mayer, 15 August 1938.

[19] Erika Weinzierl, *Zu wenig Gerechte*, 37.

[20] Yad Vashem Archives, 0–5/1–2; Rosenkranz, *Verfolgung*, 157.

[21] *The Times*, 7 October 1938.

[22] Evan Burr Bukey, 'Die Stimmung in der Bevölkerung während der Nazizeit', in Talos et al., *NS-Herrschaft*, 78–9.

[23] In Schmidt, *1938 . . . und was dann?*, 297; Goebbels, *Tagebücher I, VI*, 312.

[24] Botz, *Nationalsozialismus*, 486.

[25] Scholz and Heinisch, *Wiener Pfarrer*, 95.

[26] Liebmann, *Innitzer*, 198.

[27] Liebmann, *Innitzer*, 204.

[28] Bock, *Stifte unter dem Hackenkreuz*, 90.

[29] Stephenson, *Home Front*, 140.

[30] DGFP, D IV 303.

[31] Goebbels, *Tagebücher I, VI*, 141.

[32] Goebbels, *Tagebücher I, VI*, 139.

[33] DGFP, D IV, 54, 56.

[34] Goebbels, *Tagebücher I, VI*, 158.

[35] Roger Manvell and Heinrich Fraenkel, *Doctor Goebbels*, London 1959, 170–2.

[36] Goebbels, *Tagebücher I, VI*, 158.

[37] Hassell, *Diaries*, 18.

[38] François-Poncet, *Souvenirs*, 342–3; Goebbels, *Tagebücher I, VI*, 131.

[39] Groscurth, *Tagebücher*, 151.

[40] Reich, *Zweier Zeugen Mund*, 231–3.

[41] Henriette Mandl in Reich, *Zweier Zeugen Mund*, 300.

[42] Rosenkranz, *Verfolgung*, 158.

[43] BBD, C11/12/2 1938.

[44] Quoted in BBD, E3/282.

[45] Edward Crankshaw, *Gestapo, Instrument of Tyranny*, London 1956, 89.

[46] Sybil Milton, 'Menschen zwischen Grenzen: Die Polenausweisung 1938', in Historisches Museum, *Novemberpogrom*, 48–9.

[47] Roos, *Polen und Europa*, 371.

[48] *Ciano's Diary*, 113.

[49] Roos, *Polen und Europa*, 356.

[50] Quoted in Read, *Devil's Disciples*, 507.

[51] Moseley, *Mussolini's Shadow*, 45; *Ciano's Diary*, 185.

[52] Hans-Jürgen Döscher, *Reichskristallnacht – Die Novemberpogrome*, Frankfurt/Main and Berlin 1988, 51.

[53] Klepper, *Tagebücher*, 669.

[54] Marcel Reich-Ranicki, *The Author of Himself*, London 2000, 107–8.

[55] See Trude Maurer, 'Abschiebung und Attentat: die Ausweisung der polnischen Juden und der Vorwand für die "Kristallnacht"', in Walter Pehle, ed., *Der Judenpogrom – von der 'Reichskristallnacht' zum Völkermord*, Frankfurt/Main 1988.

[56] *Der Stürmer* 44, November 1938. [57] Groscurth, *Tagebücher*, 158–9.

CHAPTER 11: NOVEMBER

[1] *Ciano's Diary*, 188.

[2] Klepper, *Tagebücher*, 673.

[3] Irving, *Göring*, 230–1.

[4] Goebbels, *Tagebücher I*, VI, 174.

[5] Goebbels, *Tagebücher I*, VI, 166.

[6] Grunberger, *Social History*, 518.

[7] Döscher, *Reichskristallnacht*, 58–64.

[8] Kate Connolly, 'Historian Says Jewish Boy Killed His Nazi Lover', in the *Guardian*, 31 October 2001.

[9] Elisabethe Klamper, 'Herschel', in Historisches Museum, *Judenpogrom*, 58.

[10] George Lane-Fox Pitt-Rivers, *The Czech Conspiracy*, London 1938, 13.

[11] Wolfgang Benz, 'Der Ruckfall in der Barbarei', in Pehle, ed., *Judenpogrom*, 15.

[12] Quoted in Padfield, *Himmler*, 238–9.

[13] See Giles MacDonogh, *After the Reich – From the Fall of Vienna to the Berlin Airlift*, London 2007.

[14] Goebbels, *Tagebücher I*, VI, 178.

[15] Goebbels, *Tagebücher I*, VI, 180.

[16] Lang, *Wolff*, 104, 106.

[17] Hamann, *Winifred Wagner*, 298.

[18] Lang, *Wolff*, 105.

[19] Lang, *Wolff*, 105.

[20] Uwe Dietrich Adam, 'Wie spontan war der Pogrom?', in Pehle, ed., *Judenpogrom*, 79; Raul Hilberg, *The Destruction of the European Jews*, I, 38–9.

[21] Goebbels, *Tagebücher I*, VI, 180.

[22] Goebbels, *Tagebücher I*, VI, 181.

[23] Benz in Pehle, ed., *Judenpogrom*, 22.

[24] Hassell, *Diaries*, 20.

[25] Benz in Pehle, ed., *Judenpogrom*, 40.

[26] Gilbert, *Kristallnacht*, 31.

[27] *Manchester Guardian*, 11 November 1938.

[28] Goebbels, *Tagebücher I*, VI, 182.

[29] Adam in Pehle, ed., *Judenpogrom*, 78.

[30] Burleigh, *Third Reich*, 332.

[31] Hamann, *Winifred Wagner*, 297.

[32] Gilbert, *Kristallnacht*, 109.

[33] Gilbert, *Kristallnacht*, 94–5.

[34] Engelmann, *Hitler's Germany*, 121.

[35] Gilbert, *Kristallnacht*, 42.

[36] Quoted in Giles MacDonogh, *Berlin*, London 1997, 433.

[37] Gay, *German Question*, 134–5.

[38] Beck, *Underground Life*, 36–7.

[39] Gilbert, *Kristallnacht*, 46.

[40] Gräfin von Maltzan, *Memoirs*, 57.

[41] Beck, *Underground Life*, 36.

[42] Gilbert, *Kristallnacht*, 44, 48–9.

[43] Jonny Moser, 'Die "Reichskristallnacht" in Wien', in Historisches Museum, *Judenpogrom*, 61.

[44] Erika Weinzierl, *Nur wenig Gerechte*, 65.

[45] Gilbert, *Kristallnacht*, 64–5.

[46] Rosenkranz, *Verfolgung*, 161–2.

[47] Rosenkranz, *Verfolgung*, 159.

[48] Goebbels, *Tagebücher I*, VI, 182.

[49] Burleigh, *Third Reich*, 326, quoting Hassell, *Diaries*, 28.

[50] Hilberg, *Destruction*, I, 39.

[51] Bloch, *Ribbentrop*, 222.

[52] Manvell and Fraenkel, *Doctor Goebbels*, 157.

[53] Hilberg, *Destruction*, I, 40.

[54] Walzer and Templ, *Unser Wien*, 32; Moser, 'Reichskristallnacht', in Historisches Museum, *Judenpogrom*, 62.

[55] Gilbert, *Kristallnacht*, 118.

[56] See Benz in Pehle, ed., *Judenpogrom*.

[57] Benz in Pehle, ed., *Judenpogrom*, 47.

[58] Heilig, *Men Crucified*, 154; Gilbert, *Kristallnacht*, 26.

[59] Safrian, *Eichmann*, 23.

[60] Tooze, *Wages*, 277.

[61] Quoted in Bankier, in Historisches Museum, *Judenpogrom*, 79.

[62] Hilberg, *Destruction*, I, 45.

[63] Bankier, in Historisches Museum, *Judenpogrom*, 81.

[64] Goebbels, *Tagebücher I, VI,* 198.

[65] Goebbels, *Tagebücher I, VI,* 185.

[66] Safrian, *Eichmann,* 47–8.

[67] Walzer and Templ, *Unser Wien,* 57.

[68] Engel, 'Archive des Grauens'.

[69] Gilbert, *Kristallnacht,* 179.

[70] Gilbert, *Kristallnacht,* 183.

[71] Klepper, *Tagebücher,* 688.

[72] Kautsky, *Teufel und Verdamte,* 29.

[73] Moser, *Juden Verfolgung,* 9.

[74] Erwin Stein, ed., *Arnold Schoenberg – Letters,* London 1964, 205.

[75] Klemperer, *Tagebücher,* 435.

[76] Giles MacDonogh, *The Last Kaiser: William the Impetuous,* London 2000, 456.

[77] *Ciano's Diary,* 193.

[78] *Daily Herald,* 9 November 1938.

[79] *Der Stürmer* 46, November 1938.

[80] *Der Stürmer* 45, November 1938.

[81] Gilbert, *Kristallnacht,* 143.

[82] Gilbert, *Kristallnacht,* 172.

[83] Chandler, 'Church of England', 237.

[84] See, for example, Ulrich Heinemann, *Ein konservativer Rebell: Fritz–Dietlof Graf von der Schulenberg und der 20 Juli,* Berlin 1990, 93–4.

[85] Goebbels, *Tagebücher I, VI,* 189.

[86] Burleigh, *Third Reich,* 333.

[87] Jamie Bulloch and Katharina Bielenberg, *Peter Bielenberg,* privately printed memoir, c. 2001, 80–1.

[88] Groscurth, *Tagebücher,* 157.

[89] Groscurth, *Tagebücher,* 162.

[90] Klepper, *Tagebücher,* 682.

[91] MacDonogh, *Good German,* 118–19.

[92] Meehan, *Unnecessary War,* 55–6.

[93] Stephenson, *Home Front,* 144.

[94] Kershaw, *Final Solution*, 175.

[95] Grunberger, *Social History*, 138–9.

[96] Gilbert, *Reichskristallnacht*, 151–2.

[97] Hilberg, *Destruction*, 134–5.

[98] Tooze, *Wages*, 277–9.

[99] Goebbels, *Tagebücher I*, VI, 219.

[100] Mendelsohn and Detwiler, *Holocaust*, VI, London 1982, 5; McClure, *Rublee*, 260.

[101] McClure, *Rublee*, 262.

[102] McClure, *Rublee*, 266–7.

[103] Mendelsohn and Detwiler, *Holocaust*, V, 149.

[104] Meehan, *Unnecessary War*, 98–9.

[105] Meehan, *Unnecessary War*, 99.

[106] *Daily Express*, 7 November 1938.

[107] FLA Germany Files GE9.

[108] BBD, E3/282.

[109] Rosenkranz, *Verfolgung*, 181.

[110] Naomi Shepherd, *Wilfred Israel*, London 1984, 146–7, 149.

[111] Diana Hopkinson, *The Incense Tree*, London 1968, 163.

[112] Hopkinson, *Incense Tree*, 163.

[113] BBD, Acc 3121 C2/2/4/1, Ruth Horowitz to Dr B. Homa, 21 July 1950.

[114] Hilberg, *Destruction*, 127.

[115] Gräfin von Maltzan, *Memoirs*, 58; MacDonogh, *Berlin*, 380.

[116] Stephenson, *Home Front*, 145.

[117] Lambeth Palace, Lang Papers, 38/224. *Daily Telegraph*, 26 November 1938.

[118] Rosenkranz, *Verfolgung*, 167.

[119] Smith, *Foley*, 133.

[120] Engelmann, *Hitler's Germany*, 128–31.

[121] *The Times*, 27 October 1938.

[122] Lambeth Palace, Lang Papers, 38/255, Bell to Alan Don, 30 November 1938. Mrs Baker's letter is missing.

[123] Lambeth Palace, Lang Papers, 38/260, Alan Don to Batty, 5

December 1938.

[124] Lambeth Palace, Lang Papers, 38/264, 265, 266, 6–7 December 1938.

[125] Lambeth Palace, Lang Papers, 38/311, 313, 322.

CHAPTER 12: DECEMBER

[1] FLA Yarnall, Factual Notes, in FSC/GE/5.

[2] Darton, *Friends Committee*, 50–1.

[3] Rosenkranz, *Verfolgung*, 182.

[4] FLA Germany Files, GE9, Ethel Houghton to Bernard Lawson, 4 February 1939.

[5] Hilberg, *Destruction*, 125–6.

[6] Conwell-Evans, *None So Blind*, 116.

[7] Bloch, *Ribbentrop*, 229.

[8] DGFP, D IV, 481.

[9] Mendelsohn and Detwiler, *Holocaust*, VI, 22; DGFP, D IV, 351.

[10] Sir Frederick Leith-Ross, *Money Talks: Fifty Years of International Finance*, London 1958, 254.

[11] McClure, *Rublee*, 269–74.

[12] PRO W16643, 17 December 1938. Hoare to Josiah Wedgwood; *Bulletin of the Co-ordinating Committee for Refugees*, February 1939.

[13] PRO 371, House of Lords Debates, 14 December 1938.

[14] PRO W16614/48, 16 December 1938.

[15] PRO W16580 45.

[16] PRO T15833 580 635, 7 December 1938.

[17] Rosenkranz, *Verfolgung*, 186.

[18] PRO W1 6645/94, 17 December 1938.

[19] PRO W1 6645, 17 December 1938.

[20] Jeremy Noakes, 'Social Outcasts in the Third Reich', in Richard Bessel, ed., *Life in the Third Reich*, Oxford 1987, 90.

[21] Michael Burleigh and Wolfgang Wipperman, *The Racial State: Germany 1933–1945*, Cambridge 1991, 120–1.

[22] *Der Stürmer* 50, December 1938.

[23] Klemperer, *Tagebücher*, 448.

[24] Groscurth, *Tagebücher*, 164.

[25] Reich, *Zweier Zeugen Mund*, 253–5.

[26] Schuschnigg, *Requiem*, 85.

[27] Groscurth, *Tagebücher*, 163.

[28] Goebbels, *Tagebücher I*, VI, 226.

CONCLUSION

[1] Conversation with the late Peter Bielenberg, summer 1988.

[2] MacDonogh, *Good German*, 122–3.

[3] Rosenkranz, *Verfolgung*, 169–70.

[4] Döw – Akten 20000/R244. Judgment of the Volksgericht, Berlin, 15 September 1939: 1 J 172/38g; Auschwitz Sterbe-Index Nr 10163/1943.

[5] Judith Fels-Margulies, 'Anmerkungen', in an otherwise untitled and undated document.

[6] Tooze, *Wages*, 283.

[7] Goebbels, *Tagebücher I*, VI, 245.

[8] Kershaw, *Final Solution*, 109.

[9] Breker, *Strahlungsfeld*, 93, 98; Ruldolf Wolters, *Neue deutsche Baukunst*, Prague 1943, 12.

[10] Eberle and Uhl, *Hitler Book*, 36.

EPILOGUE

[1] Kaus, *Und was für ein Leben*, 184.

[2] Information from Gisela Müller.

[3] See my article 'Otto Horcher, Caterer to the Third Reich' in *Gastronomica*, Winter 2007. Also 'The Reichsmarschall's Table', BBC Radio 4, first broadcast 14 March 2005.

[4] Laura Wärndorfer, *Meine einhundertzwanzig Jahre*, MS autobiography, n.d., 50.

[5] Walzer and Templ, *Unser Wien*, 42–3.

INDEX